# THE PENGUIN BOOK OF
## *International Women's Stories*

Selected and with an introduction
by Kate Figes

VIKING

VIKING

Published by the Penguin Group
Penguin Books Ltd, 27 Wrights Lane, London w8 5tz, England
Penguin Books USA Inc., 375 Hudson Street, New York, New York 10014, USA
Penguin Books Australia Ltd, Ringwood, Victoria, Australia
Penguin Books Canada Ltd, 10 Alcorn Avenue, Toronto, Ontario, Canada m4v 3b2
Penguin Books (NZ) Ltd, 182–190 Wairau Road, Auckland 10, New Zealand

Penguin Books Ltd, Registered Offices: Harmondsworth, Middlesex, England

First published 1996
10 9 8 7 6 5 4 3 2 1
First edition

This selection and introduction copyright © Kate Figes, 1996
The moral right of the editor has been asserted

The acknowledgements on pp. 460–2 constitute an extension to this copyright page

Set in 10/13 pt Monotype Garamond
Typeset by Datix International Limited, Bungay, Suffolk
Printed in England by Clays Ltd, St Ives plc

A CIP catalogue record for this book is available from the British Library
ISBN 0 670 86981 3

Kate Figes was born in 1957 and graduated with a BA in Arabic and Russian from the Polytechnic of Central London. She worked for six years for the publishing house Pandora Press before moving to *Cosmopolitan* magazine, where she is Fiction Editor. Her first book, *Because of Her Sex: The Myth of Equality for Women in Britain*, was published in 1994. She also edited *The Cosmopolitan Book of Short Stories*, published in 1995.

# CONTENTS

# INTRODUCTION

The thirty-three stories in this collection have been selected from as many different countries as existing translations will allow in order to reveal and contrast the range and depth of talent of stories by women around the world. Inevitably personal taste has entered the selection process. I have chosen stories that were so deeply satisfying and complete that I didn't want to disturb the powerful, lingering images left in their wake by immediately reading another one.

Geography wrestled with personal taste throughout the selection of these stories. For every writer included, twenty North American or British women writers have had to be excluded. While there has been a flourishing of writing by women in the English language, scant resources have been invested in translating foreign fiction into English. Even so, one cannot help but be impressed by the range of styles and subject-matter and the way in which women throughout the world have used the literary form as a means of expression.

The stories included may not necessarily be set in each writer's home country, but they all tell tales with universal appeal. Childhood fantasies and fears may vary according to culture, but the emotions are recognizable everywhere, from the thrill of doing precisely what your mother says you should never, ever do, as in Janet Frame's 'The Reservoir', to being forgotten and never found in a game of hide and seek, as in Anita Desai's 'Games at Twilight'. Family life is family life the world over, and María Elena Llano's story charts some of the tensions and ties of blood relationships, while Helen Simpson's masterful 'Heavy Weather' is surely one of the best portrayals of young motherhood ever written.

As the world shrinks through television, air travel and telecommunications, cultures have clashed and crossed and produced some remarkable fiction. Alice Walker's 'Nineteen Fifty-five' opens the anthology with a chilling, funny and intimate tale about the black singer-songwriter Gracie May Still and the white superstar – a thinly disguised Elvis – who steals her songs and then feels so guilty that he overwhelms her with expensive gifts she doesn't want. Bi Shumin's 'Broken Transformers' describes how the flood of American toys into China creates problems of etiquette when a coveted, expensive transformer is broken by a small boy's friend. 'One has to admire the Americans,' she writes. 'Who else would come up with the idea of turning the belly of a fighter into a robot's head and then proceed to create a machine that executes the transition so flawlessly?' Irene Dische's 'The Jewess' tells the story of a young American accountant who travels to Berlin after the Second World War to claim his inheritance, a department store left to him by a father he can barely remember. It captures the emotional confusion of German Jews in exile masterfully. Bharati Mukherjee's story of an Indian wife welcoming her estranged Indian husband to New York highlights the stark clash of expectations between those cultures, while Alison Lurie's wry 'Fat People' contrasts fat, rich America with thin, poor India. She also captures with chilling accuracy Western women's love–hate relationship with food.

Literature and politics are uneasy bedfellows and, like men, women writers have plenty to say. Belisa Crepusculario, the central character in Isabel Allende's 'Two Words', travels the country selling words and uses them to great effect. The story has even greater power when we realize that Belisa is an anagram of the author's name. Luisa Valenzuela's 'Blue Water-man' depicts angry resistance to the omnipotence and corruption of the official who controls the thirst of an entire village, while Bessie Head's moving story 'Jacob: the Story of a Faith-healing Priest' offers spiritual redemption rather than revolution as a solution to corruption. Nadine Gordimer's succinct 'Comrades' captures the guilt and despair of a white South African woman as she tries to help a group of young black students by offering them a lift in her car, and 'Before' by Annie Saumont reminds us how communities that once shared so much are ripped apart by war, seemingly overnight. Shena Mackay's 'Perpetual Spinach' is warm, funny, brilliant about neighbours, gentrification and the entrenched British class system.

While Chinese state literature boasts of its numerous women writers, unsurprisingly I found no politically overt fiction. The Cultural Revolution and the famine of the late 1950s are still largely taboo, but Chinese women are beginning to write more honestly about the hurdles of daily life. In other foreign stories, it is interesting to note the portrayal of male central characters. Vassily Mikhailovich in Tatyana Tolstaya's 'The Circle' is as reflective and preoccupied with growing older as any woman, and Banana Yoshimoto's unnamed male character in 'Newlywed' is as unhappy with the constraints of marriage as any trapped housewife.

There is an abundance of humour in these stories. Whether it is the natural humour of character in Hanan Al Shaykh's touching 'The Funfair' or the wit of one-liners in Lorrie Moore's 'You're Ugly, Too', these stories add joy to the average day. Women's fiction has in recent years said so much about women's lives: about repression, relationships and failed dreams. Stories such as 'Woman Hollering Creek' by Sandra Cisneros, about a battered pregnant wife, or the spiked revenge against men's' neglect or wrongdoing in 'Hairball' by Margaret Atwood or 'Cream Sauce' by Mary Flanagan are brilliant, heart-rending examples of women's attempts to overcome their impotence and take control of their lives. But these are not the only issues that women writers can or want to write about. A whole range of subject-matter is here.

'The joy and beauty of a short story is that I can read them in one sitting, like drinking a gin and tonic . . . and I can return to them again and again like favourite pictures,' says the writer Helen Simpson. These pictures are windows on a world where women's lives and expectations are rapidly changing. They are tiny tastes from a flourishing of new and exciting talent worldwide.

# Nineteen Fifty-five

*Alice Walker was born in Eatonton, Georgia, an all-black town, in 1944. She was the youngest of eight children of a poor share-cropper family and at eight years old lost the sight of one eye when her brother accidentally shot her. Because of her handicap, she was awarded a scholarship to Speiman, a leading black college, where she studied literature. She has taught at Wellesley College and the University of Massachusetts as a consultant in black history. In 1983 she won the American Book Award and the Pulitzer Prize for her third novel,* The Color Purple, *which was subsequently turned into a film by Steven Spielberg. Her novels describe much of the suffering of black women at the hands of not only whites but also black men, and it is her portrayal of black male cruelty that has stirred such controversy in the USA.*

*1955*

The car is a brand-new red Thunderbird convertible, and it's passed the house more than once. It slows down real slow now, and stops at the curb. An older gentleman dressed like a Baptist deacon gets out on the side near the house, and a young fellow who looks about sixteen gets out on the driver's side. They are white, and I wonder what in the world they doing in this neighborhood.

Well, I say to J. T., put your shirt on, anyway, and let me clean these glasses offa the table.

We had been watching the ballgame on TV. I wasn't actually watching, I was sort of daydreaming, with my foots up in J. T.'s lap.

I seen 'em coming on up the walk, brisk, like they coming to sell something, and then they rung the bell, and J. T. declined to put on a shirt but instead disappeared into the bedroom where the other television is. I turned down the one in the living room; I figured I'd be rid of these two double quick and J. T. could come back out again.

Are you Gracie Mae Still? asked the old guy, when I opened the door and put my hand on the lock inside the screen.

And I don't need to buy a thing, said I.

What makes you think we're sellin'? he asks, in that hearty Southern way that makes my eyeballs ache.

Well, one way or another and they're inside the house and the first thing the young fellow does is raise the TV a couple of decibels. He's about five feet nine, sort of womanish looking, with real dark white skin and a red pouting mouth. His hair is black and curly and he looks like a Loosianna creole.

About one of your songs, says the deacon. He is maybe sixty, with white hair and beard, white silk shirt, black linen suit, black tie and black shoes. His cold gray eyes look like they're sweating.

One of my songs?

Traynor here just *loves* your songs. Don't you, Traynor? He nudges Traynor with his elbow. Traynor blinks, says something I can't catch in a pitch I don't register.

The boy learned to sing and dance livin' round you people out in the country. Practically cut his teeth on you.

Traynor looks up at me and bites his thumbnail.

I laugh.

Well, one way or another they leave with my agreement that they can record one of my songs. The deacon writes me a check for five hundred dollars, the boy grunts his awareness of the transaction, and I am laughing all over myself by the time I rejoin J. T.

Just as I am snuggling down beside him though I hear the front door bell going off again.

Forgit his hat? asks J. T.

I hope not, I say.

The deacon stands there leaning on the door frame and once again I'm thinking of those sweaty-looking eyeballs of his. I wonder if sweat makes your eyeballs pink because his are sure pink. Pink and gray and it strikes me that nobody I'd care to know is behind them.

I forgot one little thing, he says pleasantly. I forgot to tell you Traynor and I would like to buy up all of those records you made of the song. I tell you we sure do love it.

Well, love it or not, I'm not so stupid as to let them do that without making 'em pay. So I says, Well, that's gonna cost you. Because, really, that song never did sell all that good, so I was glad they was going to buy it up. But on the other hand, them two listening to my song by themselves, and nobody else getting to hear me sing it, give me a pause.

Well, one way or another the deacon showed me where I would come out ahead on any deal he had proposed so far. Didn't I give you five hundred dollars? he asked. What white man – and don't even need to mention colored – would give you more? We buy up all your records of that particular song: first, you git royalties. Let me ask you, how much you sell that song for in the first place? Fifty dollars? A hundred, I say. And no royalties from it yet, right? Right. Well, when we buy up all of them records you gonna git royalties. And that's gonna make all them race record shops sit up and take notice of Gracie Mae Still. And they gonna push all them other records of yourn they got. And you no doubt will become one of the big-name colored recording artists. And then we can offer you another five hundred dollars for letting us do all this for you. And by God you'll be sittin' pretty! You can go out and buy you the kind of outfit a star should have. Plenty sequins and yards of red satin.

I had done unlocked the screen when I saw I could get some more money out of him. Now I held it wide open while he squeezed through the opening between me and the door. He whipped out another piece of paper and I signed it.

He sort of trotted out to the car and slid in beside Traynor, whose head was back against the seat. They swung around in a U-turn in front of the house and then they was gone.

J. T. was putting his shirt on when I got back to the bedroom. Yankees beat the Orioles 10–6, he said. I believe I'll drive out to Paschal's pond and go fishing. Wanta go?

While I was putting on my pants J. T. was holding the two checks.

I'm real proud of a woman that can make cash money without leavin' home, he said. And I said *Umph*. Because we met on the road with me singing in first one little low-life jook after another, making ten dollars a night for myself if I was lucky, and sometimes bringin' home nothing but my life. And J. T. just loved them times. The way I was fast and flashy and always on the go from one town to another. He loved the way my singin' made the dirt farmers cry like babies and the womens shout Honey, hush! But that's mens. They loves any style to which you can get 'em accustomed.

*1956*

My little grandbaby called me one night on the phone: Little Mama, Little Mama, there's a white man on the television singing one of your songs! Turn on channel 5.

Lord, if it wasn't Traynor. Still looking half asleep from the neck up, but kind of awake in a nasty way from the waist down. He wasn't doing too bad with my song either, but it wasn't just the song the people in the audience was screeching and screaming over, it was that nasty little jerk he was doing from the waist down.

Well, Lord have mercy, I said, listening to him. If I'da closed my eyes, it could have been me. He had followed every turning of my voice, side streets, avenues, red lights, train crossings and all. It give me a chill.

Everywhere I went I heard Traynor singing my song, and all the little white girls just eating it up. I never had so many ponytails switched across my line of vision in my life. They was so *proud*. He was a *genius*.

Well, all that year I was trying to lose weight anyway and that and high blood pressure and sugar kept me pretty well occupied. Traynor had made a smash from a song of mine, I still had seven hundred dollars of the original one thousand dollars in the bank, and I felt if I could just bring my weight down, life would be sweet.

*1957*

I lost ten pounds in 1956. That's what I give myself for Christmas. And J. T. and me and the children and their friends and grandkids of all description had just finished dinner – over which I had put on nine and a half of my lost ten – when who should appear at the front door but Traynor. Little Mama, Little Mama! It's that white man who sings '— — —'. The children didn't call it my song anymore. Nobody did. It was funny how that happened. Traynor and the deacon had bought up all my records, true, but on his record he had put 'written by Gracie Mae Still'. But that was just another name on the label, like 'produced by Apex Records'.

On the TV he was inclined to dress like the deacon told him. But now he looked presentable.

Merry Christmas, said he.

And same to you, Son.

I don't know why I called him Son. Well, one way or another they're all our sons. The only requirement is that they be younger than us. But then again, Traynor seemed to be aging by the minute.

You looks tired, I said. Come on in and have a glass of Christmas cheer.

J. T. ain't never in his life been able to act decent to a white man he wasn't working for, but he poured Traynor a glass of bourbon and water, then he took all the children and grandkids and friends and whatnot out to the den. After while I heard Traynor's voice singing the song, coming from the stereo console. It was just the kind of Christmas present my kids would consider cute.

I looked at Traynor, complicit. But he looked like it was the last thing in the world he wanted to hear. His head was pitched forward over his lap, his hands holding his glass and his elbows on his knees.

I done sung that song seem like a million times this year, he said. I sung it on the Grand Ole Opry, I sung it on the Ed Sullivan show. I sung it on Mike Douglas, I sung it at the Cotton Bowl, the Orange Bowl. I sung it at Festivals. I sung it at Fairs. I sung it overseas in Rome, Italy, and once in a submarine *underseas*. I've sung it and sung it, and I'm making forty thousand dollars a day offa it, and you know what, I don't have the faintest notion what that song means.

Whatchumean, what do it mean? It mean what it says. All I could think was: These suckers is making forty thousand a *day* offa my song and now they gonna come back and try to swindle me out of the original thousand.

It's just a song, I said. Cagey. When you fool around with a lot of no count mens you sing a bunch of 'em. I shrugged.

Oh, he said. Well. He started brightening up. I just come by to tell you I think you are a great singer.

He didn't blush, saying that. Just said it straight out.

And I brought you a little Christmas present too. Now you take this little box and you hold it until I drive off. Then you take it outside under that first streetlight back up the street aways in front of that green house. Then you open the box and see . . . Well, just *see*.

What had come over this boy, I wondered, holding the box. I looked out the window in time to see another white man come up and get in the car with him and then two more cars full of white mens start out behind him. They was all in long black cars that looked like a funeral procession.

Little Mama, Little Mama, what is it? One of my grandkids come running up and started pulling at the box. It was wrapped in gay Christmas paper – the thick, rich kind that it's hard to picture folks making just to throw away.

J. T. and the rest of the crowd followed me out the house, up the street to the streetlight and in front of the green house. Nothing was there but somebody's gold-grilled white Cadillac. Brandnew and most distracting. We got to looking at it so till I almost forgot the little box in my hand. While the others were busy making 'miration I carefully took off the paper and ribbon and folded them up and put them in my pants pocket. What should I see but a pair of genuine solid gold caddy keys.

Dangling the keys in front of everybody's nose, I unlocked the caddy, motioned for J. T. to git in on the other side, and us didn't come back home for two days.

*1960*

Well, the boy was sure nuff famous by now. He was still a mite shy of twenty but already they was calling him the Emperor of Rock and Roll.

Then what should happen but the draft.

Well, says J. T. There goes all this Emperor of Rock and Roll business.

But even in the army the womens was on him like white on rice. We watched it on the News.

*Dear Gracie Mae* [he wrote from Germany],

*How you? Fine I hope as this leaves me doing real well. Before I come in the army I was gaining a lot of weight and gitting jittery from making all them dumb movies. But now I exercise and eat right and get plenty of rest. I'm more awake than I been in ten years.*

*I wonder if you are writing any more songs?*

*Sincerely,*
*Traynor*

I wrote him back:

*Dear Son,*

*We is all fine in the Lord's good grace and hope this finds you the same. J. T. and me be out all times of the day and night in that car you give me – which you know you didn't have to do. Oh, and I do appreciate the mink and the new self-cleaning oven. But if you send anymore stuff to eat from Germany I'm going to have to open up a store in the neighborhood just to get rid of it. Really, we have more than enough of everything. The Lord is good to us and we don't know Want.*

*Glad to here you is well and gitting your right rest. There ain't nothing like exercising to help that along. J. T. and me work some part of every day that we don't go fishing in the garden.*

*Well, so long Soldier.*

*Sincerely,*
*Gracie Mae*

He wrote:

*Dear Gracie Mae,*

*I hope you and J. T. like that automatic power tiller I had one of the stores back home send you. I went through a mountain of catalogs looking for it – I wanted something that even a woman could use.*

*I've been thinking about writing some songs of my own but every time I finish one it don't seem to be about nothing I've actually lived myself. My agent keeps sending me other people's songs but they just sound mooney. I can hardly git through 'em without gagging.*

*Everybody still loves that song of yours. They ask me all the time what do I think it means, really. I mean, they want to know just what I want to know. Where out of your life did it come from?*

*Sincerely,*
*Traynor*

*1968*

I didn't see the boy for seven years. No. Eight. Because just about every-body was dead when I saw him again. Malcolm X, King, the president and his brother, and even J. T. J. T. died of a head cold. It just settled in his head like a block of ice, he said, and nothing we did moved it until one day he just leaned out the bed and died.

His good friend Horace helped me put him away, and then about a year later Horace and me started going together. We was sitting out on the front porch swing one summer night, dusk-dark, and I saw this great procession of lights winding to a stop.

Holy Toledo! said Horace. (He's got a real sexy voice like Ray Charles.) Look *at* it. He meant the long line of flashy cars and the white men in white summer suits jumping out on the drivers' sides and standing at attention. With wings they could pass for angels, with hoods they could be the Klan.

Traynor comes waddling up the walk.

And suddenly I know what it is he could pass for. An Arab like the ones you see in storybooks. Plump and soft and with never a care about weight. Because with so much money, who cares? Traynor is almost dressed like someone from a storybook too. He has on, I swear, about ten necklaces. Two sets of bracelets on his arms, at least one ring on every finger, and some kind of shining buckles on his shoes, so that when he walks you get quite a few twinkling lights.

Gracie Mae, he says, coming up to give me a hug. J. T.

I explain that J. T. passed. That this is Horace.

Horace, he says, puzzled but polite, sort of rocking back on his heels, Horace.

That's it for Horace. He goes in the house and don't come back.

Looks like you and me is gained a few, I say.

He laughs. The first time I ever heard him laugh. It don't sound much like a laugh and I can't swear that it's better than no laugh a'tall.

He's gitting fat for sure, but he's still slim compared to me. I'll never see three hundred pounds again and I've just about said (excuse me) fuck it. I got to thinking about it one day an' I thought: aside from the fact that they say it's unhealthy, my fat ain't never been no trouble. Mens always have loved me. My kids ain't never complained. Plus they's fat. And fat like I is I looks distinguished. You see me coming and know somebody's *there*.

Gracie Mae, he says, I've come with a personal invitation to you to my house tomorrow for dinner. He laughed. What did it sound like? I couldn't place it. See them men out there? he asked me. I'm sick and tired of eating with them. They don't never have nothing to talk about. That's why I eat so much. But if you come to dinner tomorrow we can talk about the old days. You can tell me about that farm I bought you.

I sold it, I said.

You did?

Yeah, I said, I did. Just cause I said I liked to exercise by working in a garden didn't mean I wanted five hundred acres! Anyhow, I'm a city girl now. Raised in the country it's true. Dirt poor – the whole bit – but that's all behind me now.

Oh well, he said, I didn't mean to offend you.

We sat a few minutes listening to the crickets.

Then he said: You wrote that song while you was still on the farm, didn't you, or was it right after you left?

You had somebody spying on me? I asked.

You and Bessie Smith got into a fight over it once, he said.

You *is* been spying on me!

But I don't know what the fight was about, he said. Just like I don't know what happened to your second husband. Your first one died in the Texas electric chair. Did you know that? Your third one beat you up, stole your touring costumes and your car and retired with a chorine to Tuskegee. He laughed. He's still there.

I had been mad, but suddenly I calmed down. Traynor was talking very dreamily. It was dark but seems like I could tell his eyes weren't right. It was like some*thing* was sitting there talking to me but not necessarily with a person behind it.

You gave up on marrying and seem happier for it. He laughed again. I married but it never went like it was supposed to. I never could squeeze any of my own life either into it or out of it. It was like singing somebody else's record. I copied the way it was sposed to be *exactly* but I never had a clue what marriage meant.

I bought her a diamond ring big as your fist. I bought her clothes. I built her a mansion. But right away she didn't want the boys to stay there. Said they smoked up the bottom floor. Hell, there were *five* floors.

No need to grieve, I said. No need to. Plenty more where she come from.

He perked up. That's part of what that song means, ain't it? No need to grieve. Whatever it is, there's plenty more down the line.

I never really believed that way back when I wrote that song, I said. It was all bluffing then. The trick is to live long enough to put your young bluffs to use. Now if I was to sing that song today I'd tear it up. 'Cause I done lived long enough to know it's *true*. Them words could hold me up.

I ain't lived that long, he said.

Look like you on your way, I said. I don't know why, but the boy seemed to need some encouraging. And I don't know, seem like one way or another you talk to rich white folks and you end up reassuring *them*. But what the hell, by now I feel something for the boy. I wouldn't be in his bed all alone in the middle of the night for nothing. Couldn't be nothing worse than being famous the world over for something you don't even understand. That's what I tried to tell Bessie. She wanted that same song. Overheard me practicing it one day, said, with her hands on her hips: Gracie Mae, I'ma sing your song tonight. I *likes* it.

Your lips be too swole to sing, I said. She was mean and she was strong, but I trounced her.

Ain't you famous enough with your own stuff? I said. Leave mine alone. Later on, she thanked me. By then she was Miss Bessie Smith to the World, and I was still Miss Gracie Mae Nobody from Notasulga.

The next day all these limousines arrived to pick me up. Five cars and twelve bodyguards. Horace picked that morning to start painting the kitchen.

Don't paint the kitchen, fool, I said. The only reason that dumb boy of ours is going to show me his mansion is because he intends to present us with a new house.

What you gonna do with it? he asked me, standing there in his shirt-sleeves stirring the paint.

Sell it. Give it to the children. Live in it on weekends. It don't matter what I do. He sure don't care.

Horace just stood there shaking his head. Mama you sure looks *good*, he says. Wake me up when you git back.

*Fool*, I say, and pat my wig in front of the mirror.

*

The boy's house is something else. First you come to this mountain, and then you commence to drive and drive up this road that's lined with magnolias. Do magnolias grow on mountains? I was wondering. And you come to lakes and you come to ponds and you come to deer and you come up on some sheep. And I figure these two is sposed to represent England and Wales. Or something out of Europe. And you just keep on coming to stuff. And it's all pretty. Only the man driving my car don't look at nothing but the road. Fool. And then *finally*, after all this time, you begin to go up the driveway. And there's more magnolias – only they're not in such good shape. It's sort of cool up this high and I don't think they're gonna make it. And then I see this building that looks like if it had a name it would be the Tara Hotel. Columns and steps and outdoor chandeliers and rocking chairs. Rocking chairs? Well, and there's the boy on the steps dressed in a dark-green satin jacket like you see folks wearing on TV late at night, and he looks sort of like a fat Dracula with all that house rising behind him, and standing beside him there's this little white vision of loveliness that he introduces as his wife.

He's nervous when he introduces us and he says to her: This is Gracie Mae Still, I want you to know me. I mean . . . and she gives him a look that would fry meat.

Won't you come in, Gracie Mae, she says, and that's the last I see of her.

He fishes around for something to say or do and decides to escort me to the kitchen. We go through the entry and the parlor and the breakfast room and the dining-room and the servants' passage and finally get there. The first thing I notice is that, altogether, there are five stoves. He looks about to introduce me to one.

Wait a minute, I say. Kitchens don't do nothing for me. Let's go sit on the front porch.

Well, we hike back and we sit in the rocking chairs rocking until dinner.

Gracie Mae, he says down the table, taking a piece of fried chicken from the woman standing over him, I got a little surprise for you.

It's a house, ain't it? I ask, spearing a chitlin.

You're getting *spoiled*, he says. And the way he says *spoiled* sounds funny.

He slurs it. It sounds like his tongue is too thick for his mouth. Just that quick he's finished the chicken and is now eating chitlins *and* a pork chop. *Me* spoiled, I'm thinking.

I already got a house. Horace is right this minute painting the kitchen. I bought that house. My kids feel comfortable in that house.

But this one I bought you is just like mine. Only a little smaller.

I still don't need no house. And anyway who would clean it?

He looks surprised.

Really, I think, some peoples advance *so* slowly.

I hadn't thought of that. But what the hell, I'll get you somebody to live in.

I don't want other folks living 'round me. Makes me nervous.

You *don't*? It *do*?

What I want to wake up and see folks I don't even know for?

He just sits there downtable staring at me. Some of that feeling is in the song, ain't it? Not the words, the *feeling*. What I want to wake up and see folks I don't even know for? But I see twenty folks a day I don't even know, including my wife.

This food wouldn't be bad to wake up to though, I said. The boy had found the genius of corn bread.

He looked at me real hard. He laughed. Short. They want what you got but they don't want you. They want what I got only it ain't mine. That's what makes 'em so hungry for me when I sing. They getting the flavor of something but they ain't getting the thing itself. They like a pack of hound dogs trying to gobble up a scent.

You talking 'bout your fans?

Right. Right, he says.

Don't worry 'bout your fans, I say. They don't know their asses from a hole in the ground. I doubt there's a honest one in the bunch.

That's the point. Dammit, that's the point! He hits the table with his fist. It's so solid it don't even quiver. You need a honest audience! You can't have folks that's just gonna lie right back to you.

Yeah, I say, it was small compared to yours, but I had one. It would have been worth my life to try to sing 'em somebody else's stuff that I didn't know nothing about.

He must have pressed a buzzer under the table. One of his flunkies zombies up.

Git Johnny Carson, he says.

On the phone? asks the zombie.

On the phone, says Traynor, what you think I mean, git him offa the front porch? Move your ass.

So two weeks later we's on the Johnny Carson show.

Traynor is all corseted down nice and looks a little bit fat but mostly good. And all the women that grew up on him and my song squeal and squeal. Traynor says: The lady who wrote my first hit record is here with us tonight, and she's agreed to sing it for all of us, just like she sung it forty-five years ago. Ladies and Gentlemen, the great Gracie Mae Still!

Well, I had tried to lose a couple of pounds my own self, but failing that I had me a very big dress made. So I sort of rolls over next to Traynor, who is dwarfted by me, so that when he puts his arm around back of me to try to hug me it looks funny to the audience and they laugh.

I can see this pisses him off. But I smile out there at 'em. Imagine squealing for twenty years and not knowing why you're squealing? No more sense of endings and beginnings than hogs.

It don't matter, Son, I say. Don't fret none over me.

I commence to sing. And I sound – wonderful. Being able to sing good ain't all about having a good singing voice a'tall. A good singing voice helps. But when you come up in the Hard Shell Baptist church like I did you understand early that the fellow that sings is the singer. Them that waits for programs and arrangements and letters from home is just good voices occupying body space.

So there I am singing my own song, my own way. And I give it all I got and enjoy every minute of it. When I finish Traynor is standing up clapping and clapping and beaming at first me and then the audience like I'm his mama for true. The audience claps politely for about two seconds.

Traynor looks disgusted.

He comes over and tries to hug me again. The audience laughs.

Johnny Carson looks at us like we both weird.

Traynor is mad as hell. He's supposed to sing something called a love ballad. But instead he takes the mike, turns to me and says: Now see if my imitation still holds up. He goes into the same song, *our* song, I think, looking out at his flaky audience. And he sings it just the way he always did. My voice, my tone, my inflection, everything. But he forgets a couple of lines. Even before he's finished the matronly squeals begin.

He sits down next to me looking whipped.

It don't matter, Son, I say, patting his hand. You don't even know those people. Try to make the people you know happy.

Is that in the song? he asks.

Maybe. I say.

*1977*

For a few years I hear from him, then nothing. But trying to lose weight takes all the attention I got to spare. I finally faced up to the fact that my fat is the hurt I don't admit, not even to myself, and that I been trying to bury it from the day I was born. But also when you git real old, to tell the truth, it ain't as pleasant. It gits lumpy and slack. Yuck. So one day I said to Horace, I'ma git this shit offa me.

And he fell in with the program like he always try to do and Lord such a procession of salads and cottage cheese and fruit juice!

One night I dreamed Traynor had split up with his fifteenth wife. He said: *You meet 'em for no reason. You date 'em for no reason. You marry 'em for no reason. I do it all but I swear it's just like somebody else doing it. I feel like I can't remember Life.*

The boy's in trouble, I said to Horace.

You've always said that, he said.

I have?

Yeah. You always said he looked asleep. You can't sleep through life if you wants to live it.

You not such a fool after all, I said, pushing myself up with my cane and hobbling over to where he was. Let me sit down on your lap, I said, while this salad I ate takes effect.

In the morning we heard Traynor was dead. Some said fat, some said heart, some said alcohol, some said drugs. One of the children called from Detroit. Them dumb fans of his is on a crying rampage, she said. You just ought to turn on the TV.

But I didn't want to see 'em. They was crying and crying and didn't even know what they was crying for. One day this is going to be a pitiful country, I thought.

# The Circle

Translated by Antonina W. Bollis

*Tatyana Tolstaya was born in Leningrad in 1951 and is the granddaughter of Alexei Tolstoy. Her father is a physicist and an accomplished linguist who taught her two languages, and many of her seven siblings are involved in the arts. After graduating from Leningrad State University in 1974 with a degree in classics and Russian literature, she married, moved to Moscow and became a junior editor in a publishing house, where she worked for eight years before devoting herself to full-time writing. She has published two collections of short stories,* On the Golden Porch *(1987) and* Sleepwalker in a Fog *(1992). Her major inspiration is Vladimir Nabokov, and her stories are said to be difficult to translate because her style is rich and complex with a combination of high romanticism and low urban slang.*

The world is ended, the world is distorted, the world is closed, and it is closed around Vassily Mikhailovich.

At sixty, fur coats get heavy, stairs grow steep, and your heart is with you day and night. You've walked and walked, from hill to hill, past shimmering lakes, past radiant islands, white birds overhead, speckled snakes underfoot, and you've arrived here, and this is where you've ended up; it's dark and lonely here, and your collar chokes you and your blood creaks in your veins. *This* is sixty.

This is it, it's over. Here no grass grows. The soil is frozen, the earth is narrow and stony, and ahead only one sign glows: exit.

But Vassily Mikhailovich didn't want this.

He sat in the hallway of the beauty parlour and waited for his wife. Through the open door he could see the crowded room, partitioned with

mirrors, where three . . . three women his own age were squirming in the
hands of mighty blonde furies. Could he call the things that were multi-
plying in the mirrors 'ladies'? With growing horror, Vassily Mikhailovich
peered at what sat closest to him. A curly-haired siren planted her feet
firmly, grabbed *it* by the head, pulled it back on to a waiting metal basin,
and splashed it with boiling water: steam rose; she lathered wildly; more
steam, and before Vassily Mikhailovich could cry out she had fallen upon
her victim and was choking it with a white terry-towel. He looked away. In
another chair – my God – long wires were attached to a reddened, albeit
very happy head, with protruding diodes, triodes, and resistors . . . In the
third chair, he realized, was Yevgeniya Ivanovna, and he went over to her.
What at home went by the name of her hair was now wrinkled up,
revealing her scalp, and a woman in a white coat was dabbing at it with a
stick dipped in some kind of liquid. The odour was stifling.

'Take off your coat!' several voices cried.

'Zhenya, I'm going for a walk, just taking a turn,' Vassily Mikhailovich
said, waving his arm. He had felt weak in the legs since morning, his heart
was thumping and he was thirsty.

In the lobby stiff green sabres grew hilt-down out of large pots, and
photographs of bizarre creatures with unpleasant glints in their eyes
stared from the walls under incredible hair – towers, icing, rams' horns; or
ripples, like mashed potatoes in fancy restaurants. And Yevgeniya
Ivanovna wanted to be one of them.

A cold wind blew, and small dry flakes fell from the sky. The day was
dark, empty, brief; its evening had been born with the dawn. Lights burned
brightly and cosily in the small stores. A tiny, glowing, sweet-smelling
store, a box of miracles, had grown on to the corner. You couldn't get in:
people were pushing and shoving, reaching over heads with their chits,
grabbing little somethings. A fat woman was trapped in the doorway, she
clutched the jamb, she was being carried away by the flow.

'Let me out! Let me get out!'

'What's in there?'

'Lip gloss!'

Vassily Mikhailovich joined the jostling. *Woman, woman*, do you exist? . . .
What are you? . . . High up a Siberian tree your hat blinks its eyes in fear; a
cow gives birth in suffering so you can have shoes; a lamb is sheared

screaming so you can warm yourself with its fleece; a sperm whale is in its death throes; a crocodile weeps; a doomed leopard pants, fleeing. Your pink cheeks come from boxes of flying dust, your smiles from golden containers with strawberry filling, your smooth skin from tubes of grease, your gaze from round transparent jars . . . He bought Yevgeniya Ivanovna a pair of eyelashes.

. . . Everything is predestined and you can't swerve from the path – that's what bothered Vassily Mikhailovich. You don't pick wives: they simply appear out of nowhere by your side, and you're struggling in fine netting, bound hand and foot; hobbled and gagged, you're taught thousands and thousands of stifling details of transient life, put on your knees, your wings clipped; and the darkness gathers, and sun and moon still run and run chasing each other along a circle, *the circle, the circle.*

It was revealed to Vassily Mikhailovich how to clean spoons, and the comparative physiology of meatballs and patties; he knew by heart the grievously brief lifespan of sour cream – one of his responsibilities was destroying it at the first signs of mortal agony – he knew the birthplaces of brooms and whisks, he could distinguish grains professionally, had in his head all the prices of glassware, and every autumn wiped window panes with ammonium chloride to eradicate the ice cherry orchards that planned to grow by winter.

At times Vassily Mikhailovich imagined that he would finish this life and begin a new one in a new image. He fussily selected his age, an era, his looks: sometimes he wanted to be born a fiery southern youth; or a medieval alchemist; or the daughter of a millionaire; or a widow's beloved cat; or a Persian king. Vassily Mikhailovich calculated, compared, deliberated, made conditions, grew ambitious, rejected all suggested possibilities, demanded guarantees, huffed, grew tired, lost his train of thought; and, leaning back in his armchair, stared long and hard in the mirror at himself – the one and only.

Nothing happened. Vassily Mikhailovich was not visited by a six-winged seraph or any other feathery creature with offers of supernatural services; nothing burst open, there was no voice from the heavens, no one tempted him, carried him aloft, or hurled him down. The three-dimensionality of existence, whose finale was ever approaching, suffocated Vassily Mikhailovich; he tried to get off the tracks, drill a hole in the sky, leave through a drawing of a door. Once, dropping off sheets at the laundry, Vassily Mikhailovich stared into the blossoming clover of cotton expanses, and noticed that the seven-digit notation sewn on to the north-east corner resembled a telephone number; he secretly called, and was graciously welcomed, and began a boring joyless affair with a woman named Klara. Klara's house was just like Vassily Mikhailovich's, with the same clean kitchen, although the windows faced north, and the same cot, and as he got into Klara's starched bed Vassily Mikhailovich saw yet another telephone number in the corner of the pillow case; he doubted that his fate awaited him there, but, bored by Klara, he called and got through to a woman, Svetlana, with a nine-year-old son; in Svetlana's linen cupboard, clean folded linen lay with pieces of good soap in between the layers.

Yevgeniya Ivanovna sensed that something was up, looked for clues, rummaged in his pockets, unfolded scraps of paper, unaware that she was sleeping in the pages of a large telephone directory with Klara's telephone number in it, or that Klara dreamed in Svetlana's telephone number, or that Svetlana reposed, as it turned out, in the number of the accounting department of the social security office.

Vassily Mikhailovich's women never did learn of one another's existence; but, of course, Vassily Mikhailovich did not exactly pester them with information about himself. And where would he have got a surname, a job, an address or, say, a postal code – he, the phantom of blanket covers and pillow cases, born of chance whims of the laundry office?

Vassily Mikhailovich stopped the experiment. Not because of the social security office; it was just that he realized that the attempt to escape the system of coordinates was a failure. It wasn't a new, unheard-of road with breathtaking possibilities that opened before him, not a secret path into the beyond, no; he had simply felt around in the dark and grabbed the usual wheel of fate and if he went around it hand over hand, along the curve, along the circle, he would eventually end up with himself, from the other side.

For, after all, somewhere in the bustling crowd, in the thick tangle of back streets, a nameless old woman is tossing a sack of worn linen marked with a seven-digit cryptogram through a small wooden window: you are enciphered in it, Vassily Mikhailovich. In all fairness, you belong to the old woman. She has every right to you – what if she makes her demand? You don't want that? Vassily Mikhailovich – *no, no, no* – didn't want a strange old woman, he was afraid of her stockings, and her feet, and her yeasty smell, and the creak of bedsprings under her white elderly body, and he was sure she'd have a tea mushroom growing in a three-litre jar – a slippery eyeless silent creature, living years very quietly on the windowsill without splashing even once.

But the one who holds the thread of fate in his hands, who determines meetings, who sends algebraic travellers from Point A to Point B, who fills pools from two pipes, had already marked with a red X the intersections where he was to meet Isolde. Now, of course, it was quite some time since she had passed away.

He saw Isolde at the market and followed her. A peek from the side at her face blue with cold, at her transparent grapelike eyes, and he knew: she would be the one to bring him out of the tight pencil case called the universe. She wore a shabby fur coat with a belt and a thin knitted hat – one of those caps sold in their dozens by the stocky, heavy women who blocked the entrances to the market; women who like suicides are banned within the gates, turned away from proper stalls, and whose shadows, hard in the frost, wander in crowds along the blue fence, holding in their outstretched hands piles of woolly pancakes – raspberry, green, canary, rustling in the wind – while the early November flakes fall, fall, blowing and whistling, hurrying to wrap the city in winter.

And Vassily Mikhailovich, his heart contracting with hope, watched the meek Isolde, chilled to the bone, to an icy crunch, wander through the black crowd and nip inside the gates and run her finger along the long, empty counters, looking to see if there was anything tasty left.

The northern blizzards had blown away the hothouse sellers of capricious summer produce, those sweet marvels created on high by warm air from pink and white flowers. But the last faithful servants of the soil stood firm, frozen to the wooden tables, grimly offering their cold underground catch: for in the face of annual death nature gets scared, turns round, and grows head down, giving birth in the final moments to coarse, harsh, clumsy creatures – the black dome of radish, the monstrous white nerve of horseradish, the secret potato cities.

And the disappointed Isolde wandered on, along the light-blue fence, past the galoshes and plywood crates, past the tattered magazines and wire brooms, past the drunkard offering white porcelain plugs, past the man indifferently fanning out coloured photographs; on and on, sad and shivering, and a pushy woman was now spinning a bright woollen wheel right before her blue face, and singing its praises, and scratching it, tugging at it with a big-toothed metal brush.

Vassily Mikhailovich took Isolde by the arm and offered her some wine, and his words glistened with winey sparkle. He led her to a restaurant and the crowd parted for them, and the cloakroom attendant took her raiment as if it were the magical swan feathers of a fairy bather who had come from the heavens to a small forest lake. The columns emitted a soft marble aroma, and roses floated in the dim lighting. Vassily Mikhailovich was almost young, and Isolde was like a wild silvery bird, one of a kind.

Yevgeniya Ivanovna sensed Isolde's shadow, and she dug pits, put up barbed wire, and forged chains to keep Vassily Mikhailovich from leaving. Lying next to Yevgeniya Ivanovna with his heart pounding, he saw with his inner eye the cool calm of fresh snow glowing on the midnight streets. The untouched whiteness stretched, stretched, smoothly turned the corner: and on the corner, a Venetian window filled with pink light; and within it, Isolde lay awake listening to the unclear blizzard melody in the city, to the dark winter cellos. And Vassily Mikhailovich, gasping in the dark, mentally sent his soul to Isolde, knowing that it would reach her along the sparkling arc that connected them across the city, invisible to the uninitiated:

> *Night trains jangle in my throat,*
> *It comes, and grabs, and grows silent once more.*
> *The crucified hangs above a deep hole*
> *Where angels of death buzz like gnats:*
> *'Give up! You're locked in a square,*
> *We'll come, release you, and begin once more.'*
> *O woman! Apple tree! Candle flame!*
> *Break through, chase away, protect, scream!*
> *Hands tied, mouth contorted,*
> *A black maiden sings in the dark.*

Vassily Mikhailovich chewed through the chain and ran away from Yevgeniya Ivanovna; he and Isolde sat holding hands, and he flung open wide the doors to his soul's treasures. He was as generous as Ali Baba, and she was astonished and trembled. Isolde did not ask for anything: not a crystal toilette, not the Queen of Sheba's coloured sash; she would be happy to sit for ever at his side, burning like a wedding candle, burning without extinguishing with a steady quiet flame.

Soon Vassily Mikhailovich had told her everything he had to tell. Now it was Isolde's turn: she had to wrap her weak blue arms around him and step with him into a new dimension, so that lightning, with a flash, would shatter the ordinary world like an eggshell. But nothing of the kind happened. Isolde just trembled and trembled, and Vassily Mikhailovich grew bored. 'Well, Lyalya?' he would say with a yawn.

He paced the room in his socks, scratched his head, smoked by the window, and stuck the butts in the flower pots, packed his razor in his suitcase: he planned to go back to Yevgeniya Ivanovna. The clock ticked, Isolde wept, not understanding, vowing she would die, there was slush beneath the window. Why make a scene? Why didn't she grind some meat and make patties instead? I said I was leaving, that meant I was leaving. What was unclear about that?

Yevgeniya Ivanovna was so glad she baked a carrot pie, washed her hair, polished the floors. He celebrated his fortieth birthday first at home, then in a restaurant. They packed the uneaten fish and jellied meat in plastic bags, and there was enough for lunch the next day. He got good presents: a radio, a clock with a wooden eagle, and a camera. Yevgeniya Ivanovna had been dreaming of being photographed at the beach in the surf. Isolde did not control herself and sort of ruined the party. She sent some stuff wrapped in paper and an unsigned poem, in her childish handwriting:

> *Here is a gift for you in parting:*
> *Candle stub,*
> *Shoe laces and a plum stone.*
> *Look closely and smile crookedly.*
> *This was*
> *Your love until it died:*

*Fire, and skipping, and sweet fruit*
*Above the abyss, and the brink of disaster.*

She was no longer alive.

And now he was sixty, and the wind blew up his sleeves, into his heart, and his legs refused to go. Nothing, nothing was happening, nothing lay ahead, and really there was nothing behind, either. For sixty years he'd been waiting for them to come and call him and show him the mystery of mysteries, for red dawn to blaze over half the world, for a staircase of rays to rise from earth to heaven and for archangels with trombones and saxophones or whatever they used to blare their unearthly voices, welcoming the chosen one. But why were they taking so long? He'd been waiting his whole life.

He hastened his step. While they shaved Yevgeniya Ivanovna's neck, boiled her head, and bent her hair with metal hooks, he could reach the market and have some warm beer. It was cold, his fur coat was cheap, a fur coat in name only – fake leather lined with fake fur – which Yevgeniya Ivanovna had bought from a black marketeer. 'She skins crocodiles for herself, though,' thought Vassily Mikhailovich. They had gone to the black marketeer – for crocodile shoes, the fur coat, and other trifles – in the evening, searching a long time for the right house. It was dark on the landing, they felt around, having no matches. Vassily Mikhailovich swore softly. To his amazement he felt a peephole at knee level on one of the doors.

'That's the right place, then,' his wife whispered.

'What does she do, crawl around on all fours?'

'She's a dwarf, a circus midget.'

With bated breath he felt the nearness of a miracle: beyond the vinyl-covered door, perhaps the one and only door in the world, gaped the passageway into another universe, breathed living darkness, and a tiny, translucent elf soared among the stars, trembling on dragonfly wings, tinkling like a bell.

The dwarf turned out to be old, mad, mean, and didn't let them touch any of the things. Vassily Mikhailovich surreptitiously looked at the bed with the stepladder, the children's chairs, the photographs hung low, just above the floor, testimony to the faded charms of the Lilliputian. There, in the pictures, standing on the back of a dolled-up horse, in ballet costume, in glass circus diamonds, happy, tiny, the young black marketeer waved through the glass, through time, through a lifetime. And here, pulling enormous adult clothing out of the closet with tiny wrinkled hands, the evil troll ran back and forth, the guardian of underground gold, and the Gulliver shadow cast by the low-hanging lamp also ran back and forth. Yevgeniya Ivanovna bought the fur coat, and the crocodile shoes, and a winking Japanese wallet, and a scarf with Lurex threads, and an Arctic fox fur for a hat from the horrible child, and while they made their way down the dark stairs, supporting each other, she explained to Vassily Mikhailovich that you clean Arctic fox with potato-flour grains heated on a dry skillet, and that the skin side of the fur should be kept away from water, and that she now had to buy a half metre of plain ribbon. Vassily Mikhailovich, trying not to remember any of this, thought about what the dwarf had been like in her youth, and whether dwarves can marry, and that if they were to jail her for illegal trading, the prison cell would seem so big and frightening to her, every rat would be like a horse, and then he imagined that the young black marketeer was imprisoned in a gloomy barred castle with nothing but owls and bats, wringing her doll-like hands, it was dark and he was creeping towards the castle with a rope ladder over his shoulder through the evil grounds; only the moon ran behind the black branches like a silver apple, and the dwarf clutched the bars of her window and squeezed through, transparent as a lollipop in the moonlight, and he climbed up, lacerating his fingers on the mossy medieval stones, and the guards were asleep leaning on their halberds, and a raven steed pawed the ground below ready to gallop around the sawdust arena, on the red carpet, round and round the circle.

The time allotted to Vassily Mikhailovich was running out. The ocean was behind him, but the unexplored continent had not blocked his path, new lands had not floated out of the mist, and with anguish he could make out the dreary palms and familiar minarets of India, which the miscalculating Columbus had thirsted for and which meant the end of the road for Vassily Mikhailovich. The trip around the world was coming to an end: his caravel, having circled life, was sailing up from the other side and was entering familiar territory. The familiar social security office, where the pensions fluttered on flagpoles, hove into view, then the opera house, where Svetlana's son, wearing stage eyebrows, sang about the ephemerality of life to the loud applause of Yevgeniya Ivanovna.

'If I run into Isolde,' Vassily Mikhailovich made a bet with fate, 'my path is over.' But he was cheating: Isolde had passed away a long time ago.

Sometimes he still got signals: you are not alone. There are glades in the groves of people, where in hermits' cabins live the ascetics, the chosen who reject the bustle, who seek the secret loophole out of prison.

News arrived: strange objects were appearing, at first glance insignificant, useless, but imbued with a secret meaning; indicators leading to nowhere. One was Cheburashka, a daring challenge to school Darwinism, an old shaggy evolutionary link fallen out of the measured chain of natural selection. Another was Rubik's Cube, a breakable, changeable, but always whole hexahedron. Having stood four hours in the cold along with thousands of grim fellow sect members, Vassily Mikhailovich became the owner of the marvellous cube and spent weeks twisting and twisting its creaking movable facets, until his eyes grew red, waiting in vain for the light to another universe to shine at last from the window. But sensing one night that of the two of them, the real master was the cube, which was doing whatever it wanted to with helpless Vassily Mikhailovich, he got up, went to the kitchen, and chopped up the monster with a cleaver.

In anticipation of revelation he leafed through typewritten pages that taught you to breathe a green square in through one nostril at dawn and to chase it with mental power up and down your intestines. He spent hours standing on his head with his legs crossed in someone's apartment near the railway station, between two unshaven, also upside-down engineers, and the rumble of the trains outside the house speeding into the distance shook their upraised striped socks. And it was all in vain.

Ahead was the market, spattered with booths. Twilight, twilight. Illuminated from inside were the icy windows of the booth where winter sells a snowy pulp covered with chocolate on a splintery stick and the colourful gingerbread house where you can buy various kinds of poisonous smoke and a folding spoon and chains of special very cheap gold; and the desired window where a group of black figures huddled, hearts warmed by happiness, and where a beery dawn glowed translucently with wandering flames in the thick glass of mugs. Vassily Mikhailovich got in the queue and looked around the snowy square.

There was Isolde, legs spread apart. She was blowing beer foam on to her cloth boots, horrible-looking, with a cracked drunken skull and red wrinkled face. Lights were coming on and the first stars were rising: white, blue, green. The icy wind came from the stars to the earth, stirring her uncovered hair, and after circling around her head, moved on to the dark doorways.

'Lyalya,' said Vassily Mikhailovich.

But she was laughing with new friends, stumbling, holding up her mug: a big man was opening a bottle, another man struck the edge of the counter with a dried fish, they were having a good time.

'My heart sings with joy,' Isolde sang. 'Oh, if I could feel this way for ever.'

Vassily Mikhailovich stood and listened to her sing without understanding the words and when he came to, a struggling Isolde was being led away by the militiamen. But that couldn't be Isolde: she had passed away a long time ago.

And he, it seemed, was still alive. But now there was no point to it. Darkness pressed against his heart. The hour of departure had struck. He looked back one last time and saw only a long cold tunnel with icy walls, and himself, crawling with a hand extended, grimly smothering all the sparks that flashed on the way. The queue shoved and hurried him, and he took a step forward, no longer feeling his legs, and gratefully accepted from gentle hands his well-earned cup of hemlock.

# The Jewess

*Irene Dische grew up in the 1950s in the 'Fourth Reich' Washington Heights – a German-Jewish colony in Manhattan. Her parents were German-Austrian immigrants, her father a respected scientist, her mother Deputy Medical Examiner of New York City. In 1969 she was sent to summer school to study the harpsichord at the 'Mozarteum' in Salzburg, but she cashed in her tuition fees, travelled through northern Africa and dropped out of high school instead. She became an assistant to Louis B. Leakey, the paleontologist, in East Africa, and he helped her to get into Harvard University to study anthropology. A week after his death in 1972 Dische changed her university course to literature. In the mid 1970s she moved to Berlin, where she wrote for Enzensberger's version of the* New Yorker, *called* Transatlantik, *and later for* Die Zeit. *She has also written and directed a film,* Zacharias, *and written an opera film,* Bassa Saddam. *Her first novel,* Pious Secrets, *was published in 1989. It went straight into the West German bestseller list, and she was awarded the German Critics' Prize. She now lives in Berlin with her husband and two children.*

### Charles is Recognized

When the dark-haired, nondescript accountant from Oregon first stepped on to German concrete at Frankfurt Airport, he made the following gesture: the index and middle fingers of his right hand grazed his forehead, slid down to his chest and flapped over the left, then the right side of his rib-cage.

At once the trouble began. As he collected his baggage and asked about transferring to an inland flight to Berlin, people gawked. A mistake to talk German! He was immediately recognized. The baggage clerk had seen his passport. Bedlam broke out among his prejudices. 'Oh, you're not

German. But your German is so good. Why is your German so good?'

'It's not good at all, many mistakes, my parents were German.' The man named Charles Allen in the passport had trouble lying.

'Aha.' The clerk concentrated. 'And when did your parents leave Germany?'

'1955.'

'The flight to Berlin leaves from Gate 4,' the clerk said, suspecting he had been fooled.

'Your German is flawless. When did your relations ever leave Germany?' asked Charles Allen's neighbour on the flight to Berlin. The American looked past him, through the window at the clouds and replied '1950.'

'So you say you are an American – and I say impossible! *They* can't ever learn a foreign language,' cried the taxi-driver, swerving the steering wheel in consternation.

And so it went. 'My parents were German.' This Mr Allen explained in his deep, unsteady voice.

Then his interrogators suspected. It seemed to Allen that only politeness prevented them from pouncing and tearing him into bleeding pieces: 'When did they leave Germany?' they snarled.

'1945,' Charles Allen told the cab-driver. This implied that his parents had been good comrades who knew when to leave. The answer '1955' meant they were mere unpatriotic opportunists, turning their backs for economic reasons, pitiable in view of the current weakness of the dollar, and the low, 2 per cent inflation in the Heimat.

But not everyone was gullible. The taxi-driver steering absent-mindedly along the Kurfürstendamm to the Pension Zentral remarked, 'Your German is much too good for an American. Then you are very smart.'

And of course cleverness is the classic give-away.

### Charles Gives Himself Advice

Do not behave cleverly. Read your newspaper alone in the dowdy *pension* dining-room. Do not talk to the concierge who has seen your passport unless absolutely necessary. Speak English, even with the other steady lodger, Herr Nadler, who only understands German. Concentrate on speaking English without any accent, Rs belong in the trough of your mouth, and not rattling at the back of your throat. Smile often. Wash behind your ears, polish your loafers. Admit to nothing.

### Charles Runs out of Advice

Possibly because he was not home in Athens, Oregon, the Dodgers had lost three consecutive games, and the Yankees were looking better every day. There was a hot spell in Central Europe. Two weeks passed, in which he ignored the business matter that had brought him to Berlin.

Instead, he led the life of the *pension*. He took all his meals with Herr Nadler, his neighbour, a permanent guest. He found eating anything other than sweets a task, and when he had been good and mastered his meal then he rewarded himself with a sensual act: reading the sports page of an American newspaper while lying on his bed.

For a few hours every afternoon he ventured outside dressed in his national colours, red tie, white shirt, and blue trousers and jacket. He only visited places and restaurants mentioned in his tourbook. He kept a business letter in the front pocket of his trousers, as though he might actually see to his business. The envelope's sharp edges pricked his groin. He tugged at it, and the old women of Berlin glared at him.

He returned home late in the evenings to watch the unsatisfactory German sports games on the lounge television until he was tired enough to sleep. In this way he spent the last days of summer.

Then the seasons changed in the former capital. A permanent mist settled and soaked summer till its deep colours ran like cheap dyes, leaving days in metallic greys and a rust like dried blood. The rain tramped on the tiles.

One morning the concierge came into the dining-room evil-tempered because of an increase in the price of individual servings of butter. She shouted into the hearing-aid that twined from Herr Nadler's ear. 'If only you were young again, Herr Nadler. You're honourable. You tried to save your motherland from Big Money once before. You'd do something now!'

Herr Nadler looked confused and muttered, '*Selbstverständlich, Frau . . . Frau . . .*'

The concierge's words blasted Charles Allen out of his lethargy. Brushing breadcrumbs from his mouth, he groped for the pocketed envelope. The concierge forgot Herr Nadler and watched the American tugging at his trousers.

## A Duty

According to the letter, Charles Allen was an heir. He had inherited an estate consisting of several bank accounts with no more than spare change in them, and a business and retail outlet called Die Schöne Heimat. The value of the stock had not been assessed, and the store was closed. The letter warned Charles Allen of his duty. He must decide within six months, by the beginning of November, whether to claim the inheritance. The name of the deceased was buried in the middle of the text. It read, 'Johannes Allerhand'.

When Charles first read this, the name rang like chimes on a door blown open by the wind. No one came in. Later, he remembered that 'Johannes Allerhand' referred to his father.

Charles Allen recalled a pudgy, thick-featured, balding man standing proudly in front of a Studebecker. A few spoken sentences went with this image, every one about an antique store that the Nazis had burned down on a night called 'Crystal' in the autumn of 1938. It seemed to Charles that his father had never spoken about anything else.

It had certainly seemed so to his mother, Irma Allen. Charles remembered her complaining that, long before he was born, she had done her best to change the subject. In 1939, she packed two suitcases and dragged him to the boat in Bremerhaven. She called him 'Johannes' when he boarded, and 'John' by the time they disembarked. From New York she scolded him across the country by Greyhound, finally picking a small town called Athens in Oregon to settle because of the wonderful scenery.

But the acquisition of a five-room wooden bungalow, an American passport, an American-born son, and a job as a waiter at Joey's Barbecue, could not reorient this Johannes-turned-John. His wife kept at it. She cajoled him into the rotary office to change the family name from Allerhand to Allen, she had everyone baptized and after a few Sundays at church, she began to believe what she practised.

His adult son straining to recollect could only find his father on the periphery of his most important childhood memories. On Charles's fourth birthday, John Allen said there was no toy train in all America to compare with the old German ones. For Christmas he wished for his shop back. When Charles fell down a flight of stairs at five, John Allen picked him up and comforted him by telling him again about the 'accident' that had cost him his business.

One Sunday morning, while driving home from mass, John Allen heard news on the car radio: the German government was reimbursing former citizens who had lost property during the Third Reich. John Allen parked the Studebecker and said, 'I'm going to walk. I can't drive when I'm excited.'

He left the family in the back seat, ran home, and packed his old suitcase. He left for Germany the next morning. He was supposed to be back in Athens for Charles's first day of school. He never even wrote.

His wife stood in for him at Joey's until the owner lost patience with her because she never smiled. Then she went to work as a live-in housekeeper at an order of nuns called Immaculate Conception, where speaking was forbidden. At school Charles heard the sound of voices as a strange noise. His English never lost its German accent.

Irma Allen died the day her son passed his driving test. She was buried in the convent cemetery while he missed the first game of the World Series. Charles studied accounting for two years and took over the management of the convent finances. No one ever asked him questions, no one ever suspected about his family history. When notification of his father's death arrived from Germany, the mailman asked if he could have the stamps.

Charles ripped them off with part of the return address. He thought: Who cares? Let someone else keep the inheritance.

But his annual vacation was due again. For the past two years he had declined the chance to take even a day off. This time the Mother Superior said, 'You must take a break.' Charles obeyed. He went to a travel agency and, since no other destination occurred to him, he booked himself a thirty-day trip to Berlin.

## The Inheritance Remembered

By the time Charles Allen reached the twenty-eighth day of his first vacation, he felt on easy terms with Berlin. He had sampled all the city's tourist attractions, and most of the sweet desserts offered at its better coffee houses. His twenty-eighth morning in the *pension* seemed no different from the twenty-seven preceding it, until the concierge started to fret about Herr Nadler's honour.

The elderly Herr Nadler was the concierge's comfort. In a changing world, there was something permanent about him. He had the muscle-tone of a former warrior who works out on the parquet before breakfast, and, no matter the circumstances, his posture always stayed aligned along its ramrod. His appearance had a crispness and whiteness that the concierge wished for her tablecloths.

Charles's posture was poor, and his love of honour underdeveloped. He even hated the word, because the omission of the aspirated H seemed a mutilation of the English by the French. He liked to think that German, at least, had reliable, emphatic syllables. The concierge's were slurred by outrage as she addressed her guests about the price of butter and praised Nadler because he fought for his country instead of trying to cheat people. She considered money as necessary but distasteful as faeces.

Hearing her words, urgency possessed Charles Allen. He hurried out of the breakfast room, abandoning a perfectly good half-pat of butter.

## A Dutiful Visitor

Charles Allen was not a shopper. Antiques bored him and he disliked all forms of shabbiness. He would have skirted the store, if he had not inherited it. The façade repelled him, soot covered the front window, rust overgrew and twisted the metal sign that read, 'Die Schöne Heimat'. A dim light shone at the back, and the door stood slightly ajar.

Charles entered with the manner of a clerk intent upon carrying out a transaction quickly and impersonally. A tall, bulky man picked his way slowly towards him through a clutter of antiques. As he advanced, he called, 'Esther! A customer!' Charles had no time to deny it.

A small woman flashed up to him, a confusing image of reds and blacks that made him turn away, even as she addressed him. 'Are you buying or selling? We're actually closed.'

Charles faced the man, who shrugged his shoulders at the attention. 'She's the boss.' He wore a tailored suit, and his round face gleamed with a close shave. 'I'm just old Baruch, the assistant, I have nothing to say.

Maybe we give him a chance, Esther. He has something worth buying, you don't know.'

Charles Allen clawed forth his official letter, which rustled loudly as he unfolded it. 'I've come about this,' he said to the floor.

The woman did not even acknowledge the paper. She said, 'So it's Allerhand's son. Good son. Turning up to claim what is his. Rubbish son!' She snapped her fingers and pointed at the door. Her companion's head jerked to look in the direction she pointed.

Charles Allen slunk to the door, brushing a stack of books that began to tumble slowly. Then she shouted in a hoarse voice, 'Spoiled American Jew!'

### Charles Runs Away

As Charles Allen scrambled out, his jacket caught in the door, and a seam tore loudly. Everything about him seemed to be coming apart. He ran. He wasn't very fast. On the next corner, a hand yanked at his arm. 'Why don't you just wait a minute?' And it was she, the woman called Esther. He could no longer avoid looking at her and saw that her black hair reached down to her waist, and that a red crooked mouth dominated her pale face. He felt without really thinking that she must be too old to be pretty, well over thirty. A silver Star of David shone in her décolletage.

'Oh, don't get carried away by a little unfriendliness. Who isn't spoiled nowadays? The war's over. It kept people in line. I'm spoiled too. A spoiled German Jewess. So now we're even. And I happen to be a beast, to top it off. Because I was treated like a beast. So please don't blame me. Look, I did everything for Allerhand. For over fifteen years. I *made* Allerhand and my reward is, when he dies, his relations show up with their palms held out. We're not talking about an ordinary sort of business here, but a complicated one – and it's the only occupation someone like me can have in Germany.'

'You're right,' yipped Charles on the street corner. 'You keep the shop, it's only fair. Fair play, it's an American ideal I believe in.' His hand drew up to his heart. 'It wasn't my idea to come here, I'll go back to Oregon tomorrow. Excuse me for bothering you. Really, I didn't know. I'm going –'

The apologies disarmed her. 'You're not like your father, are you?'

She wasn't like his mother.

He had never spoken to a woman who put colour on her face. He couldn't decipher what it did to her beyond obscuring her features. He noted that the redness of her lips accentuated the whiteness of her teeth, but the colour was smeared in one corner by a large scar. Her figure was sturdy. No, she was not Charles Allen's type, although he had no experience with women at all, and by thirty-five years of age he had long given up the expectation that he ever would. But he had his principles: he preferred blondes.

'I'm a businesswoman,' she resumed, 'so let's talk *Tacheles*.' She spoke the Yiddish word without effort. 'You want something – everyone wants something! And I want something too. That's honest.'

She moved close to him. 'And I don't want you to turn down the inheritance, even if it seems the easiest way for you. I want you to accept it, and let me continue to manage it, as I've always done. Otherwise, Die Schöne Heimat goes to the government. You can't possibly want to give your inheritance to the German state, that would be too grotesque.'

'I'll give it to you,' he said, trying to back away.

'Well, that sounds better.' Suddenly she smiled at him. 'Don't you want to go see your father?'

### Charles Goes to See His Father

'You can call me Frau Becker.'

'I'm Mr Allen.'

'You're lying. Your name's Mr Allerhand.'

'Allen. Charles Allen. Changed name, maybe. But I never had another. You're Esther, aren't you? Esther Becker.'

'You can call me Esther if my last name is too tough. You have no sense of privacy in the land of the free. I'm sure you have never seen anything like my car, even in America, Charles.'

Charles Allen had never paid attention to cars before; now he made an effort. The black Mercedes had a telephone, a bar, and leather bucket seats. 'Eighty thousand,' she said. She drove clumsily, both hands on the steering wheel, accelerating with little jerks. Charles watched the Star of David swing around her bosom. 'What are you looking at?' she protested, her hand flying up to her neck, pulling her jacket closed. 'It's cowardly to inspect someone like that. Like a border policeman. Inspect yourself first.'

And at the next traffic light she glanced with condescending quickness, as if it sufficed to take in his short black hair, his rather handsome face, the neat dreary suit he always wore, the undemonstrative tie and thin leather belt, the shiny loafers on his flat feet. 'There are two kinds of Jews in the world,' she concluded. 'The aggressive kind like me, and the passive, intelligent ones, just waiting for a beating. Like you.

'Your father was the only mixture of the two kinds I have ever known. He didn't look like a bully, but he was a bully, a sentimental bully. He used to cry about the human race, about Germany – the Schwarzwald! The Rhine! – Actually, the only thing that really moved him was his own feelings. Are you listening?'

'Yes.'

'When he came here, he was just one of a lot of fellows with big noses and changed names turning up to claim reparations money. He wasn't very sensible about his money, though, the way the others were. He spent every penny to buy back the store he had owned before the war. He tried to sell souvenirs there – bottles of Berlin air, toy bears, and antiques. Listening?'

'Yes.'

'The population was humiliated and starving, only the occupying soldiers had any money. But then he had some luck. He stumbled on other things to buy and sell. As a foreigner, he could travel back and forth between the zones. He became a specialist in Nazi loot. Isn't that ironic? No one asked him any questions, he was allowed to possess valuables when no one else was.

'The Germans never hated the Jews more than after the war, when it seemed the Chosen People had inherited the earth – moral superiority – and money.

'So Allerhand made a lot of money, and was still not happy. He began to feel guilty about being rich, he felt he had to do something for the money he earned. When the Wall went up he made that his business. So he became less rich, and by the time we met he was struggling again.'

They drove away from the city centre, west, until she stopped the car at the edge of a forest of very old tall trees. A metal fence staked a clearing in the woods. After they passed through a modest entrance gate, Charles saw the gravestones, grey welts along the forest floor. The starlings blew in black clouds through the trees.

Johannes Allerhand's grave was only marked by a wooden plaque. His son stood over it and felt the cold seep down into his shoes. He sidled closer to Esther and then another sensation assaulted him: an awareness of her smallness and roundness and warmness, of her woman's voice and the softness of her hair. First only his body had this awareness, it simply bypassed his intelligence. When his mind became privy to the sensation, he lost the last of his already modest ability to make small talk.

'You might say here lies a bad father to several,' she said, speaking with such gayness that Charles wondered whether she was not rather indifferent to death. He was glad to disapprove of her a little. 'He looked after me when I was younger. And when he was older I looked after him. It wasn't easy. He was very moody. If he was angry, he wouldn't talk and his silence could last weeks and then months, and was a dreadful punishment. Over the years he became more and more like the old Jewish God: humourless, all-knowing and cruel. I couldn't imagine him ill. He never was. I never saw him injured. I used to laugh, he has no blood at all.

'He never spoke about you, ever. I found out he had a son when he died. On the store documents you were listed as an owner. He must have had you in mind thirty years ago when he first came to Germany. But after that – cancel any illusions if you have them – he forgot about you.'

### Inside Esther, a Mysterious Landscape

By the time Allerhand was buried, she appeared to have forgotten that he had died. She hardly enjoyed herself at his funeral – the rabbi was expensive, he was charging them his enemy tariff, and he performed listlessly. The five friends of the deceased in attendance were more appalled by his death than saddened by it, although they cried a fair amount and prayed loudly with the rabbi. The weather was just right: the ground was no longer frozen, so that Esther didn't worry about the gravediggers having trouble digging a hole. And it wasn't lovely enough to make a death seem poignant. But winter had definitely come to an end, the sky was clear and windy, and the crocuses were burrowing slowly through the soil. Esther had never felt sentimental about nature, but she recognized a pretty day; Allerhand must be enjoying it, wherever he was.

The party after the burial was enjoyable. Quite a number of people who had made themselves a nuisance to Allerhand during his lifetime showed up at Esther's apartment to sit around drinking beer, eating pretzels and cake, and telling fond jokes about the deceased, until they laughed or cried. Esther's tears ran black with mascara as if some of the cemetery soil was lodged in her eyes. Her weeping was not accompanied by any of the usual side-effects. Just as she was cackling at a remark whispered by the baby-faced Baruch, or launching into an anecdote or a mouthful of cake, these black tears suddenly cascaded down her face. The whites of her eyes gradually turned pink and then red, and she kept whipping the moisture off her face and protesting, 'Dammit, *why* am I crying?'

When the doorbell rang, the guests stopped moving. Someone turned off the dance music on the radio. Esther suspected it could be Allerhand returning, the whole thing a stupid joke, but she found the courage to open the door. She giggled at the sight: Frau Bilka, the landlady, fat enough to fill the doorway, holding red roses against the black dress she had put on for the occasion. 'I want to pay my respects,' the frumpy blonde said, as if the old fashion of the phrase was itself an important ingredient of consolation.

'We don't need your respects, Frau Bilka,' Esther told her. 'Really we don't. We'd prefer you kept your dog from making such a lot of noise in the morning when he attends to his bowels. And next winter shovelling the snow from the front walk a bit more punctually, before it's frozen solid. That would be a way to pay your respects. But thank you for coming, and have a pleasant day, just the way I'm having.' She closed the door again. Inside, she quoted herself to everybody. 'That woman hated Johannes. Why should I be charitable?' Then she gave a booming laugh, which was a signal for the party to resume.

Nothing interrupted the festivities again, certainly not any talk about Allerhand's death. No one said as much as 'Why did he do it! He had everything going for him in his old age. And in such a vile manner, so that his closest friends had their stomachs turn at the thought!'

## The Jewess Explains the Jews

They left the cemetery in the dark. On the brightly lit Kurfürstendamm Charles said he would return to his hotel, but she stopped him. 'You won't. We have to talk. I'm inviting you.' And she clamped her small hand around his arm and steered him to one of those vast coffee houses, where the elderly indulge their need for rococo. The ceiling was glutted with chandeliers and slowly drifting smoke, while down below the old women sat bent over coffees and *Torte*, their grey heads neat as tombstones.

Charles ordered *Apfelstrudel* with vanilla sauce and devoted himself to the pastry like a monk to prayer. He did not listen to Esther who, after settling her coat on the back of the chair and her mind on the least expensive cake on the menu, began a monologue about the virtues of saving money. She was far gone when she noticed her escort's inattentiveness. 'Baruch says I am a financial genius,' she exclaimed.

'Yes.'

'But it is just a question of energy. And instinct. You have to know what to buy when. And whether a risk is worth taking. Last month, after Johannes died, I bought thirty thousand pairs of shoes from Bangkok; that was a comfort to me. They cost only 1.85 marks a pair. It took our women two weeks to scratch the Thai labels off. And then we sold them to a wholesaler for 4.85 a pair. That netted us 90,000 marks. Now they retail at 29.95 a pair, a price no customer can resist. Of course, I'll have a load of taxes to pay. You know?'

'Yes.'

'You eat cake just like one of these old biddies,' she laughed angrily. Then he pushed aside his plate in shame.

She consulted the menu. 'Eight marks for our measly cake and coffee. The waitress doesn't deserve a tip at all either. But I'll round it up for her. No, I'll leave her 20 pfennig. No, 25, that's a round sum, isn't it, 8.25.' She rummaged in her purse. Charles handed her change.

'That'll do, although she doesn't deserve it,' Esther said. 'These coffee houses make me so nervous with all those old Nazis sitting around enjoying themselves.'

The waitress approached the table, and Esther waved her away. 'Let me finish what I was saying, without anyone interrupting us.' The waitress moved away again. 'Listen to me now,' she demanded. 'Pretend you're a man.'

He tried; he made an effort to appear interested, his face set in a mask he remembered seeing on dark, handsome leading men in the movies when they were listening to a blonde angel talk about her last tennis match at Southampton. But then he thought with irritation that Esther was not blonde and she was much too old for the interest of a leading man, and with an ugly scar. Yet she impressed him.

The waitress was not impressed. She loomed over their table. There were other customers waiting for places. She had taut yellow curls, and a sarcastic expression. Esther said very loudly, 'These Aryans are simply not able to imagine the suffering of a Jewess in Germany.'

The waitress turned away and busied herself with the neighbouring table. 'It's still an Original Sin to be Jewish here, and no baptism will clean it off you,' Esther's voice pursued her.

'My parents had friends who hid them in Berlin until 1943. My father had nothing better to do in the attic of an office building than to impregnate his wife. Then he was terrified of the consequences, and sent her away wrapped in a rug in the back of a diplomat's car. She landed in Alsatia where she had contacts. They hid her in a farmer's barn. They visited her at night. The farmer didn't know.

'When her contacts didn't come any more, she slipped out and scavenged. And she loathed the baby growing in her stomach. She dreaded my birth because she thought my first cry of life would alert the farmer that she was hiding in his barn. She's hated me ever since.'

The waitress stared at them from a distance.

'That's wonderful,' Charles said.

'What's wonderful?' she said.

He shook his head. 'Excuse me, I mean, you're so honest. About such a thing. It amazes me.'

'Then bring me home now.'

## Too Early to Go to Bed

He told himself there could be no harm in bringing her home. They didn't talk as they walked and his thoughts fluttered like birds competing for a roost: the Dodgers won against the Orioles today; there's no harm in walking; it must be terribly late, time for bed; the street lights turn her black hair silver and her pale face black; with her messy mouth.

They had reached her apartment.

'Come up,' she said.

'I shouldn't. The hotel closes at midnight.'

'Then there's lots of time.' She fumbled with the keys. 'A *pension*, not a hotel then. You must be on a very cheap trip.'

'No, it isn't. It cost $749 all-inclusive. That's a lot.

'Even a trip to Las Vegas, for instance, is cheaper, with the best hotel accommodation.'

They reached a door, with a bronze plaque reading 'Becker'.

'You're like me, remembering a number like $749. I like that.

'Welcome to Esther's place,' she said, flinging the door open.

'What a place!' he admitted. Vegetation filled it, growing from the high ceiling downwards along special shelves to the floor. Nor were these common-cut flowers like roses, tulips or daisies. The gardener was discriminating: honeysuckle and grape vines twisted along a trellis heavy with fruit. Fuchsia grew in rows and amaryllis in big pots. In one corner fanned a lilac shrub. A table stood beneath the grape vine, with four chairs around it. The carpet beneath was lawn. 'Plastic,' said Esther, 'is my passion.

'Ghastly, isn't it? We Jews have no taste. I read an article once on why. It comes from generations always having to move on. We don't form attachments to furniture. It's too combustible. I keep only the necessities. Jewellery, coins, that's what we like. And plastic flowers you don't have to water.' She led him down a long hall to an immaculate kitchen. 'This is where your father died.

'He never ate until I told him to. One day I said, "Hans, come home with me, you must eat an egg with *Bratkartoffeln*." He sat down at the kitchen table, and I set his place, with fork, knife, a plate, his glass. I put down salt and pepper. Then I fried him an egg, with my back turned towards him. I was just thinking: Maybe he doesn't have to have *Bratkartoffeln*, toast will do, it's cheaper, when I turned around. And he was lying with his face on the plate.'

She smiled politely. The scar on her upper lip stretched. 'What's that scar?' he asked, 'on your mouth?'

'I was twenty when I met him. He was like a father to me, but a possessive father – no man was good enough for me. So in a way, he had the best fifteen years of my life for himself. Then he disappeared.

'I'm annoyed, that's all. Sad, no, why should I be sad? I'm a survivor. Who do I have here? A few friends, like Baruch. A mother who has hated me since before I was born.

'My mother is half-dead now. I have a half-dead mother in a home for the half-dead. I used to visit her on Sabbath, although those visits were the most arduous work I did all week. On Sabbath, good Jewish children visit their parents and hope they die soon. It's an old tradition. And my mother is deranged. Her memory is a black hole, that sucks in everything. The one thing it spits out again is how much I owe her, as a daughter. For hiding me in her stomach. For bearing me at all. I should be grateful to her bodily functions.'

Then she resumed her tour. 'This is my bedroom. You can look at it, why not!'

### Her Bedroom

Her bedroom had a bed.

To the male virgin, a woman's bed is a monument of overwhelming grandeur. His heart thrashes. He is terrified of using his nose, and smelling scents strange and wrenching beyond imagination, so he pants through his mouth. Glimpse of a wardrobe. Then his vision is snared in the pillows and sheets, like a bunny in bramble.

'Let me show you the extra room,' Esther said calmly.

### The Extra Room

'Why don't you just sleep here tonight?'

He made no reply.

'It's easier than going back to that cheap *pension*. I usually have a lodger. I'm just looking for a new one now. It's actually a maid's room. I make a small profit for the trouble and risk I go to; they can use the kitchen, and the hall toilet, not the bathroom. And it's furnished. Not with my things. With your father's.'

Furnished meant jammed with gleaming ebony pieces, it meant the limitation, or rather the elimination, of any human movement beyond walking three steps, opening a wardrobe, sitting down at a dressing-table with three mirrors that tripled the furniture, or lying down on the medieval bed. One wall was taken up with a shadow picture. A black woman knelt on the white page, her head thrown back, her long hair pulled by the devil. In his other hand the devil brandished a whip.

'Your father claimed I posed for that,' Esther said. Then she blew him a kiss.

He could hear her next door running the water in the bath. Charles relaxed, took off his shoes, and sat upright on the bed. The water gurgled in the bathroom, a glass rattled, the cabinet opened and closed. He leaned cautiously against the headboard and fell asleep.

## *Charles Needs Good Luck*

In Berlin, dawn is greeted by the concierges entering their courtyards and crowing, 'There's to do! There's to do! There's always to do!' Those who cannot sleep on must endure the racket of *Tüchtigkeit* – dutifulness – a dreadful noise in any profession but the concierge has the most powerful instruments at her disposal: the garbage bin and the hose, the broom and the hacking cough.

Charles Allen woke up with impressions of Esther in his ears, in his nose, on his arms. He stood up, checked his three reflections in the mirror. The left side showed his prominent nose with curved nostrils; the middle reflected a man who felt embarrassed by his mouth and black-lashed eyes, as if their large size was a demand for attention he really did not seek, and the right side was filled out by an ill-kempt sort in a wrinkled suit.

He ran his fingers through his hair, and smoothed his suit. Then he gave a friendly nod to the girl being flogged and the Christ being crucified, and sought out the kitchen.

'Ready for breakfast?' called a motherly voice. 'I'm going to make you an egg.'

She was warm-hearted, she was interested in his well-being, she was womanly. The three Ws that make a female, speculated Charles, driving his fork into the egg yolk.

'You can stay here with me for a few days while we sort out the business,' she said, when he had finished. 'You'll save. Let's go get your suitcase.'

Charles Allen agreed. 'I can save 80 marks a day,' he said, trying to share her interest in money. He enjoyed leaning back to make room for her to sponge off the table.

'You'll save 40 marks. It'll cost you 40 marks to stay a night at my place, with breakfast.'

It was Sabbath. 'Die Schöne Heimat' was closed. After noon, everything would be locked up until Monday. 'It used to depress me that for forty-eight hours I couldn't go shopping or do any business,' Esther said. 'That was my Sunday Depression. Then I found out that lots of businesses are open around the clock.'

Nevertheless, the day passed pleasurably. Esther doted on him. She allowed him to read his newspaper; fed him at regular intervals; tidied up around him; and, best, did not engage him in too much conversation.

In the evening, she drove him to the Pension Zentral where the concierge fussed about waiting up the entire previous night to let Herr Allen in, who hadn't come at all. She wondered why he was moving out two days ahead of time, since he would have to pay for them anyway.

Charles Allen paid. As she double-checked the number of bills, the landlady became sentimental about Americans, remembering John Kennedy for his youthfulness and honesty. She fetched Herr Nadler and they stood at the door like an honour guard as Charles Allen trudged out with his suitcase. When Charles reached the bottom of the steps he turned back to look, and Herr Nadler grunted, 'Good luck to you.'

Why should I need good luck? Charles wondered. He calculated that by staying with Esther he saved half the money he would pay for a hotel, so he could afford to stay twice as long. He told himself this was a reason to stay.

He was sitting upon the narrow bed reading the newspaper when Esther came in to say goodnight to him. She sat down next to him and said, 'We can sign a contract on Monday, you can leave here with happy memories.' She placed her hand palm up on his knee. He cowered. She laughed, and stood up again.

Much later she made a lot of noise walking up and down the hall in front of his door; her footsteps were a drumroll of suspense.

## Charles Suffers

On Monday, after a long, idyllic weekend, Charles faced the mirror in his room and reflected about his future. He saw himself explaining his odd state of mind to the Mother Superior. 'The decision about the inheritance has proven complicated,' he spoke boldly. He imagined the Mother Superior laughing happily and then breaking into the song 'Climb Every Mountain'.

He watched his face turn red with shame. He knew he was much too cowardly to confide in her. But confide what, for heaven's sake? he asked himself. The word twisted around in his mouth: flesh.

Every minute that Charles was near Esther, taboos were crunching in his psyche. He had already broken the biggest taboo of all – he had felt curiosity. Now he wanted to satisfy this curiosity by studying her. In this way, he expected to enjoy her. It never crossed his mind that, in order to do this, he might have to leave the vantage point of a Catholic virgin.

But that morning he caught only a glimpse of her as she sped by him on her way to the bathroom. He posted himself outside and listened. She emerged after a long time, dressed in a black suit, her hair a black mass over her carefully decorated, girlish face. She practically knocked him over coming out, and then snapped at him. 'What are you hanging around here for? I can't bear anyone seeing me asleep, or just gotten up, I hate pasty swollen sleepy faces. Stop staring at me, please.'

Later, she came and told him to take a bath. 'You may as well look good for your last morning in Berlin.' Those moments in the sanctum of her bathroom, surrounded by a vast array of her cosmetics, proved the happiest of his day.

By the time she knocked for him to hurry, she had orchestrated breakfast. He absorbed the image of her standing at the old stove in the yellow light of the kitchen. He noted exactly how she opened the oven with the pot holder, how she had to hop backwards, and then blink, grabbing a napkin to check her mascara, before removing the rolls and spreading them with butter. 'Have some honey, it's good for your potence,' she said.

She seemed to like his passivity, the greed with which he ate her buttered rolls. She obviously drew out the moment when she slid the spoon into the honey, rolled it to keep the syrup from dripping. As she slipped it into his mouth she said, 'This breakfast is the long and short of a pleasant relationship.' She said, 'I'm kind of sorry you're leaving.'

He swallowed and told her, 'I think I'll stay and think about the store for a few more days. There's no hurry. I have till the ninth of November to decide.' He licked the honey from his lips, and she startled him by clattering the sticky spoon on the table.

'Oh, sure, fine,' she said. 'I guess you're not going to be so generous with the store after all. "Take it," you said. Because you were scared of me. Then, when I'm nice to you, you want to keep it. Sure, fine, you can stay with me if you like. Till the ninth. But then you'll be just a lodger here, do you understand? Nothing fancier. Not a friend, not a sonny boy I have to mother. Pay rent, and you can stay. But you can make up your mind about the shop without me. I'm going now. You can wait here for me.'

He followed her out of the kitchen and watched her hurtle around the apartment. She locked the door to her room, to the kitchen, even to the bathroom, pointing out the guest toilet he could use. She didn't want him near her personal things, she said, enunciating the word 'personal' so that it left a puncture wound in his ambitions. He accompanied her to the threshold and watched despondently for her high-heeled boot to click on the first step, then her slow disappearance down the staircase, marked by a shortened torso, and finally only the parting in the middle of her head.

He waited for her to return. He waited at home, and then he waited at a coffee shop. He drizzled the sugar on the table to spell the word WWW, the three Ws that make a woman. When the waitress approached he brushed it hastily on the floor. Back in Esther's apartment he sat on his bed reading the *Tribune*'s baseball scores and suddenly his lips formed the word, 'W-W-W-ait,' and then bitterly, 'good luck.' In his head, he heard himself shout: I can't wait! He could not understand why his waiting did not force her to come back.

He found he could no longer remember what she looked like. He drew up his own addition to the 'Most Wanted' list:

Esther Becker:
*Hair Colour*: Black, like billions of other people in the world.
*Shape of Face*: Oval, far from 'perfect' at the jowls and below the chin.

*Colour of Eyes*: Thick black paste on them. The eyebrows absent, replaced by two sweeps of a pencil.

*Mouth*: An abnormal mouth: the upper left corner is stained by a scar. She has a way of pursing her lips before each smile, and she has perfect, even, white teeth worthy of Hollywood.

*Hands*: Sparrow-sized, they flutter about when she talks. Like a Hollywood hand, every finger wears its own ring, except for the ring finger. Apparently her nails can't grow long.

He wrote, '*Torso*:' and left it blank, continuing with:

*Feet*: Size 35, my age!

He read through his work, realized he didn't know what colour eyes she had, hated himself for being so sloppy in his research, and turned on the television.

Late at night, Charles left 40 marks on the plastic coffee table beneath the living-room grape bower and tried to sleep. Much later, he became aware of her return. He listened as she paced down the hall, he heard exactly and with interest how she used the toilet, how she turned off lights on her way to her bedroom, and snapped her door shut.

He fell asleep, and awoke with the relief that follows an illness. He laughed as the concierge banged the garbage-bin lids in her rooster rage, and he said to himself, 'There's to do today!' He pulled the curtains, saw the blue sky, and exulting, went to find Esther. But she had already left.

The apartment was uncompromising.

Charles Allen's ability to absorb feeling reached its saturation point. Suddenly, his suffering ended. He became aggressive. She could not forbid him to look for her.

### Charles Finds What He Wants

Finding Esther wasn't hard. 'Die Schöne Heimat' was located just a few corners away. There, in person, was the object of his study, bending over, so that all he saw through the glass door was her backside and the back of her boots.

He began to address her even as he was stepping over the threshold. 'I'd like to see the store records, that's why I've come. I'm an accountant.

I'll just look through them and bother no one,' and all the time he was grinning with delight.

## Charles Learns About Business

'What really brings you to your own store?' asked Baruch. He polished a heavy silver menorah. 'Your father's last acquisition, not many buyers for a seven-arm menorah from Alsatia, even though it's very rare, nineteenth-century. I'm going to offer it to Father Renard as a special holder for votive candles; the real money's in Christian articles, diamond rosaries, antique crucifixes, thuribles, pyx, and relics. Renard takes everything. We pick up a lot from Italy, where they don't lock the churches.'

He held up the menorah. 'The shop lives from . . .'

'The shop lives from candles and furniture,' Esther interrupted. 'We buy and sell.' She unloaded dusty ledgers from a locked shelf. 'We introduced East German candles to West Berlin. We get them from a firm in Dresden, we call them Holy Land candles. Most candles come from the old "family firms" in Fulda. They grew big making candles for Hitler's army chaplains to burn at field masses.'

Baruch reproached her. 'So dry, Esther. You got to make it colourful for him, so he'll enjoy himself. There's nothing wrong with the candles made in Fulda except that they're either fancy or silly, nothing looks like a candle any more. Your father had this idea about importing plain, white, cheap candles from the Communist countries. If you want to know the truth,' he put the menorah down with a sigh, 'Johannes Allerhand had no sense of humour, and was always worrying about aesthetics.'

'It wasn't a question of humour or aesthetics at all,' corrected Esther. She piled the ledgers on a table. 'He thought he was contributing to *détente*. Here, Charles, you wanted something to do. Have a good time.'

Baruch put the menorah down and tapped a forefinger on the table. 'This, for example, is a typical example of what Esther calls "Buy and Sell". A Gale table, legally acquired yesterday from the stupid. I saw an ad in the papers, "An old table with a picture of a river carved into the top". This woman wanted 100 marks for it; I got her down to 75. It'll sell for 5,000.'

'He's interested in the books, Baruch, not in your fables.'

They left Charles alone with the stacks of ledgers. He heard them quarrelling in the back room about Baruch's garrulousness.

The first store records were dated 1956, and showed that Johannes Allerhand had paid for the store with a lump sum.

Apparently the year 1956 was a poor one; the store just broke even.

Nineteen fifty-seven was just as bad.

Nineteen fifty-eight was bad too. The economic boom of the Sixties bypassed 'Die Schöne Heimat'. The store's defeat was neatly recorded. 'This business made no money!' Charles marvelled.

'We do it for pleasure.' Esther took the ledgers and returned them to the cabinet. 'There are other sources of income,' she added.

She locked the cabinet. 'Are you absolutely sure you're Allerhand's son?'

### Inside Esther, a Mysterious Landscape

Johannes Allerhand followed Esther up the four flights of stairs, falling farther and farther behind her. She hated the fact that she could walk so much faster than he. 'Hurry up, will you?' she called down at each landing. She could see part of his slowly moving shoulder and fedora. He panted. He was too fat, and he was too old. When he reached the apartment door, she had slammed it shut, and he had to ring the bell. She took a long time coming to open the door again. 'I've already started lunch,' she said. 'Although you shouldn't eat anything.' She let him in, and smiled grudgingly.

'You let me decide that myself,' he replied. He was still strong as an ox emotionally: he didn't care enough about her to mind her contempt. 'I wouldn't mind having some *Bratkartoffeln*.' He looked at her maliciously. 'You be a nice girl and make me some *Bratkartoffeln*. With bacon.'

She had no bacon. 'You're old and horrible,' she replied. 'One oughtn't allow you to eat ever again. Starve you to death, for humanitarian reasons.'

He began to laugh and then he stopped laughing and said, 'No. You depress me. I'm beginning to regret things.'

'Don't ask me to count up all the things I regret,' she replied, now only reluctantly continuing the squabble. She unbuttoned his coat for him. She had already set the kitchen table for two, and when she turned away from him he was sitting at his place, holding his knife and fork expectantly; the eagerness for food always touched her. But she was not going to make him his potatoes. She made fried eggs; they sizzled and the pan banged.

She turned around, holding the pan, to slide the eggs on to his plate, and then she saw what he had done: he had put the knife way back into his mouth, propped the end on the table, and let his head fall down on it. It held him upright, but as she watched, his head rolled over on to the plate.

'You filthy despicable pig, how I hate you,' she told him.

## Esther Begins to Educate Charles

'What's missing in Charles is common sense,' said Baruch. 'It's all blah-blah inside his brain. Maybe you should clarify the situation for him here.'

'Clarify?' asked Esther.

'Talk to him. Go for a walk.'

'He's too badly dressed. I don't want to be seen with him.'

Esther and Baruch crowded around Charles, pulled him up from his chair, and felt his middle. 'You're much too thin,' Esther said. 'You'll need a warmer coat. You can have one of these here. I bought two hundred of them.'

Charles stood up straight. The coat was black mink. 'Now you need a hat,' she said. 'I've got a nice grey fedora lying around somewhere.'

Later, he regretted that he had refused the hat. Esther spoke about nothing else but how handsome hats looked on men, in particular fedoras, she had a weakness for them, she could not bear a man without a hat, and then, to say no to such a fine model, she could not forgive him. She took him on a walk anyway, because she said he had to learn a bit about his father. He thought she was still trying to prove a point about that hat when she took him to a wide-open space where nothing prevented the wind from rushing into his ears. Two cranes heaped the sand and rubble into dunes. One side of the area was marked by the grey, ordinary barrier covered with gay graffiti that arouses such emotions in the tourist's heart – the Wall. The tourists all wear hats, Esther pointed out. She wound her red scarf around her ears. She always wore the wool scarf, she admitted, even in a summer heat. It was a talisman.

'It was the only thing my mother saved from her trip to Alsatia. She wore it when she was hiding in that barn. She had it on when I was born.

I found it in her closet a few years ago. She didn't want to give it to me. But to whom does my birth count more, to her or to me? Anyway, I need to be indulged.'

The wind buffeted the two cranes but the whirring of the machinery remained constant and so rather soothing. Finally, she changed the subject. 'They're smoothing out bad ground. Here lies the Gestapo building,' she said, 'where Eichmann pushed his little pen.'

He was embarrassed. She was going to see his reaction to something that jarred him. He tried to cover up. 'So what!' he cried. He blushed and argued, 'The Wall is much more interesting. The graffiti are surely the most entertaining in the world! Look at that one: "Berlin is the asshole of the world".' He realized as he chattered that he must appear foolish. 'And this: "No High Jumping Permitted".'

She watched him. He giggled, and his body swayed, buffeted by the roaring winds of his shame. He went on, '"Humpty Dumpty was Here", well, I guess I am like Humpty, no one will ever be able to put me together again.'

Suddenly the motors of the cranes were silenced. The day turned as quiet as it was grey, and the lights of the watchtowers on the other side of the Wall went on. He shivered, seeing that she was watching him. In panic, he turned towards her, and slapped his arm awkwardly around her shoulder; and, when she did not withdraw, he placed the other arm around her and tightened the embrace.

## The Embrace

Heat rose from the opening of Esther's coat and bathed Charles's face. He trembled, and steadied himself on her shoulders. His face sank into the long hair that enveloped her neck and the rough red scarf, where he smelled a scent he knew to be woman's perfume. He did not disintegrate. He became aware of his palms sliding along a soft material, and of his torso pressing a warm, yielding surface. He did not burn up or melt down, he was merely indecisive, and, to his astonishment and relief, a bit bored. And she? She accepted the gesture, she neither warmed to it, nor repelled it. She stood absolutely still. After a moment, he recalled his arms one by one, soldiers who had gone out on a mission without orders, smiled at her and remarked, 'I'm sorry.'

### Esther's Lesson

Released, she did not reply but rummaged around in her handbag until she found a jewellery case. Inside the case was a tattered newspaper clipping. She said, 'This place is special to me. This is where I was born again.' She handed the clipping to Charles.

It showed a young woman crawling out of a hole beneath the old red-bricked Wall. The scene had been shot at night: outside the spotlight created by the photographers' blitz, everything was swampy. In the foreground, a bulky male figure in a fedora, with his back turned to the photographer, extended his hand to help the young woman out of her last millimetres of confinement. The girl was looking up at her rescuer. The girl was Esther.

'Who is that?' asked Charles, pointing to the man.

'Your father.'

### Charles is Unsettled

Charles did not wish to continue the walk. He did not want to see the new museum, or the kinky café on Stresemann Strasse, or afterwards attend a party at a rich man's house. He did not want to talk, he did not want to listen, he did not want to know anything about Esther, Berlin, or his father.

Charles wanted to go home.

'And where is home?'

'Drop me off at the store, please. I want to have another look at those books before I go back to America.'

'The books will tell you nothing. Accountants aren't God, you know. And we are missing a party.'

At the store he picked out the volumes 1963–1967 which corresponded to the years the Wall was made of red brick. Charles knew from his guided tours that, after the East Germans replaced the brick with grey cement, tunnel escapes became impossible. Quite a number of people had been put out of work, including, perhaps, his father. From the books he learned that in 1965 Johannes Allerhand had taken a manager on to his payroll named Esther Becker. He paid her a sum of 6,000 marks per annum, 'plus commissions'. The commissions were not noted.

The merchandise seemed to correspond to Baruch's description – religious candles bought from a firm in Israel that organized exports from the East Bloc, and sold them at a profit to West German churches. There were no unusual expenditures at all until 1967, when Allerhand had bought an office-supply shop and then sold it again two weeks later at a loss.

'Can you explain about this purchase of an entire office store, please?'

'We needed office equipment,' she told him, 'without having to show a receipt for it. So we bought a full store and sold an empty one.'

'It's a secret to buy office equipment?'

'D'you realize we're missing a good party because of your nonsense?' she said.

He ignored her. She watched him as he quietly, patiently, leafed through the store records. Seeing him in that pose, Esther suffered an unpleasant memory. It enclosed her, like a locked room.

## Inside Esther, a Mysterious Landscape

There comes a moment in a relationship between two people when the power leaves one of them and alights on the other. So it happened with Allerhand and the woman he employed as his manager and assistant. One minute she was unpacking an antique tea set in the back room, and he was berating her after he heard a cup jingling. She should take more care. It was a dull, hot Sunday night in August. She was cool in a cotton dress, her hair in a long braid down her back, while the heat erupted under his expensive starched shirt. They were interrupted by a knock on the back door.

Allerhand grumbled. He did not want to be bothered. 'Put that box away, will you,' he told Esther. Then he unlocked the door.

There stood humble Herr Feigl, malformed Herr Rosen, and voluble but unintelligible Herr Rother. His colleagues. They sidled into the room in soft shoes and pastel linen suits, they peered around, cleared their throats, did not smile once, and passed on a message, one after the other, first with Herr Feigl's raspy voice, then with the Yiddish accent of Herr Rosen, and finally with the rapid mispronounced syllables of the Polish Herr Rother: the Herr Direktor did not like what Allerhand was doing with his business practices. The Herr Direktor felt Herr Allerhand was giving the Jews a bad name. 'Die Schöne Heimat' Company should switch businesses, go into something lucrative but legal, like furs or diamonds. Candles and antiques were a paltry front for a wicked, politically explosive commerce.

Of course, Allerhand should have thrown them out. Instead, he tried to defend himself. He said he was doing Jews a service, maybe not the Jews who ran jewellery shops or fur-import companies, but the other Jews, the ones stranded in the East who still needed help.

Then Allerhand became sad. What an irony it was, how repellent and trivial. Tears welled up in his deep-set black eyes, he walked straight up to them and said, 'Please leave me alone now to my disappointment.' But he was a failure. Instead of leaving, they smirked and said, 'From a converted Jew we have to take such shenanigans? No!'

Then Allerhand's self-righteousness failed him. He jerked around to Esther. And this turning around to her was a begging for help, and a surrender of his supremacy in their relationship. At once, she took over.

'That'll be all now,' she sneered. 'I've suffered enough for my Judaism not to be pestered by some frustrated businessboys who happen to belong to my faith.' And she pushed them along as though they were schoolchildren until she could close the door behind them.

Johannes Allerhand sat in his store crying, crying for the loss of his dignity. Esther stood at the door, her back turned towards him, and listened to his sobs as if they were chamber music.

## Esther Explains

'Office equipment is useful for forging papers. Not only ownership papers, receipts, sales records, and warranties of authenticity, but also visas and travel documents, for those who need them.

'Now can we go to the party? I want to see my friends.'

Charles hated friends. But Esther obviously liked them. The party host was definitely a friend: he whispered, 'Don't disgrace me, darling,' to Esther as they entered his heavy-set villa.

Henry Rosen was celebrating his son's bar mitzvah with the other Rosens from Tel Aviv, Caracas, Cincinnati and Johannesburg. In his son's honour, he had also invited all of his business colleagues, who included almost as many Christians as he knew. When the elderly parent inquired which schoolmates the bar mitzvah boy wanted to invite, the child had replied, 'No one, please.'

Rosen intended to spend the evening standing next to his boy in the front hall, introducing him. 'My son, Lonny. His teachers don't think much of him, but that's because he doesn't try.' Lonny kept his head down. He had not heard anything his father said in several years, but the diamonds sewn into the blue velvet cappy on his head were impossible to ignore.

'Disgrace you? If you don't want me to disgrace you, then you shouldn't have invited me,' Esther told the host. 'But you want me to disgrace you.'

They went to the cloakroom and added their coats to a mass of fur. Charles hadn't seen Esther change her clothes. She wore what he at first took to be a rabbit costume, a white dress with black patches, a paw pattern at the cuff, and a puff like a bunny tail at the back. Rosen evidently expected something unusual. He followed Esther into the cloakroom, waited until she disrobed and then sighed with relief. 'Nice, Esther, real evening dress.'

She turned on him. 'Don't criticize.'

'Did I criticize?'

'People have to accept me the way I am. Or they're not worth bothering about anyway.

'Let's find Baruch,' she said to Charles. 'These here aren't my friends at all.' Rosen smiled and returned to his post. The crowd parted for Esther, and it seemed to Charles that the other guests regarded her critically. It must be her odd dress, he thought, or her wild black hair, or her pulling *me* along by the hand.

'There are my friends,' she said, when they reached the farthest end of the room. Charles recognized Baruch's fat face on the other side of a coffee table. Esther marched him into the limelight. 'Introducing Johannes's little son, Charles!'

'Hans's son?' voices asked.

'He had a son?'

'A convert!' Esther poked him down into a chair. She adjusted the bunny tail, and squeezed in next to him. Her thighs reverberated when she talked. 'Charles'll have to tell you about the conversion . . . Oh, it's dreadfully funny . . . I mustn't start to laugh . . . From the beginning, Charles, when the priest was so bored with babies, and pepped up when he saw a flock of Jewish lambs . . .'

A group of faces regarded Charles Allen and he replied mechanically, 'It was nothing. The altar boy said, "Oh, wow!" when he saw us, and the priest took him outside again and I heard him scold, "We do not say 'Oh, wow!' at a conversion."'

'He's been ashamed of being Jewish ever since,' Esther said. 'I was caught lying about it just once. I was playing the clapping-question game in the courtyard – you know the game? You make a circle, and one child stands in the middle. Then everyone in the circle claps their hands and fires questions at the child in the centre, who has to answer "Yes" or "No" on the beat of the clapping hands. "Do you like the colour red?" "Does your mother wear perfume?" Clap, clap. The joke is you ask normal, banal questions and then suddenly you try this question: "Are you in love with so-and-so?", and the child in the middle goes to pieces denying it.'

'But, why don't we play now?!' someone said. 'Henry's parties are always so boring.'

Someone else agreed. 'I adore games about liars!'

A consensus was reached: the company wanted Baruch in the middle.

Baruch resisted. 'Inge won't like it, will you?'

A chubby, sultry, middle-aged woman at his side replied, 'Inge will love it!'

'Baruch in the middle! I'll finish my story later,' said Esther. Charles felt her weight shift against him, as she whispered, 'Inge's Protestant!'

Baruch lowered himself on the glass coffee table. 'You better answer honestly,' warned Inge, and set a rapid rhythm.

The others leaned forward in their chairs, eager for spectacle. Two identical twins from the Soviet Union clapped madly out of turn. They hardly understood German yet, Esther told Charles. They were the product of a Lithuanian woman raped by a German soldier. To commemorate their father, she had given them Nordic names: Volker and Friede. The bastards grew up in the provinces, inseparable in thought, word and deed. At their fifth arrest for shoplifting from an Intershop [Western currency only], a psychiatrist diagnosed kleptomania, and Soviet officials asked them if they wouldn't like to emigrate to Israel. They missed their connecting flight to Tel Aviv in West Berlin, and stayed put. After their fifth arrest for shoplifting from Karstadt, the twins were brought to the attention of the Jewish community's welfare office. There they found a foothold in the person of Henry Rosen, who put them to work in his real-estate business. They hadn't been in trouble since.

Clap, clap!

'Have you been to Vilna?' asked the first twin.

'No,' said Baruch.

'Have you been to Riga?' asked the second.

'No imagination,' answered Baruch.

'Is your real name Baruch?' called Esther.

'According to my mother, yes,' replied the victim.

'Are the police looking for you?' asked her neighbour, a young man named Leon.

'They've never looked for me!' asserted Baruch.

'Are you in love with Inge?' asked Inge.

'If necessary,' said Baruch, heaving himself off the coffee table. 'This game is for the poor liars among us. And those without appetites. I heard the buffet is open. Excuse me.'

The twins followed. 'They follow him everywhere. He can't go to the toilet alone,' Inge complained. 'How about you, Leon, aren't you hungry?'

Leon was watching his biceps as he pumped his arm. 'Without clapping my hands, I want to know what our convert is doing here among us. His profession. That sort of thing.'

'I'm an accountant,' said Charles Allen.

Inge cheered. 'An accountant! How unusual. And you, Leon, what do you do?'

'I'm a crook,' replied the polite young man.

This conversation went on until Baruch reappeared looking red and ruffled. 'This is some celebration,' he said. 'Esther, you and your heir better hurry before that buffet disappears.'

Charles was released from the pressure of Esther's thigh, only to be forced to eat in public, an act that turned his face red, not from exertion so much as shame: this public opening of his mouth, public salivating and chewing and swallowing, wet-lipped, Adam's apple bobbing, with Leon and Esther standing and watching him.

'And what is the ending of your clapping-game story?' Leon asked, checking his reflection in the gaze of the women around him.

'Speech! Speech!' cried Henry Rosen.

'I'm going to tell you about how I came to Germany from Israel. By way of explaining my pride in this bar mitzvah. I came back to Germany not as a Jew but as an Israeli. In Israel I was in the Air Force as a fighter pilot. I was strong. I came here to look around, and I liked what I saw. Germany is the land of opportunity, the freest country in Europe! So I decided to stay. As an Israeli guest, I was always careful to behave correctly here. I am a hundred and fifty per cent correct! And nevertheless I've been very successful here, and I have made enough money to have such a big bar mitzvah. And I *wanted* to have an expensive party because you never know with money: here today, gone tomorrow. And at least Lonny will always have this as a memory. I'm grateful to this country for giving me a chance to supply Lonny with this precious memory! Tonight, I want to take this opportunity to thank Germany!'

He twirled and waved at the corner, where a band of musicians waited to strike the first note of the German National Anthem.

Henry Rosen made his way through the crowd, shaking hands, puffing up with all the compliments, leaving his son still standing at the entrance, his head bowed under the psychological ton of special blue-velvet cappy.

'Esther! Darling! Isn't this beautiful!' Rosen had reached them. 'And you're beautiful. I should have married you, maybe. What a beauty. And now you have a new friend, who is he, he looks nice, a little young for you, introduce me.'

'Charles, this is my old heartthrob Henry.'

'You're right, that's exactly it, heartthrob. I feel it right now.'

'If only you had nice teeth, Henry. I could never have a man with such bad teeth. Bad teeth, bad bones. I would never let you kiss me.'

Henry Rosen looked dazed. 'Nobody ever told me that before,' he said, his forefinger tapping his brown front teeth. 'Not one woman. Not even Wanda.' He moved away, tears in his eyes. The orchestra played a moderate foxtrot.

'The end of your stupid story, Esther,' persisted Leon.

'Leave her alone, Leon,' said Baruch, dancing by with Inge.

'We're celebrating our own anniversary tonight,' said Inge. 'My fifth year as welfare recipient.'

Baruch stepped back and she danced on without him, and while she moved her legs she moved her mouth – she told them her history, how she had briefly held a job as a secretary, hurt her back on a skiing holiday, and as she couldn't work as a secretary any more she was waiting for the welfare office to provide her with an acceptable alternative. Baruch listened from the sidelines, his eyes passionate. When she finished he grabbed her around the waist, hoisted her above his head and said, 'After the nuclear holocaust, my Inge will survive with the rats.'

Turkish waiters appeared with sugary Negev wine in champagne glasses. The band took a break, Esther's friends regrouped around the coffee table again. This time Esther sat right down in Charles's lap, placed her arms around his neck, and laid her head on his shoulder. She closed her eyes. Charles could feel her breath against his neck. He peered around her, trying to ignore what was happening to him, and followed Inge and Baruch arguing about whether they were in love. Esther stirred in his lap. 'I'm used to you,' Baruch argued, 'nothing else. I'm used to the television programmes you like to watch, and your fried potatoes.'

'And I'm used to your conceit and your bad character,' said Inge.

'Esther, wake up and finish the story!' Leon called from the other end of the coffee table. 'About being caught lying. I am famished for stories about exposed liars.'

'No, please don't finish the story, I can't hear it one more time,' pleaded Baruch.

Esther sat up in Charles's lap.

She finished her story. 'Well, we played this clapping game constantly when I was a child. I adored it. But one day I was afraid to play because I was madly in love with a little boy named Fabian. So when I came in the middle I dreaded the question, "Are you in love with Fabian?" But instead they asked, clap, clap, "Are all your grandparents Aryan?"'

'"And you started to cry,' Baruch sneered.

Esther ignored him. 'And I started to cry. My mother heard me from upstairs, she came running down and the children asked her, what was wrong, why was I crying, and she said, "Oh, she's sensitive about everything, the poor girl." She took me upstairs, everyone thought she was going to comfort me, and then upstairs, she beat the shit out of me.'

'Oh Esther,' complained Baruch, 'you and that boring story again. Ten times ago, I first prayed that God would spare me the torture of ever hearing it again. God lets me suffer. I was in Auschwitz, isn't that enough? I shouldn't have to listen to these stories! The Germans are behaving decently to the Jews. What more do you want?' He cupped his belly with both huge hands. 'Look at this. *Sauerbraten, Knödel, Torte, Bier.* As for your mother: I've never even seen her. Does she exist? Is she a monster?'

### Esther Leaves a Party

'Not that vase!'

  'Watch the coat rack!'

  'Such an embarrassment.'

  'Help with the coats, there are hundreds of coats . . .'

  'Oh, what a disgrace to me.'

### A Seduction Attempt

'Blind, deaf and dumb. Now I understand what he sees in Inge. His type is responsible for all the trouble. Sometimes I hate Baruch enough to think he deserved his concentration camp. He would sell his own people for a penny, he's only interested in money, and completely insensitive – if that's not subhuman, what is?'

She sat on the kerb, her feet in the street. Charles hovered around her, worrying what passers-by would think, or worse, remark. He said nothing at all to her and after a while she stood up all of a sudden and walked off. He watched her go, and then ran after her in panic.

She did not speak to him, but permitted him to walk beside her. Soon he felt her hand snaking into the crook of his arm. It was not dangerous, just a hand, not as bad as the thigh had been, yet it left an eerie feeling in his arm. He was delighted that she was not running off without him, but at the same time he could barely control his desire to shake her off. They turned down her street and she pressed against him. When they reached her door he took advantage of the stairwell to pull out of her grasp, so that the viper arm lashed at her side.

He reached the guest room ahead of her. She followed him, shedding her coat on the way, continuing on towards him in her rabbit dress, cornering him next to the dressing-table. The mirror captured his mink coat from the back, and her gradual approach. She was holding something. Then she helped him out of the coat, tossing it carelessly on the bed – in his despair he thought: At least the bed is now fully occupied with coats and no one can expect me to sit or lie down on it – and then she placed something on his head.

'Turn around, sit down, and look at yourself,' she said.

He did as he was told and saw a swarthy young man in a blue suit with a white cappy on his head. In the background a woman in white, a Star of David glittering at her bosom. Fascinated, he watched as her arms slid around his chest and her cheek came down to his. In the mirror he saw how she bent down to him, and how, driven by the image, he responded: a Jewish lover.

The image proved fleeting. No sooner did he turn his head, than it was gone. Charles struggled briefly out of a kiss to seek his reflection again, but the cappy tumbled off his head, and he found only his familiar self in the mirror.

Esther slid down around his knees and buried her head in his lap. He felt terribly embarrassed. He shook her off by standing up, and apologized. 'I'm sorry, I prefer blondes. I can't help it.'

She stood up after him and said, 'I prefer blonds myself. Never mind. It was just a thought. You can keep the cappy.'

Charles thought she looked cheerful. He decided to forget the incident. She left quickly. As he passed the living-room table, he laid a 50-mark bill on the coffee table; he thought the extra 10 marks would make her happy. He wanted to make her happy.

### Esther Cleans Up

The next morning her footsteps beat in a furious percussion down the hall, and she appeared in his doorway, babbled something about filthy and lazy, and how she could take no more. She disappeared.

'Look what happens to the bathroom when I don't lock it up!' she called. He trotted after her, beguiled by her astonishing array of cosmetics. She was scrubbing the sink. 'I've never seen such a mess!' Then the floor. She whirled around with her sponge until she knocked a shelf and all the beautiful women on the bottles and boxes toppled and spun off. He wanted to help her, and picked up a container. But she snatched this out of his hand before he could even look at it and cried, 'Get out of here!'

He returned to his room, sat down on his bed and reread a *Herald Tribune*. When she flounced in after him he pretended not to notice her.

'The worst dirt comes from coins,' she said, putting a wet 10-pfennig piece on the table. 'Have you noticed how black your hands get from a wet coin?'

## Inside Esther, a Mysterious Landscape

On a weekday the promenade along the lake was not overrun by families, and then Allerhand, who professed to hate the sight of children, took his assistant for a walk there.

'Isn't it glorious? One should be grateful for such a beautiful day,' Johannes Allerhand said, his voice directed towards nature as much as towards his companion. She was thirty years younger than he, but he had insisted on straining with a blanket and the picnic basket, and she did not offer to help, for fear of annoying him.

'The trees, the sky, the water – Germany!' The water had a film of petrol. This did not discourage swimmers from dropping their clothes along the soggy banks of the lake and diving in nude, as if they had been overpowered by the same sentiments that wrenched at Allerhand. The two turned away from the water on to a dirt path that led into the woods. Soon they left the path, and with Johannes Allerhand leading, pushed through the underbrush until they reached a small clearance where the sun shone through. Allerhand spread the blanket. 'Go ahead, lie down.'

He took off his hat and shirt, and stood with his broad back and bald head towards her, chin up, eyes closed. 'And I thought I was too old to feel this.' He walked from tree to tree, touching the bark at his knee-level.

When he found the scar in the wood he returned to Esther, opened the picnic basket and took out a child's shovel. He dug a hole at the base of the tree beneath the mark. He did not exert himself, nor did he dig as casually as a child either; he frowned until his plastic shovel tapped metal, and then he scooped an ordinary container from the dirt.

Esther was not watching him any more; she had fallen asleep. He dusted off the box, opened it, removing a packet of West German passports which he leafed through with pleasure. He refilled the hole again, fooling around with the earth for a while before he returned to the hamper, and took out a bottle of wine. He sat down on the blanket at Esther's feet and drank greedily. Esther was watching him through half-closed eyes. She smiled.

'Nature gives me an appetite,' he said. He knelt down and put his hand on her calf, running it down to take off her shoes.

## Mother Exists

Charles's eyes had a ravenous appetite. He saw the light perspiration on her forehead and her upper lip. He watched for each effect that speaking and swallowing and breathing had on her scarred mouth, and on her pretty teeth.

'What do you think about going back to America!' she cried. 'Spare me this mess, and your forever staring.'

'Yes, I could still go back to Oregon,' he answered, as he examined the way her hair fell over her shoulders. 'Get my old job back right away.'

'And what about the store?'

'Just keep it.'

'That's not enough! You have to sign it over to me. But we can do that, all we need is a piece of paper, and you write down, "Charles Allen sells his inheritance to Esther Becker for 1 mark." We both sign, finished.'

'I don't even want to sign anything.'

'And what do you want? Read the sports page, of course. Eat, sleep, and regular bowels. Fit for the slaughter house,' she said. 'The Nazis would have tied you to a spit and roasted you! Look, let me write up a statement, all you have to do is sign it. You come with me this morning. That's what you've always wanted. Stare at me till you're sated. Stare and then sign.'

She bought a *Herald Tribune*, and folded it open for him at the baseball news. He read in the car next to her. He could step out of the car without putting the paper down, estimate the location of the kerb without losing his place on the page, and hold a door open for Esther, his eyes riveted to the text. 'My mother lives here,' said Esther. Then he looked up. They were inside an institution.

Esther's mother existed: small, straight and wearing a fancy dress with lots of lace and ribbons. 'Dressed like a Christmas present again, aren't you?' Esther said, approaching her from the back. 'Vain till the bitter end.'

Her mother heard but did not register the assault. Her name, Frau Becker, was printed on a button stuck into her lapel. She turned the pages of a magazine, and did not stop when Esther came up to her. Herr Brumm, Fräulein Gierlich, and Frau Harzbach, sharing a table with her, also turned pages, although they were in the midst of heated discussion about food prices.

'Why do you still worry about prices,' teased Esther, 'when you no longer have to buy anything?' The pages of *Tip*, *Stern*, *Brigitte* flapped.

'It was cheaper in the past,' said Fräulein Gierlich, 'but it wasn't as easy to get. Potatoes you could buy, but meat? Hundred grams a week per person. A child can eat that for dinner. War! No meat during wartime. Terrible days, I'm glad they're over.'

'Yes, terrible days, with that Hitler fooling us. And afterwards, even worse,' said Frau Harzbach.

'But before the war, we had our own vegetable stand at Fehrberliner Platz,' said Herr Brumm. 'The higher-ups came to us after work. And queued up.'

'But you have visitors, Frau Becker, crank your head around and look!' Frau Becker eased her head around like a ship making a wide turn, and regarded the figure standing next to her. 'Oh, it's you,' she said, 'how nice. My daughter,' she told the others, 'has come to visit me.'

'We know your daughter: Fräulein Becker, isn't it?' said Herr Brumm, greedy to look at someone younger than seventy.

'With a friend, it looks like.' Frau Harzbach pointed at Charles Allen. 'Nice young man. Look, Frau Becker, now turn your head to the other side.'

Frau Becker turned and stared. Then she nodded, in Charles's direction. '*Ach*, that's better,' she wheezed.

## Ach, *That's Better*

*Ach*, that's better. Later, Charles Allen wondered what she meant. He had not thought of asking Frau Becker. After just a minute with the elderly,

Esther was seized with such impatience that she had to say goodbye again. She bade her mother for a word alone at another table in the lobby.

From a distance, Charles saw how Esther took a pen and several pieces of paper out of her purse, and how she laid the pages down for her mother to sign at the bottom. Then Esther kissed her on the cheek, and left her abruptly. Charles watched Esther walk towards him, while in the background her mother took some trouble getting back up on her feet, looking uncertainly after her daughter. Charles waved goodbye. He could make out Frau Becker's look of surprise, and how she switched her cane from the right hand to the left, in order to wave back.

'Waving to an old woman is no great contribution to the family business. If you want to get involved with me, then help us,' Esther chided him. 'Even my mother helps us. She signs everything. They never bother senior citizens. Too venerable. The entire generation. One doesn't want to pry into their thoughts.'

## Esther Organizes the Afternoon

In 'Die Schöne Heimat' Esther and Baruch cornered Charles with a bottle of wine. Neither one mentioned the previous night's argument. They were too intent on manipulating their quarry. They filled his glass. 'Charles, you can help us with Father Renard's ikon,' said Esther.

'We've been wondering who can take care of that for us,' said Baruch. '*Prost*, you're perfect, Charles. Father Renard isn't very curious, and the figurine is beautiful, it comes from a little church near Versailles. Friede and Volker took a four-day guided tour to Paris and spotted it there. Father Renard only likes to buy from the deceased, so we told him it comes from an estate. Pass the bottle.'

'He can take it over to St Josef's right now. As Dr Allerhand,' said Esther. 'Keep drinking, Baruch, so you keep your wits about you . . .'

'I'm no doctor,' said Charles. 'I'm not going to pretend at all. I don't know how.'

Baruch's voice turned soft, wounded. 'We've had no one to replace your father, someone who knows how to behave in a church. I got beaten up in school too, Esther, for making fun of Catholics.' He made a sign of the cross and chanted, '"I can play dominoes . . . Better than you can play dominoes . . . I bet you ten to one I can beat you at domino-o-o-es."'

'Pretend, no. But I can shake Father Renard's hand, and genuflect, if that's what you mean.' Charles gave in.

It was a simple game: Baruch was going to play chauffeur with Esther's Mercedes, and Esther was going to label the box, 'Estate of Stella Wanderling' and Charles was going to wash his hands and practise telling the mirror, 'Charles Allen with the ikon you ordered. My father couldn't bring it around himself, as he is unfortunately deceased.'

He was not going to talk about the ikon because he was not going to lie at all. As he scrubbed his bony impractical hands, Charles looked in the mirror and reflected that the Yankees had traded their best second baseman and would live to regret it. Minutes later a car honked in front of the door. The Mercedes arrived, with Baruch in a chauffeur's uniform. His neck bulged at the collar. He ran around to open the back door for Charles.

Father Renard's church was an emergency measure in red brick taken by Rome during the 'hunger years', the late-Forties when food for the soul was also in short supply. Its spire had once been a symbol of growth for the neighbourhood and could be seen for kilometres. Now it did not affect the skyline of more than one block.

But a Mercedes made an impression. Turkish children gathered, and kept their eyes on the Mercedes star. Baruch parked on the sidewalk, and the crowd grew. He stepped out and addressed the children, 'Touch this once and I'll shoot your mothers during dinner.'

The children backed off.

The church was empty, blue light filtered in through the modern stained-glass windows and candles flickered at the stations of the cross that circled the nave. The American made a sign of the cross. Baruch tapped his temples.

The church office might have belonged to any small administration. An elderly woman counted and sorted coins. 'I make a mistake, I lose my head,' she said.

Father Renard was looking through the receipts. He was a picture-book cleric: mild-eyed, fine-featured, with so little vanity that one could not define his appearance. 'So you're Dr Allerhand. Johannes Allerhand's son.' He weighted the words so that they sounded like consolation.

'"Die Schöne Heimat" has supplied us with supplies for ten years now, and we're very satisfied. High quality, at reasonable prices. A bit short on the paperwork, it's like shopping discount. But again and again, a remarkable piece, an ikon, a *Teffilin* – we're ecumenical in our interests – a rood, what have you. We have the most beautiful chapel in Berlin. And now this Madonna. Let's have a look.'

He waited at a kind of attention, the way he heard his confessions, stiff-limbed to keep from erupting into joyfulness. Charles Allen unpacked the ikon. The Madonna was stocky, black hair rimmed her veil, her skin a bluish-white. She looked, Charles thought, almost like his own Jewess. 'Beautiful,' murmured the priest, and produced his wallet. 'This one is for me privately.'

## Brotherhood

During a card game around Baruch's Gale table, Esther announced she had made a decision. 'It's the Christmas season again soon,' she said, 'and I want to get out of the candle business.' She dealt the canasta deck.

Charles Allen sorted his cards. His hand was exciting. 'Start, Esther,' he begged.

'I am always having good ideas,' Henry Rosen complained, 'about Christmas, sales schemes for houses. Last year I had: Give your loved one what she's always wanted, an extra room! And today I suddenly had an idea for the most Christian of occasions, the anniversary of a pogrom.

'The Jewish community has a new director. He'd love to make a spectacular show of pride for his members, boost morale, something visible. Why not candles? A candle-lit march to commemorate *Kristallnacht*. Very chic.'

The others had not yet ordered their hands. Charles was impatient. 'I have a good hand. Will anyone play?' asked Charles.

'Oh, Henry,' said Esther, 'if the Jewish community needs candles, I'd love to supply them. I'll expand our order, they can have a special friendship price. After all these years when they were on such bad terms with Johannes.'

'Esther, will you play?' urged Charles.

'Will I what?' snapped Esther. 'You're a little idiot. Your father lost everything he had on *Kristallnacht* – and you're about to lose your good hand. Because we have to go now.' She tossed her hand on the table.

Charles Allen shuffled the cards together and scuttled to keep up with the others.

It was warm for late October, an evening for a drive through the city with the windows rolled down and the radio turned up. But then it was a night to turn off the radio, and turn off the headlights and turn silently into the courtyard of a warehouse. More cars arrived with their radios off, and their lights dimmed.

They waited. Charles wondered at Baruch's stern, intent demeanour. When a jalopy arrived with six giggling Turkish women in Bavarian scarves, Baruch climbed out of the Mercedes and jerked his finger across his throat. Then their silence had something forced about it, as though they were faking quiet, one could almost hear them continuing to chortle in their heads.

The silence ended with a truck rumbling into the courtyard. Baruch stumbled around the yard backwards, helping the driver steer into place. Finally everyone including Charles left their seat. He stood in the middle of a chain formed by the men to unload bundles from the truck, passing them from hand to hand, piling them at Esther's feet. She and Inge ripped open their thick plastic coverings and scooped out soft, dark fur coats. They held them briefly to their noses and cheeks, before handing them on to the six Turkish women who sat in a circle on folding stools and with dexterous hands removed the labels.

## Charles's Long Night

Having committed his first crime, Charles Allen wanted to drink orange juice and then sleep. Esther granted him his first wish. 'If you want to, you can fall in love with me. I'm lonely, you know.'

'I do not fall in love, any more than I fall into a sewer.'

'And if I dyed my hair blonde?'

When he picked up the newspaper, she left the guest room. He put down the newspaper and stared at his door. Turning his head, he could see the high white door with the brass handle reflected as a white light in his window, and he could see it as a triptych in his dressing-table mirror. Faint as a tone from the back of the orchestra, he heard Esther reach her room.

She would be unzipping her dress now, he thought, her arm crooked over her shoulder, her left arm pulling the dress straight at the back, thrusting out her stomach – he had seen his mother do it – and then the dress would slide off her shoulders past her knees and she would step out of it, in a white slip. Next she would be throwing back the covers of her bed. Charles read his newspaper.

He imagined her sleeping now. Charles had seen Woman Asleep. In public places, on park benches, at bus depots and at the swimming pool, they closed their eyes, they had no shame. He had seen his mother asleep in her bed, it had shocked him.

The Orioles had bought a mediocre first baseman; but so what!

Charles dropped the paper on the floor. He passed along the hall through Esther's plastic greenhouse, and drew up to the door of her bedroom. He pushed it open and stared. The street light outside penetrated the long white curtains, and shone on her head. She was sleeping on her side, her black hair in a nest on the pillow, her hand in a fist next to her cheek. She looked very young. Then he retreated. He had seen something else. On her bedside table stood a glass of water, and in it, glowing, rested a set of white teeth.

### So It Happened that Charles Began Spending His Afternoons with Esther's Demented Mother

From then on, winter laid siege to the city. The dead linden and oak leaves were raked into rotting banks, the damp air had a searing, chemical smell, the days flickered with a weak light that was trimmed back by the early afternoon.

The press noted the robbery of a truckload of fur coats, the driver had been drugged by two Turkish employees who had serviced him at his regular gas station. He had never seen them there before, and would presumably never see them again. The event commanded no more than one newspaper paragraph. Esther clipped the article and laid it on Charles's dressing-table. She treated him as a lodger and friend. Her suggestive manner – the way she patted him on the shoulder, or touched his hand while making a point – no longer worried him after Esther confessed that her last lodger had been his father. Obviously having a man sleeping in her apartment meant nothing special to her.

At the end of October, Charles wrote the Mother Superior of the

Order of the Immaculate Conception in Athens, Oregon, a letter asking forgiveness for his delayed return. His decision whether to keep the inheritance had to be made by *Kristallnacht*. The coincidence outraged Esther, and she was always chafing about the officials from the Bureau of Inheritance who were historically callous enough to make the ninth of November a deadline for a Jew to make a decision about property. Charles began to look for companionship in someone who did not trouble him so much. He was becoming bored with Esther's constant talk about Jews.

So it happened that Charles began spending his afternoons at the old-age home with Esther's demented mother. He never thought of bringing her flowers or chocolates, he just showed up and read his newspaper while she leafed through her magazine. Occasionally they talked about Esther who was busy preparing a final sale of Holy Land candles for the Christmas season. She was offering the candles so cheaply that parishes all over Berlin were putting in double and triple orders. Esther never signed any agreements, she passed on any documents that needed a signature to her mother who co-operated, confiding in Charles later, 'I'm too old to quarrel with her any more; we've always had different opinions about everything.' On occasion, Charles too would scrawl his name on a page, without ever asking her why; it seemed a small price to pay for his inability to decide what to do with the store. And the scope of this sale impressed him. Only the Jewish community had hesitated about buying the Holy Land candles.

It didn't interest Charles when, at the bar mitzvah of another community boy, Herr Rosen had broached the subject of 'special' candles for the *Kristallnacht* celebration to the new community rabbi. A band from Tel Aviv had just come on stage, the rabbi kept turning his head trying to clear the rock-and-roll out of his ears. He understood Rosen's undertone despite the decibels: the new rabbi could make a city-wide impression with a big celebration: candles supplied from the Holy Land instead of an old Nazi factory in Fulda, candles borne in the hands of thousands in a march through downtown Berlin ending in front of the Jewish community centre.

Although the image appealed to Rabbi Schwarz, canniness made him hesitate. Herr Rosen was so frustrated at his inability to make a deal that he promised to throw in a seventeenth-century menorah from Alsatia at a special price. Now the community chief couldn't resist. The community needed an impressive menorah. He had grown up in New York and he said, 'Make me a reasonable offer on that menorah and you have a deal on the candles.'

But Esther didn't want to sell the menorah. 'It's from my birthplace, I'm not selling it.'

'It doesn't belong to you, does it?' argued Baruch. 'It belongs to Hans's son.'

'Only after he accepts the inheritance. Until then, the manager decides what to do with the merchandise.'

Rosen had come around directly to the store from the bar mitzvah. He called Esther crude names but the adjective that set everyone's head nodding in agreement was 'ungrateful'. Henry appealed to Baruch's superior judgement. 'Talk her out of it, you're her friend.' But Baruch didn't like to question Esther on business policy, and he said Charles should decide what to do with the menorah.

Charles wanted to shrug, say, 'Let Esther choose,' and reach for his newspaper. But her tenacity made him suspicious. The menorah was Johannes Allerhand's last acquisition for 'Die Schöne Heimat'. Was she sentimental about his father? The thought disgusted Charles. 'Schwarz can have it,' he said. 'What's the use of having it lie around here? For 1,000 marks.'

'Father Renard is the only reliable buyer,' Esther battled. 'And that menorah happens to be hot from a museum. Interpol is looking for it.'

'There's one place they won't dream of looking,' said Baruch. 'And we have to keep on good terms with the community.'

'But 1,000 isn't enough!' cried Esther. 'We can get 2,500 or 3,000 for it. It was sold at auction for 95,000. Money is all I have these days,' she said bitterly.

'A thousand is enough,' decided Charles.

So Rosen passed the menorah on to the rabbi with a fake bill of sale from Christie's and the stipulation that no attention must be drawn to it, questions were to be answered 'no comment' until the old aunt who had given it to him, and who would be dreadfully offended, no longer lived. Rabbi Schwarz calculated that he needed one candle for each member of the community, and an equal number of visitors, optimism became the nth power in his calculation and he ordered ten thousand candles, which amounted to half a ton.

In all, Esther ordered two tons of the Holy Land candles which were shipped from Dresden with a special clearance from a corrupt official in East Berlin, crossing the border in a truck with Fulda licence plates. Charles himself directed the truck to the different delivery points in Berlin sitting in the caboose next to the driver accepting huge cash payments for the candles. When they had finished their rounds, he handed the East German a bank cheque from 'Die Schöne Heimat'. The cheque, Esther told him later as she opened a bottle of champagne, was not covered. Charles, the accountant, should have known that. The cheque would bounce sky-high. There was nothing the candle company could do about it since accepting a Western cheque was illegal in East Germany. 'You're up to your neck,' Esther laughed, 'in money.'

It was the eighth of November. If Charles Allen did not reject his inheritance by the next day – 'anniversary of our humiliation', Esther called it – then he would own 'Die Schöne Heimat'.

Charles left Esther and Baruch dividing bundles of marks into three piles. They insisted he take his share because they weren't scoundrels. He left his portion in plain sight on the same antique table where he had once attempted to make sense of his father's business, and excused himself, polite as an altar boy. Charles needed to know something.

At the old-age home, Frau Becker closed the magazine, hesitated, and then answered him. 'The one she had before was much too old for her. I never knew his first name. He used to bring me chocolates. I think he was trying to charm me. In East Germany he brought me coffee. I couldn't say no to coffee, we had none. But I told him to keep his chocolate for himself. He was rather fat. He died. Esther told me that.

'I am not really on speaking terms with my daughter, but that's her decision. She has never been a good child. But times were hard, you know, when she was small. My husband felt so helpless and he never got over it. It was such a humiliation, what happened to us. Afterwards he was not a man any more. I had to do everything. It's something I never talk about here. And my husband died of it, died of the broken heart.'

'I know, Frau Becker,' Charles said, recalling Esther's words, 'how terrible it was for you being Jewish in Germany back then, Esther has told me how you had to hide in a haystack in Alsatia. Pregnant and alone. And all that. Terrified that the Nazis would find you when the baby screamed. I am –' He stopped. She had jerked forward in her seat, the magazine flopping off her lap, and was staring at him. 'I am Jewish too,' said Charles Allen, and he tried, covertly, by pretending to scratch his forehead, and then dropping his hand to his chest, to make a sign of the cross.

'Go, please,' begged the old woman. 'Esther tells everyone that story? Please, leave me alone now.' She was trembling, her mouth hanging open. Charles fled.

## *Last Shopping Day before* Kristallnacht

Charles Allen left the old-age home just as the street lights were turned on, and shop windows began to sparkle. Soon they reflected the pulsating red of police lights. He followed this to the Jewish community house where the *Kristallnacht* procession was just arriving. It proved a magnificent crowd of emotional people but not many Jews among them, they had stayed home in fright. Instead, schools of pupils and their teachers, university societies, various SPD unions, and the entire Christian Democratic leadership came, each individual holding a thick, white, brightly burning candle. Traffic was chaotic, and the helpless drivers cursed the marchers.

The procession halted when it reached the front of the community house, dissolving into a crowd plied by policemen and a contingent of nicely dressed, earnest young men distributing leaflets about the Auschwitz lie. The crowd grew silent when Rabbi Schwarz appeared on the top of the stairs of the Jewish community house. Everyone knew he had lost his parents and all his siblings in Auschwitz. He raised the huge seven-armed menorah high over his head with its candles blazing. Silhouetted in black on the rooftop behind him lay the police sharpshooters.

## *Esther's Birth into a Mysterious Landscape*

The reporters were already at the Wall, alerted by the old man whose life's work was alerting reporters to an escape. The reporters tipped the tipster handsomely; it was his only source of income, for the courts had refused to pay this embarrassingly prominent former official a pension. His name had not always been Schmidt, but now he had become well known as

Wall-watcher Schmidt, and even if the times changed back again, as he often fantasized, he would have probably stayed with the new name.

The reporters slipped him small bills and considered him a nuisance. He always hung around at the site of the escape, tripped over their equipment, and horned in on the honour. This time was no different. Schmidt and three photographers and a crowd of locals watched as the heavyset, elderly man in a grey fedora, who refused to face the cameras and refused to name himself, began digging frantically with a shovel at a particular point at the Wall. The man who the press referred to as 'the stranger' kept his back to the cameras so all they had to shoot was a hat, a short neck, and a huge, dark overcoat.

Meanwhile Schmidt was making such a pest of himself trying to help dig this tunnel that the photographers could no longer concentrate and lost precious seconds when they should have positioned themselves differently, so that the unidentified man remained in the foreground of their photographs and then Schmidt was offended and started playing fisticuffs so that they missed the moment altogether, which they knew was the high point of this particular escape, when 'the stranger' reached his arm deep into the tunnel and pulled, stemming himself with one foot against the Wall. In this position he strained as if he were pulling all of East Berlin through the tunnel.

Luckily the photographers were able to shake Schmidt off in time to get a shot when he succeeded in lifting out a raven-haired girl with a Star of David around her neck. She came out into freedom looking only into her rescuer's eyes, with an expression of trepidation and surprise the public could not fathom and attributed to the news photographers.

### *Esther and Charles Celebrate* Kristallnacht

Poor Charles, chilled and frightened by the *Kristallnacht* festivities, hurried home. From the street he saw the yellow light of her warm living-room and Esther on a ladder hanging paper garlands in the window. Inside, the smell of roast lamb made him so meek that he allowed Esther to throw her arms around his neck and say, 'Darling, we have to celebrate! Don't you understand? – We've bought ourselves a bit of financial security. Don't worry, the East Germans will never dare to prosecute. You and I are having guests. Like a normal couple. You have to pretend.'

She tied a flowered apron around his waist, handed him a dish towel and instructed him so cheerfully in the fine art of drying dishes that he could not help wondering whether he had found happiness at last.

At seven thirty the doorbell rang. Esther swore: it was too early, nothing was finished yet. But it was not one of the invited guests; it was Esther's mother, in thick shoes and an ugly raincoat, panting hideously. She carried a plastic shopping bag with a picture of a white baby seal on it and the inscription, 'Save the Seals'. Esther put her hand to her forehead. '*Oi weh*, what an honour.'

Helga Becker entered, rummaging in the bag as she went. She extracted a piece of stiff official paper, a document. She stood in the middle of the living-room, holding this between her yellow thumb and forefinger. She squinted at the paper and read aloud, '"Birth certificate of Margeret Becker, born 1944 in the St Gertrauden Krankenhaus in Berlin. No abnormalities. Father's profession: Lawyer. Member of the Party, and of the SS. Mother: Hausfrau." Read it for yourself.' She handed it to Charles Allen, canny and intent, continuing, 'After the war he wasn't allowed to work so I supported us as a cleaning lady. I've had a hard life, I haven't always been in a good mood. And then at fifteen Margeret gets ideas. Insists her name is Esther. Dyes her beautiful hair black. Blonde hair, she had, like an angel. It must take litres to keep it that colour.' She dropped a photograph on the coffee table under the bower. It showed a slender little girl with blonde braids, sitting in the lap of a pale, tired-looking man.

Esther regarded her mother with detachment. Then she addressed Charles. 'This is not my real mother at all. I didn't want to tell you because you are such a bunny rabbit: the Nazis found my real mother when I was born, and they murdered her.

'This is my stepmother, who has always hated me. She used to beat me. She knocked out my teeth when I was ten.'

The two women turned to each other as if Charles himself was choreographing them: their profiles were identical.

For the first time since his arrival in Berlin Charles Allen showed emotion. He couldn't control his voice because a rage had punched up into his throat, and he cried, 'Get out, and leave Esther alone!' He pointed his pale, weak, trembling hand at the door, he did not think how silly he looked in his posy apron. The old woman lost her nerve then. When she left he slammed the door majestically behind her. He returned purposefully, and picked up the photograph of the child.

The child was pretty, but where she smiled there were no teeth showing. There was a raw, red scar on her upper lip.

He put the photo down carelessly and moved towards the woman who had been his host for the past months, and as he went he pulled off his apron. His rage had reached his groin now. She tried to push him away. She put her small hands on his chest and pushed. Although he was tall, he was slight, but he was not to be stopped, the energy in him was burning a fuel of thirty-five years: he pulled her apart, her clothes, her clenched arms and legs, his actions ran their course on the plastic lawn like a simple motor: he raped her.

## Charles is Recognized

When Father Renard unlocked the church on the morning of the ninth of November and went inside to say good morning to his thuribles, pyx, relics and crucifixes, he saw the devil.

The priest refrained from using the name of the Lord in vain, stepped outside the church again where he leaned against the door breathing heavily. The additional oxygen made him sceptical that the devil should trouble to come in his church. But he found no other explanation for a being with a red tail inside his locked doors. Unless he had hidden there after the *Kristallnacht* service the night before, with the intention of thieving, only to be locked in, a common thief, perhaps, there must be another explanation for the red tail. Now Father Renard decided it was safe to turn on the coronas and look. The tail proved to be an old, red-wool scarf, one end dangling, the other stuck beneath the seat of a man sleeping propped up against a suitcase in a pew. At the ringing of Father Renard's footsteps, and the sudden light, the man opened his eyes. Father Renard peered at him. 'Oh!' he cried. 'It's you! Mr Allerhand! Naughty boy, sleeping here. Just like your father used to do. In the morning I would hear his confession. It was always very interesting. But why the suitcase?'

To Father Renard's disappointment, Charles Allen's only words were of thanks, and then the 'devil' left, red scarf wrapped around his neck, ends tucked into a thin raincoat. The weather had turned wintry. The priest watched him and saw how he stopped after a few yards to put on a peculiar white cap. After another few yards, he suddenly pulled the cap off again and flagged a taxi with it. As he was wrestling his suitcase into the car, the cap dropped into the street – Father Renard shouted, 'Wait!' The taxi pulled away. The priest chased the car for a block, clutching the wet white cap, but to no avail. He would put in in his office for safe-keeping.

When Father Renard dusted the sleeper's pew, he found a postcard there. It was stamped properly and addressed to the Office of Inheritance. Father Renard did not like to pry, yet he could not help reading the short text. But it was uninteresting, full of negatives, something about not accepting an inheritance and not wishing to know any more about it. The priest thought the young man's carelessness with his possessions should be punished, but mailed the postcard for him nevertheless.

# The Fun-fair

*Hanan Al Shaykh was born in Lebanon to a Muslim family, brought up in Beirut and educated in Cairo. She was a successful journalist in Cairo and in Beirut; she married a Christian Lebanese engineer and lived with him and their two children in the Arabian Gulf. Since 1982 they have lived in London because of the civil war. She has written three highly acclaimed novels,* The Story of Zahra, Women of Sand *and* Myrrh, *which was chosen by* Publisher's Weekly *as one of the fifty best books of 1992, and, most recently,* Beirut Blues. *She is also the author of several collections of short stories.*

My fiancé Farid insisted that I should go with him and his family to visit his grandmother's grave on the eve of the feast. I'd always thought this custom was for old or lonely people who felt comfortable sitting with their dead relatives. They say there's nothing like visiting a cemetery for curing depression. I hadn't been aware of my own parents visiting family graves on special days, although once when I was little I prayed fervently that somebody I didn't know in the family would die so that I could go inside one of the buildings people put up around their graves. I'd gone with our cook to her house overlooking the cemetery – an occasion which seems to have remained imprinted on my mind – and from then on I'd pictured the dead people living in those burial chambers, like us in our houses, only different, perhaps like pharaohs. I thought they probably moved about without making any sound, or stayed in bed all the time.

In those days the tombs seemed strange to me, with their engraved cupolas the colour of sand. They stood among a few faded trees and mounds of sandy earth which were perfect for rolling down. The cats and dogs whose voices I could hear I was sure were the guardians of these tombs.

We called in at Farid's parents' house. As I made to reply to his father's greeting his mother appeared from nowhere and asked me disapprovingly why I wasn't wearing the diamond ear-rings.

'Diamonds for the cemetery?' I asked.

'Why not?' she nodded. 'Everyone's going to be there, I know, and they'll say, why did he only give her a ring when they were engaged?'

Then she vanished and returned with a brooch of precious stones and came towards me to pin it on my dress. I took a step backwards, insisting as diplomatically as I could that I didn't like brooches. Turning again towards her room she replied impatiently, 'All right. Wear my marcasite ear-rings. But everybody will recognize them.'

I looked beseechingly at Farid and he said to her, 'I don't want her to wear any jewellery.'

Only then did she notice the bunch of white roses I was holding. She took them from me, smelling them and calling on the Prophet in her delight, then rushed to put them in a vase with some other flowers. The price of them had made me hesitate, but they'd looked to me as if they were just waiting for someone to appreciate their fragrant beauty. I justified buying them on the grounds that they weren't for me, and that anyway from now on there was no need for me to feel a pang of conscience every time I bought something expensive, since I was going to marry a wealthy man. Farid told his mother that the flowers were for the grave. 'What a shame. They're lovely,' she replied, continuing to arrange them in the vase.

Farid signalled to me, and I understood that I shouldn't pursue the subject of the flowers. I looked about me in an attempt to escape from my embarrassment at her behaviour and pretended to be interested in the content of the baskets by the door: pastries for the feast day, bread in unusual shapes and old clothes and shoes.

I sat next to my fiancé in the front of the car, with his mother and father and adolescent sister in the back. The eve of the feast was like the feast itself, the crowded streets throbbing with noise and excitement and everywhere the sound of fireworks exploding. I remembered how as children we would wander the streets all day at this time of year and ride the fairground swings, rushing to empty the peach-coloured sand·from our socks and shoes as soon as we reached home. Every year when the feast came round, it felt as if we were celebrating it for the first time. My mother would prepare the tray of *kunafa* and would take it to the communal oven. Although we stood there for ages, our eyes fixed on the baker so that he would remember our tray, he always took it out late and the pastries would be rock-hard. All the same we ate them with noisy relish. I remembered the handbag I had especially for the feast, the socks I wore even at the height of summer, the shiny shoes, the hair ribbons. We used to visit all our relatives, including those who lived at a distance and were hardly related to us at all. We would knock on their doors and wish them well, not meaning what we said. We knew the uncle who said he had no change on him was lying and would sit for ages on his doorstep before we rushed off to the swings and the pickle-sellers, discussing the rumour that the feast was going to last a day or two longer this year for the children's benefit.

People spent the whole of this feast-day eve in the cemetery. The children wore their brightest clothes. Amplified voices recited the Quran, and at the same time popular songs blared out from radios and cassette-recorders. There were women selling dates and palm leaves. One was smoking and the others shared a joke, their tattooed chins quivering with laughter. Fool beans and *falafel*, fruit juice and pickles of many varieties and colours were all on sale at the entrance to the cemetery. I thought I would have a display of pickles in jars like that in my own house.

Farid's mother stopped at the first vendor she came to, a woman without a tooth in her head, and chose a large quantity of oranges, tangerines and palm leaves. She haggled with her for some time, then gave her a sum of money and walked off. 'Lady! Lady!' the woman called after her. When she tried to ease herself up off the ground, I begged Farid to pay her what she was asking: 'Poor thing, it's a shame on a day like this.'

We hurried to catch up with Farid's mother, elegant in spite of her plumpness, springing over the mud and earth and gravel like a gazelle. She carried her purchases, leaving the baskets to Farid, his father and sister, who looked increasingly morose. I found myself walking along beside her. She glanced at her watch and asked if I thought the sun would come out later, then lowering her voice she explained, 'I want to go to the club. Have a swim and lie in the sun.'

I smiled at her. The noise was deafening. There was the clatter of saucepans and the roar of Primus stoves where the women had spread themselves out to cook in the narrow alleyways and the open spaces between the tombs. The shrieks of children mingled with the voices of the Quran reciters who moved from grave to grave and in and out of the tombs. In vain they tried to raise their voices and their audience – families wanting private recitations for their dead – had to give them all their attention to catch what they were saying. Most of the working reciters were elderly, despite the fact that there were young ones about, leaning against tombstones looking bored. I watched Farid's mother darting from one to another, and all of them promising to find their way to her sooner or later, with the help of the cemetery caretaker. When one of the younger ones approached her offering his services, she pretended not to notice him. Angrily Farid asked her why she had snubbed him and she answered, 'Old men have more merit in the eyes of the Lord.'

Perhaps she meant because the young faces didn't bear the marks of grief and suffering as the old ones did.

We went into a courtyard with a little garden round it where there were graves with pink and white ornamental headstones. Farid said they belonged to his father's grandfather and the grandfather's two brothers who had asked to be buried in this garden, which looked green and moist as if someone had recently watered it. Then we crossed the courtyard into the main family tomb and found it crammed with members of the family, a Quran reciter and dishes of dates and cucumbers and tangerines. The grave itself was festooned with palm leaves. 'Why are we sitting in here, right next to the grave?' I wondered.

I saw disappointment, then anger, on the face of my fiancé's mother, which she was unable to conceal. 'You must have spent the night here,' was her first comment to the assembled company. Nobody answered her, but to her amazement they stood up and greeted us, disregarding the recitation of the Quran: Farid's three paternal aunts, his grandfather, the husbands of two of the aunts and their children. They made room for us on wooden chairs, disfigured by time and neglect, and we all sat down except for Farid's mother who began spreading more palm leaves over the grave until it had almost vanished from sight. Then she took out pastries, bread, dates, cucumbers, tangerines and glasses for tea. She put some pastries and dates in a bag and went up to the Quran reciter, thrusting the bag into his hands. He stopped in the middle of his recitation to mumble his thanks and handed the bag to a boy who was sitting at his feet counting out notes and coins before putting them in his pocket.

Farid's mother asked him all of a sudden how much he took from each family. 'Depends how much time they want,' the boy answered slyly.

'How much?' she insisted. 'Last year, for example?' 'Last year was last year,' he replied. Then, peering into the bag, he named an amount which made Farid's mother gasp. 'That's the same as a check-up at the doctor's,' she remarked. I met my fiancé's eyes and we almost laughed aloud.

There was uproar outside, then the caretaker appeared, accompanied by a sheikh. When they heard the recitation in progress, the sheikh tried to retreat, but Farid's mother grabbed his hand and pulled him in. In spite of the family's obvious disapproval she led him over to where her daughter was sitting, while he murmured, 'I mustn't poach from someone else.'

Impatiently she answered him, 'Just relax. He'll get his share and you'll get yours.'

The sheikh obeyed and sat listening to his colleague, nodding his head with feeling, while the aunts' faces registered annoyance. One of them sighed and another turned her face away. Farid's mother declared, 'It's not a feast every day, and we want to be sure our dead go to heaven.'

Then she approached the caretaker, wishing him well, and counted out some money into his hand, enunciating the amount in an audible voice. 'I hope this place isn't opened up again as soon as our backs are turned?' she inquired sharply.

'What do I carry a weapon for?' countered the caretaker.

'No. You know what I mean,' she said. 'We heard that the previous caretaker used to let our tomb as if it was a hotel.'

'That's why he's the previous caretaker. You know I don't even let kids come through here.'

I thought that relief was at hand when from outside the smell of kebab and meatballs wafted in, making my nostrils twitch. The blind reciter rose to his feet and was led away by the boy, while the newcomer began chanting prayers. I looked around the room, at the faces, especially the aunts'. They shifted their gaze from me to Farid's mother, to his sister and back again. When our eyes met we exchanged smiles, as if they knew what I was thinking and agreed: 'It doesn't matter that Farid's mother's difficult, and I don't have any sort of a relationship with her. Farid's family all love him, even though he does exactly what she says.'

The reciter paused to clear his throat and immediately one of the aunts turned to me and said she hadn't expected me to be so pretty in spite of the descriptions she'd heard and only an illness had kept her away from my engagement party. Another asked if we'd found a flat and what area we were thinking of. I answered these questions in all innocence at first, but from their expressions and the way Farid kept trying to catch my eye, I felt that I must be on sensitive ground as far as his mother was concerned. Sure enough, she interrupted and said there was no urgency about renting a place, her house had big rooms and was Farid's as much as it was hers.

When I replied to the aunts that we were planning a simple wedding, just the family, Farid's mother announced, as if she hadn't heard a word I'd said, that we'd be holding it in one of the big hotels. When I told them that my wedding dress was second-hand, and had been worn first in the Twenties, she was quite unable to hide her alarm. It was then I realized a state of war existed between Farid's mother and the aunts and regretted ever opening my mouth. From their loaded questions and the way they looked at one another after each of my replies, I could tell that they were using me to attack her in her most vulnerable spot. She protested, almost in a scream, 'God forbid! You're wearing a dress that someone else has worn, to your wedding? That's out of the question!'

'Is it white?' inquired one of the aunts, provoking Farid's mother to still greater anguish.

'White, black, what's the difference?' she shouted. 'It's out of the question. Marisa has to make it. I promised her. She'll be upset.'

'Upset!' remarked one of them laughing. 'She's got more work than she can handle. She'll be delighted.'

'I know you're jealous because Marisa's going to make it,' screamed back Farid's mother.

For a moment I forgot where I was. The walls were grey and the visitors' chairs blocked out the tombstone and the palm leaves. We could have been in somebody's sitting room. Farid's father and the third aunt's husband interrupted the argument, coming to stand behind their wives' chairs. 'The clothes. Aren't you going to give them to the caretaker?' asked Farid's father, changing the subject.

His wife sighed, annoyed with herself. 'I forgot all about them,' she replied. 'Let's hope death forgets me!' Then she whispered something in his ear. When he didn't make any comment, she said, 'Who'd like some tea?' She went over into a corner where there was a Primus stove I hadn't noticed before. As she pumped it, she asked, 'What do you think about building on to the tomb? Another room, a little kitchen, a bathroom?'

Nobody answered. They were all absorbed in their own private conversations. She repeated, 'We need to extend the tomb. Farid's father agrees. What do you say?'

'Extend it!' scoffed one of the aunts. 'To hear you talking anyone would think a tomb was just like a flat or a house!'

'What I meant,' Farid's mother corrected herself, 'is that we should buy an old abandoned tomb.'

Another aunt seized on her words: 'And have our dead mixed up with other people's? That's madness!'

'I mean we should buy a plot of ground, even if it's a little way off.'

The voices rose and fell. Farid's cousins and sister whispered scornfully to each other. Farid brought me a glass of tea. Meanwhile, his mother continued to ask querulously, at intervals, 'What do you say?'

'What do we say?' answered one of the aunts at last. 'Nobody's in a position to lay out money on tombs and suchlike, that's what we say.'

Farid's mother drew a triumphant breath: 'Farid's got a marvellous job, thank God, and . . .'

I looked with embarrassment at Farid, who was shaking his head like someone who wanted help. He said sheepishly, 'Why do you need to mention that?'

His mother must have felt from this response that he was siding with his aunts against her, but she went on, 'I mean God's made you rich enough to pay for the new tomb.'

She seemed to gain strength from his silence, and had the look of a cat when the mouse is finally cornered. But the spiteful looks of the other women snatched victory from her grasp. 'We know your stories,' they seemed to say. 'You want to tell your friends that you've got a big new tomb. A villa! A three-storey villa with marble stairs and wrought-iron gates!'

'Have you ever heard of anyone visiting the family tomb and sitting almost on top of the graves?' shouted Farid's mother. 'We must have a separate room to sit in.'

'We used to be able to use the one you gave the caretaker,' interrupted one of the aunts.

'At least there's only him and his wife,' persisted Farid's mother. 'Surely that's better than having a family taking it over, with children clambering over our tombstones like apes, and then not being able to get rid of them?'

'And what's wrong with being buried in the garden?' continued the aunt in a superior tone. 'You don't have to be inside the room.'

'Your father's grandfather liked the idea of being buried in the garden – that's his business,' yelled Farid's mother. 'I and my family want to be buried inside.'

In a whisper, as if divulging a secret, Farid's father said, 'Listen to me. Land prices are going to soar. People are going to start living in these buildings on a regular basis. And anyway what's wrong with our family having the very best?'

'I know,' answered his sister. 'But is it reasonable to expect you to pay while we stand with our arms folded? You know, the children are at university and there are the monthly payments to keep up with and all our other commitments . . .'

'I'm ready to fall in with anything,' said her husband.

His intervention seemed to irritate Farid's mother and she snapped back at him, 'In any case, your wife won't be buried here. She'll go with your family.'

His wife ignored her and said, 'Look. Just look around. This tomb's big. You couldn't call this a small area.'

But Farid's mother came back at her with a reply which unnerved me like a physical blow. All along I hadn't believed that the family's scheming and arguing over the peaceful grave in its midst could be serious. I told myself it must be a family joke, and anyway it had nothing to do with me, even Farid's helping to pay.

Standing in the middle of the room, Farid's mother declared, 'No. It's not as big as you imagine. There's me, there's my husband, and now Farid's about to become two, and then there'll be his children.'

Her words frightened me. Death wasn't as distant as it had been. I didn't think of it, like a child, as something that wouldn't happen to me. Trying to make a joke, I said, 'Should we be planning for our afterlife when we're not yet married?'

'We're saying prices are going to soar,' intervened Farid's father, seizing on the same pretext as before.

I knew that all eyes were on me, especially the aunts', begging me to save them from Farid's mother's claws. But I lacked the strength even to save myself and abandoned myself to the terrifying thought that one day I'd be here in this room underneath a tombstone like that, with one for Farid and each of my children. We'd all end up here and our children's children would sit like us now, sipping tea, arguing, eating dates.

The raised voices of the men, joining in with the women now, brought me back to the present. Farid came to my rescue, taking my hands in his soothingly, and I mumbled, 'It's crazy to think about it now.'

I don't know how Farid's mother heard what I said; I hardly heard it myself, but she remarked smugly, 'Our lives are in God's hands.'

This angered me and, unconscious of what I was saying, like a child who wanted to contradict for the sake of contradicting, I replied, 'I don't want to be buried here.'

'You don't have any choice,' she said. 'When you become part of the family, that's what you have to do. Even your own family wouldn't agree to bury you with them.'

I felt as though she was already shovelling earth down on top of me. 'No!' I screamed. 'No!' I jumped up and rushed to the door. Farid's mother paid no attention even when Farid took hold of me and said reprovingly to her, 'Are you happy now?'

'She has to understand, my dear,' she said to him, 'that whoever lives with us must die with us.'

I broke free and ran. He came after me. Outside in the cemetery's main square I caught my breath and leant against a tombstone while I fastened my sandal. Children were playing with a ball there, disregarding the comments of their mothers and the older women who sat resting from the labours of their cooking. 'The dead must be trembling with anxiety down there,' remarked one.

I composed myself at last, perhaps at this spectacle of everyday life, or the glimpse of a bird abandoning itself to space, beautiful and oblivious to what was happening below. We stopped beside the car. I knew we would have to wait for his family. I felt I wanted to be free of his hand holding tightly on to mine. I turned my face away, contemplating the washing spread out to dry, the empty bowl resting against one grave, the cooking pot sitting on another, as if it was a table, and the owners of these objects going about their business – victims of the housing crisis, who had squatted in abandoned tombs, rented at the going rate, or simply occupied family tombs prematurely, and adapted them to suit their lives. I saw television and radio aerials in place; and yet Farid's mother wanted a bigger space to house her graves.

When I saw Farid's mother, father and sister appearing in the distance, I felt the breath being knocked out of me. So we were one family, living together, dying together?

Farid's father must have told his wife to keep quiet, as she hadn't uttered a word from the moment she entered the car. His sister tried to make peace with me, and told me about a friend of hers who was a social scientist and was doing a study of the people who lived alongside the dead. She said how the women would be trilling for joy at the birth of a baby, and would fall silent suddenly if they noticed a funeral procession approaching. Their noises of rejoicing would turn to keening, while the men rushed to find which tomb the music was coming from, or the news broadcast, so they could silence it. As soon as the funeral was over, life would return to normal.

But I remained silent. Surrounded by their loud voices, I felt like the ant I'd noticed on the floor of the tomb. It had moved uncertainly along, not knowing that any moment it could be trodden on and crushed to death. I realized I'd changed my mind about marriage, and I wanted to get out of the car straight away before I was suffocated by Farid's mother. I had a vision of the aunts like three witches preparing to serve us all up to the Devil.

I thought I would tell Farid that the reason I'd changed my mind about marrying him wasn't to do with the tomb or where I would be buried. On the contrary, I'd loved all the commotion, and the cemetery itself was like a fun-fair. Anyway, I didn't like being alone even while I was alive.

Then I decided against this last sentence. I was haunted by the scene of the family in the tomb, and their voices were still ringing in my ears. I resolved to try to like being alone, alive or dead.

# A Wilderness Station

*Alice Munro was born in Canada in 1931 and grew up in a 'fringe community of Wingham', a small town in south-western Ontario. She spent many years running a bookshop before becoming a writer. Her book* The Beggar Maid *was shortlisted for the Booker Prize, and she is also the author of seven collections of short stories, including most recently* Open Secrets, *from which this story comes. Again and again critics have been overwhelmed by her narrative powers and her empathy with unremarkable lives and unambitious people. Her work is deeply rooted in the past and in landscape, and she has declared herself absolutely loyal to the short-story form. 'I started to write short stories because my life didn't allow me time to write a novel. That's what I thought – I had small children, and I could never count on a big chunk of time. And now that I could arrange for the time a novel needs, I'm not interested in writing one. I love short stories, reading them, writing them. There's an excitement about them – a world seen in a quick glancing light . . .'*

I

Miss Margaret Cresswell, Matron, House of Industry, Toronto, to Mr Simon Herron, North Huron, January 15, 1852.

Since your letter is accompanied by an endorsement from your minister, I am happy to reply. Requests of your sort are made to us frequently, but unless we have such an endorsement we cannot trust that they are made in good faith.

We do not have any girl at the Home who is of marriageable age, since we send our girls out to make a living usually around the age of fourteen or fifteen, but we do keep track of them for some years or usually until they are married. In cases such as yours we sometimes recommend one of these girls and will arrange a meeting, and then of course it is up to the two parties involved to see if they are suited.

There are two girls eighteen years of age that we are still in touch with. Both are apprenticed to a milliner and are good seamstresses, but a marriage to a likely man would probably be preferred to a lifetime of such work. Further than that cannot be said, it must be left to the girl herself and of course to your liking for her, or the opposite.

The two girls are a Miss Sadie Johnstone and a Miss Annie McKillop. Both were born legitimately of Christian parents and were placed in the Home due to parental deaths. Drunkenness or immorality was not a factor. In Miss Johnstone's case there is however the factor of consumption, and though she is the prettier of the two and a plump rosy girl, I feel I must warn you that perhaps she is not suited to the hard work of a life in the bush. The other girl, Miss McKillop, is of a more durable constitution though of leaner frame and not so good a complexion. She has a waywardness about one eye but it does not interfere with her vision and her sewing is excellent. The darkness of her eyes and hair and brown tinge of her skin is no indication of mixed blood, as both parents were from Fife. She is a hardy girl and I think would be suited to such a life as you can offer, being also free from the silly timidness we often see in girls of her age. I will speak to her and acquaint her with the idea and will await your letter as to when you propose to meet her.

## II

Carstairs *Argus*, Fiftieth Anniversary Edition, February 3, 1907. Recollections of Mr George Herron.

On the first day of September, 1851, my brother Simon and I got a box of bedclothes and household utensils together and put them in a wagon with a horse to pull it, and set out from Halton County to try our fortunes in the wilds of Huron and Bruce, as wilds they were then thought to be. The goods were from Archie Frame that Simon worked for, and counted as part of his wages. Likewise we had to rent the horse off him, and his boy that was about my age came along to take it and the wagon back.

It ought to be said in the beginning that my brother and I were left alone, our father first and then our mother dying of fever within five weeks of landing in this country, when I was three years old and Simon eight. Simon was put to work for Archie Frame that was our mother's cousin, and I was taken on by the schoolteacher and wife that had no child of their own. This was in Halton, and I would have been content to go on living there but Simon being only a few miles away continued to visit and say that as soon as we were old enough we would go and take up land and be on our own, not working for others, as this was what our father had intended. Archie Frame never sent Simon to school as I was sent, so Simon was always bound to get away. When I had come to be fourteen years of age and a husky lad, as was my brother, he said we should go and take up Crown Land north of the Huron Tract.

We only got as far as Preston on the first day as the roads were rough and bad across Nassageweya and Puslinch. Next day we got to Shakespeare and the third afternoon to Stratford. The roads were always getting worse as we came west, so we thought best to get our box sent on to Clinton by the stage. But the stage had quit running due to rains, and they were waiting till the roads froze up, so we told Archie Frame's boy to turn about and return with horse and cart and goods back to Halton. Then we took our axes on our shoulders, and walked to Carstairs.

Hardly a soul was there before us. Carstairs was just under way, with a rough building that was store and inn combined, and there was a German named Roem building a sawmill. One man who got there before us and already had a fair-sized cabin built was Henry Treece, who afterwards became my father-in-law.

We got ourselves boarded at the inn where we slept on the bare floor with one blanket or quilt between us. Winter was coming early with cold rains and everything damp, but we were expecting hardship or at least Simon was. I came from a softer place. He said we must put up with it so I did.

We began to underbrush a road to our piece of land and then we got it marked out and cut the logs for our shanty and big scoops to roof it. We were able to borrow an ox from Henry Treece to draw the logs. But Simon was not of a mind to borrow or depend on anybody. He was minded to try raising the shanty ourselves, but when we saw we could not do it I made my way to Treeces' place and with Henry and two of his sons and a fellow from the mill it was accomplished. We started next day to fill up the cracks between the logs with mud and we got some hemlock branches so we would not be out money anymore for staying at the inn but could sleep in our own place. We had a big slab of elm for the door. My brother had heard from some French-Canadian fellows that were at Archie Frame's that in the lumber camps the fire was always in the middle of the shanty. So he said that was the way we should have ours, and we got four posts and were building the chimney on them, house-fashion, intending to plaster it with mud inside and out. We went to our hemlock bed with a good fire going, but waking in the middle of the night we saw our lumber was all ablaze and the scoops burning away briskly also. We tore down the chimney and the scoops being green basswood were not hard to put out. As soon as it came day, we started to build the chimney in the ordinary way in the end of the house and I thought it best not to make any remark.

After the small trees and brush was cleared out a bit, we set to chopping down the big trees. We cut down a big ash and split it into slabs for our floor. Still our box had not come which was to be shipped from Halton so Henry Treece sent us a very large and comfortable bearskin for our cover in bed but my brother would not take the favour and sent it back saying no need. Then after several weeks we got our box and had to ask for the ox to bring it on from Clinton, but my brother said that is the last we will need to ask of any person's help.

We walked to Walley and brought back flour and salt fish on our back. A man rowed us across the river at Manchester for a steep price. There were no bridges then and all that winter not a good enough freeze to make it easy going over the rivers.

Around Christmastime my brother said to me that he thought we had the place in good enough shape now for him to be bringing in a wife, so we should have somebody to cook and do for us and milk a cow when we could afford one. This was the first I had heard of any wife and I said that I did not know he was acquainted with anybody. He said he was not but he had heard that you could write to the Orphanage Home and ask if they had a girl there that was willing to think about the prospect and that they would recommend, and if so he would go and see her. He wanted one between eighteen and twenty-two years of age, healthy and not afraid of work and raised in the Orphanage, not taken in lately, so that she would not be expecting any luxuries or to be waited on and would not be recalling about when things were easier for her. I do not doubt that to those hearing about this nowadays it seems a strange way to go about things. It was not that my brother could not have gone courting and got a wife on his own, because he was a good-looking fellow, but he did not have the time or the money or inclination, his mind was all occupied with establishing our holding. And if a girl had parents they would probably not want her to go far away where there was little in comforts and so much work.

That it was a respectable way of doing things is shown by the fact that the minister Mr McBain, who was lately come into the district, helped Simon to write the letter and sent word on his own to vouch for him.

So a letter came back that there was a girl that might fit the bill and Simon went off to Toronto and got her. Her name was Annie but her maiden name I have forgotten. They had to ford the streams in Hullet and trudge through deep soft snow after leaving the stage in Clinton, and when they got back she was worn out and very surprised at what she saw, since she said she had never imagined so much bush. She had in her box some sheets and pots and dishes that ladies had given her and that made the place more comfortable.

Early in April my brother and I went out to chop down some trees in the bush at the farthest corner of our property. While Simon was away to get married, I had done some chopping in the other direction towards Treeces', but Simon wanted to get all our boundaries cut clear around and not to go on chopping where I had been. The day started out mild and there was still a lot of soft snow in the bush. We were chopping down a tree where Simon wanted, and in some way, I cannot say how, a branch of it came crashing down where we didn't expect. We just heard the little branches cracking where it fell and looked up to see it and it hit Simon on the head and killed him instantly.

I had to drag his body back then to the shanty through the snow. He was a tall fellow though not fleshy, and it was an awkward task and greatly wearying. It had got colder by this time and when I got to the clearing I saw snow on the wind like the start of a storm. Our footsteps were filled in that we had made earlier. Simon was all covered with snow that did not melt on him by this time, and his wife coming to the door was greatly puzzled, thinking that I was dragging along a log.

In the shanty Annie washed him off and we sat still a while not knowing what we should do. The preacher was at the inn as there was no church or house for him yet and the inn was only about four miles away, but the storm had come up very fierce so you could not even see the trees at the edge of the clearing. It had the look of a storm that would last two or three days, the wind being from the north-west. We knew we could not keep the body in the shanty and we could not set it out in the snow fearing the bobcats would get at it, so we had to set to work and bury him. The ground was not frozen under the snow, so I dug out a grave near the shanty and Annie sewed him in a sheet and we laid him in his grave, not staying long in the wind but saying the Lord's Prayer and reading one psalm out of the Bible. I am not sure which one but I remember it was near the end of the Book of Psalms and it was very short.

This was the third day of April, 1852.

That was our last snow of the year, and later the minister came and said the service and I put up a wooden marker. Later on we got our plot in the cemetery and put his stone there, but he is not under it as it is a foolish useless thing in my opinion to cart a man's bones from one place to another when it is only bones and his soul has gone on to Judgement.

I was left to chop and clear by myself and soon I began to work side by side with the Treeces, who treated me with the greatest kindness. We worked all together on my land or their land, not minding if it was the one or the other. I started to take my meals and even to sleep at their place and got to know their daughter Jenny who was about of my age, and we made our plans to marry, which we did in due course. Our life together was a long one with many hardships but we were fortunate in the end and raised eight children. I have seen my sons take over my wife's father's land as well as my own since my two brothers-in-law went away and did well for themselves in the West.

My brother's wife did not continue in this place but went her own way to Walley.

Now there are gravel roads running north, south, east, and west and a railway not a half mile from my farm. Except for woodlots, the bush is a thing of the past and I often think of the trees I have cut down and if I had them to cut down today I would be a wealthy man.

The Reverend Walter McBain, Minister of the Free Presbyterian Church of North Huron, to Mr James Mullen, Clerk of the Peace, Walley, United Counties of Huron and Bruce, September 10, 1852.

I write to inform you, sir, of the probable arrival in your town of a young woman of this district, by the name of Annie Herron, a widow and one of my congregation. This young person has left her home here in the vicinity of Carstairs in Holloway Township, I believe she intends to walk to Walley. She may appear at the Gaol there seeking to be admitted, so I think it my duty to tell you who and what she is and her history here since I have known her.

I came to this area in November of last year, being the first minister of any kind to venture. My parish is as yet mostly bush, and there is nowhere for me to lodge but at the Carstairs Inn. I was born in the west of Scotland and came to this country under the auspices of the Glasgow Mission. After applying to know God's will, I was directed by Him to go to preach wherever was most need of a minister. I tell you this so you may know what sort I am that bring you my account and my view of the affairs of this woman.

She came into the country late last winter as the bride of the young man Simon Herron. He had written on my advice to the House of Industry in Toronto that they might recommend to him a Christian, preferably Presbyterian, female suitable to his needs, and she was the one recommended. He married her straight away and brought her here to the shanty he had built with his brother. These two young lads had come into the country to clear themselves a piece of land and get possession of it, being themselves orphans and without expectations. They were about this work one day at the end of winter when an accident befell. A branch was loosed while chopping down a tree and fell upon the elder brother so as to cause instant death. The younger lad succeeded in getting the body back to the shanty and since they were held prisoner by a heavy snowstorm they conducted their own funeral and burial.

The Lord is strict in his mercies and we are bound to receive his blows as signs of his care and goodness for so they will prove to be.

Deprived of his brother's help, the lad found a place in a neighbouring family, also members in good standing of my congregation, who have accepted him as a son, though he still works for title to his own land. This family would have taken in the young widow as well, but she would have nothing to do with their offer and seemed to develop an aversion to everyone who would help her. Particularly she seemed so towards her brother-in-law, who said that he had never had the least quarrel with her, and towards myself. When I talked to her, she would not give any answer or sign that her soul was coming into submission. It is a fault of mine that I am not well-equipped to talk to women. I have not the ease to win their trust. Their stubbornness is of another kind than a man's.

I meant only to say that I did not have any good effect on her. She stopped appearing at services, and the deterioration of her property showed the state of her mind and spirit. She would not plant peas and potatoes though they were given to her to grow among the stumps. She did not chop down the wild vines around her door. Most often she did not light a fire so she could have oat-cake or porridge. Her brother-in-law being removed, there was no order imposed on her days. When I visited her the door was open and it was evident that animals came and went in her house. If she was there she hid herself, to mock me. Those who caught sight of her said that her clothing was filthy and torn from scrambling about in the bushes, and she was scratched by thorns and bitten by the mosquito insects and let her hair go uncombed or plaited. I believe she lived on salt fish and bannock that the neighbours or her brother-in-law left for her.

Then while I was still puzzling how I might find a way to protect her body through the winter and deal with the more important danger to her soul, there comes word she is gone. She left the door open and went away without cloak or bonnet and wrote on the shanty floor with a burnt stick the two words: 'Walley, Gaol'. I take this to mean she intends to go there and turn herself in. Her brother-in-law thinks it would be no use for him to go after her because of her unfriendly attitude to himself, and I cannot set out because of a deathbed I am attending. I ask you therefore to let me know if she has arrived and in what state and how you will deal with her. I consider her still as a soul in my charge, and I will try to visit her before winter if you keep her there. She is a child of the Free Church and the Covenant and as such she is entitled to a minister of her own faith and you must not think it sufficient that some priest of the Church of England or Baptist or Methodist be sent to her.

In case she should not come to the Gaol but wander in the streets, I ought to tell you that she is dark-haired and tall, meagre in body, not comely but not ill-favoured except having one eye that goes to the side.

Mr James Mullen, Clerk of the Peace, Walley, to the Reverend Walter McBain, Carstairs, North Huron, September 30, 1852.

Your letter to me arrived most timely and appreciated, concerning the young woman Annie Herron. She completed her journey to Walley unharmed and with no serious damage though she was weak and hungry when she presented herself at the Gaol. On its being inquired what she did there, she said that she came to confess to a murder, and to be locked up. There was consultation round and about, I was sent for, and it being near to midnight, I agreed that she should spend the night in a cell. The next day I visited her and got all particulars I could.

Her story of being brought up in the Orphanage, her apprenticeship to a milliner, her marriage, and her coming to North Huron, all accords pretty well with what you have told me. Events in her account begin to differ only with her husband's death. In that matter what she says is this:

On the day in early April when her husband and his brother went out to chop trees, she was told to provide them with food for their midday meal, and since she had not got it ready when they wanted to leave, she agreed to take it to them in the woods. Consequently she baked up some oatcakes and took some salt fish and followed their tracks and found them at work some distance away. But when her husband unwrapped his food he was very offended, because she had wrapped it in a way that the salty oil from the fish had soaked into the cakes, and they were all crumbled and unpleasant to eat. In his disappointment he became enraged and promised her a beating when he was more at leisure to do it. He then turned his back on her, being seated on a log, and she picked up a rock and threw it at him, hitting him on the head so that he fell down unconscious and in fact dead. She and his brother then carried and dragged the body back to the house. By that time a blizzard had come up and they were imprisoned within. The brother said that they should not reveal the truth as she had not intended murder, and she agreed. They then buried him – her story agreeing again with yours – and that might have been the end of it, but she became more and more troubled, convinced that she had surely been intending to kill him. If she had not killed him, she says, it would only have meant a worse beating, and why should she have risked that? So she decided at last upon confession and as if to prove something handed me a lock of hair stiffened with blood.

This is her tale, and I do not believe it for a minute. No rock that this girl could pick up, combined with the force that she could summon to throw it, would serve to kill a man. I questioned her about this, and she changed her story, saying that it was a large rock that she had picked up in both hands and that she had not thrown it but smashed it down on his head from behind. I said why did not the brother prevent you, and she said, he was looking the other way. Then I said there must indeed be a bloodied rock lying somewhere in the wood, and she said she had washed it off with the snow. (In fact it is not likely a rock would come to hand so easily, with all such depth of snow about.) I asked her to roll up her sleeve that I might judge of the muscles in her arms, to do such a job, and she said that she had been a huskier woman some months since.

I conclude that she is lying, or self-deluded. But I see nothing for it at the moment but to admit her to the Gaol. I asked her what she thought would happen to her now, and she said, well, you will try me and then you will hang me. But you do not hang people in the winter, she said, so I can stay here till spring. And if you let me work here, maybe you will want me to go on working and you will not want me hanged. I do not know where she got this idea about people not being hanged in the winter. I am in perplexity about her. As you may know, we have a very fine new Gaol here where the inmates are kept warm and dry and are decently fed and treated with all humanity, and there has been a complaint that some are not sorry – and at this time of year, even happy – to get into it. But it is obvious that she cannot wander about much longer, and from your account she is unwilling to stay with friends and unable to make a tolerable home for herself. The Gaol at present serves as a place of detention for the Insane as well as criminals, and if she is charged with Insanity, I could keep her here for the winter perhaps with removal to Toronto in the spring. I have engaged for a doctor to visit her. I spoke to her of your letter and your hope of coming to see her, but I found her not at all agreeable to that. She asks that nobody be allowed to see her excepting a Miss Sadie Johnstone, who is not in this part of the country.

I am enclosing a letter I have written to her brother-in-law for you to pass on to him, so that he may know what she has said and tell me what he thinks about it. I thank you in advance for conveying the letter to him, also for the trouble you have been to, in informing me as fully as you have done. I am a member of the Church of England, but have a high regard for the work of other Protestant denominations in bringing an orderly life to this part of the world we find ourselves in. You may believe that I will do what is in my power to do, to put you in a position to deal with the soul of this young woman, but it might be better to wait until she is in favour of it.

The Reverend Walter McBain to Mr James Mullen, November 18, 1852.

I carried your letter at once to Mr George Herron and believe that he has replied and given you his recollection of events. He was amazed at his sister-in-law's claim, since she had never said anything of this to him or to anybody else. He says that it is all her invention or fancy, since she was never in the woods when it happened and there was no need for her to be, as they had carried their food with them when they left the house. He says that there had been at another time some reproof from his brother to her, over the spoiling of some cakes by their proximity to fish, but it did not happen at this time. Nor were there any rocks about to do such a deed on impulse if she had been there and wished to do it.

My delay in answering your letter, for which I beg pardon, is due to a bout of ill health. I had an attack of the gravel and a rheumatism of the stomach worse than any misery that ever fell upon me before. I am somewhat improved at present and will be able to go about as usual by next week if all continues to mend.

As to the question of the young woman's sanity, I do not know what your Doctor will say but I have thought on this and questioned the Divinity and my belief is this. It may well be that so early in the marriage her submission to her husband was not complete and there would be carelessness about his comfort, and naughty words, and quarrelsome behaviour, as well as the hurtful sulks and silences her sex is prone to. His death occurring before any of this was put right, she would feel a natural and harrowing remorse, and this must have taken hold of her mind so strongly that she made herself out to be actually responsible for his death. In this way, I think many folk are driven mad. Madness is at first taken on by some as a kind of play, for which shallowness and audacity they are punished later on, by finding out that it is play no longer, and the Devil has blocked off every escape.

It is still my hope to speak to her and make her understand this. I am under difficulties at present not only of my wretched corpus but of being lodged in a foul and noisy place obliged to hear day and night such uproars as destroy sleep and study and intrude even on my prayers. The wind blows bitterly through the logs, but if I go down to the fire there is swilling of spirits and foulest insolence. And outside nothing but trees to choke off every exit and icy bog to swallow man and horse. There was a promise to build a church and lodging but those who made such promise have grown busy with their own affairs and it seems to have been put off. I have not however left off preaching even in my illness and in such barns and houses as are provided. I take heart remembering a great man, the great preacher and interpreter of God's will, Thomas Boston, who in the latter days of his infirmity preached the grandeur of God from his chamber window to a crowd of two thousand or so assembled in the yard below. So I mean to preach to the end though my congregation will be smaller.

*Whatsoever crook there is in one's lot, it is of God's making.* Thomas Boston.

*This world is a wilderness, in which we may indeed get our station changed, but the move will be out of one wilderness station unto another.* Ibid.

Mr James Mullen to the Reverend Walter McBain, January 17, 1853.

I write to you that our young woman's health seems sturdy, and she no longer looks such a scarecrow, eating well and keeping herself clean and tidy. Also she seems quieter in her spirits. She has taken to mending the linen in the prison which she does well. But I must tell you that she is firm as ever against a visit, and I cannot advise you to come here as I think your trouble might be for nothing. The journey is very hard in winter and it would do no good to your state of health.

Her brother-in-law has written me a very decent letter affirming that there is no truth to her story, so I am satisfied on that.

You may be interested in hearing what the doctor who visited her had to say about her case. His belief is that she is subject to a sort of delusion peculiar to females, for which the motive is a desire for self-importance, also a wish to escape the monotony of life or the drudgery they may have been born to. They may imagine themselves possessed by the forces of evil, to have committed various and hideous crimes, and so forth. Sometimes they may report that they have taken numerous lovers, but these lovers will be all imaginary and the woman who thinks herself a prodigy of vice will in fact be quite chaste and untouched. For all this he – the doctor – lays the blame on the sort of reading that is available to these females, whether it is of ghosts or demons or of love escapades with Lords and Dukes and suchlike. For many, these tales are a passing taste given up when life's real duties intervene. For others they are indulged in now and then, as if they were sweets or sherry wine, but for some there is complete surrender and living within them just as in an opium-dream. He could not get an account of her reading from the young woman, but he believes she may by now have forgotten what she has read, or conceals the matter out of slyness.

With his questioning there did come to light something further that we did not know. On his saying to her, did she not fear hanging? she replied, no, for there is a reason you will not hang me. You mean that they will judge that you are mad? said he, and she said, oh, perhaps that, but is it not true also that they will never hang a woman that is with child? The doctor then examined her to find out if this were true, and she agreed to the examination, so she must have made the claim in good faith. He discovered however that she had deceived herself. The signs she took were simply the results of her going so long underfed and in such a reduced state, and later probably of her hysteria. He told her of his findings, but it is hard to say whether she believes him.

It must be acknowledged that this is truly a hard country for women. Another insane female has been admitted here recently, and her case is more pitiful for she has been driven insane by a rape. Her two attackers have been taken in and are in fact just over the wall from her in the men's section. The screams of the victim resound sometimes for hours at a stretch, and as a result the prison has become a much less pleasant shelter. But whether that will persuade our self-styled murderess to recant and take herself off, I have no idea. She is a good needlewoman and could get employment if she chose.

I am sorry to hear of your bad health and miserable lodgings. The town has grown so civilized that we forget the hardship of the hinterlands. Those like yourself who choose to endure it deserve our admiration. But you must allow me to say that it seems pretty certain that a man not in robust health will be unable to bear up for long in your situation. Surely your Church would not consider it a defection were you to choose to serve it longer by removing to a more comfortable place.

I enclose a letter written by the young woman and sent to a Miss Sadie Johnstone, on King Street, Toronto. It was intercepted by us that we might know more of the state of her mind, but resealed and sent on. But it has come back marked 'Unknown'. We have not told the writer of this in hopes that she will write again and more fully, revealing to us something to help us decide whether or not she is a conscious liar.

Mrs Annie Herron, Walley Gaol, United Counties of Huron and Bruce, to Miss Sadie Johnstone, 49 King Street, Toronto, December 20, 1852.

Sadie, I am in here pretty well and safe and nothing to complain of either in food or blankets. It is a good stone building and something like the Home. If you could come and see me I would be very glad. I often talk to you a whole lot in my head, which I don't want to write because what if they are spies. I do the sewing here, the things was not in good repare when I came but now they are pretty good. And I am making curtains for the Opera House, a job that was sent in. I hope to see you. You could come on the stage right to this place. Maybe you would not like to come in the winter but in the springtime you would like to come.

Mr James Mullen to the Reverend Walter McBain, April 7, 1853.

Not having had any reply to my last letter, I trust you are well and might still be interested in the case of Annie Herron. She is still here and busies herself at sewing jobs which I have undertaken to get her from outside. No more is said of being with child, or of hanging, or of her story. She has written once again to Sadie Johnstone but quite briefly and

I enclose her letter here. Do you have an idea who this person Sadie Johnstone might be?

I don't get any answer from you, Sadie, I don't think they sent on my letter. Today is the First of April, 1853. But not April Fool like we used to fool each other. Please come and see me if you can. I am in Walley Gaol but safe and well.

Mr James Mullen from Edward Hoy, Landlord, Carstairs Inn, April 19, 1853.

Your letter to Mr McBain sent back to you, he died here at the inn February 25. There is some books here, nobody wants them.

## III

Annie Herron, Walley Gaol, to Sadie Johnstone, Toronto. Finder Please Post.

George came dragging him across the snow. I thought it was a log he dragged. I didn't know it was him. George said, it's him. A branch fell out of a tree and hit him, he said. He didn't say he was dead. I looked for him to speak. His mouth was part way open with snow in it. Also his eyes part way open. We had to get inside because it was starting to storm like anything. We dragged him in by the one leg each. I pretended to myself when I took hold of his leg that it was still the log. Inside where I had the fire going it was warm and the snow started melting off him. His blood thawed and ran a little around his ear. I didn't know what to do and I was afraid to go near him. I thought his eyes were watching me.

George sat by the fire with his big heavy coat on and his boots on. He was turned away. I sat at the table, which was of half-cut logs. I said, how do you know if he is dead? George said, touch him if you want to know. But I would not. Outside there was terrible storming, the wind in the trees and over top of our roof. I said, Our Father who art in Heaven, and that was how I got my courage. I kept saying it every time I moved. I have to wash him off, I said. Help me. I got the bucket where I kept the snow melting. I started on his feet and had to pull his boots off, a heavy job. George never turned around or paid attention or helped me when I asked. I didn't take the trousers or coat off of him, I couldn't manage. But I washed his hands and wrists. I always kept the rag between my hand and his skin. The blood and wet where the snow had melted off him was on the floor under his head and shoulders so I wanted to turn him over and clean it up. But I couldn't do it. So I went and pulled George by his arm. Help me, I said. What? he said. I said we had to turn him. So he came and helped me and we got him turned over, he was laying face down. And then I saw, I saw where the axe had cut.

Neither one of us said anything. I washed it out, blood and what else. I said to George, go and get me the sheet from my box. There was the good sheet I wouldn't put on the bed. I didn't see the use of trying to take off his clothes though they were good cloth. We would have had to cut them away where the blood was stuck and then what would we have but the rags. I cut off the one little piece of his hair because I remembered when Lila died in the Home they did that. Then I got George to help me roll him on to the sheet and I started to sew him up in the sheet. While I was sewing I said to George, go out in the lee of the house where the wood is piled and maybe you can get in enough shelter there to dig him a grave. Take the wood away and the ground is likely softer underneath.

I had to crouch down at the sewing so I was nearly laying on the floor beside him. I sewed his head in first folding the sheet over it because I had to look in his eyes and mouth. George went out and I could hear through the storm that he was doing what I said and pieces of wood were thrown up sometimes hitting the wall of the house. I sewed on, and every bit of him I lost sight of I would say even out loud, there goes, there goes. I had got the fold neat over his head but down at the feet I didn't have material enough to cover him, so I sewed on my eyelet petticoat I made at the Home to learn the stitch and that way I got him all sewed in.

I went out to help George. He had got all the wood out of the way and was at the digging. The ground was soft enough, like I had thought. He had the spade so I got the broad shovel and we worked away, him digging and loosening and me shovelling.

Then we moved him out. We could not do it now one leg each so George got him at the head and me at the ankles where the petticoat was and we rolled him into the earth and set to work again to cover him up. George had the shovel and it seemed I could not get enough dirt on to the spade so I pushed it in with my hands and kicked it in with my feet any way at all. When it was all back in, George beat it down flat with the shovel as much as he could. Then we moved all the wood back searching where it was in the snow and we piled it up in the right way so it did not look as if anybody had been at it. I think we had no hats on or scarves but the work kept us warm.

We took in more wood for the fire and put the bar across the door. I wiped up the floor and I said to George, take off your boots. Then, take off your coat. George did what I told him. He sat by the fire. I made the kind of tea from catnip leaves that Mrs Treece showed me how to make and I put a piece of sugar in it. George did not want it. Is it too hot, I said. I let it cool off but then he didn't want it either. So I began, and talked to him.

You didn't mean to do it.

It was in anger, you didn't mean what you were doing.

I saw him other times what he would do to you. I saw he would knock you down for a little thing and you just get up and never say a word. The same way he did to me.

If you had not have done it, some day he would have done it to you.

Listen, George. Listen to me.

If you own up what do you think will happen? They will hang you. You will be dead, you will be no good to anybody. What will become of your land? Likely it will all go back to the Crown and somebody else will get it and all the work you have done will be for them.

What will become of me here if you are took away?

I got some oat-cakes that were cold and I warmed them up. I set one on his knee. He took it and bit it and chewed it but he could not get it down and he spit it on to the fire.

I said, listen. I know things. I am older than you are. I am religious too, I pray to God every night and my prayers are answered. I know what God wants as well as any preacher knows and I know that he does not want a good lad like you to be hanged. All you have to do is say you are sorry. Say you are sorry and mean it well and God will forgive you. I will say the same thing, I am sorry too because when I saw he was dead I did not wish, not one minute, for him to be alive. I will say, God forgive me, and you do the same. Kneel down.

But he would not. He would not move out of his chair. And I said, all right. I have an idea. I am going to get the Bible. I asked him, do you believe in the Bible? Say you do. Nod your head.

I did not see whether he nodded or not but I said, there. There you did. Now. I am going to do what we all used to do in the Home when we wanted to know what would happen to us or what we should do in our life. We would open the Bible any place and poke our finger at a page and then open our eyes and read the verse where our finger was and that would tell you what you needed to know. To make double sure of it just say when you close your eyes, God guide my finger.

He would not raise a hand from his knee, so I said, all right. All right, I'll do it for you. I did it, and I read where my finger stopped. I held the Bible close in to the fire so I could see.

It was something about being old and gray-headed, *oh God forsake me not*, and I said, what that means is that you are supposed to live till you are old and gray-headed and nothing is supposed to happen to you before that. It says so, in the Bible.

Then the next verse was so-and-so went and took so-and-so and conceived and bore him a son.

It says you will have a son, I said. You have to live and get older and get married and have a son.

But the next verse I remember so well I can put down all of it. *Neither can they prove the things of which they now accuse me.*

George, I said, do you hear that? *Neither can they prove the things of which they now accuse me.* That means that you are safe.

You are safe. Get up now. Get up and go and lay on the bed and go to sleep.

He could not do that by himself but I did it. I pulled on him and pulled on him until he was standing up and then I got him across the room to the bed which was not his bed in the corner but the bigger bed, and got him to sit on it then lay down. I rolled him over and back and got his clothes off down to his shirt. His teeth were chattering and I was afraid of a chill or the fever. I heated up the flat-irons and wrapped them in cloth and laid them down one on each side of him close to his skin. There was not whisky or brandy in the house to use, only the catnip tea. I put more sugar in it and got him to take it from a spoon. I rubbed his feet with my hands, then his arms and his legs, and I wrung out cloths in hot water which I laid over his stomach and his heart. I talked to him then in a different way quite soft and told him to go to sleep and when he woke up his mind would be clear and all his horrors would be wiped away.

A tree branch fell on him. It was just what you told me. I can see it falling. I can see it coming down so fast like a streak and little branches and crackling all along the way, it hardly takes longer than a gun going off and you say, what is that? and it has hit him and he is dead.

When I got him to sleep I laid down on the bed beside him. I took off my smock and I could see the black and blue marks on my arms. I pulled up my skirt to see if they were still there high on my legs, and they were. The back of my hand was dark too and sore still where I had bit it.

Nothing bad happened after I laid down and I did not sleep all night but listened to him breathing and kept touching him to see if he was warmed up. I got up in the earliest light and fixed the fire. When he heard me, he waked up and was better.

He did not forget what had happened but talked as if he thought it was all right. He said, we ought to have had a prayer and read something out of the Bible. He got the door opened and there was a big drift of snow but the sky was clearing. It was the last snow of the winter.

We went out and said the Lord's Prayer. Then he said, where is the Bible? Why is it not on the shelf? When I got it from beside the fire he said, what is it doing there? I did not remind him of anything. He did not know what to read so I picked the 131st Psalm that we had to learn at the Home. *Lord my heart is not haughty nor mine eyes lofty. Surely I have behaved and quieted myself as a child that is weaned of his mother, my soul is even as a weaned child.* He read it. Then he said he would shovel out a path and go and tell the Treeces. I said I would cook him some food. He went out and shovelled and didn't get tired and come in to eat like I was waiting for him to do. He shovelled and shovelled a long path out of sight and then he was gone and didn't come back. He didn't come back until near dark and then he said he had eaten. I said, did you tell them about the tree? Then he looked at me for the first time in a bad way. It was the same bad way his brother used to look. I never said anything more to him about what had happened or hinted at it in any way. And he never said anything to me, except he would come and say things in my dreams. But I knew the difference always between my dreams and when I was awake, and when I was awake it was never anything but the bad look.

Mrs Treece came and tried to get me to go and live with them the way George was living. She said I could eat and sleep there, they had enough beds. I would not go. They thought I would not go because of my grief but I wouldn't go because somebody might see my black and blue, also they would be watching for me to cry. I said I was not frightened to stay alone.

I dreamed nearly every night that one or other of them came and chased me with the axe. It was him or it was George, one or the other. Or sometimes not the axe, it was a big rock lifted in both hands and one of them waiting with it behind the door. Dreams are sent to warn us.

I didn't stay in the house where he could find me and when I gave up sleeping inside and slept outside I didn't have the dream so often. It got warm in a hurry and the flies and mosquitoes came but they hardly bothered me. I would see their bites but not feel them, which was another sign that in the outside I was protected. I got down when I heard anybody coming. I ate berries both red and black and God protected me from any badness in them.

I had another kind of dream after a while. I dreamed George came and talked to me and he still had the bad look but was trying to cover it up and pretend that he was kind. He kept coming into my dreams and he kept lying to me. It was starting to get colder out and I did not want to go back in the shanty and the dew was heavy so I would be soaking when I slept in the grass. I went and opened the Bible to find out what I should do.

And now I got my punishment for cheating because the Bible did not tell me anything that I could understand, what to do. The cheating was when I was looking to find something for George, and I did not read exactly where my finger landed but looked around quick and found something else that was more what I wanted. I used to do that too when we would be looking up our verses in the Home and I always got good things and nobody ever caught me or suspected me at it. You never did either, Sadie.

So now I had my punishment when I couldn't find anything to help me however I looked. But something put it into my head to come here and I did, I had heard them talking about how warm it was and tramps would be wanting to come and get locked up, so I thought, I will too, and it was put into my head to tell them what I did. I told them the very same lie that George told me so often in my dreams, trying to get me to believe it was me and not him. I am safe from George here is the main thing. If they think I am crazy and I know the difference I am safe. Only I would like for you to come and see me.

And I would like for that yelling to stop.

When I am finished writing this, I will put it in with the curtains that I am making for the Opera House. And I will put on it, Finder Please Post. I trust that better than giving it to them like the two letters I gave them already that they never have sent.

## IV

Miss Christena Mullen, Walley, to Mr Leopold Henry, Department of History, Queen's University, Kingston, July 8, 1959.

Yes I am the Miss Mullen that Treece Herron's sister remembers coming to the farm and it is very kind of her to say I was a pretty young lady in a hat and veil. That was my motoring-veil. The old lady she mentions was Mr Herron's grandfather's sister-in-law, if I have got it straight. As you are doing the biography, you will have got the relationships worked out. I never voted for Treece Herron myself since I am a Conservative, but he was a colorful politician and as you say a biography of him will bring some attention to this part of the country – too often thought of as 'deadly dull'.

I am rather surprised the sister does not mention the car in particular. It was a Stanley Steamer. I bought it myself on my twenty-fifth birthday in 1907. It cost twelve hundred dollars, that being part of my inheritance from my grandfather James Mullen who was an early Clerk of the Peace in Walley. He made money buying and selling farms.

My father having died young, my mother moved into my grandfather's house with all us five girls. It was a big cut-stone house called Traquair, now a Home for Young Offenders. I sometimes say in joke that it always was!

When I was young, we employed a gardener, a cook, and a sewing-woman. All of them were 'characters', all prone to feuding with each other, and all owing their jobs to the fact that my grandfather had taken an interest in them when they were inmates at the County Gaol (as it used to be spelled) and eventually had brought them home.

By the time I bought the Steamer, I was the only one of my sisters living at home, and the sewing-woman was the only one of these old servants who remained. The sewing-woman was called Old Annie and never objected to that name. She used it herself and would write notes to the cook that said, 'Tea was not hot, did you warm the pot? Old Annie.' The whole third floor was Old Annie's domain and one of my sisters – Dolly – said that whenever she dreamed of home, that is, of Traquair, she dreamed of Old Annie up at the top of the third-floor stairs brandishing her measuring stick and wearing a black dress with long fuzzy black arms like a spider.

She had one eye that slid off to the side and gave her the air of taking in more information than the ordinary person.

We were not supposed to pester the servants with questions about their personal lives, particularly those who had been in the Gaol, but of course we did. Sometimes Old Annie called the Gaol the Home. She said that a girl in the next bed screamed and screamed, and that was why she – Annie – ran away and lived in the woods. She said the girl had been beaten for letting the fire go out. Why were you in jail, we asked her, and she would say, 'I told a fib!' So for quite a while we had the impression that you went to jail for telling lies!

Some days she was in a good mood and would play hide-the-thimble with us. Sometimes she was in a bad mood and would stick us with pins when she was evening our hems if we turned too quickly or stopped too soon. She knew a place, she said, where you could get bricks to put on children's heads to stop them growing. She hated making wedding dresses (she never had to make one for me!) and didn't think much of any of the men that my sisters married. She hated Dolly's beau so much that she made some kind of deliberate mistake with the sleeves which had to be ripped out, and Dolly cried. But she made us all beautiful ball gowns to wear when the Governor-General and Lady Minto came to Walley.

About being married herself, she sometimes said she had been and sometimes not. She said a man had come to the Home and had all the girls paraded in front of him and said, 'I'll take the one with the coal-black hair.' That being Old Annie, but she refused to go with him, even though he was rich and came in a carriage. Rather like Cinderella but with a different ending. Then she said a bear killed her husband, in the woods, and my grandfather had killed the bear, and wrapped her in its skin and taken her home from the Gaol.

My mother used to say, 'Now, girls. Don't get Old Annie going. And don't believe a word she says.'

I am going on at great length filling in the background but you did say you were interested in details of the period. I am like most people my age and forget to buy milk but could tell you the color of the coat I had when I was eight.

So when I got the Stanley Steamer, Old Annie asked to be taken for a ride. It turned out that what she had in mind was more of a trip. This was a surprise since she had never wanted to go on trips before and refused to go to Niagara Falls and would not even go down to the Harbor to see the fireworks on the First of July. Also she was leery of automobiles and of me as a driver. But the big surprise was that she had somebody she wanted to go and see. She wanted to drive to Carstairs to see the Herron family, who she said were her relatives. She had never received any visits or letters from these people, and when I asked if she had written to ask if we might visit she said, 'I can't write.' This was ridiculous – she wrote those notes to the cooks and long lists for me of things she wanted me to pick up down on the Square or in the city. Braid, buckram, taffeta – she could spell all of that.

'And they don't need to know beforehand,' she said. 'In the country it's different.'

Well, I loved taking jaunts in the Steamer. I had been driving since I was fifteen but this was the first car of my own and possibly the only Steam car in Huron County. Everybody would run to see it go by. It did not make a beastly loud noise coughing and clanking like other cars but rolled along silently more or less like a ship with high sails over the lake waters and it did not foul the air but left behind a plume of steam. Stanley Steamers were banned in Boston, because of steam fogging the air. I always loved to tell people, I used to drive a car that was banned in Boston!

We started out fairly early on a Sunday in June. It took about twenty-five minutes to get the steam up and all that time Old Annie sat up straight in the front seat as if the show were already on the road. We both had our motoring-veils on, and long dusters, but the dress Old Annie was wearing underneath was of plum-colored silk. In fact it was made over from the one she had made for my grandmother to meet the Prince of Wales in.

The Steamer covered the miles like an angel. It would do fifty miles an hour – great then – but I did not push it. I was trying to consider Old Annie's nerves. People were still in church when we started, but later on the roads were full of horses and buggies making the journey home. I was polite as all get-out, edging by them. But it turned out Old Annie did not want to be so sedate and she kept saying, 'Give it a squeeze,' meaning the horn, which was worked by a bulb under a mudguard down at my side.

She must not have been out of Walley for more years than I had been alive. When we crossed the bridge at Saltford (that old iron bridge where there used to be so many accidents because of the turn at both ends), she said that there didn't used to be a bridge there, you had to pay a man to row you.

'I couldn't pay but I crossed on the stones and just hiked up my skirts and waded,' she said. 'It was that dry a summer.'

Naturally I did not know what summer she was talking about.

Then it was, Look at the big fields, where are the stumps gone, where is the bush? And look how straight the road goes, and they're building their houses out of brick! And what are those buildings as big as churches?

Barns, I said.

I knew my way to Carstairs all right but expected help from Old Annie once we got there. None was forthcoming. I drove up and down the main street waiting for her to spot something familiar. 'If I could just see the inn,' she said, 'I'd know where the track goes off behind it.'

It was a factory town, not very pretty in my opinion. The Steamer of course got attention, and I was able to call out for directions to the Herron farm without stopping the engine. Shouts and gestures and finally I was able to get us on the right road. I told Old Annie to watch the mailboxes but she was concerned with finding the creek. I spotted the name myself, and turned us in at a long lane with a red brick house at the end of it and a couple of these barns that had amazed Old Annie. Red-brick houses with verandas and key windows were all the style then, they were going up everywhere.

'Look there!' Old Annie said, and I thought she meant where a herd of cows was tearing away from us in the pasture-field alongside the lane. But she was pointing at a mound pretty well covered with wild grape, a few logs sticking out of it. She said that was the shanty. I said, 'Well, good – now let's hope you recognize one or two of the people.'

There were enough people around. A couple of visiting buggies were pulled up in the shade, horses tethered and cropping grass. By the time the Steamer stopped at the side veranda, a number were lined up to look at it. They didn't come forward – not even the children ran out to look close up the way town children would have done. They all just stood in a row looking at it in a tight-lipped sort of way.

Old Annie was staring off in the other direction.

She told me to get down. Get down, she said, and ask them if there is a Mr George Herron that lives here and is he alive yet, or dead?

I did what I was told. And one of the men said, that's right. He is. My father.

Well, I have brought somebody, I told them. I have brought Mrs Annie Herron.

The man said, that so?

(A pause here due to a couple of fainting-fits and a trip to the hospital. Lots of tests to use up the taxpayers' money. Now I'm back and have read this over, astounded at the rambling but too lazy to start again. I have not even got to Treece Herron, which is the part you are interested in, but hold on, I'm nearly there.)

These people were all dumbfounded about Old Annie, or so I gathered. They had not known where she was or what she was doing or if she was alive. But you mustn't think they surged out and greeted her in any excited way. Just the one young man came out, very mannerly, and helped first her then me down from the car. He said to me that Old Annie was his grandfather's sister-in-law. It was too bad we hadn't come even a few months sooner, he said, because his grandfather had been quite well and his mind quite clear – he had even written a piece for the paper about his early days here – but then he had got sick. He had recovered but would never be himself again. He could not talk, except now and then a few words.

This mannerly young man was Treece Herron.

We must have arrived just after they finished their dinner. The woman of the house came out and asked him – Treece Herron – to ask us if we had eaten. You would think she or we did not speak English. They were all very shy – the women with their skinned-back hair, and men in dark-blue Sunday suits, and tongue-tied children. I hope you do not think I am making fun of them – it is just that I cannot understand for the life of me why it is necessary to be so shy.

We were taken to the dining-room which had an unused smell – they must have had their dinner elsewhere – and were served a great deal of food of which I remember salted radishes and leaf lettuce and roast chicken and strawberries and cream. Dishes from the china cabinet, not their usual. Good old Indian Tree. They had sets of everything. Plushy living-room suite, walnut dining-room suite. It was going to take them a while, I thought, to get used to being prosperous.

Old Annie enjoyed the fuss of being waited on and ate a lot, picking up the chicken bones to work the last shred of meat off them. Children lurked around the doorways and the women talked in subdued, rather scandalized voices out in the kitchen. The young man, Treece Herron, had the grace to sit down with us and drink a cup of tea while we ate. He chatted readily enough about himself and told me he was a divinity student at Knox College. He said he liked living in Toronto. I got the feeling he wanted me to understand that divinity students were not all such sticks as I supposed or led such a stringent existence. He had been tobogganing in High Park, he had been picnicking at Hanlan's Point, he had seen the giraffe in the Riverdale Zoo. As he talked, the children got a little bolder and started trickling into the room. I asked the usual idiocies . . . How old are you, what book are you in at school, do you like your teacher? He urged them to answer or answered for them and told me which were his brothers and sisters and which his cousins.

Old Annie said, 'Are you all fond of each other, then?' which brought on funny looks.

The woman of the house came back and spoke to me again through the divinity student. She told him that Grandpa was up now and sitting on the front porch. She looked at the children and said, 'What did you let all them in here for?'

Out we trooped to the front porch, where two straight-backed chairs were set up and an old man settled on one of them. He had a beautiful full white beard reaching down to the bottom of his waistcoat. He did not seem interested in us. He had a long, pale, obedient old face.

Old Annie said, 'Well, George,' as if this was about what she had expected. She sat on the other chair and said to one of the little girls, 'Now bring me a cushion. Bring me a thin kind of cushion and put it at my back.'

I spent the afternoon giving rides in the Stanley Steamer. I knew enough about them now not to start in asking who wanted a ride, or bombarding them with questions, such as, were they interested in automobiles? I just went out and patted it here and there as if it was a horse, and I looked in the boiler. The divinity student came behind and read the name of the Steamer written on the side. 'The Gentleman's Speedster'. He asked was it my father's.

Mine, I said. I explained how the water in the boiler was heated and how much steam-pressure the boiler could withstand. People always wondered about that – about explosions. The children were closer by that time and I suddenly remarked that the boiler was nearly empty. I asked if there was any way I could get some water.

Great scurry to get pails and man the pump! I went and asked the men on the veranda if that was all right, and thanked them when they told me, help yourself. Once the boiler was filled, it was natural for me to ask if they would like me to get the steam up, and a spokesman said, it wouldn't hurt. Nobody was impatient during the wait. The men stared at the boiler, concentrating. This was certainly not the first car they had seen but probably the first steam car.

I offered the men a ride first, as it was proper to. They watched skeptically while I fiddled with all the knobs and levers to get my lady going. Thirteen different things to push or pull! We bumped down the lane at five, then ten miles an hour. I knew they suffered somewhat, being driven by a woman, but the novelty of the experience held them. Next I got a load of children, hoisted in by the divinity student telling them to sit still and hold on and not be scared and not fall out. I put up the speed a little, knowing now the ruts and puddle-holes, and their hoots of fear and triumph could not be held back.

I have left out something about how I was feeling but will leave it out no longer, due to the effects of a martini I am drinking now, my late-afternoon pleasure. I had troubles then I have not yet admitted to you because they were love-troubles. But when I had set out that day with Old Annie, I had determined to enjoy myself as much as I could. It seemed it would be an insult to the Stanley Steamer not to. All my life I found this a good rule to follow – to get as much pleasure as you could out of things even when you weren't likely to be happy.

I told one of the boys to run around to the front veranda and ask if his grandfather would care for a ride. He came back and said, 'They've both gone to sleep.'

I had to get the boiler filled up before we started back, and while this was being done, Treece Herron came and stood close to me.

'You have given us all a day to remember,' he said.

I wasn't above flirting with him. I actually had a long career as a flirt ahead of me. It's quite a natural behavior, once the loss of love makes you give up your ideas of marriage.

I said he would forget all about it, once he got back to his friends in Toronto. He said no indeed, he would never forget, and he asked if he could write to me. I said nobody could stop him.

On the way home I thought about this exchange and how ridiculous it would be if he should get a serious crush on me. A divinity student. I had no idea then of course that he would be getting out of Divinity and into Politics.

'Too bad old Mr Herron wasn't able to talk to you,' I said to Old Annie. She said, 'Well, I could talk to him.'

Actually, Treece Herron did write to me, but he must have had a few misgivings as well because he enclosed some pamphlets about Mission Schools. Something about raising money for Mission Schools. That put me off and I didn't write back. (Years later I would joke that I could have married him if I'd played my cards right.)

I asked Old Annie if Mr Herron could understand her when she talked to him, and she said, 'Enough.' I asked if she was glad about seeing him again and she said yes. 'And glad for him to get to see me,' she said, not without some gloating that probably referred to her dress and the vehicle.

So we just puffed along in the Steamer under the high arching trees that lined the roads in those days. From miles away the lake could be seen – just glimpses of it, shots of light, held wide apart in the trees and hills so that Old Annie asked me if it could possibly be the same lake, all the same one that Walley was on?

There were lots of old people going around then with ideas in their heads that didn't add up – though I suppose Old Annie had more than most. I recall her telling me another time that a girl in the Home had a baby out of a big boil that burst on her stomach, and it was the size of a rat and had no life in it, but they put it in the oven and it puffed up to the right size and baked to a good color and started to kick its legs. (Ask an old woman to reminisce and you get the whole ragbag, is what you must be thinking by now.)

I told her that wasn't possible, it must have been a dream.

'Maybe so,' she said, agreeing with me for once. 'I did used to have the terriblest dreams.'

# Comrades

*Nadine Gordimer was born in 1923 in Springs, a small mining town near Johannes-*
*burg in South Africa, of immigrant Jewish parents. She began to write at the age of*
*nine, and her first short story was published in a South African magazine when she*
*was only fifteen. Her first collection of short stories,* Face to Face, *was published ten*
*years later, in 1949. Her first novel,* The Lying Days, *was published in 1953. She*
*has now published ten novels and eight collections of short stories as well as a few*
*volumes of literary criticism, and some of her books have at times been banned in*
*South Africa. Her novel* The Conservationist *was the joint winner of the Booker*
*Prize in 1974, and in 1991 she was awarded the Nobel Prize for Literature, the first*
*woman to receive that prestigious prize in over twenty years.*

As Mrs Hattie Telford pressed the electronic gadget that deactivates the
alarm device in her car a group of youngsters came up behind her. Black.
But no need to be afraid; this was not a city street. This was a non-racial
enclave of learning, a place where tended flowerbeds and trees bearing
botanical identification plates civilized the wild reminder of campus
guards and dogs. The youngsters, like her, were part of the crowd loosening into dispersion after a university conference on People's Education.
They were the people to be educated; she was one of the committee of
white and black activists (convenient generic for revolutionaries, leftists
secular and Christian, fellow-travellers and liberals) up on the platform.
 – Comrade . . . – She was settling in the driver's seat when one so slight
and slim he seemed a figure in profile came up to her window. He drew
courage from the friendly lift of the woman's eyebrows above blue eyes,
the tilt of her freckled white face: – Comrade, are you going to town? –

No, she was going in the opposite direction, home . . . but quickly, in the spirit of the hall where these young people had been somewhere, somehow present with her (ah no, she with them) stamping and singing Freedom songs, she would take them to the bus station their spokesman named. – Climb aboard! –

The others got in the back, the spokesman beside her. She saw the nervous white of his eyes as he glanced at and away from her. She searched for talk to set them at ease. Questions, of course. Older people always start with questioning young ones. Did they come from Soweto?

They came from Harrismith, Phoneng Location.

She made the calculation: about two hundred kilometres distant. How did they get here? Who told them about the conference?

– We are Youth Congress in Phoneng. –

A delegation. They had come by bus; one of the groups and stragglers who kept arriving long after the conference had started. They had missed, then, the free lunch?

At the back, no one seemed even to be breathing. The spokesman must have had some silent communication with them, some obligation to speak for them created by the journey or by other shared experience in the mysterious bonds of the young – these young. – We are hungry. – And from the back seats was drawn an assent like the suction of air in a compressing silence.

She was silent in response, for the beat of a breath or two. These large gatherings both excited and left her over-exposed, open and vulnerable to the rub and twitch of the mass shuffling across rows of seats and loping up the aisles, babies' fudge-brown soft legs waving as their napkins are changed on mothers' laps, little girls with plaited loops on their heads listening like old crones, heavy women swaying to chants, men with fierce, unreadably black faces breaking into harmony tender and deep as they sing to God for his protection of Umkhonto weSizwe, as people on both sides have always, everywhere, claimed divine protection for their soldiers, their wars. At the end of a day like this she wanted a drink, she wanted the depraved luxury of solitude and quiet in which she would be restored (enriched, oh yes! by the day) to the familiar limits of her own being.

Hungry. Not for iced whisky and feet up. It seemed she had scarcely

hesitated: – Look, I live nearby, come back to my house and have something to eat. Then I'll run you into town. –

– That will be very nice. We can be glad for that. – And at the back the
tight vacuum relaxed.

They followed her in through the gate, shrinking away from the dog –
she assured them he was harmless but he was large, with a fancy collar by
which she held him. She trooped them in through the kitchen because
that was the way she always entered her house, something she would not
have done if they had been adult, her black friends whose sophistication
might lead them to believe the choice of entrance was an unthinking
historical slight. As she was going to feed them, she took them not into
her living-room with its sofas and flowers but into her dining-room, so
that they could sit at table right away. It was a room in confident taste that
could afford to be spare: bare floorboards, matching golden wooden ceiling, antique brass chandelier, reed blinds instead of stuffy curtains. An
African wooden sculpture represented a lion marvellously released from
its matrix in the grain of a Mukwa tree-trunk. She pulled up the chairs and
left the four young men while she went back to the kitchen to make
coffee and see what there was in the refrigerator for sandwiches. They had
greeted the maid, in the language she and they shared, on their way
through the kitchen, but when the maid and the lady of the house had
finished preparing cold meat and bread, and the coffee was ready, she
suddenly did not want them to see that the maid waited on her. She
herself carried the heavy tray into the dining-room.

They are sitting round the table, silent, and there is no impression that
they stopped an undertone exchange when they heard her approaching.
She doles out plates, cups. They stare at the food but their eyes seem
focused on something she can't see; something that overwhelms. She
urges them – Just cold meat, I'm afraid, but there's chutney if you like it . . .
Milk everybody? . . . Is the coffee too strong? I have a heavy hand, I know.
Would anyone like to add some hot water? –

They eat. When she tries to talk to one of the others, he says *Ekskuus?*
And she realizes he doesn't understand English, of the white man's languages knows perhaps only a little of that of the Afrikaners in the rural
town he comes from. Another gives his name, as if in some delicate

acknowledgement of the food. – I'm Shadrack Nsutsha. – She repeats the surname to get it right. But he does not speak again. There is an urgent exchange of eye-language, and the spokesman holds out the emptied sugar-bowl to her. – Please. – She hurries to the kitchen and brings it back refilled. They need carbohydrate, they are hungry, they are young, they need it, they burn it up. She is distressed at the inadequacy of the meal and then notices the fruit bowl, her big copper fruit bowl, filled with apples and bananas and perhaps there is a peach or two under the grape leaves with which she likes to complete an edible still life. – Have some fruit. Help yourselves. –

They are stacking their plates and cups, not knowing what they are expected to do with them in this room which is a room where apparently people only eat, do not cook, do not sleep. While they finish the bananas and apples (Shadrack Nsutsha had seen the single peach and quickly got there first) she talks to the spokesman, whose name she has asked for: Dumile. – Are you still at school, Dumile? – Of course he is not at school – *they* are not at school; youngsters their age have not been at school for several years, they are the children growing into young men and women for whom school is a battleground, a place of boycotts and demonstrations, the literacy of political rhetoric, the education of revolt against having to live the life their parents live. They have pompous titles of responsibility beyond childhood: he is chairman of his branch of the Youth Congress, he was expelled two years ago – for leading a boycott? Throwing stones at the police? Maybe burning the school down? He calls it all – quietly, abstractly, doesn't know many ordinary, concrete words but knows these euphemisms – 'political activity'. No school for two years? No. – So what have you been able to do with yourself, all that time? –

She isn't giving him a chance to eat his apple. He swallows a large bite, shaking his head on its thin, little-boy neck. – I was inside. Detained from this June for six months. –

She looks round the others. – And you? –

Shadrack seems to nod slightly. The other two look at her. She should know, she should have known, it's a common enough answer from youths like them, their colour. They're not going to be saying they've been selected for the First Eleven at cricket or that they're off on a student tour to Europe in the school holidays.

The spokesman, Dumile, tells her he wants to study by correspondence, 'get his matric' that he was preparing for two years ago; two years ago when he was still a child, when he didn't have the hair that is now appearing on his face, making him a man, taking away the childhood. In the hesitations, the silences of the table, where there is nervously spilt coffee among plates of banana skins, there grows the certainty that he will never get the papers filled in for the correspondence college, he will never get the two years back. She looks at them all and cannot believe what she knows: that they, suddenly here in her house, will carry the AK-47s they only sing about, now, miming death as they sing. They will have a career of wiring explosives to the undersides of vehicles, they will go away and come back through the bush to dig holes not to plant trees to shade home, but to plant land-mines. She can see they have been terribly harmed but cannot believe they could harm. They are wiping their fruit-sticky hands furtively palm against palm.

She breaks the silence; says something, anything.

– How d'you like my lion? Isn't he beautiful? He's made by a Zimbabwean artist, I think the name's Dube. –

But the foolish interruption becomes revelation. Dumile, in his gaze – distant, lingering, speechless this time – reveals what has overwhelmed them. In this room, the space, the expensive antique chandelier, the consciously simple choice of reed blinds, the carved lion: all are on the same level of impact, phenomena undifferentiated, undecipherable. Only the food that fed their hunger was real.

# An Unfinished Record

Translated by W. J. F. Jenner

*Zhang Jie was born in 1937, and although she was deeply interested in literature was persuaded to study economics at the People's University in Beijing because it would be of more use to her country. She then worked in an industrial bureau and a film studio. She started to write at the age of forty, shortly after the fall of the Gang of Four and the end of the Cultural Revolution, and she is now one of China's most popular and controversial writers. Her short story 'The Child from the Forest' won a prize in 1978 as one of the best short stories of that year, and her novel* Leaden Wings *(Virago, 1987) won China's prestigious Mao Dun Literary Prize in 1985. She is a member of the Chinese Writers' Association and now works for the Beijing branch of the China Federation of Literary and Art Circles. She joined the Communist Party at an early age. However, during the Cultural Revolution she was fiercely criticized, and much of her writing today is still considered extremely contentious.*

I know that I will never come back to this place again. As I close the window, forcing my old cat, the Grand Historian, outside for the last time. He grows cross with me for the insult of this rough treatment. Yet he's far too tolerant and dignified to scratch or yowl at me. He merely springs back on to the windowsill, crouched, staring at me through the pane, with those apparently all-seeing eyes.

The sighing of the poplars, the clamour of the traffic, the neighbour boy playing his mouth-organ are all muffled now, more distant, removed. I wonder if the lad is growing tired, attempting the same tune over and over again since this morning. But I am finished with these sounds by now and with the pain they make deep inside my ears.

I decide to be thorough and lock the window, but it's been broken for so long that the frame is coming apart and is too misshapen to shut properly. No matter how hard I try, it cannot be bolted. It is not the fault of the maintenance staff for not doing their job properly, rather I'd call it one more symptom of my hopeless indifference to making my life more comfortable. Usually I managed by tying up the frame with string, making raising the window a terrible nuisance, but luckily I've rarely opened it. I've long been as delicate as a premature baby and the night breezes or the slightest change in temperature cause me the most mysterious complaints. I'm always wishing our hospitals had insulated cubicles for decrepit old wrecks like me to find rest in.

From being shut off so long my room has always had a musty atmosphere, like that of a cellar, the desiccated odour of a room where an invalid has been enduring for a long time. But for the last few nights I've kept the window open, wanting the flower-scented spring breeze to drift into every corner and whisk away all traces of my life which has impregnated the room for all these years. It was a warm, lovely breeze but it started me off coughing, my throat thick with phlegm, like a chimney clogged with soot. If only, like a chimney, it could be swept clean.

This is probably the last thing I will be able to do for anyone else. Or is it the first? The best thing, of course, would have been to give these walls a good new coat of whitewash, but now it's too late. Sooner or later some new tenants will move in, and I don't wish them to resent any lingering part of me. But even if they do resent any hold I may have on the place, I will be beyond hearing them.

The hospital called me the day before yesterday with the message that I should come there today. The boy who spoke to me had a voice like a singer in a musical, melodious, as though he were singing a solo. He might have been urging me to go to a rendezvous with someone who'd be waiting for me, under a silk tree or by a little bridge. But instead I'll be going through the door that leads to . . . who can say what?

After that phone call I began looking back over my life, the way people who are about to die find themselves doing. It surprised me – why hadn't I done this before? Do we really have to wait until it's too late to do anything, before we remember all those countless old debts, great and small, that we've no way of settling now? Each of us can only experience the mystery of death once and it seems cruel to enter this mystery feeling unsettled, with a sense of guilt. But, in fact, my life has been pointless and dull, the most ordinary life possible, containing absolutely nothing of interest for a novelist – no dramatic tragedy, no peaks of joy. Poor soul who must write my eulogy, perhaps the shortest eulogy ever, read in two brief minutes.

My very name seems to have been designed to make things awkward for everyone. It's graceless, hard to pronounce, a stiff and commonplace-sounding name. Even though it appears on the spine of books on Ming history every couple of years or so, those thick tomes of four or five hundred pages costing well over a *yuan* are usually found on the bottom shelves of the bookshop. I always know perfectly well that when my next book comes out the previous one won't have sold out, but I can't help going to the bookshop from time to time to look and see if there are any fewer of those unsold volumes. Even one less would be a welcome sight. Then I slip away like a thief, afraid someone will discover that I'm the author of those unsold books. I've wasted all that paper, I feel, and tricked all my readers into giving me their time. It makes me heavy-hearted. I know I have little talent, but it's as if I had been bewitched into devoting all my thoughts, my soul and even my body to the study of our ancestors' history. I could not stop myself from writing. What else was there for me to live for, all alone as I am?

A moment ago Li, my neighbour, asked with some concern whether there was anything he could do for me while I was in hospital. Should he take letters and cables straight to the hospital, or wait till he could bring them along when he came to visit me? They could wait, I told him. He could get someone to take them along when it was convenient.

Apart from letters to and from publishers, magazines and a university journal which takes my articles, and very occasionally a hand-written note from another simple-minded bookworm like me wanting to argue about just where a battle was fought during some dynasty, I have virtually no private correspondence. And since I have done no work for a long time because of my illness, even letters such as these have become few and far between.

Now that I think of it, there is something to be said for having no private life: you have few attachments, and nobody has to feel distressed when you begin to fail. Still, if I do get to heaven I shall feel sad that no one on earth will be grieving for me. It's not that I don't get along with people, but that I simply haven't had the good fortune to make any friends. My colleagues in the research institute regard me with great respect and kindness. People usually treat me well, but I tend to frighten them off, or to mistake their ordinary courtesy for an expression of interest. I'm afraid I have gone on for hours and hours citing evidence to show that the Qing historian Xia Xie's *Universal Mirror of Ming History* is full of wrong judgements, not caring whether my listeners are interested, how busy they are, or if I'm trying their patience. Whenever I have to return a visit, my mind stays back with those manuscripts piled on my desk and I hope that the person I am going to see will be out. Then, by leaving a brief note, I can meet the requirements of courtesy with the minimum waste of time. If I find them in I always make meaningless remarks, such as 'It's gradually been getting a bit warmer recently,' then repeat myself three times over. These social performances generally exhaust me, and my boorishness and lack of manners leave others at a complete loss as to how to deal with me. When I get up to leave, my host's face shows relief and gratitude that he will not have to prolong this mutual torture.

My everyday life is totally organized around work, and on public holidays when I can't go to the institute cafeteria, I'm never sure about when to eat breakfast, lunch or supper. No one has more enthusiasm than I have for the development of China's food and clothing industries: I'm eager for the time when the whole business of eating can be reduced to the simplicity of the astronaut's toothpaste-tube meals. I await anxiously the new clothing to be made out of paper, as well as the quilt-covers and pillowcases, so mine won't always be like soiled rags. Of course, I like clean clothes and quilt-covers the same as everyone else, but I've had neither the time nor the inclination to bother with them.

But now these minor irritations are history and I ask myself: has there been nothing else interesting to review from my life? Is there no more than the few *yuan* I owe here and there, or the call I've forgotten to return? In a fairy tale of Hans Christian Andersen, one cold, winter's night a lonely old man on the point of death sees the whole of the past through one of his cloudy tears. And it reminds me that there has been just one tear in my long, monotonous life. Not an old man's cloudy tear, but a unique tear from my youth that had the lustre and the colour of a pearl. It is only now, when it is about to be buried with me, that I can bear to bring it up from the deep well of memory.

It was a warm summer morning. She was laughing as she came into our office, which was dark and sombre from the shadowy green vines on the wall outside the small windows. From the moment she arrived it was as if there had been another window in the room. How could she laugh so much? Whenever she laughed I laughed too, and I discovered to my delight that this made her laugh even more. I never knew what I looked like when I laughed, but from then on I was full of confidence that my face looked fine when I laughed, and that confidence made my writing suddenly speed up from one to two thousand characters a day.

I'm always losing umbrellas, one after another. It only has to rain for me to lose an umbrella – on buses, in little restaurants or bookstores I chance upon, or by newsstands. The day I left my umbrella at some academic conference, she came running after me, calling and laughing, and handed me my umbrella back. I drank in her laughter with such pleasure that I forgot to thank her.

Listening to her voice, to her laughter, and feeling that the office had an extra window in it had become the most important thing in my life. Any day on which she did not come to work might just as well have not happened. Her lightness, her conversation, her losing a button, her touch of irritation because she had been unable to buy a pretty pair of shoes all slowly infused the historical data I read and the words I wrote. I longed to share everything I had and everything I did with her.

My life seemed a lot more complicated than it had been before I knew her. I was always showing her books that I found interesting and useful, and whenever I talked to her about our admirable forebears and the history that had ebbed like a tide I felt an emotion I had never known before: happiness.

I even started going to the pictures. I recall one film. At the time everyone said that it was a thoroughly boring film, the sort you forget all about before you're even outside the cinema. But that film, with an actress who reminded me of her, turned my heart upside down. I found a new boldness I didn't know I had. I took out paper and pen and I wrote to her, asking her to meet at nine o'clock by a little bridge, just as in the film. Even the words I used were borrowed from the film. I was drunk with the image of her running to meet me under the silk tree.

I arrived an hour early, to be there ready to see her as she arrived. Nine o'clock passed. By ten o'clock she had still not come and I thought that I must have written the wrong date or time. That was very possible, even though I had taken the letter out of the envelope many times, read it through and put it back again before I posted it. I could not be sure that my mind had been clear enough at the time, or whether my nerves had been dependable. That sort of thing had happened to me before. Back in middle-school maths, for example, an exam question asked what $50/2$ was equal to. I wrote it correctly: $50/2$. I don't know how many times I checked through my answers, but for its own reasons my mind stubbornly held on to $50/3$, a fraction that could not be reduced any further. Could I in the same way have written midday or eight p.m. instead of nine a.m.?

I became hungry, but I dared not leave the little bridge to have some lunch. I kept taking my glasses off to wipe clean the lenses, so I wouldn't miss seeing her, but they stayed as hazy as ever. I wished I had not always thrust them into my pockets with keys, nailclippers and everything else, or carelessly thrown them lens-down on my desk, until they were like frosted glass. Why did they seem now even worse than ever?

I began to wonder whether she had suddenly fallen ill. I felt so anxious that my heart was hurting. Perhaps she had had an accident on the way there. If something like that really had happened, I'd never have been able to forgive myself, not even if I could have gone to hell and been punished ten times over.

The bustle of traffic and people gradually died away with the day. The street lights came on in the distance and generously cast their gentle orange glow over me, as if to soothe away my disappointment. I walked home alone, among the shadows, as if the happiness of the morning had never been.

Even before I got into the office next morning I heard her laughter as I walked on the path among the green trees. Thank heavens! She was still alive, healthy and happy. For a long time I stood under the eaves of the building, not wanting to go inside in case some other impression might weaken the happiness I had lost and now recovered. My eyes were filled with tears of gratitude, even though I did not know who I should be thanking or for what.

Laughing as sweetly as ever she spoke to me. 'Please meet my fiancé. We would like you to come to our wedding on Saturday evening.' He was strong, tall and good-looking and shook my hand heartily.

As she spoke she handed me a heavy parcel, wrapped in strong brown paper and tied with string. It was the book I had lent her. As I watched them I thought happily about their wedding, and of how well matched they were. It was just as if my agonies of self-reproach by the bridge the day before had never happened and the letter I had tortured myself for so long over sending had never existed.

The wedding ceremony was informal, with a very free and jovial atmosphere, like a group of friends meeting spontaneously. That was very much her way of doing things. It was the first time I had been in a crowd without feeling awkward and uncomfortable.

The bridegroom sat down right next to me and told me he was a geologist. He explained to me with great gusto how the stress that caused earthquakes is built up, and how infrared remote sensing was going to replace the geologist's compass, hammer and magnifying-glass in prospecting for the earth's natural resources. He talked to me not as if he were the groom, but as if he were a guest who had come along to offer his congratulations.

I smiled. His way of making conversation without bothering whether he was killing the person he was talking to was a bit like mine. He was very fond of his work and believed that geology was definitely very useful to the world and a truly wonderful science. I admired him and even started wondering whether I had made a mistake in studying history instead of geology all those years ago. He casually handed me a cigarette. He was evidently too happy and enthusiastic to care about such details as whether I was a smoker or wanted to smoke.

Of course I accepted the cigarette – I couldn't turn his kind offer down. He was the man she loved, and on top of that I liked him myself. I didn't know whether I was meant to swallow the evil-smelling fumes or to inhale them. From the health posters I had seen in hospitals about smoking causing lung cancer I guessed that you had to draw them into your lungs. I could not have remembered wrongly; the hospital was a place I knew very well, the place I went to most often apart from my office and my room. I choked on the first puff, but tried as hard as I could not to cough although the effort made my eyes water. It did not go at all well and I was afraid all this would alarm him and make him blame himself for causing one such misery.

She came over to us smiling, her eyes dazzling. She handed me an exquisite crystal glass and wanted me to drink a toast to them. I accepted the glass of wine and at once a humming started in my head. The drink was so strong, yet my heart remained light. It was very odd that I should have felt that way, but I was as happy as if I were getting married myself.

It was late at night when I left the place where those two people had surrounded me with happiness. It was mid-October, still quite warm, and I was in a cheerful frame of mind. I flung my jacket over my shoulders and strolled back through the moonlight. I didn't know whether it came from the cigarette or the drink, but I felt as if I were floating through the air. In a gust of light breeze I seemed to hear people whispering or laughing quietly from the locust and poplar trees by the roadside.

I remembered the Schubert 'Serenade' stanzas the bridegroom had just been singing:

> *Softly my songs*
> *Cry to you through the night*

and I remembered her expression as he sang.

A pale longing welled up in my heart. I longed to have a soft shoulder beside me, longed to have someone leaning her adorable curly head against my shoulder. I would have put my jacket around her like a gallant Spanish knight wrapping his woman in his cloak.

I tripped over a stone, and looked down to see my shadow on the ground, the shoulders as narrow as a child's. I looked as if I had three less ribs than anyone else, and seemed to be painfully bent forward. It suddenly occurred to me that I was an old fool – no woman would ever want to rest her head on a shoulder like mine.

> *Oh my dearest, a cry to the beloved is carried on*
> *the wind, on such a night as this . . .*

As soon as I was back in my room I flung myself across my little bed, stretched out to the side of the bedside table and on it wrote the first letter of her name: S. I felt no particular misery or grief. Gradually my eyes misted up, and the letter seemed to turn into a winged angel flying lightly above my head. I closed my tired eyelids. I must have had a happy dream that night, but it was such a long time ago that I can no longer remember it clearly.

She soon left our institute and started travelling all over the country with her geologist. And the years passed. I realize that by now she must be as decrepit as I am, but as long as I don't see her again I'll remember her as she was when we parted, always laughing for no good reason, radiant and cheerful like someone who has slept and dreamt well the night before.

People say that love is endless longing, heartache and madness, wild exhilaration, pain like hell frozen over, cruel sleepless nights. I've never in all my life experienced such complicated and bitter-sweet emotions. But I am very grateful to her. Even though I never stood in front of her window night after night, waiting for her shadow to appear, she still brought me good fortune. Because of her I knew the delight and felt the brightness that emanate from an extra window, and was happy even with just her single initial by my side.

I suppose I should be going, but there is still so much unfinished business to be done. Why am I trying to sort it out now in this last minute? I had intended to catalogue all the books now shoved into the shelves at random, and to arrange them by period so that they will be easier for their next owner to refer to. And I haven't yet corrected the proofs of the article on Zhu Yuanzhang, the founder of the Ming dynasty, and the Red Turban Army of peasant rebels.

All I managed to complete last night were two small tasks that were within my powers. I rubbed out the initial written on the side of my table, and burned that sheet of brown wrapping paper – so brittle it went to pieces at the touch – and the piece of string. I didn't want those things I've treasured for so many years to be casually thrown away as rubbish when my effects are sorted out after I'm dead, and I wasn't prepared to let a stranger's hand rub that initial out.

As I watched the last spark fly away I thought of all these years, of how I kept them as treasures because she had breathed on them and touched them. It was as if I had been a thief all these years, a thief who had stolen what she had never given me, what had never belonged to me – a tiny fragment of her life. It was probably the most shameful thing I have ever done. If I could I'd kneel before her and beg her to forgive me. She is so good and sweet and generous that I'm sure she'd have forgiven me and said, 'In a long life everyone does something wrong.'

As I lift the net bag with my washing things in it my toothbrush slips out through a hole and when I lean over to pick it up I take another look around the room that has shared half a lifetime with me. My old table stands isolated in the middle of the room, there irrelevant and uncon-nected, like some obscure island in the Pacific that not even the most third-rate explorer would bother with. The springs of my folding bed gave out a long time ago, and it sags very low to the floor. The yellowing and blackened walls have an air of decrepitude, just like my dried-up face, as they lean feebly together around my jumble of furniture. Even the books on the shelves look sick and crippled, without even one fine leather volume with gold lettering to give the bookshelves a touch of distinction. All the large softcover books lie on their sides, drooping out over the shelves like wilting foliage taken too long ago from a tree. Dusty cobwebs sway from the ceiling and in the corners of the room.

The sight of this dispirited room fills me with regret, as if I have wasted its youth for nothing. It could have been as clean, bright and tidy as other rooms. And as I see this, a new nameless feeling begins to overwhelm me. I cannot give it a name, but from it I sense that my whole life from beginning to end has been lacking in something.

Lacking what? My eyes sweep the cluttered bookcases, across the books I've scrimped and saved for a lifetime to buy, or written with my own sweat and blood. I realize that I have all of these things to leave to a lot of people, but no one unique thing to leave to one special person. And this is the lack, this is what is missing.

I know that Dong, from the personnel department of the institute, will finally sign in the space on the operation form where the next of kin's signature is needed. But if only there could be one beloved face, wrinkled like mine, sitting on the bench outside the operating theatre, anxious for me, quietly sobbing for me. If only on my bedside table there could be good things to eat prepared by her own hand. My head, which has worked through mountains of waste paper like a mechanical recording machine, has at last shown its boundless creative genius in imagining the food. These delectable treats look, smell and taste delicious as I eat them from the aluminium canteen that's been scrubbed till it shines.

But, in fact, the time for these imaginings is finished. Soon my ashes will lie in their urn, which will be placed on an obscure shelf to gather dust for three years, until at last they are flung away. Nobody will want to keep them. And even less will anyone want to mingle her ashes with mine.

There is a soft noise at the window. The Grand Historian's ugly face is pressed against the glass, his expression one of concentration and bewilderment. His usual coldness and superiority have vanished. I look away at once, not wanting him to see the loneliness in my heart. We have seen many things together and he should not feel bereft as I leave him. He scratches at the pane with his front paws like someone knocking at a door.

Years ago I picked him up in the street and brought him home. There wasn't an uglier, lazier cat in the world. His short tail was like a piece of rag. His greyish, dull fur was so dirty that you couldn't tell his true colour. He had been sitting in the middle of the road, not moving or making a sound, while the torrent of bicycle, lorry and car wheels flowed past him. He just sat there like a pile of rubbish that had been dumped on the road, as if he had stopped caring whether he lived or died. It would only have taken a small turn by a single wheel to squash him flat.

I gave him a bath in my foot-bowl and I'm inclined to think he failed to understand my good intentions and reckoned that I was trying to skin him alive. He drew blood where he clawed the back of my hand as he jumped on to my radio, which was playing at the time and felt warm to his paws. He stared at me with caution and silence. After several days of very close observation he acknowledged me as a friend, but even then, with a touch of condescension. Whenever I sat at my desk writing furiously he always looked at me with a certain superciliousness. His manner said: 'What you're scribbling is all useless nonsense, old friend.' When I read my articles aloud to myself, wagging my head, he lazily shut his eyes and purred rhythmically. And when I gazed with adoration at the letter written on the side of the table every night before going to sleep he sat by my pillow with his head on his front paws and stared at my face with a pitying, mocking stare. I am still covered from head to foot with little red flea bites, just as I was when he first came to me.

Every morning he used to stroke my thinning white hair with his paw, telling me to stop lying in bed gazing vacantly at the ceiling. Whenever I sat down to take a rest and shut my dim old eyes he'd spring on to my lap, or lick my hands with their protruding blue veins and slack, wrinkled skin, or grasp my wrists and nip my fingers, but very carefully so that he never hurt me.

It was because of him that I finally started paying some attention to feeding us properly and sometimes treated us with cold meat. I would spread it out on the greasy wrapping paper, and as he crouched on the other side of it facing me, we would take our time savouring the meat together. Sometimes my imagination would run free and I'd think that if we could both have had a drink, we would have clinked glasses and drunk to each other. Thank God for sending me an animal soul, so patient and understanding, never using its tongue to harass or harm me. I am praying that the next tenant will adopt the Grand Historian and that maybe even he will liven up a bit. I'm sure he can, and that someone will take him in, but I can't be certain.

I have been silently hoping that the next tenant will be someone full of life who will decorate this room like other rooms with sheer white curtains, a gleaming crystal fixture hanging from the ceiling, a woven tablecloth, a beautiful landscape painting on the wall and a vase of pale-yellow roses . . . A girl would be best. She'd be bound to have her boyfriend mend the window bolt so she could open it wide and allow the moonlight to come flooding in, the breeze to waft in the scent of locust blossom in May, and perhaps even strains of Schubert's 'Serenade'. Then the room will have the joy and pleasure I was never able to bring to it.

What else is there left? Oh, yes, so many longings I still feel, vividly, acutely, now that the time is used up. They have not faded but hang suspended in my heart.

I used to think that all my emotions belonged in the past, to history, but I know that I yearn for the future just like everyone else. Even as life draws to a close, I realize that I have never understood myself completely . . . If only . . .

But now it certainly is too late to do more, to be more, in this lifetime.

# Too Much Rain, or, the Assault of the Mold Spores

*Ellen Gilchrist was born by the Mississippi River in Issaquena County. She got her first job when she was fourteen, writing a column for the local Franklin, Kentucky, newspaper. At nineteen she married an engineering student, with whom she had three children. After her marriage ended she enrolled at Millsaps College, where she took a creative-writing course taught by Eudora Welty. She has published several collections of short stories, including* Victory over Japan, Drunk with Love *and* Light Can be Both Wave and Particle.

The spring Miss Crystal got her allergies was no joke. Creating jobs, Mr Manny called it, and it did turn out to be quite an industry. By the time her nose quit running and she could talk again, there were fifteen different carpenters, four painters, two attic men, and half the teen-agers in the neighborhood who knew the combinations to every door in the house. Two, two, four, two, three, is the front-door combination in case there is anyone left in New Orleans who doesn't know it yet. There is nothing left in this house to steal anyway as Miss Crystal has turned out to be allergic to house dust as well as to mold spores and she is not taking any chances on any accumulating on any bric-à-brac. The allergy doctor showed Miss Crystal a blown-up photograph of a dust mite and that was the end of every book and statue and flower vase and piece of antique furniture in this house. We have gone completely modern for our interior with everything painted white and some new chairs by Mr Mies van der Rohe who does not believe in chairs having arms on them. Also we have pulled up the carpets and put in black and white tiles that show every smudge and heel print and require a pair of floor cleaners coming in every Friday to vacuum and buff. So much for the house. It was Miss Crystal's body that was the real battlefield. She even insisted that I go down and be tested even though I have never been allergic to anything in my life and wasn't showing any signs. Still, she pled and pled and finally I went on down and let them test me. They put sixty holes in your back and then you wait in this freezing-cold room for twenty minutes and then they come back in to see if any of the holes have started itching or turning red. Then they put sixty more on your right arm with stronger chemicals in them and if that doesn't get a reaction they put sixty on your left arm. They were just debating whether to put a fourth set on my leg when I called a halt. Only one of all the holes had turned red and it was to a plant that grows up in Minnesota where I am not planning on going anytime soon and besides, I had to lead a youth group at four and it was growing late.

Another note. There was this nurse in white giving allergy shots to little children. The whole time I was waiting to be tested I had to watch that going on. She was standing in the hall with this tray full of dirty little bottles of different sorts of things people are allergic to. Ragweed, maple pollen, cedar dust, geraniums, and so forth. Each little child would come up and stick their arm out and she would dip a needle down into two or three of the jars, never watching what she was doing, just chatting with the parents and jabbing the needle in and out of the jar necks. Then she'd grab the child's arm and stick the needle in. I have never seen a nurse I trusted less. I wouldn't take those shots for anything in the world from that woman and I told Miss Crystal so. If you take them, I warned, demand another nurse.

The first thing the allergy doctor tried on Miss Crystal was having her stay in the house and putting her on some nose spray and a drug called Seldane that dries you up without putting you to sleep. I'd stick with Benadryl, I told her. You know you have strange reactions to prescription drugs. I have to take it, she replied. I have to put my faith in someone, so I have picked out Dr Allensby.

So she began to take these Seldane tablets twice a day, once every twelve hours, and things picked up. Not only had her doctor recom- mended them but they were also recommended by a medical book we bought recently. Three days go by and all is going well. She is even able to go out in the yard to oversee the gardener.

The third afternoon she went down to the video store to get Crystal Anne a video and the girl in the store started talking to her about allergies and how everyone is getting them now and isn't it strange that it happened right when the pollution is getting worse and don't tell her it is only plants and trees making people in the United States get sick.

'I've got mine under control,' Miss Crystal says. 'I'm taking this new drug called Seldane. It's great. It makes you kind of hyper but I can stand it. It's better than not breathing.'

'Oh, my God,' the girl says. 'My brother and I took that last year. It made us have terrible dreams. Very, very lifelike dreams.'

'What did you say?' Miss Crystal says. 'What did you just say?' It turns out she had been having terrible dreams for three nights but had not put the two things together. In the worst dream she and I are standing in a parking lot watching Mr Manny drive the Lexus off the top of a cliff with the baby in the backseat. Mr Manny is Miss Crystal's baby-faced and excessively brilliant husband. They have a mixed marriage which is doing better after many trials and tribulations. They met at a party in Pass Christian during the third day of the Six-day War, when Miss Crystal was in her pro-Israeli syndrome and while Mr Manny was obsessed with blonde Christian women, due to his having been sent to New England to school when he was thirteen years old. All of this came out in therapy. So they forged this troubled marriage out of these materials and they have this precious little girl, Crystal Anne, who is one of the two mainstays of my life. The other is my niece, Andria, who is at LSU leading the anti-establishment crusade. I have never been able to have a child of my own and for many years now I have seen that as a blessing in disguise. You get your heart tied up in children and you lose all sense of how to care for them and teach them to be strong. But back to Miss Crystal's dream.

The Lexus falls on its nose as we watch in terror and disbelief. Then a voice comes from the car. It is Mr Manny's voice and he says everything is all right. He gets out of the car and then he reaches in the back seat and brings out the baby. They are both all right although they were not wearing seat belts. I think this dream is only a justification for Miss Crystal and Miss Lydia refusing to wear seat belts when they are together. Miss

Lydia is Miss Crystal's best friend. She is a famous painter out in California who gets up to seventeen thousand dollars for every painting that she paints. Still, she and Miss Crystal are bad to act like adolescents when they get together. Many of their worst habits are on the wane now but they still like to ride around New Orleans with no seat belts. They say it is to prove there is no security, but I think it is more about not messing up their dresses when they are going out.

But back to the medical problems. You cannot win at this allergy game. Once your body goes auto-immune on you it is just one long trip to the doctor or the drugstore. Meanwhile, every tree and plant in New Orleans was bursting with blooms. Putting out pollen morning, noon, and night. 'I am no longer part of the beauty of the world,' Miss Crystal cried out at least once a day. 'Now I have to hate the things I used to love so dearly.'

'You never did pay much attention to flowers,' I consoled her. 'You'd rather be on the tennis court any day.'

'I can't even play tennis with this going on,' she answered. 'I can see the pollen falling from the trees. The more I breathe, the more Seldane I have to take.'

Here's what Mr Manny decided we should do. All go to Florida and stay a few weeks and, if Miss Crystal gets well, buy a house there for her to live in when the going gets rough in New Orleans.

It was Monday when we decided we should leave. By Tuesday afternoon we were out at the airport, only of course by then Mr Manny had decided he couldn't leave his work. Now that he has quit his law firm and gotten into environmental work he is a worse workaholic than he was when he was only doing it to make money. He is fighting to save the wetlands and has almost completely stopped wearing ties.

So it was only Miss Crystal and Crystal Anne and myself who were boarding the plane. Crystal Anne and I sat together and Miss Crystal sat across the aisle reading a *Vogue* magazine and stopping every few minutes to blow her nose. 'We will be there in two hours,' I told her several times. 'Buck up your courage. We have solved worse problems than this.'

'You're right,' Miss Crystal answered. 'This is a very small problem. A problem we can fix.'

'I was going to be the lilac fairy in the school play,' Crystal Anne noted for the third time. 'I'll never get to be the lilac fairy again.'

'You are going to Florida instead,' I told her. 'Many little girls would give their eye teeth for a week off from school to see the ocean.'

We arrived in St Petersburg in the middle of the afternoon and a van from the hotel picked us up and carried us into town. It is a very spread-out city and quite clean and the hotel Mr Manny had gotten for us was this very swanky hotel on the beach with an indoor pool and one outside near the ocean. Crystal Anne loves pools, although she also likes to swim in the ocean. Personally I do not like water that has chlorine in it. It reminds me too much of washday down in Boutte when my auntie would have water boiling with so much bleach in it the smell would fill the town.

We settled down in two rooms with a door that opened between them. There were balconies that looked out on to the beach and the Gulf of Mexico. Crystal Anne was enchanted by the balconies and kept going from one to the other putting her dolls on the chairs and making little nests for them overlooking the sea. She is eight years old now, just as sweet as an angel, which she has been ever since the day that she was born. Born sweet and stayed sweet. Also, she has a very fine brain and she knows how to use it. She is like Mr Manny in that. She does not let outside influences change the way she sees things. If she has a flaw, it is that she is very rigid about her likes and dislikes. If she likes someone, she will stick up for them no matter what. If she takes a dislike to them, watch out. Well, she took a dislike to Mr Hotchkiss, which Miss Lydia later said only proved once again that a little child should lead us.

But we had barely arrived and Mr Hotchkiss had not showed up yet and so we took off our traveling clothes and went down to the pool to let Crystal Anne practice swimming.

The people around the pool were very friendly. There was a couple from Maine who had met each other at a support meeting they went to after their spouses died. His had died and hers had died so they got together and have lived happily ever after for two years. They each talked a lot about the people they used to be married to. It seemed that was most of their conversation, plus some jokes he was making about the fact that she was fifteen years younger than he was and other jokes about the fact that she smoked. She mostly talked about sailing the British Virgin Islands with her dead husband who was her age and what a good sailor he was and their narrow escapes.

I began to get the picture. Her on the sailboat with her young good-looking husband, the two of them tanned and sort of devil-may-care and smoking all the time. Him in a nice house with the mother of his children. Both of them happy and content and him never giving a thought to a younger woman until his wife died and forced him into it. He was very fat and jolly and glad to talk, and she was not pretty but she was vivacious and I began to take to her.

Another woman who said she was forty-eight was lying on a deck chair and she got into our conversation and began to tell all about her young husband and how her mother pretended not to know she was married to a man half her age and was supporting him. I really liked this woman a lot. Miss Martha Ann Hamblin from St Louis, Missouri. She was a snow-bird, which means she goes to Florida to get away from snowstorms. Her husband was with her on the trip but he was off somewhere shopping for clothes. She was very vivacious too and had a pretty face. She kept laughing when she'd tell things about herself and she and Miss Crystal were establishing a rapport.

There weren't many other children at the pool. Just a fat girl about eight and another girl maybe twelve years old. Crystal Anne tried to make friends with the fat girl but the fat girl only wanted to play in her water wings and wouldn't dive or swim laps. I feel a great sympathy for fat children and always want to take over and change their diet although my niece Andria tells me that psychiatrists say many fat children are born to be that way and have a slow metabolism and should not be made fun of or have people always after them trying to change their diet.

We spent most of the afternoon by the pool or walking down to the ocean and back. Miss Crystal said she felt like a new woman from breathing the salt air. Crystal Anne was trying to get in one hundred laps before the sun went down. She was up to seventy-six when we made her give up and went up to our rooms to dress for dinner. The air down here in Florida is soft and fine and full of salt. So puffy and romantic. It is easy to see why all these people from up north come down here and decide to stay. Balmy is the word I'm searching for. Balmy is the only word for it.

There were two dining-rooms in the hotel. The Palm Court, which is the finest one, and a more casual area called Sixteen Palms. We tossed a coin and the Palm Court won, so we dressed up in our best clothes and put the heated rollers on Crystal Anne's hair and dressed her in her new pink linen dress and down we went to have our first resort meal. There weren't too many people in the Palm Court when we got there, so we took a seat at the best table looking out toward the sea and began to talk about the salt air and why it always seems to mend anything that is wrong with you. We were laughing and carrying on and making fun of the menu when this very handsome man with black hair came in and took a seat at a small table facing us. He was very elegant, tall and thin and wearing a white linen suit like you see in movies set in Europe. He had on these little wire spectacles that made him look even more distinguished. While he was studying the menu the headwaiter came over and told him there was a telephone call for him and would he like a phone, but he said no, he wouldn't take it, he was eating dinner and would the headwaiter take a message.

Our dinner had been served but Miss Crystal had lost all interest in food. She started sitting up very straight in her chair and asking Crystal Anne things that I know couldn't really be of any interest to her. Also, she had taken off her glasses.

I have seen Miss Crystal get that way before, like she has seen a way out of a tunnel that she thought had no end. Like she had been asleep for days and all of a sudden woke up and started blinking.

She was not looking at him. Although by now he was occasionally raising his eyes above the little glasses and looking at her. That was about all that happened that night, except that he finished dinner before we did and passed by our table on his way to go stand on the patio and drink a brandy. 'What a lovely child,' he said, as he passed our table, this very cultured accent like he was from Boston or England or somewhere far away. Miss Crystal blushed and Crystal Anne bristled like he had said she was ugly. 'I hate it when people do that,' she said. 'It's rude to act like children don't know you are talking about them.'

*

The next morning, no sooner had we gone down to the beach and gotten settled on our striped beach chairs, when he came walking down to the water's edge. He had on a pair of blue jeans and a starched white shirt and some leather handmade sandals. In the morning light he looked even handsomer than he had the night before. He walked past us and stood a long time at the water's edge, letting us admire his back.

I should stop here and tell you something about Miss Crystal that you might miss if you only heard me tell the things she says and does. She is very lovely to look at. Not just the features of her face. She has a kind of glow about her, something coming from deep within that draws people to her. Everything she does has a kind of gracefulness and charm. I do not love her for nothing. It is because she has this glow of kindness, from the inside going out and it has always reached out to me. She does not think of me as a maid or a servant and I do not think of her as my employer. Not to mention that I have always been the highest-paid housekeeper in New Orleans and I have never had to ask for a raise. For a while there it looked as if Miss Crystal and Mr Manny were in a race to see which one could pay more money to anyone who works for them. When Miss Crystal gave me the down payment for a house, Mr Manny went right out and bought the gardener a pick-up truck. Andria has paced up and down my living-room a dozen times telling me this is a bad thing and we are all living in a fool's paradise but I do not care. Andria has set her sights on being a television anchor-woman and so it is necessary that she see everything in the most cynical light.

Back to Florida and the scene on the beach when Mr William Hotchkiss from Atlanta, Georgia, showed up and went to stand at the water's edge looking out. We did not know at the time that it was Crystal Anne who was making him sad. It turned out he had a small daughter who had died several years before, carrying with her to the grave half his liver, which had failed to save her life. He had lain down beside her on a table at Mayo's Clinic and let them take out half his liver and stuff as much as they could fit into her tiny, sick body. After she died, his wife went completely crazy and started sleeping with everyone in sight and it ended in divorce. Now he was on a leave of absence from his job and was traveling around the country trying to find a place to think straight. He had come to St Petersburg because once, as a young man, he had sailed from there in an old patched-up sailboat with two other young men and made it to the Virgin Islands after having to build a de-salinator for water and making a rudder out of a dinghy seat. All of this came out later in conversation. For now, Miss Crystal was sitting up straight in her beach chair, Crystal Anne was getting nervous, and I was doing my usual thing, which is watch and reserve judgment until more information comes in. I have learned this counseling teenagers at my church.

'I'm not perfect,' Miss Crystal says, meeting my eyes. 'Life is short, Traceleen. Whatever winter offers, I will take.'

'I see you're feeling better,' is all I would say to that.

'I feel terrific, to tell the truth.' She stood up and put her baby-blue beach coat on over her suit. 'I think I'll take a swim. The Gulf of Mexico, think about it, connecting to the Atlantic Ocean, the deep blue sea.' She walked over in the direction of Mr Hotchkiss, and I guess she must have said hello, or, haven't we met somewhere before? or, isn't it a nice day? because in a few minutes they were walking along the water's edge like they were old friends. She was telling him about her allergies, I suppose, because he was nodding his head.

I should stop and tell you something about this day. It was paradisiacal. Balmy and blue, soft, soft air, brilliant sun, low clouds on the horizon and everywhere the sound of the sea lapping on the sandy shores. My powers of observation fail me. Silk is the only word that fits this day.

Crystal Anne noticed her mother talking to Mr Hotchkiss and she came out of the water and walked back over to me. About that time a man from the hotel came along and asked if we wouldn't like an umbrella and I said yes and he began to set up this very large green-and-white-striped umbrella above our heads. 'Who is Momma talking to?' Crystal Anne asked. 'Is she going to start flirting with men again?'

'Would you care to play tic-tac-toe?' I answered. 'I brought a pad and pencils in case you'd like to play some games.'

'Is that the man we saw last night at dinner?'

'I think so. Yes, I think it's the same man. He must be lonely. Down here at a hotel all by himself.'

'If she starts flirting with men, I'm going home.' Crystal Anne put on her hooded beach coat and pulled the hood up over her hair. 'Why does she always have to do that?'

'Play me some games,' I answered. 'Leave your momma alone. Your momma is only talking to that man.'

That night they started dancing. It was in the Palm Court again. There was a band playing South American dance music and Mr Hotchkiss came to our table while we were waiting for the main course and asked Miss Crystal if she'd like to dance. They went out on to the dance floor and started dancing like they'd been dancing together all their lives. By now Miss Crystal had heard most of his story and her interest in him was furthered by sympathy.

She was wearing blue again, a long blue silk sheath with a little jacket. I had on my cerise cotton suit and Crystal Anne was wearing white with a pink sash, looking exactly like an angel.

That night she insisted on sleeping in my room with me. 'I don't like Mr Hotchkiss,' she said, when we had turned off the lights and said our prayers. 'I don't like the way he looks at me.'

'He came down here because his little girl died and his wife went crazy on him. It won't hurt us to be nice to him.'

'She's going to let him go to Disney World with us. Just because his little girl died doesn't mean he ought to dance with Momma all the time. If he goes to Disney World, I won't go.' She rolled over with her face to the wall and put a pillow over her head and held it there.

'Go to sleep, honey. We're not in charge of everything that happens.'

'We're on a planet,' she said, rolling back over and throwing the pillow on the floor. 'It's just a planet circling the sun. All around is darkest space.'

'God is here,' I put in.

'Maybe he is and maybe he's not. If he is, he's doing a terrible job.'

In the end only Crystal Anne and I went to Disney World. Miss Crystal stayed at the hotel taking dancing lessons. Crystal Anne and I had a pretty good time. We had our photographs made and a five-minute video of us talking to Donald Duck. We rode about two dozen rides and ate lunch in

Rapunzel's Tower and bought sweatshirts and sunglasses and got home about five in the afternoon completely exhausted. At least I was.

We went up to our rooms and Crystal Anne threw herself down on Miss Crystal's bed and started pouting. I was in the next room with the door open between the rooms.

'Did you have fun at Disney World?' Miss Crystal asked.

'No.'

'Why not?'

'I wanted you to be there. People look at me funny when I'm with Traceleen.'

'Why is that?'

'They think a maid is taking care of me.'

'Do you think that?' I couldn't get up and close the door. I didn't know what to do. I coughed, but they did not seem to hear. I coughed again. 'Come in here, Traceleen,' Miss Crystal said. 'This concerns you too.'

'Black people should be at home taking care of their own families,' Crystal Anne said. 'That's what everybody thinks.'

'I don't have any children but you,' I answered. 'This is my job, Crystal Anne. Also, my heart's desire. I love being in Florida with you. You know it's true.'

'You're mad about Mr Hotchkiss, aren't you?' Miss Crystal had decided to bite the bullet.

'I think it's going to be like it was in Maine with Allen. You and Daddy will get a divorce and I'll have to live in two houses like Augusta Redmon.'

'I am only getting to know Mr Hotchkiss so that when Lydia comes down here she will have someone to go out with. I'm trying to get Lydia to come and join us. I haven't told you yet because I wasn't sure she could come. Well, there it is, now you know and don't be disappointed if she doesn't come.' Miss Crystal looked at me across Crystal Anne's head. It was the biggest lie I had ever heard her tell her child. The worst lie she had told since she quit drinking. It was a lie that was destined to draw me in. I took the bait. 'See there, honey. It's not what you thought it was.' Crystal Anne looked at me out of the bottom of her eyes. It is impossible to lie to her. Many children are that way. It is a gift they have.

'I'm going swimming,' she said. 'I want to get in some laps before dinner.'

As soon as Crystal Anne left the room Crystal got on the phone and called Miss Lydia in California and began to plead with her to come and join us. 'I'll buy the airplane ticket,' she said. 'I'll pay for everything. You better come and meet this man. He's a ten. You know you don't like any other kind.'

So the upshot of it was Miss Lydia agreed to come the following day. It turned out she was in a lull between painting jobs anyway and thought she might drum up some portrait business among the snowbirds.

That night Miss Crystal went to work telling Mr Hotchkiss all about how happily married she was and how careful everyone has to be around Crystal Anne because she is so sensitive and can read minds. Also, how fortunate everyone in St Petersburg was going to be when the best painter in the United States showed up for a visit and let ordinary people talk to her. I think Miss Crystal probably overdid it. Mr Hotchkiss was so lonely and guilt-ridden over his liver not being strong enough to save his child that he was ripe for any kind of attention. We could have run in somebody with only half the personality of Miss Lydia and he would have been thrilled to meet her.

So Miss Lydia joined the party. She is a catalyst I guess you could call it. The ingredient that makes the pot boil over. She got off the airplane wearing this little black California outfit and carrying a rolled-up canvas under her arm. It was her latest painting, a portrait of a famous writer sitting beside a bowl of huge white roses. *Homage to Van Gogh*, it is called and we all agreed it was the best thing she had ever painted.

Why she would roll it up and carry it across the United States on an airplane is beyond me but she says it is because of anxiety. She is continually worried that an earthquake will destroy one of her paintings before she has time to finish it or put it in a contest.

'I have just found out that much of what I have always thought of as anxiety is just plain fear,' she started telling Mr Hotchkiss as soon as they were introduced. (It is not the old-fashioned way to get a man interested in you but I try to keep an open mind about such things. In the old days we would look up at a man and say, where did you get those big brown eyes? or something more along that line.) 'All these years I assumed I was suffering the ordinary anxiety and depression common to artists when all along it was just plain old Midwestern fear.'

'Imagine that,' Mr Hotchkiss said.

'I could have told you that,' Miss Crystal puts in. 'You've never been depressed, Lydia. Being afraid of earthquakes when you live on the San Andreas Fault is not neurotic. Why don't you move to New Orleans and live near me?'

'I might,' she answered, and got this dark and serious look on her face and sat up straighter. 'I'm rereading the *Chronicles of Dune*. I want to be a Bene Gesserit nun and have power over every aspect of my life. I am training myself to be constantly aware. And read body language.' She looked directly at Mr Hotchkiss, who was sitting like a perfect gentleman. He didn't move a muscle when she said that and I began to think maybe I had underrated him.

'Well,' Miss Crystal said. 'I think I'll join Crystal Anne in the pool. I want to get in a swim before dinner.' Miss Crystal got up and went to join her daughter and Mr Hotchkiss suggested that Lydia change her shoes and accompany him on a walk.

Lydia agreed and went off to her room leaving Mr Hotchkiss and me alone. He looked off toward the sea, very gentle and companionable, and I reached in my bag for my knitting. I am knitting a pair of golf-club covers for my niece Andria. It is tricky work and I forgot myself in it for a while. 'I took up knitting once,' Mr Hotchkiss said. 'When I was in the navy. I knitted seven scarves, each one longer than the last. The last one was seven feet long. It was my masterpiece.'

'What sort of vessel were you on?' I asked.

'A nuclear sub. Imagine being young and unimaginative enough to do that.' He laughed a gentle laugh and I thought for a moment he might cry. It is a strange thing about very handsome men as they grow older. Either they become great to match their beauty or a sort of fading begins. Their smiles lose all excitement. It's as if great beauty makes promises it cannot keep.

Miss Lydia reappeared, wearing shorts and a shirt and white socks and tennis shoes. She swept him up and took him off down the beach.

About that time who should come walking out of the hotel but Mr

Manny. He had finished up his work and decided to come down and surprise us. He came walking out of the hotel still wearing his suit and tie. Crystal Anne spotted him from the pool. She came tearing across the concrete and threw herself into his arms, getting him soaking wet.

Miss Crystal was slower in her welcome but I could see it was sincere. The things that have gone on between this pair that I have witnessed! Still, the love they have is always greater than their problems. They are smart enough for each other and can make each other laugh. 'I look terrible,' is the first thing Miss Crystal said. 'My hair's wet. Why didn't you tell me you were coming? Come on, go up to my room while I get dressed.'

'Crystal Anne and I will get a snack in the coffeeshop,' I volunteered. Nothing makes me happier than the thought that Miss Crystal and Mr Manny might spend an hour in bed. It looked like this might be the afternoon, so I grabbed up Crystal Anne and took her inside to eat bacon, lettuce, and tomato sandwiches and drink iced tea.

'Where did Lydia go with Mr Hotchkiss?' she asked me. We were taking dainty little bites of our sandwiches, our backs straight, our napkins in our laps. Crystal Anne and I are not part of the messiness of life in the nineties.

'Lydia can take care of herself,' I answered. 'She has lived through two earthquakes all alone in a little house in a redwood forest. I wouldn't worry about her taking a walk with a man from Atlanta, Georgia.'

'What does Mr Hotchkiss do for a living?' She sat up even straighter and knit her eyebrows together in a perfect imitation of Miss Crystal's father.

'We haven't asked,' I answered. 'You know it is impolite to question people about their livelihoods. People will volunteer this information when they are ready.'

'I don't like it when men don't go to work.' She picked a piece of tomato out of her sandwich and laid it on her plate. 'They should go to work in the daytime.'

'Judge not that ye be not judged,' is all I would say to that. We finished up our sandwiches and iced tea. Crystal Anne had added so much sugar to her tea that the bottom of the glass looked like a beach. She removed the ice, then took her red-and-white-striped straw and fashioned the sugar into a tiny sand castle. 'Are you going to eat that sugar?' I asked.

'Yes,' she said. She took her iced-tea spoon and very carefully filled it with the castle and put it into her beautiful little pink mouth. I would rather have a meal with Crystal Anne than any king or queen on the earth. I have never had a meal with her that did not turn out to be memorable.

We wrapped up our bread crusts for the gulls and signed our bill and walked down to the beach to give the crusts away. There was no sign of Lydia and Mr Hotchkiss. We walked along beside the water for a while, then we went up to our rooms to dress for dinner.

At seven that night Lydia and Mr Hotchkiss had not been heard from. At seven thirty we went to dinner without them. At nine Miss Crystal began to want to call the police.

At ten fifteen the phone finally rang. It was Lydia calling from a bar in Tampa, begging them to come and save her. 'He's drunk,' she told Miss Crystal. 'He said he'll kill himself if I leave him. He said he has no reason to live.'

'I knew he was a kidnapper,' Crystal Anne said, when Manny and Crystal had gone off to save Lydia. 'You all go crazy if I speak to a stranger and Mother just takes up with a man she meets in a hotel and lets him take Lydia off like that.'

'Your mother does the best she can,' I answered. 'You are too smart a little girl to start disliking your beloved mother just because she has flights of imagination.'

An hour and a half later Manny and Crystal reappeared with Lydia. 'I have spent my life trying to escape that bar,' Lydia said. 'Then I end up in it with this dull goddamn man from Atlanta. Will I ever learn?'

'Why did you go?' Crystal Anne had moved in closer. I couldn't believe we were letting her take part in this conversation.

'Because I felt sorry for him. And because he said he wanted me to paint his dead child. From a photograph, of course. He didn't bat an eyelash when I said twenty thousand dollars.'

'Why don't you paint Crystal Anne instead?' Manny asked. 'For, say, half that amount.'

Which is how a spring that began with pollen, mold, and dust mites ended up in a glorious portrait of Crystal Anne wearing a green-and-white sprigged dimity garden dress and holding a hat in her hand. Beside her are squirrels and robins and bluejays and a turtle and her cat and many other of the creatures that she loves so dearly. Lydia stayed with us while she painted it and while she was doing the drawings Crystal Anne would add an animal every time she saw Lydia in a good mood. The painting is called *The Menagerie* and a copy of it was the cover of *New Orleans* magazine for August of last year. It has completely dominated the living-room of our house and looks perfect with the stark floors and armless Mies van der Rohe chairs.

Actually, we would not have had to move all that furniture and paint all those walls if we had waited a few months. It turns out that Miss Crystal's allergies were really caused by all the antibiotics that she took when she had her teeth capped. What few allergies she has now can be controlled by nose spray and are only caused by the budding of the trees in spring and the going-to-seed of plants in the fall. Talking about things like that is work for a poet. If Mr Alter hadn't killed himself he might be here to turn this experience into literature. In his absence I have tried to do the best I can. Here is my poem.

> *When the dew point rises*
> *When the buds appear*
> *'When Aprile with its sweete showeres'*
> *Fills the world with moisture*
> *This is the hour when the upper respiratory system*
> *Goes into high gear*
> *And we must accept*
> *We are not in charge here.*

SANDRA CISNEROS

# *Woman Hollering Creek*

*Sandra Cisneros is the daughter of a Mexican father and a Mexican-American mother. She grew up in a Puerto Rican district of Chicago and now teaches at the University of Texas. She is the author of a novel,* The House on Mango Street, *and a volume of poetry,* My Wicked Wicked Ways. *This short story comes from her collection* Woman Hollering Creek.

The day Don Serafín gave Juan Pedro Martínez Sánchez permission to take Cleófilas Enriqueta DeLeón Hernández, as his bride, across her father's threshold, over several miles of dirt road and several miles of paved, over one border and beyond to a town *en el otro lado* – on the other side – already did he divine the morning his daughter would raise her hand over her eyes, look south, and dream of returning to the chores that never ended, six good-for-nothing brothers, and one old man's complaints.

He had said, after all, in the hubbub of parting: I am your father, I will never abandon you. He *had* said that, hadn't he, when he hugged and then let her go. But at the moment Cleófilas was busy looking for Chela, her maid of honor, to fulfill their bouquet conspiracy. She would not re-member her father's parting words until later. *I am your father, I will never abandon you.*

Only now as a mother did she remember. Now, when she and Juan Pedrito sat by the creek's edge. How when a man and a woman love each other, sometimes that love sours. But a parent's love for a child, a child's for its parents, is another thing entirely.

This is what Cleófilas thought evenings when Juan Pedro did not come home, and she lay on her side of the bed listening to the hollow roar of the interstate, a distant dog barking, the pecan trees rustling like ladies in stiff petticoats – *shh-shh-shh, shh-shh-shh* – soothing her to sleep.

In the town where she grew up, there isn't very much to do except accompany the aunts and godmothers to the house of one or the other to play cards. Or walk to the cinema to see this week's film again, speckled and with one hair quivering annoyingly on the screen. Or to the center of town to order a milk shake that will appear in a day and a half as a pimple on her backside. Or to the girlfriend's house to watch the latest *telenovela* episode and try to copy the way the women comb their hair, wear their make-up.

But what Cleófilas has been waiting for, has been whispering and sighing and giggling for, has been anticipating since she was old enough to lean against the window displays of gauze and butterflies and lace, is passion. Not the kind on the cover of the *¡Alarma!* magazines, mind you, where the lover is photographed with the bloody fork she used to salvage her good name. But passion in its purest crystalline essence. The kind the books and songs and *telenovelas* describe when one finds, finally, the great love of one's life, and does whatever one can, must do, at whatever the cost.

*Tú o Nadie.* 'You or No One'. The title of the current favorite *telenovela*. The beautiful Lucía Méndez having to put up with all kinds of hardships of the heart, separation and betrayal, and loving, always loving no matter what, because *that* is the most important thing, and did you see Lucía Méndez on the Bayer aspirin commercials – wasn't she lovely? Does she dye her hair do you think? Cleófilas is going to go to the *farmacía* and buy a hair rinse; her girlfriend Chela will apply it – it's not that difficult at all.

Because you didn't watch last night's episode when Lucía confessed she loved him more than anyone in her life. In her life! And she sings the song 'You or No One' in the beginning and end of the show. *Tú o Nadie.* Somehow one ought to live one's life like that, don't you think? You or no one. Because to suffer for love is good. The pain all sweet somehow. In the end.

\*

*Seguín.* She had liked the sound of it. Far away and lovely. Not like *Monclova. Coahuia.* Ugly.

*Seguín, Tejas.* A nice sterling ring to it. The tinkle of money. She would get to wear outfits like the women on the *tele*, like Lucía Méndez. And have a lovely house, and wouldn't Chela be jealous.

And yes, they will drive all the way to Laredo to get her wedding dress. That's what they say. Because Juan Pedro wants to get married right away, without a long engagement since he can't take off too much time from work. He has a very important position in Seguin with, with ... a beer company, I think. Or was it tires? Yes, he has to be back. So they will get married in the spring when he can take off work, and then they will drive off in his new pick-up – did you see it? – to their new home in Seguin. Well, not exactly new, but they're going to repaint the house. You know newlyweds. New paint and new furniture. Why not? He can afford it. And later on add maybe a room or two for the children. May they be blessed with many.

Well, you'll see. Cleófilas has always been so good with her sewing machine. A little *rrrr, rrrr, rrrr* of the machine and *¡zas!* Miracles. She's always been so clever, that girl. Poor thing. And without even a mama to advise her on things like her wedding night. Well, may God help her. What with a father with a head like a burro, and those six clumsy brothers. Well, what do you think! Yes, I'm going to the wedding. Of course! The dress I want to wear just needs to be altered a teensy bit to bring it up to date. See, I saw a new style last night that I thought would suit me. Did you watch last night's episode of *The Rich Also Cry*? Well, did you notice the dress the mother was wearing?

*La Gritona.* Such a funny name for such a lovely *arroyo.* But that's what they called the creek that ran behind the house. Though no one could say whether the woman had hollered from anger or pain. The natives only knew the *arroyo* one crossed on the way to San Antonio, and then once again on the way back, was called Woman Hollering, a name no one from these parts questioned, little less understood. *Pues, allá de los indios, quién sabe* – who knows, the townspeople shrugged, because it was of no concern to their lives how this trickle of water received its curious name.

'What do you want to know for?' Trini the laundromat attendant asked in the same gruff Spanish she always used whenever she gave Cleófilas change or yelled at her for something. First for putting too much soap in the machines. Later, for sitting on a washer. And still later, after Juan Pedrito was born, for not understanding that in this country you cannot let your baby walk around with no diaper and his pee-pee hanging out, it wasn't nice, ¿entiendes? Pues.

How could Cleófilas explain to a woman like this why the name Woman Hollering fascinated her. Well, there was no sense talking to Trini.

On the other hand there were the neighbor ladies, one on either side of the house they rented near the *arroyo*. The woman Soledad on the left, the woman Dolores on the right.

The neighbor lady Soledad liked to call herself a widow, though how she came to be one was a mystery. Her husband had either died, or run away with an ice-house floozie, or simply gone out for cigarettes one afternoon and never came back. It was hard to say which since Soledad, as a rule, didn't mention him.

In the other house lived *la señora* Dolores, kind and very sweet, but her house smelled too much of incense and candles from the altars that burned continuously in memory of two sons who had died in the last war and one husband who had died shortly after from grief. The neighbor lady Dolores divided her time between the memory of these men and her garden, famous for its sunflowers – so tall they had to be supported with broom handles and old boards; red red cockscombs, fringed and bleeding a thick menstrual color; and, especially, roses whose sad scent reminded Cleófilas of the dead. Each Sunday *la señora* Dolores clipped the most beautiful of these flowers and arranged them on three modest headstones at the Seguin cemetery.

The neighbor ladies, Soledad, Dolores, they might've known once the name of the *arroyo* before it turned English but they did not know now. They were too busy remembering the men who had left through either choice or circumstance and would never come back.

Pain or rage, Cleófilas wondered when she drove over the bridge the first time as a newlywed and Juan Pedro had pointed it out. *La Gritona*, he had said, and she had laughed. Such a funny name for a creek so pretty and full of happily ever after.

\*

The first time she had been so surprised she didn't cry out or try to defend herself. She had always said she would strike back if a man, any man, were to strike her.

But when the moment came, and he slapped her once, and then again, and again, until the lip split and bled an orchid of blood, she didn't fight back, she didn't break into tears, she didn't run away as she imagined she might when she saw such things in the *telenovelas*.

In her own home her parents had never raised a hand to each other or to their children. Although she admitted she may have been brought up a little leniently as an only daughter – *la consentida*, the princess – there were some things she would never tolerate. Ever.

Instead, when it happened the first time, when they were barely man and wife, she had been so stunned, it left her speechless, motion-less, numb. She had done nothing but reach up to the heat on her mouth and stare at the blood on her hand as if even then she didn't understand.

She could think of nothing to say, said nothing. Just stroked the dark curls of the man who wept and would weep like a child, his tears of repentance and shame, this time and each.

The men at the ice house. From what she can tell, from the times during her first year when still a newlywed she is invited and accompanies her husband, sits mute beside their conversation, waits and sips a beer until it grows warm, twists a paper napkin into a knot, then another into a fan, one into a rose, nods her head, smiles, yawns, politely grins, laughs at the appropriate moments, leans against her husband's sleeve, tugs at his elbow, and finally becomes good at predicting where the talk will lead, from this Cleófilas concludes each is nightly trying to find the truth lying at the bottom of the bottle like a gold doubloon on the sea floor.

They want to tell each other what they want to tell themselves. But what is bumping like a helium balloon at the ceiling of the brain never finds its way out. It bubbles and rises, it gurgles in the throat, it rolls across the surface of the tongue, and erupts from the lips – a belch.

If they are lucky, there are tears at the end of the long night. At any given moment, the fists try to speak. They are dogs chasing their own tails before lying down to sleep, trying to find a way, a route, an out, and – finally – get some peace.

In the morning sometimes before he opens his eyes. Or after they have finished loving. Or at times when he is simply across from her at the table putting pieces of food into his mouth and chewing. Cleófilas thinks, This is the man I have waited my whole life for.

Not that he isn't a good man. She has to remind herself why she loves him when she changes the baby's Pampers, or when she mops the bathroom floor, or tries to make the curtains for the doorways without doors, or whiten the linen. Or wonder a little when he kicks the refrigerator and says he hates this shitty house and is going out where he won't be bothered with the baby's howling and her suspicious questions, and her requests to fix this and this and this because if she had any brains in her head she'd realize he's been up before the rooster earning his living to pay for the food in her belly and the roof over her head and would have to wake up again early the next day so why can't you just leave me in peace, woman.

He is not very tall, no, and he doesn't look like the men on the *telenovelas*. His face still scarred from acne. And he has a bit of a belly from all the beer he drinks. Well, he's always been husky.

This man who farts and belches and snores as well as laughs and kisses and holds her. Somehow this husband whose whiskers she finds each morning in the sink, whose shoes she must air each evening on the porch, this husband who cuts his fingernails in public, laughs loudly, curses like a man, and demands each course of dinner be served on a separate plate like at his mother's, as soon as he gets home, on time or late, and who doesn't care at all for music or *telenovelas* or romance or roses or the moon floating pearly over the *arroyo*, or through the bedroom window for that matter, shut the blinds and go back to sleep, this man, this father, this rival, this keeper, this lord, this master, this husband till kingdom come.

A doubt. Slender as a hair. A washed cup set back on the shelf wrong-side-up. Her lipstick, and body talc, and hairbrush all arranged in the bathroom a different way.

No. Her imagination. The house the same as always. Nothing.

Coming home from the hospital with her new son, her husband. Something comforting in discovering her house slippers beneath the bed, the faded housecoat where she left it on the bathroom hook. Her pillow. Their bed.

Sweet sweet homecoming. Sweet as the scent of face powder in the air, jasmine, sticky liquor.

Smudged fingerprint on the door. Crushed cigarette in a glass. Wrinkle in the brain crumpling to a crease.

Sometimes she thinks of her father's house. But how could she go back there? What a disgrace. What would the neighbors say? Coming home like that with one baby on her hip and one in the oven. Where's your husband?

The town of gossips. The town of dust and despair. Which she has traded for this town of gossips. This town of dust, despair. Houses farther apart perhaps, though no more privacy because of it. No leafy *zócalo* in the center of the town, though the murmur of talk is clear enough all the same. No huddled whispering on the church steps each Sunday. Because here the whispering begins at sunset at the ice house instead.

This town with its silly pride for a bronze pecan the size of a baby carriage in front of the city hall. TV repair shop, drugstore, hardware, dry cleaner's, chiropractor's, liquor store, bail bonds, empty storefront, and nothing, nothing, nothing of interest. Nothing one could walk to, at any rate. Because the towns here are built so that you have to depend on husbands. Or you stay home. Or you drive. If you're rich enough to own, allowed to drive, your own car.

There is no place to go. Unless one counts the neighbor ladies. Soledad on one side, Dolores on the other. Or the creek.

Don't go out there after dark, *mi'jita*. Stay near the house. *No es bueno para la salud. Mala suerte.* Bad luck. *Mal aire.* You'll get sick and the baby too. You'll catch a fright wandering about in the dark, and then you'll see how right we were.

The stream sometimes only a muddy puddle in the summer, though now in the springtime, because of the rains, a good-size alive thing, a thing with a voice all its own, all day and all night calling in its high, silver voice. Is it La Llorona, the weeping woman? La Llorona, who drowned her own children. Perhaps La Llorona is the one they named the creek after, she thinks, remembering all the stories she learned as a child.

La Llorona calling to her. She is sure of it. Cleófilas sets the baby's Donald Duck blanket on the grass. Listens. The day sky turning to night. The baby pulling up fistfuls of grass and laughing. La Llorona. Wonders if something as quiet as this drives a woman to the darkness under the trees.

What she needs is . . . and made a gesture as if to yank a woman's buttocks to his groin. Maximiliano, the foul-smelling fool from across the road, said this and set the men laughing, but Cleófilas just muttered, *Grosera*, and went on washing dishes.

She knew he said it not because it was true, but more because it was he who needed to sleep with a woman, instead of drinking each night at the ice house and stumbling home alone.

Maximiliano who was said to have killed his wife in an ice-house brawl when she came at him with a mop. I had to shoot, he had said – she was armed.

Their laughter outside the kitchen window. Her husband's, his friends'. Manolo, Beto, Efraín, el Perico. Maximiliano.

Was Cleófilas just exaggerating as her husband always said? It seemed the newspapers were full of such stories. This woman found on the side of the interstate. This one pushed from a moving car. This one's cadaver, this one unconscious, this one beaten blue. Her ex-husband, her husband, her lover, her father, her brother, her uncle, her friend, her co-worker. Always. The same grisly news in the pages of the dailies. She dunked a glass under the soapy water for a moment – shivered.

He had thrown a book. Hers. From across the room. A hot welt across the cheek. She could forgive that. But what stung more was the fact it was *her* book, a love story by Corín Tellado, what she loved most now that she lived in the US, without a television set, without the *telenovelas*.

Except now and again when her husband was away and she could manage it, the few episodes glimpsed at the neighbor lady Soledad's house because Dolores didn't care for that sort of thing, though Soledad was often kind enough to retell what had happened on what episode of *María de Nadie*, the poor Argentine country girl who had the ill fortune of falling in love with the beautiful son of the Arrocha family, the very family she worked for, whose roof she slept under and whose floors she vacuumed, while in that same house, with the dust brooms and floor cleaners as witnesses, the square-jawed Juan Carlos Arrocha had uttered words of love, I love you, María, listen to me, *mi querida*, but it was she who had to say No, no, we are not of the same class, and remind him it was not his place nor hers to fall in love, while all the while her heart was breaking, can you imagine.

Cleófilas thought her life would have to be like that, like a *telenovela*, only now the episodes got sadder and sadder. And there were no commercials in between for comic relief. And no happy ending in sight. She thought this when she sat with the baby out by the creek behind the house. Cleófilas de . . .? But somehow she would have to change her name to Topazio, or Yesenia, Cristal, Adriana, Stefania, Andrea, something more poetic than Cleófilas. Everything happened to women with names like jewels. But what happened to a Cleófilas? Nothing. But a crack in the face.

Because the doctor has said so. She has to go. To make sure the new baby is all right, so there won't be any problems when he's born, and the appointment card says next Tuesday. Could he please take her. And that's all.

No, she won't mention it. She promises. If the doctor asks she can say she fell down the front steps or slipped when she was out in the backyard, slipped out back, she could tell him that. She has to go back next Tuesday, Juan Pedro, please, for the new baby. For their child.

She could write to her father and ask maybe for money, just a loan, for the new baby's medical expenses. Well then if he'd rather she didn't. All right, she won't. Please don't anymore. Please don't. She knows it's difficult saving money with all the bills they have, but how else are they going to get out of debt with the truck payments? And after the rent and the food and the electricity and the gas and the water and the who-knows-what, well, there's hardly anything left. But please, at least for the doctor visit. She won't ask for anything else. She has to. Why is she so anxious? Because.

Because she is going to make sure the baby is not turned around backward this time to split her down the center. Yes. Next Tuesday at five thirty. I'll have Juan Pedrito dressed and ready. But those are the only shoes he has. I'll polish them, and we'll be ready. As soon as you come from work. We won't make you ashamed.

Felice? It's me, Graciela.

No, I can't talk louder. I'm at work.

Look, I need kind of a favor. There's a patient, a lady here who's got a problem.

Well, wait a minute. Are you listening to me or what?

I can't talk real loud 'cause her husband's in the next room.

Well, would you just listen?

I was going to do this sonogram on her – she's pregnant, right? – and she just starts crying on me. *Híjole*, Felice! This poor lady's got black-and-blue marks all over. I'm not kidding.

From her husband. Who else? Another one of those brides from across the border. And her family's all in Mexico.

Shit. You think they're going to help her? Give me a break. This lady doesn't even speak English. She hasn't been allowed to call home or write or nothing. That's why I'm calling you.

She needs a ride.

Not to Mexico, you goof. Just to the Greyhound. In San Anto.

No, just a ride. She's got her own money. All you'd have to do is drop her off in San Antonio on your way home. Come on, Felice. Please? If we don't help her, who will? I'd drive her myself, but she needs to be on that bus before her husband gets home from work. What do you say?

I don't know. Wait.

Right away, tomorrow even.

Well, if tomorrow's no good for you . . .

It's a date, Felice. Thursday. At the Cash 'n' Carry off I-10. Noon. She'll be ready.

Oh, and her name's Cleófilas.

I don't know. One of those Mexican saints, I guess. A martyr or something.

Cleófilas. C-L-E-O-F-I-L-A-S. Cle. O. Fi. Las. Write it down.

Thanks, Felice. When her kid's born she'll have to name her after us, right?

Yeah, you got it. A regular soap opera sometimes. *Qué vida, comadre. Bueno* bye.

All morning that flutter of half-fear, half-doubt. At any moment Juan Pedro might appear in the doorway. On the street. At the Cash 'n' Carry. Like in the dreams she dreamed.

There was that to think about, yes, until the woman in the pick-up drove up. Then there wasn't time to think about anything but the pick-up pointed toward San Antonio. Put your bags in the back and get in.

But when they drove across the *arroyo*, the driver opened her mouth and let out a yell as loud as any mariachi. Which startled not only Cleófilas, but Juan Pedrito as well.

*Pues*, look how cute. I scared you two, right? Sorry. Should've warned you. Every time I cross that bridge I do that. Because of the name, you know. Woman Hollering. *Pues*, I holler. She said this in a Spanish pocked with English and laughed. Did you ever notice, Felice continued, how nothing around here is named after a woman? Really. Unless she's the Virgin. I guess you're only famous if you're a virgin. She was laughing again.

That's why I like the name of that *arroyo*. Makes you want to holler like Tarzan, right?

Everything about this woman, this Felice, amazed Cleófilas. The fact that she drove a pick-up. A pick-up, mind you, but when Cleófilas asked if it was her husband's, she said she didn't have a husband. The pick-up was hers. She herself had chosen it. She herself was paying for it.

I used to have a Pontiac Sunbird. But those cars are for *viejas*. Pussy cars. Now this here is a *real* car.

What kind of talk was that coming from a woman? Cleófilas thought. But then again, Felice was like no woman she'd ever met. Can you imagine, when we crossed the *arroyo* she just started yelling like a crazy, she would say later to her father and brothers. Just like that. Who would've thought?

Who would've? Pain or rage, perhaps, but not a hoot like the one Felice had just let go. Makes you want to holler like Tarzan, Felice had said.

Then Felice began laughing again, but it wasn't Felice laughing. It was gurgling out of her own throat, a long ribbon of laughter, like water.

# Jacob: the Story of a Faith-healing Priest

*Bessie Head was born in South Africa in 1937 and died in 1986. She is one of Africa's best-known women writers with such novels to her name as* When Rain Clouds Gather, Matu *and* A Question of Power. *Her short-story collections are* Tales of Tenderness and Power *and* The Collector of Treasures, *and she is also the author of one historical account,* Serowe: Village of the Rain Wind.

The quiet, sleepy village of Makaleng was about thirty miles from a big railway station in Northern Botswana. Makaleng village was quiet and sleepy because the people were fat and well fed. Envious visitors to the village often exclaimed that there must be something wrong with the sky overhead, because whilst the rest of the country was smitten by drought year after year, Makaleng village never failed to receive its yearly quota of twenty-two inches of rain. Whenever people stood in groups and shook their heads sadly about another of those summers of no rain and no crops, someone would always interrupt to say:

'But I've just come from Makaleng village. The people there are eating water-melon and fresh green mealies. And from their lands they are about to harvest bags and bags of corn.'

Thus, Makaleng was one of those far-away wonders of the world which people sometimes visited but never thought of inhabiting. It never occurred to people perishing of drought and hunger to rush there in droves, settle there, and produce their crops and raise their cattle in ease and comfort. As it was, good fortune was added to good fortune in Makaleng. The village had a small population of about five hundred people and a big, broad sandy river cut its way through the central part of the village.

In the summer this river flowed in torrents of muddy water, and in winter gigantic pools of water shimmered like mercury in the potholes of its sandy bed.

The summer grass of Makaleng was a miracle too. It shot seven feet high into the sky like a thick, dense jungle which terrified the small boys who herded the cattle. The small boys had a secret joke among themselves about the summer grass of Makaleng. They never set foot in it. Early each morning they would stand at its perimeter and drive the cattle into this dark jungle of stalks and leaves to graze. Once the last swishing tail had disappeared, they would retreat as far as possible, hugging their arms around their bony chests so afraid were they of the terror that lived all summer long in the dense grass. For some hours a deep silence would reign over the grazing area; then all of a sudden, the agonized bellows of the cattle and their mad, stampeding feet would send the birds into the air with startled shrieks and make the cattle-boys jump for their sticks. A ferocious vampire-fly bred in the long grass and pierced its deep, sharp mouth-parts into the skin of either man or beast to suck up the blood. The pain caused by its sting was excruciating. Yet the cattle never seemed to learn. For once they had stampeded out of the grass and had had the flies beaten off them by the cattle-boys, they allowed themselves to be driven back again into this terrible grazing area. And that's how the cattle were grazed all summer. Maybe cattle-grazing in this manner was a hard job, but if so only the small boys who herded the cattle knew it to be so and maybe by sunset, when they herded the cattle home, they had temporarily forgotten the vampire-fly. They laughed and joked among themselves, and as soon as they entered their yards, they started fights with their sisters.

It's not certain what the authorities thought about the village of Makaleng and its good twenty-two inches of rain, or whether the area was suited to agricultural development or not. Someone had muttered something about the soil; it became too easily waterlogged. Nor did the ordinary people of the country visit Makaleng because the people there were eating fresh green mealies in a drought year. Oh no, Makaleng village was famous in the hearts of ordinary people because it had two prophets.

The one prophet, Jacob, lived on the sunrise side of the village. The other prophet, Lebojang, lived on the sunset side. Prophet Jacob was very poor and lived in a mud hut. He walked around with no shoes. Prophet Lebojang was very rich. He lived in a great mansion and drove around in a very posh car.

It was not the habit of Prophet Lebojang to notice the existence of Prophet Jacob, except that on one occasion Prophet Jacob had entered his yard on the death of a relative. But Prophet Jacob attended all funerals from the sympathy and kindness of his heart; he was unperturbed by the cold reception given him by Lebojang and his followers, and the fact that he was overlooked when plates of food were handed round. Much more terrible things had Lebojang done to him on his arrival in Makaleng. There was a time when lightning used to strike the hut of Prophet Jacob, though there was not a cloud in the sky. There was a time when an enormous hissing snake would suddenly manifest itself in the hut of Prophet Jacob, but neither lightning, nor snakes, nor poisoned food and water could take the life of Prophet Jacob. At first, Prophet Jacob had wanted to flee the hatred of Prophet Lebojang, but one night when the persecution and torture had reached its peak, he heard, so he told two close friends, the Voice of his God in the silence of his hut. It said:

'Haven't I always prepared a table for you in the presence of your enemies? Then why don't you trust me to take care of you?'

And that was enough for Prophet Jacob. He no longer feared to stay in Makaleng. It was never quite clear to those who loved Prophet Jacob just who his God was. At times he would refer to him as Jesus. At times his God, in moments of inspiration, appeared to be the width and depth of his own experience and suffering. This he in turn called the Voice which had come to him at all the turning points of his life, forcing him into strange and incomprehensible acts.

There was a time when Prophet Jacob had been as rich a man as Prophet Lebojang. He had been the owner of a store in the big railway village thirty miles from Makaleng. He had had a car, a beautiful wife who loved beautiful clothes, and two pretty daughters. To enable him to give his wife all that she desired, Jacob had even established a big beer-brewing business from which he earned huge profits. After twelve years of this rich and sumptuous living, during which time Jacob drank heavily and lived in the roar of prosperity, a bolt from the blue turned him into a man of rags and tatters overnight. It happened like this: one week his wife had a sudden desire to visit relatives living in another part of the country. She took the two small girls with her and Jacob was left alone. The night of the day of his wife's departure he retired early. At about midnight there was a thunderous, crashing sound at the door. Jacob sprang awake and found his bedroom filled with thieves. Some of the thieves held him down while his hands were tied behind his back and his mouth gagged. As he lay helpless on the floor, the thieves quietly and calmly removed every piece of furniture and clothing from the house. They had already completely emptied the store. All he had left was a few hundred rands in the bank, and he lay there weeping in the darkness. In this darkness and silence he heard the Voice of his God.

'Jacob,' it said quietly, 'why have you forgotten me? It is I who have brought this trouble on you so that you may do my work. From now on you shall only have your daily bread.'

Even though he strained his eyes in the darkness, hoping to get some glimpse of a form which uttered these words, he could see no one. But the words burned into his mind like fire. Not for one moment did he doubt that it was the Voice of his God. And that was enough for Jacob. Amazed neighbours found him the next morning still trussed up and gagged, lying on the floor of his bedroom in the ransacked house behind the ransacked store.

'You must call the police at once,' they said. 'The sooner you report a burglary, the sooner the police will catch up with the thieves.'

But Jacob only stared back at them absentmindedly. His mind had withdrawn itself from preoccupations with business. Besides, how could he explain the truth to them? How could he tell them he had heard a Voice in the night and that the Voice had claimed responsibility for the thefts? Hadn't the Voice said so? It wasn't a matter that could be mentioned to the police either. It was better to remain silent than to tell the truth. The neighbours watching him remain silent and unmoving on the floor, clucked, clucked sympathetically and shook their heads. Among themselves they said:

'This sudden trouble has unhinged the mind of our friend, Jacob. Look, he can't utter a word.'

Some of the women began to weep loudly. They could not forget the days of starvation in their own homes and the way in which Jacob had never turned a hungry child away from his door. Jacob was widely commended as a good man because of his generosity, and their weeping was meant to be an unspoken rebuke to God. Why did he strike down the good man, always? They wept this way when any of their children died and unconsciously created legends about their saintliness.

Two weeks later, Jacob's wife returned to this changed situation. As she breezed into the house with her high-heeled shoes and big, wide, red-painted mouth, it seemed to Jacob that he was seeing the type of woman he had married for the first time. He said to himself: 'I shall tell her the truth. If she is really my wife, she will give up these ways and join me in the work I have to do.'

'Darling,' she gushed, flinging off a brilliant red turban and kicking off her shoes. 'I've already heard the news. All up and down the line people are talking of nothing else. They even say it has unsettled your mind. I said: "Bosh! we'll make it up in no time." And so here I am, all ready to give it a go.'

She paused and looked at him with a brilliant smile. He looked back at her, almost choked with fear. Had they really not communicated with each other throughout these twelve years of married life? Her mood was so foreign, as though their lives had never flowed together. But what really choked him was his own nature which had constantly sought security; he had never loved any other woman because of this desire for emotional security. Now he was to lose this too. Still, he said the fatal words, so gravely and so finally:

'We are not going back to the old ways of trading in liquor,' he said. 'I have to do the work of the Lord.'

She laughed, ha! ha! ha!, in a gay and brittle way. Life had never had any depth for her. She was always in such a rush. She was also a woman of practical common sense with no whims or fancies.

'You aren't serious, darling?' she said, with raised eyebrows.

'I am,' he said.

'But who is this Lord?' she said. 'No one has ever seen him. There's nothing we Africans have but the Lord. We sit down and pray to the Lord all the time but he doesn't bring us one ounce of sugar. It would be a different thing if he came down to earth and we could see him. But no one takes the Lord seriously, darling. He doesn't come down.'

'You may say so,' Jacob replied, 'but I have heard the Voice of the Lord and I cannot disobey it.'

He had in his hand the last R10.000 he had withdrawn from the bank. He handed it to his wife, stood up, and walked out of the empty house not looking back once, not even at his two wide-eyed little girls. The Voice of the Lord had told him to go to Makaleng.

It was not the first time Jacob had tasted wealth and had wealth removed from him, overnight. He was born into wealth. His father was a German who had come to Botswana with an eye to the cattle-speculating business. Many a man had reached near millionairehood on cattle speculating because it was quick, easy money. The German had married a Motswana woman and established a cattle ranch, mostly used as a transit farm for fattening all the lean cattle he bought as a speculation from the local people. The ranch was not many miles from the village of Makaleng and it did not take him many months to organize his cattle business and have thousands of rands in the bank. His wife also bore him twins, two boys – one of whom she named Jacob, and the other Isaac, these names having been obtained from her studies of the Bible. If questioned about this part of his life, Jacob cannot remember it too well. He vaguely remembers wearing shoes and being well clothed and sleeping in a bed with sheets. But of his father and mother he has little recollection. One day, not long after Jacob and Isaac had turned six years old, his father and mother took a trip by car into the village of Makaleng. As they were crossing the narrow bridge which spanned the broad river in a heavy downpour, the car skidded and went over the edge into the muddy torrent below. Both were killed.

As from nowhere, along came an uncle, the brother of Jacob's mother, weeping bitter tears over the death of his sister. He approached a certain chief of Makaleng and offered to act as guardian of the two boys until they were old enough to inherit their father's wealth. What happened subsequently has often made people say that the then chief of Makaleng village had a share in the robbery of the children's inheritance. It was his duty to see that the guardianship of the children was conducted in an honourable way yet, to the many aghast comments from the people of Makaleng, he only turned a deaf ear. The uncle, the brother of Jacob's mother, became overnight the richest man in Makaleng. His brood of twelve children walked about in shoes and socks. He acquired a brick house and a car and was seen to wave about thick wads of money in the hotel bar of the big railway village. On the other hand, his sister's children, Jacob and Isaac, who now lived with him, were seen to walk about the village without shoes, dressed in the discarded rags and tatters of their uncle's children. What little was left after the wholesale slaughter and sale of the fifty thousand cattle was given to the two small boys, Jacob and Isaac, to herd in the traditional way in the vampire-fly, grazing-ground of Makaleng. Not once after that did the uncle's children have to soil their hands with work. They had acquired two slaves.

Those who are born to suffer experience suffering to its abysmal depths. The damage to the two children did not stop at the expropriation of their inheritance. It was now claimed by the uncle and all the relatives that since the children were not pure Batswana by birth, they were therefore of an inferior species. They were fed according to their status. They were given plain porridge with salt and water at every meal, day in and day out, year in and year out. Their sleeping quarters were a ramshackle hut at the bottom of their uncle's yard. They slept on pieces of sacking and lived out their whole lives in that dog house.

Jacob is old now. He relates these experiences of his childhood without bitterness. He will also tell you that his uncle, as though prompted by a subconscious guilt, sent him and his brother to the night school of Makaleng village together with all the small cattle-herding boys who could not attend school during the day. He even remembers the way they were taught to sing the alphabet and clap their hands.

There is a point in his story when you begin to doubt Jacob's sanity and that of his God. Somehow you don't doubt his adult experiences and his conversations with God, but you doubt cruelty and stress placed on a young and helpless child. It's when he tells you about what happened when he was twelve years old that a bad light is thrown on Jacob's God. At this time Jacob's twin brother Isaac died, worn out by the poor diet and hard labour. A deep and terrifying loneliness possessed the heart of the small boy who was left behind that night. He had lost the only living being who had shared some love with him in a world peopled by monsters. There is much said about the love and sharing to be found within tribal societies and much of this is true – but true too is Jacob's uncle. Any child trapped in this cycle of cruelty can find no way out except to cry lonely, hot tears in the dark night.

At this point, says Jacob, while he lay alone in his broken-down hut, weeping, he first heard the Voice of his God.

'Jacob,' it said, 'one day I shall call you to do my work. All the suffering you endure now is but a preparation for the work you have to do.'

Jacob sat up startled, dashing the tears from his eyes. At that time also his eyes searched for a presence or form in the room but there was nothing, only the strong impression of having heard a Voice. You lean forward eagerly towards the now old man; his God seems very dubious, so you ask: did he bring a little piece of meat on the morrow to eat with that dreadful porridge? Did he change the world and give a jersey to a little boy shivering in tattered clothes? To all your questions Jacob responds with a look of baffled surprise. It has not occurred to him to ask his God for anything all these long long years. He has been too busy fulfilling the orders and strange commands of that Voice. It didn't seem as though Jacob's God wanted him to have anything for himself, even when he was little. No meat came. No jersey. It makes you feel something is wrong because even in old age Jacob hasn't got shoes. It makes you feel like breaking down and weeping because even in old age Jacob hasn't got shoes. So you say, almost violently: does he love you, this God? Why do you let him disrupt your life like that?

Jacob keeps silent a moment sorting this out. Then he tells you that every time he heard that Voice a great peace would fill his heart; that peace gave him the courage to do whatever the Voice requested of him. To an outsider there never seemed to be much coherence in what was going on between Jacob and his God. But the way in which he expressed this relationship in deeds arrested the attention. Everything about him was very beautiful and simple and deeply sincere. He had too, one of the oddest churches in the whole wide world.

On his arrival in the village of Makaleng after parting company from his wife, Jacob set about constructing a mud hut which was to be used both as accommodation for himself and his church. His uncle and the chief of

Makaleng who had stolen the inheritance of himself and his brother were long since dead. At the time of his uncle's death the relatives had squabbled and torn each other to pieces over what remained of the wealth which was not theirs. These relatives lived on the sunset side of the village and were the followers of Prophet Lebojang. The relatives, like Prophet Lebojang, affected in public not to be aware of the sudden and unexpected return of Jacob. He had been away from the village for almost fourteen years, having walked out of his uncle's home as soon as he realized that he could stand on his own two feet and earn his living. But secretly, like all thieves, they were at first intensely interested in the activities of Jacob on the sunrise side of the village, fearing that he might still start a commotion about his stolen inheritance. They also knew about all the black-magic spells Prophet Lebojang was casting on Prophet Jacob. No one quite knew why Prophet Lebojang did not have Prophet Jacob killed outright once the black-magic powers had failed to destroy him. Some think that the Voice of Prophet Jacob's God might have spoken to Prophet Lebojang and told him under no circumstances to harm Prophet Jacob. This was a rumour in the village, said to have issued from the mouth of Prophet Lebojang.

But the activities of Prophet Jacob on the sunrise side of the village soon had the relatives and Prophet Lebojang rolling on the ground with laughter. After he had completed his hut, Prophet Jacob purchased for himself some cheap material which he shaped into a priestly cloak and in one corner pinned a small cross. He next made a wooden table and carved three wooden candlesticks. Those candlesticks he placed on the table and always, when he wanted to pray, he placed a jug of fresh, clean water near the candlesticks. Curious people would often question him about the water jug and he would reply simply that his God had ordered him to put the water there. After each session of prayer, he was to put the water in bottles and then give it freely to anyone who suffered from ailments or sorrow. His God had assured him that the blessed water would remove all people's troubles.

It took great simplicity of heart to approach a church such as the one conducted by Prophet Jacob. Prophet Jacob had no shoes, so he conducted his services in his bare feet. Many, many strange churches, variants on the Christian religion, exist in Botswana but they all have a bit of glitter and dash. They have funds behind them. Sometimes, like Prophet Lebojang, they put both God and the Devil on the same altar for many years and nothing happens except a great increase in wealth. In contrast to all of them, Prophet Jacob only had the Voice of his God, whom he obeyed. From this Voice he received the strictest orders about how to conduct himself. He was never, never under any circumstances to canvass for membership. People would be sent to him. Also, the bare minimum for his daily bread would be given him and this he must break in half and share with whomsoever should step in the door. From these commands Prophet Jacob never deviated one inch.

The next surprise Jacob received was the type of congregation sent to him by his God. One afternoon, towards sunset, as Jacob sat in the silence of his hut, the door was slowly pushed open and six small black heads peered cautiously in.

'We have come to the church, *maruti*,'* the children said.

Jacob leapt to his feet in great joy and hastened to put on his cloak. The words of the children corresponded to a dream he had had. In the dream he had sung a song. It went like this:

> *Look, I shall be coming again on clouds of glory,*
> *When you see me children,*
> *You must say: Dumelang! Allelujah!*

The song had a very gay rhythm. The little girls got carried away by it, their skirts swishing up and down as they kept time to the beat by clapping their hands vigorously. From that day onwards there was a never-ending bustle of activity in the yard of Jacob, and these activities spread themselves throughout the whole of the sunrise side of the village. The children constantly brought him information of someone ailing there, someone ailing here, and soon it became a not uncommon sight to see Jacob trailing behind a group of children, all singing and making their way to a hut to help someone in sorrow. In all cases the sorrow or ailments would be removed and people would quietly rise up and go about their daily business.

After the first reaction of surprised amusement, no one paid much

*Maruti: a priest.

attention to the church of Jacob because of his poverty and because his congregation was composed entirely of children. No adults joined the church, though through the efforts of the children many of them received a blessing from Jacob's God. A few would approach Jacob wistfully and ask to become members of his church, but he would always reply:

'Please first go to your *maruti* and ask his permission.'

This permission was never granted. Yet Jacob's reputation spread quietly and persistently; people pointed out his goodness to like-minded people. Thus, when the lorry brought visitors to Makaleng, half the people made their way to the hut of Jacob and half to the mansion of Lebojang. It was almost as though there were no meeting place between the people who went to Jacob and the people who went to Lebojang. Lebojang's relationship with people was that of a businessman. You paid your money and that was that.

If you dressed well and looked rich, a servant would immediately approach you and lead you into Lebojang's plush lounge. There you would be constantly plied with all the good things from Lebojang's pantry until he was free to interview you. If you were in rags and tatters, you sat out all day in the yard and, the interview being over, you would then wander about the village in search of provisions. Lebojang enriched himself from rich and poor alike but he only gave the good things in his pantry to those who had the least need of them. But whether rich or poor, all came to Lebojang for the same purpose – to make use of his stunning powers.

A woman would travel many miles to report to Lebojang that for a long time she had concealed a purse of money under her mattress. One day she had found the purse of money removed and it had been impossible to trace the thief. Lebojang would keep silent awhile, then fix his penetrating eyes on the woman.

'Do you have a friend named Bontle?' he would ask. And the amazed woman would merely nod her head.

'Well,' Lebojang would say. 'It is she who stole your purse on the twenty-fifth of February.'

Or again, a woman would say that she had no end of trouble from her husband, who had suddenly taken to drinking heavily. And Lebojang would say:

'Does he have a friend named Toto? Well, this Toto has one aim in mind and that is to take you as his sweetheart. Therefore he leads your husband to drink.'

Such was the power of Lebojang; he would come out with names and dates and prophecies. His charges for these services were very high. It did not matter to him that people were secretly poisoned or driven mad by his prophecies; he simply took his money and that was that. But at least these prophecies of names and dates could bear the light of day. Once his other deeds became known people were to ponder deeply on the nature of evil.

The other half of the lorry-load of visitors to Makaleng had no tales of lost purses or drunken husbands but a terrible anguish of heart. They said to Jacob:

'I have so many troubles. I don't know how to sort them out.'

The practical issues were never discussed. A man in that gathering would have no work for a year and his family would be destitute. After seeing Jacob and participating in the worship of his church, the man would strike a job in two or three days; not anything spectacular, but his poverty would be eased. There was something else too that developed in a quite natural way – an exchange of gifts system. No one ever left Jacob's hut without a parcel. Many grateful seekers of help brought gifts to Jacob; a bag of corn, a bag of sugar, a box of eggs, and so on. These gifts in turn filled many destitute people with good things so that they did not leave Jacob's home hungry. Then, too, the church really belonged to the children. They would come in towards the close of day, and the adults would sit to one side as respectful spectators while Jacob and the children conversed with the Lord. No one seemed to question the uniqueness of this, how it was possible for children, at the age when their teeth fall out, to turn up promptly at sunset for sermons. Not that they comprehended anything, not even Jacob's simple sermons.

So, in this way, following their two strange occupations, a routine and ritual established itself around the lives of the prophets of Makaleng. Prophet Lebojang increased in wealth, until it was said at the time he met his doom that he was a near-millionaire. Prophet Jacob increased only in his love for the Lord. Seemingly, in gratitude for this, the Lord arranged one more turning point in the life of Prophet Jacob. After many years of living alone, the Lord sent him a wife named Johannah.

*

Johannah was a tall, striking handsome woman with a beautifully carved mouth around which a faint smile always lingered. She also had a thick cluster of eyelashes around her pitch-black eyes. These two striking features had brought her lots of trouble. She was the sort of woman men would look at twice. Less attractive women were more in tune with the feeling of the times; there was no such thing as marriage left. Johannah had always received proposals of marriage and produced four children always with a view to marrying their fathers, but at the critical moment, the man simply disappeared.

For some years Johannah lived in the yard of her elder brother, who was married. Because of her position as an unmarried woman with children, she assumed the major responsibilities of running the home; washing, cooking for the family and mending the clothes of her brother's children as well as her own. Her brother's wife never soiled her hands with work; either she lay in bed until eleven o'clock in the morning or stood up, dressed herself in smart clothes and spent the day visiting relatives and friends. At least, Johannah reasoned, there was no need for her brother to employ a servant for his fancy wife. Johannah was careful to see that there was no waste in food and other household expenses. In spite of all the services she offered, her brother's manner abruptly changed towards her. He was often angry and impatient with his sister because he was nagged by his wife who had said to him:

'Two of Johannah's children have now reached school-going age. Are you going to foot the bill?'

Thus it was that Johannah found herself confronted by a family conference. Relatives gathered in the yard and to them Johannah's brother put his complaint; he could not afford to support all Johannah's children as well as his own. They spent some time discussing her misdeeds with rising wrath, flinging around such terms as harlot and loose woman who took her sins lightly. Johannah listened to it all with an amused smile, especially her sister-in-law's loud, irate tone. Once Johannah was no longer in the yard would she do all the housework? At last Johannah was allowed to speak. She raised her head proudly and quoted an old proverb:

'I agree with all that has been said about me,' she said. 'But I am a real woman and, as the saying goes, the children of a real woman do not get lean or die.'

Johannah spent many days wandering hither and thither in search of employment but without success. It was during her wanderings from home to home for possible employment as a house servant that she was told about the Prophet Jacob of Makaleng village who had brought work and comfort to the hearts of many people. One morning before dawn she set out on foot to the village of Makaleng, arriving there about mid-morning.

Like all the visitors to Prophet Jacob, she did not notice his poverty or the simplicity of his church but right away began confiding the troubles and disappointments of her life. Now and then she would cry a little as she recalled one promise of marriage after another and then the stress of being left alone with fatherless children. She cried in such a peculiar way that even Jacob, who was concentrating his mind on her tale of sorrow, diverted his attention to her tears. They kept welling up in abrupt little bundles which were then caught in the thick cluster of her eyelashes and deposited neatly into her lap. Not one splash soiled the smooth curved surface of her cheekbones. They were very much an expression of the concentrated emotional intensity of the woman, as though, like her tears, she only saw one thing at a time, in the immediate present, and could not be troubled much about the past. He noted that it was only on actually recalling a disillusionment in words that an abrupt bundle of tears would appear; everything about her was open and straightforward.

'I have come to see that the faults are all mine,' she said. 'Each time it was I who believed that the father of my child would marry me. I have paid heavily for this error of judgement. But the saying is still there: the children of a real woman cannot fall into the fire.'

Then she lapsed into an abrupt waiting silence, keeping her pretty eyes in a steadfast gaze on her lap. Jacob also hesitated. She was the only visitor of the day and she had arrived early. He never said prayers for visitors without the children, as they were now an inextricable part of his life. Perhaps the woman would like to prepare some food for herself? She looked extremely hungry.

'Yes, indeed,' he said, slowly. 'There are many good sayings in the world. There is the saying that the foot cannot always find its way home. It may be that I should pass your village one day and be afflicted by hunger. You would soon rush to the cooking pot to prepare something for me. Therefore I am paying you for this kindness before it is done. In the corner you will find a bag of corn and next to that a dish of meat. Prepare some food and eat.'

A brief expression of pleased surprise flitted across the woman's face. She arose in one neat, self-contained movement and set about to do as he had ordered with a grave, absorbed manner.

'So it's true,' she thought, as she dipped into the bag of corn. 'The man's goodness is expressed in deeds as well as words. How lucky for me that I took this journey. My sorrows are taken away from me this very minute.'

She had far to go on the return journey and without much waste of time Jacob sent a message to the children so that as soon as she had eaten she might receive the prayers and blessed water. In the twinkling of an eye the yard was filled from all directions with rushing feet. Johannah paused in the act of stirring the porridge to stare at the children in amazement. So this was true too; the Prophet kept a church of children. The woman who had told her this had merely shrugged and smiled. Most curious people had, out of a profound respect for Prophet Jacob, refrained from questioning him about this matter.

'I shall certainly bring my children to this church,' Johannah thought to herself. 'There is only goodness here.'

An hour later Johannah was on her way home with a swift, light step. It seemed as though a soft wind blew her home. On her head she carried a quantity of corn for herself and her children and some eggs, sugar, and tea. In her heart she carried a vivid memory of the children's singing.

'How lucky I am,' she thought. 'How wonderful this day has been.'

Alone that night in his hut Jacob found that a wandering mood possessed him. It was always the hour when his soul had soared in peace and freedom, detached from the cares of the day. But on this night it remained firmly on the earth, amusing and entertaining itself with trifles. At first it said:

'Oh, so people cry in all kinds of different ways. Some cry as though they are spitting tears out on to the dry ground.'

Then he would catch himself at this trifling amusement and mutter aloud:

'But I am in old age now. I must be fifty-five,' and he would sigh heavily thinking of his creeping old age. Then the game would start again:

'Porridge is always porridge but some people are better at cooking it than others . . .'

This went on for some time and Jacob was unaware that he was actually smiling to himself. This state of affairs was suddenly interrupted by the Voice of his God sounding loudly and clearly in his ears. It said:

'You are a very foolish man Jacob. How could you let your future wife depart so quickly?'

Being somewhat caught off-balance, for the first time Jacob replied to his God. He said:

'But I am already in old age. She looks about twenty-nine.'

And he turned with a startled expression and stared over his shoulder. But there was no further sound except . . . except an impression of soft laughter. Feeling shaken and confused, Jacob stood up and prepared his blankets on the floor.

A month went by and then one Sunday morning Johannah arrived once again with the early-morning lorry-load of visitors to Makaleng, this time bringing her four children with her. She looked very smart in a new cotton frock and brand-new low-heeled shoes. Just a day after she had paid her first visit to Prophet Jacob, she had found a job as a cook and house-keeper for a wealthy person for R10.00 a month. Somehow Prophet Jacob had already known in his heart of her coming, but since the other visitors who also crowded into his yard did not know this secret of his heart there was no one to point out that Prophet Jacob pointedly omitted to gaze in the direction of Johannah. But there was an intense joy in his heart and a glow like a candle flame in his eyes. The joy in the heart of Prophet Jacob soon affected everyone. A surprise feast was arranged on the spur of the moment. Someone suddenly walked out and bought a goat, another rice, and another some vegetables for salad, while the women ran about making preparations for the feast. The children also appeared with their freshly scrubbed faces and clean Sunday clothes and sat among the guests clapping their hands and singing the songs taught to them by Jacob. The villagers of Makaleng were amazed. Never had they heard such a commo-tion issue from the yard of Prophet Jacob.

'Perhaps Prophet Jacob is holding a marriage feast,' they said. 'Perhaps one of his visitors is getting married.'

And they hastened to wash and make their way to the yard of Prophet Jacob. But no bride and groom were in evidence. There was only joy. Not even prayers were said that day, nor was anyone given the blessed water. Each one was blessed by the joy in his own heart. By sunset, when the lorry turned up to take the visitors back to their own villages, no one wanted to leave. At last the lorry driver had to get out of his lorry and scold the people.

'Look here, people,' he shouted, 'no one pays me for overtime. I have to get back to my wife and children.'

With many wistful, lingering glances, the visitors slowly climbed into the lorry. They kept on repeating to themselves that they would surely visit Prophet Jacob the following Sunday. Since Prophet Jacob was so foolhardy as to omit gazing in any direction that might contain the presence of Johannah, he failed to see that she was not present among the visitors who climbed on to the lorry. But he stood for a long while gazing after it until the flaming red sun dropped down behind the flat horizon. The darkness and gloom that swept down on his heart was like the sudden descent of the black night on Makaleng. He sighed heavily and slowly shuffled towards his lonely hut. It was a good thing for Prophet Jacob that he had a strong heart, for as he pushed open the door of his hut the flaming sun reversed itself and shone again like a dazzling light in the gloom. There was Johannah seated on the floor with her children. Prophet Jacob could not utter a word. He stood for a long while at the door like one stunned. Johannah cried many bundles of neat tears because she could not account for her actions, only that it seemed like her death to climb into the lorry and go away. But, being fearful of this silence, she said painfully:

'You must forgive me. I am so happy here.'

Imagine the amazement of the villagers of Makaleng! That following Monday morning they had to rub their eyes in disbelief and doubt their sanity, for there was Prophet Jacob in his yard with a woman constructing a mud hut. Prophet Jacob had been celibate for so long that they had ceased to regard him as a normal man. Some of the scandalmongers of the village, hoping to get the full details of this unexpected development, immediately picked up their hoes and dishes and made their way to the yard of Prophet Jacob to help in the construction of the hut. By midday the walls were complete and Prophet Jacob had already set up the framework for the thatched roof. The scandalmongers were entertained that afternoon by all the women of the village.

'It's true,' they said. 'Prophet Jacob has acquired a new wife.'

Once the impact of it struck their sense of humour, they began to roll on the ground, laughing till the tears poured out of their eyes. In this manner it became an accepted fact that Johannah was the legal wife of Prophet Jacob.

As for Jacob, a whole new world of learning and living opened up for him. He soon found that his home was run peacefully, with clockwork precision, by a woman full of the traditions and customs of the country. Jacob had little knowledge of these customs as his upbringing had been that of an outcast living apart from the household and it was as though he was transported back into a childhood he might have had had his mother lived. His first wife had been a very different type of woman from Johannah, very modern and daring and very detribalized. If there were such things as customs which governed the behaviour of children and adults, she knew nothing about this. Now, from Johannah, he was to learn that there were strict, hard-and-fast laws governing the conduct of family life. In spite of Johannah having produced so many fatherless children, she had indoctrinated them all with the customs of her own childhood so that they were among the most disciplined children on earth. It was an easy, almost effortless act for the children to accept Jacob as their father because, according to custom, all adult people were regarded as the mothers and fathers of all children.

Jacob was amazed to note how nothing was ever out of place in his home, in spite of its having been invaded so suddenly by so many children. If a guest arrived and was served tea, it would not be long before one of the children appeared and removed the forgotten tea-tray from the floor. Then the cups and pots would be immediately rinsed out and stacked neatly away. There was always a quiet hustle and bustle to and fro. There were always chores for the little girls and boys. There was always wood and water to fetch, corn to stamp and floors to sweep, and never for a moment did the children sit idle during the daylight. Thinking of the hardship of his own childhood when he had longed to play, Jacob one day questioned his wife:

'Why so much work for the children?' he asked. 'When do they have time to play?'

She kept silent a while, staring steadfastly into her lap. Then she said, smiling faintly:

'We must teach the children the real things, husband. Is life play? No, it is hardship. Therefore it's better for the children to learn this lesson while young so that they will stand up to the hardship.'

There seemed to be much sense in her reasoning, yet it made Jacob ponder about the eagerness with which the children attended his church. It seemed to him then that his church was the only place in which they could relax, sing, and play together. He determined to have no more sermons, only singing and play. Perhaps the Lord had seen all the hardships children endured. But he did not mention this to his wife as half his mind approved of the way she brought up the children. Half of the customs too agreed with the many good things the Lord had pointed out to Jacob. From their mother's training, they broke the crust of bread and shared it equally with each other or any other child who happened to be passing by. Jacob pondered on all these things shown him by his new wife, and also the customs which she followed so strictly to teach her children the correct way of living with others.

One other thing caused a stir of amazement in Makaleng village. Jacob now had a family but his occupation brought him no funds. There were two boys of school-going age who needed clothes and school fees. Therefore Jacob spent each morning doing odd jobs about the village to have a small amount of money in hand for whatever his family might need. The women of the village said Johannah was indeed blessed to have such a good man. If Prophet Jacob had condescended to be a priest like Prophet Lebojang, he could have got people to contribute handsomely to his church. But Prophet Jacob always said: 'Please get permission from your *maruti* before you join my church.' And which priest would give this permission when it meant losing one of his pay packets?

Not long after these discussions of the people of Makaleng, the world came crashing down on Prophet Lebojang. It all began simply enough. A certain man of Makaleng village, named Kelepile, was detained on business in the big railway village thirty miles away. He had missed the last transport home and decided to make the journey by foot. As he approached Makaleng he noticed a big car parked on one side of the road and from the bushes nearby he heard voices raised in argument. Being merely curious about what people could be doing in the bushes at night, he turned and crept near. Soon he was able to hear the conversation quite clearly.

An alien voice was saying: 'It's always the case with you, Lebojang. You always want the best parts of the body.'

Lebojang appeared to be very cross. He said, 'I'm telling you, Bogosi, you won't get the money if you don't hand the heart over to me.'

The man, Kelepile, waited to hear no more. In fact, his legs were shaking with terror. He has often said that he cannot recollect how they brought him with such speed into Makaleng village. He knew well enough that the conversation was about a ritual murder, just committed. The first thought in his mind had been to save his own life but to his amazement he found his shaking legs taking him to the police station. And this was how it came about that the police surrounded Lebojang and two other men, one of whom was a witch-doctor by profession and the other a chief. They arrested the three men with the cut-up parts of a dead child in their hands. This was the first time that the doers of these evil deeds had been caught in the act. Often the mutilated bodies were found but the murderers were seldom caught.

The position was desperate. The chief and witch-doctor immediately turned state witness and shifted the blame to Lebojang. The witch-doctor was so obliging as to point out to the authorities the graves of twenty other victims to fix the case against Lebojang. They said they did this sort of murder to make potions for the cattle of rich men, like the chief, to increase. Lebojang could even make rain. Lebojang's potions had long been recommended as the best in the land. He had been making these potions and killing men, women and children for twenty years. He had also been the priest of a Christian church with a big blue cross down the back of his cloak.

Lebojang was sentenced to death. But the story did not end there. A strange thing happened after Lebojang's death. People say the soul of

Lebojang returned from the grave. At night, it kept on knocking on the doors of all the people to whom he had sold potions. Some of these people packed their belongings and fled. Some went insane. Some people also say that Lebojang's soul is like that of Lazarus. Lebojang only wanted to tell the people whom he awoke at night – his fellow ritual murderers – to desist from taking the lives of people because of the agony he was suffering now.

# Cream Sauce

*Mary Flanagan is Irish but grew up in New Hampshire. After graduating with a degree in history of art from Brandeis University, she spent three years working for a New York publisher before emigrating to England in 1969. She began writing fiction at thirty-six and in 1984 published a collection of short stories,* Bad Girls. *Her first novel,* Trust, *was published in 1987, and this was followed by* Rose Reason *in 1991.*

Lydia may not have been the world's greatest cook, but she was almost certainly the slowest. She was a fantasizer and a drunk. Moreover, she was addicted to opera. Now imagine what mealtimes at 99 Copenhagen Crescent, NW3, must have been like: tantalizing aromas accompanied by interminable waits, Callas at full decibels, the ever-present bottle of Bordeaux, the not infrequent failures which must, out of sheer physical necessity, be consumed. Her family suffered patiently.

Perhaps patiently is not the word. Perhaps their resignation grew out of causes less saintly. Elliot, for instance, was unaware of time. Of course he was unaware of time, he was a historian. How could he understand the way time siphoned off one's vital energies? While Lydia battled mundanities he lived in his study, in his mind, in the world of spirit. Eternal vistas spread themselves before *him*. Consequently, Elliot was contemptuous of other people's bad humour. Rosie and Danton, seven and ten, were engaged alternately in their charming and vicious pursuits. The world, as it should do, enthralled them, and they showed no symptoms of introversion. It occurred to Lydia that R. D. Laing would have approved of their ungovernable individualism. She supposed, wearily, that upon this she was to be congratulated.

The three of them were continually, passionately, occupied. For such types the arrival of dinner at ten thirty p.m. did not constitute disaster or even discomfort. Video games, the collapse of the Byzantine Empire, Kermit the Frog, Plato's dream or the healthy release of aggression through punching, kicking and hair pulling assure constant diversion. Actions and ideas succeed each other in a wonderful flow, each melting into the next, all things gorgeously merging to create escape. There is no waiting, for time has ceased.

Lydia sensed that only she was trapped in the disparate, in the continual performance of petty but obligatory actions which are dispensed with only in certain dreams; banal processes which must be got through and which served to keep the others afloat in their selfish personal happiness: the sorting of laundry snatched up, worn, and discarded without a thought; telephone calls to the dentist, the gas board, the plumber; the organizing of the myriad details involved in transporting two small beings from one point to another and back again; the picking up and putting away of ever-reappearing objects; the hopeless watching of a billion dust particles resettling upon a hundred scratched surfaces. Details that never meant anything. Details that required the pushing of oneself forward through time, that were a constant reminder of time. Details that made one tense, tense, tense.

'I need a loving man.' Lydia stirred the roux with one hand and refilled her glass of Médoc with the other. It was eight thirty.

She had begun life as a reasonable enough person. She had a brain, an engaging manner, and an abundance of finer feelings. But she was half-educated. The ground had been tilled and the seeds planted. Initial growth was well under way. Then, with marriage, cultivation had abruptly ceased. The result was a leggy vegetable entanglement, clamouring and competing for the limited nourishment available. She read when she could – novels and Shakespeare – and listened to opera. But everything she read and heard became somehow mixed up with dreams of the past and impossible plans for the future. How sad, how desperately sad, to be an undisciplined woman with a head full of notions. Even though some, she felt sure, were brilliant, they were, like everything else, disparate. They could not be marketed as a world view, neither could they be a world. Besides, synthesis was Elliot's department. He had staked out his territory there years ago.

It was eight forty. Danton was practising the trumpet. Rosie began to scream. She screamed and screamed and would not stop screaming. Something shattered and she stopped screaming. But Lydia could not leave the sauce, it was the critical moment. She had only just added the hot fish stock. Besides, screams could mean anything. More than likely they were screams of delight. Lydia had drunk a bottle and a half and had entered into that state where nothing mattered but the music and the memories and the *velouté* which she stirred slowly with a wooden spoon, as in a dream.

It was a quarter to nine. In any proper London middle-class household, the children would have been asleep long ago, tucked up in bed after their tea of fish fingers or cornflakes or Sainsbury fruit yoghurts – followed by the obligatory satsuma. Here the kiddipoos watched X-rated films and jumped on the bed while awaiting their Cordon Bleu repast. And what for? Whatever for, Lydia wondered, when sausages and eggs would have suited them better? It would come to that for them all if she weren't careful and failed to curb this lust for culinary elaboration, these endless preparations which began at six and continued, often, for five hours. And this after a day of details and tension and the nightmare intimacy of family life.

'I need a rich man.'

She had been forced to let Mrs Gladstone go. Since Newton and Schreiber had put back Elliot's book until the autumn (what *were* they supposed to live on now that the meagre advance had been gobbled up?) and the bank was getting ratty about the overdraft, she had been doing all the housekeeping herself. The accumulation of tasks and trivia doubled.

Elliot was a terrible business man, his beautiful mind the prey of perfidious publishers who held back his royalties to gain themselves a few pounds' extra interest at the bank. A Philistine Dutchman with a Swiss contract owed him thousands, but was Elliot bothered? Did he wake in the night consumed by anxiety and visions of deprivation? Not he. He worked on and slept on, too convinced of his own worth to stoop to bitter recriminations, let alone a lawsuit. His complacency was inhuman. He held to his theory (a cyclical, metaphysical, transcendent, and somewhat obfuscating view of history) and kept turning out his four-hundred-page books some of which, to everyone's surprise, sold.

The children grew up hyperactively. All three were having fun. But she, Lydia, had no fun, no theory, no privacy, no precious time. She was the semi-educated wife of a semi-famous man.

'"Being your slave, what should I do but tend upon the hours and times of your desire . . ."'

Elliot came into the kitchen holding an empty glass.

'Um – what?'

'I said I have no precious time at all.' She arranged the mussels around the fillets of sole.

'Excuse me, Liddy, you've had since six, I believe.' He took a handful of freshly sliced mushrooms, tilted back his fine big head (so full of brains), and ate them. He was always taking her freshly sliced or freshly grated or freshly chopped whatevers and flagrantly devouring them. It infuriated her, especially when she was forced to weigh and measure all over again.

'I usually start at six. That's when I'm allowed a glass of wine. You know that. How's the fall of Constantinople?'

'Fitting in fantastically.'

'Confirming all presuppositions?'

'Why not?' He reached for her pile of dainty pink shrimp. '*Sole dieppoise* tonight, I see.' She stayed his hand.

'Sorry, Lid. They taste better when they're stolen.' He smiled. For a split second she liked him.

'Why was Rosie screaming?' she asked.

'Was she screaming?'

'There was some horrendous crash.'

'How could I tell above Cavaradossi's howls of agony?'

Lydia was in a Puccini phase and had been listening to nothing but *Tosca* for the past three nights. Her life began at six p.m. The world-without-end hour. It began with the first glass of Bordeaux, with the first act of *Così fan tutte* or *Rhinegold*. Then she took possession of her personal domain: the kitchen, symbol of slavery, sanctuary, scene of liberation. Cooking, that blessedly inexact science, was the sole activity that sustained her. She actually looked forward to it through days of accumulated details and disparate, obligatory actions. It was her only art. As she drank and half-listened and half-remembered, everything inside her began to melt like butter in a bain-marie. She beautifully fell apart, a kind of automatic pilot took control of the dinner and left her fancy-free to roam through love and art and endless possibilities. There were moments of peace. Nothing else in her life quite did that for her. No wonder she sought to extend her evening's allotted span through overelaboration, and to master even more arcane dishes.

Elliot poured himself a glass of wine and picked up the newspaper. Oh no, he was sitting down at the kitchen table. He meant to rest his big brain by feeding it yet more information. And when her back was turned he would come and steal the shrimp. She hated the intrusion, but what could she do? People want to be in the kitchen. It's warmth and mother and life itself.

'Everything takes place here now,' Lydia thought. 'The drawing-room as scene of the action is finished. Even the bedroom, maybe, is finished. Dramas are written about kitchens, whole tragedies and farces played out in them. People double the size of their kitchens, allowing them to engulf lounges and dining-rooms; they move divans into them, set up stereo speakers. We've done the same, and at my insistence. I've opened up my theatre of operations and let in the world, damn me.' She remembered with a shudder the dinner parties she once gave, especially after Elliot's first book was published and there was such a kerfuffle. All those acquaintances swanning about, gossiping, making half-hearted offers of help, not listening to the Wagner or the Strauss, taking up her precious time. What nuisances they were and how nervous they made her. How she would long for an endless February night like this, cold outside, safe inside, alone with her cooker and her preparations. Well, all artists wished to be left alone.

It was nine fifteen. Slowly she beat the *velouté* into a mixture of egg yolks and cream then returned it to the pan. She looked through the steamy window above the sink. The moon was rising behind the branches of a bare lime tree at the end of the garden. Maria was singing '*Vissi d'arte*' as the sauce maintained a slow simmer in the bain-marie. ('Slow simmering is the secret. Allows the sauce to mature. Others skip the process, but it's essential. Let it imperceptibly thicken. Slower the better.') The previously poached sole and mussels were warm in their dish. Around her lay the numerous pots and utensils: gratin dish, sauté pan, *hachoir*, mandoline, *chinois*, various *pöelons*. The shelves were lined with ramekins, tins, flan rings, *marmites*, *diables*, and carving boards of all sizes and depths of wear. High above them stood preserving jars of fruit conserves, plums in eau-de-vie, mustard and dill pickles, piccalilli, green beans, jugged hare, and earthenware jars of preserved goose and pork. Copper moulds and timbales decked the walls. The wooden-spoon collection was formidable. Bulging from a shelf of their own were the fat greasy cookbooks whose authors were her intimate friends – Elizabeth, Julia, Louisette, Robert, Maurice, Arabella. The whole scene swam in a warm and fragrant vapour. Just for a moment life was beautiful.

'"A supernova explosion was sighted by Chinese astronomers in 1054."'

Lydia started. She had become lost in a recipe for hare with chocolate, which she had never tried and was calculating might be right for next Tuesday, simultaneously entertaining a recollection of Sidney, who had been her lover thirteen years ago. She had forgotten that Elliot was in the room.

'Dear God, he's going to edit *The Times* for me, I know it. I can feel it coming, he's in that kind of mood, his nearest approximation to expansive sociability.' She began to snap her way through a mound of haricot vert.

He read to her of the bomb, the Beirut massacres, and education vouchers, explaining for the hundredth time the way in which they all verified his theory of historical recurrence.

What a gifted exploiter he was. Could he let nothing be without forcing it to confirm his beautiful concept? Could nothing simply ramble loose, straying in its own pleasant anarchy? He was a mighty hunter was old Elliot. The moment he spied a vagrant thought, a vagrant person or event, bam! it was caught fast in the snare of, zip! it was under the net of his World View. He was inescapable, he was naïve, he was strong. He did not fret over electricity bills or train schedules or supermarket queues or holes in tights or nosebleeds or one lost mitten. What did details that consumed a thousand precious moments matter to him, snug as he was in the armour of his Idea? In his quiet way he was quite a deadly person, really.

'I need a charming man.' It was nine twenty-five.

Rosie ran into the kitchen emitting little ceaseless piccolo shrieks that were enough to shatter the eardrum.

'Danton's murdering me, he's murdering me! Oh help, help! Mummy, Elliot! Eek! Eek! Eek!'

She fell to the floor, clasping Lydia's knees, kicking and yelling as Danton beat her determinedly with a bunch of daffodils. Elliot continued to read aloud from a review by John Carey.

'Children!' Lydia shouted. 'My flowers, my sauce, ouch goddammit, my foot! *Will* you stop. Rosie, let go of me, *let go*!' She snapped a tea-towel at Rosie, who was crouched between her legs and the warming drawer, and tried without success to rescue the daffodils. Danton escaped her and ran from the room with a lunatic giggle. She managed, now in a rage, to catch hold of Rosie by the back of her jumper. As she reached out to slap her daughter's bottom, her head struck the overhead dish drainer and dislodged three saucers, two breakfast cups, and a plate which had been left her by her aunt. They shattered all over the floor as the saucepan toppled into the bain-marie.

'"The error arose in the determination of the structure of a gene of a tumour-causing virus in chickens." What turkeys these scientists are.'

Rosie howled. She ran to her father and clung to him in brilliantly simulated terror. Lydia seized the last two plates from the dish drainer and hurled them on to the floor.

'What is it, sweetie, what is it, my pet? There now, there now, what's upset my diddums so?' Elliot put down the paper at last and was caressing the inconsolable Rosie. 'Dear me, Lydia,' he was a little sharp, 'what's going on? Is all this really necessary? *Must* you be so nervous?'

'It's grief. It comes from grief.' She was down on her hands and knees, picking up the pieces, weeping and brushing her lank hair back from her face. 'Don't you remember? I mean, you're meant to be the Intellect. You read me that article', she wiped her nose on the back of her hand, 'that said how women retain the effects of every loss, every hurt.' Elliot sighed. 'That something inside them never forgets and never gets over any of it. The American psychologist – God, you read it to me, what *was* her name? It's all grief, unexpressed grief! And the sauce is ruined, I'll have to start it again. Anyway, I've stopped now. Look, I'm not crying, I'm not nervous, I'll start again. I'm sorry, sorry, sorry. Oh, Rosie!'

She tried to embrace her little girl, but Rosie was having none of it and wriggled indignantly away. A moment later she heard her laughing with Danton over a game of 'Operation'.

Elliot took up the *Guardian*, ignoring his wife's pathetic chagrin. 'If only you realized, Lydia, how contagious your hysteria is.'

'I'm sorry. I'm nervous. It comes from grief.'

He did not ask her over what it was she grieved. 'And you, remember? You told me yourself, Elliot, that there are ions or something in the brain, and these ions migrate, the sodium and the potassium –'

'Yes, yes.'

'And when they migrate from the brain to the bloodstream you've got manic depression, that's what you've got, and women are 400 per cent more prone to manic depression than men, and it's all the fault of those bloody ions.'

'Perhaps if the children were fed a bit earlier. It doesn't necessarily imply rejection, you know. Just because you had tea with the terrier for ten years . . .' He continued reading, this time in silence.

'The children are like that all day,' she started to say, but was defeated by his total lack of response. She turned the record over, got a fresh pan from the cupboard, and started the sauce again. It was nine thirty.

Interruptions, interruptions. Everything in life, even love, even children, was an interruption. All she wished for, like any artist, was to be left alone to wander inside herself, growing and rambling without restraint. Surely all souls must yearn for this simple, precious freedom.

As the butter melted she opened another bottle of wine. Elliot, without glancing up, held out his glass for a refill. Lydia looked with hatred at his composed, concentrating features.

'"I have no precious time at all to spend, nor services to do till you require."' She poured his wine.

Of course she spent too much money on it and on the ingredients for these fancy, unappreciated dinners. The overdraft, the mortal mortgage, the unpaid royalties, the bill from Berry Brothers and Rudd. What horror. But she could never give up the wine. She couldn't even switch to a Rioja or a Côtes du Rhone. Only Bordeaux really did it to her, took her where she wanted to go. It was her passport to privacy. Still, no more Margaux, she must make do with Good Ordinary Claret next time. Perhaps add

Perrier. But not tonight. Tonight she was too nervous. Tonight the ions were migrating.

She checked the potatoes. They were fine. Vegetables must appear as a separate course. '"One doesn't want them floating about the plate and getting mixed up with the sauce."' Of course that meant more dishes to wash and only maddened her in the morning.

'I need a *young* man.' Like Sidney, oh like Sidney, her lovely, her only New York Jew. Once more she sought his fugitive image: brown-eyed, olive-skinned, so unlike her fair, Protestant Elliot. She had met Sidney at the British Museum at a time in her life when she had not yet begun to be nervous. Their romance had been brief, but every so often she dreamed of him – big, rich dreams full of space and the washed light that follows a thunderstorm. They had walked by the river near Hammersmith and sat on the wall outside the City Barge, their legs dangling and touching above the low tide. They had talked and talked. Everything was funny. There was so much to say. He had been young, he had been charming, he had even had a little money. He had also died in an automobile accident, a true American death. Thirteen years. Automatic pilot switched on, and she was strolling with Sidney through endless vistas, past Florentine villas and sunny rounded hills delineated by cypress. They lay down to rest in fields and gardens, and he covered her with his long, olive-skinned body. They walked down the dark Paris street holding hands. They went into an old hotel and registered at the desk. He embraced her in the tiny lift . . .

'"If Gladstone's Home Rule Bill of 1893, which was passed by the Commons, had not been defeated in the Lords we should have no Irish problem today." Just as I've always said. You see, Lid, in the twelfth century, when Henry II invaded –'

Hell. No more sullen silence. Like a child or a cat he recovered from everything, forgot everything.

Lydia tried to find her way back to Sidney – Sidney beside the sea, great black gnarled rocks and a wild wild sky.

'"Like as the waves make towards the pebbled shore, so do our minutes hasten to their end."'

'Oh, yes.' Screams split the air. Seven-year-old screams. Not even Elliot could ignore them.

'I'll go,' was his munificent response. It was ten to ten.

No use. The fantasy was wrecked. In a moment she would be summoned to cope with catastrophe. She played Act Two of *Tosca* for the third time, drank another glass of wine, straight down, and began to mix the salad dressing. The call came like the voice of doom.

'Um, Lid, I'm awfully afraid that —'

'Oh, Christ!' She flung down her oven glove, spilling the olive oil and the wine vinegar.

'They've been bathing Avril. The floor is rather a mess.'

'But *they* were meant to be in the bath. What the hell is poor Avril doing in the bath?'

'And your make-up as well. Now try to be calm.'

She pushed past him on the stairs, blinded by tears and exerting every effort to repress the desire to tear his eyes out. She rescued the dazed and sodden sheep-dog who was redolent of Badedas and Floris Lily of the Valley. The rug was soaked through (water was, no doubt, already seeping into the living-room ceiling, the fourth time in two months). The writing was on the wall, and in her lipstick. The chaos was indescribable. Rosie had hidden under the bed in fear of further recriminations, and Danton manfully faced his mother alone. Lydia tried to check the torrent of abuse which was about to break from her. She knew what Elliot would say, how he would look, but out it came, transforming her into that termagant they all secretly knew her to be and which Sidney had never seen and never would see.

'I'm trying to listen to music, you wretched little ingrate. You know it's my only pleasure. Why do you try constantly to deprive me of it? Why do you abuse and thwart me like this and rob me of my privacy and of every little precious moment?'

'I suppose you'd better just send us to Dr Barnardo's.' Danton looked her straight in the eye.

'There's another place I've considered sending you.'

'That's enough of that.' Elliot stood in the doorway, looking, for him, almost angry, defending his children, as usual, from the mad woman he had taken to wife.

'Oh, my God, the sauce.' The mess must wait, otherwise they would be eating at midnight. Lydia fled to save the supper. She was just in time. But as she mopped up the spilled dressing, she saw in despair that Elliot had eaten all the shrimp.

She heard the three of them laughing upstairs. Tosca was stabbing Scarpia. The timing buzzer went off. Grimly, she carried on with the salad, hopeless of finding her way back to Sidney, certain that the bathroom atrocity would be left to her entirely, and that she would be on her hands and knees up there well after one a.m. while the others slept.

'Din-dins' she shouted at ten thirty-five in her best approximation of cheerfulness, determined to put everything right. There was no reply. She went to Elliot's study, barely able, by now, to focus on him. He was bent over his desk, copying something out of a large volume.

'Dinner's ready.'

'Great. Be there in a moment.'

'Where are the children?'

'Asleep, I think.'

'Asleep!' She checked their bedroom. They were passed out on top of each other with the television and the ET radio both going, unwashed, unfed, and still in their clothes. What kind of mother was she? She returned to absorbed Elliot.

'Couldn't you have kept them awake?' Her voice trembled.

'Hm?'

'Awake. The children.'

'Are they? They were so quiet I thought they were asleep.'

'Oh Elliot, they *are* asleep, and dinner is ready. God, I work so hard and for what? No one cares, no one appreciates the squandering of my precious time. I'm being slowly ground down to nothing. I need a holiday or I shall go mad. Can't we go to the sea? What about Normandy or Sicily? Elba, maybe —'

'Lydia, they were very upset after what happened. I did my best to cheer them up, but they're beginning to live in fear of your rages. Besides, they'd had no supper.' If she were the grist, Elliot was the mill.

'But I was making the supper. Supper is *made*.'

'Why not give them tea at six and put them to bed?'

'That's barbarous.'

'Anyway, I've come across a most interesting passage in Jung. It absolutely confirms what I was saying about Uniting Symbols and the motif of circle and square in the early Renaissance. Remember?' She didn't but said she did. 'Well, he's writing here about Revelations. Listen: "While the circle signifies the roundness of heaven and the all-embracing nature of the pneumatic deity, the square refers to the earth. Heaven is masculine but earth is feminine. Therefore God has his throne in heaven, while Wisdom has hers on earth, as she says in Ecclesiasticus –"'

'Amazing, Elliot. You'll fit in fantastically, I'm sure. But dinner.'

'Just want to finish copying it down. Use it in chapter eight. With you in a moment, Liddy. Smells wonderful. "In the same way that Sophia signifies God's self-reflection –"'

*There* was her real child. She went back to the kitchen. The buzzer was going, had been going, no doubt, for the past five minutes. The sauce was not ruined entirely, but it was spoiled. She would have to pass it through the *chinois*, and that meant yet another article to wash up in the morning. She began to cry, knowing she must proceed, even though she was now hopelessly drunk. The food would be cold – or at best dismally glazed over from too long a sojourn in the warming drawer – and there would be only her and Elliot to eat it. Tosca was again stabbing Scarpia. The music induced in Lydia's mind a hazy notion which she began to act upon, hardly realizing what she was about. It was as though she had gone on to automatic pilot for good.

She opened the cabinet under the sink, the common repository of homely poisons (Mrs Gladstone had kept it very well stocked), and removed the following items: window cleaner, disinfectant, Harpic, lemon-scented cleansing powder, Flash, spray furniture polish, liquid foliar feed, and a fresh green sink scrubber. She passed over the washing-up liquid since it might so incriminatingly bubble. No, she was not about to tidy up; she was proceeding with dinner. Elliot's eating the shrimp had been the last straw.

An experimental squeeze of creamy pink window cleaner confirmed that it would most probably integrate without curdling the sauce (would it now become an *aurore* rather than a *parisienne*, she wondered?). Just a little bit of everything, one must be so careful to balance the flavours, only a dash of disinfectant. She sifted together a mixture of Harpic and cleansing powder and added it to the sauce, whisking constantly, of course. She could almost think of Sidney now. She removed from the oven the glazed earthenware gratin dish which held the sole and placed it on the tiles next to the cooker. She poured on the sauce, now of a lovely amber hue imparted by the foliar feed. Over the whole she grated the crunchy green sink scrubber. The effect was delightful. She returned the dish to the oven for five minutes to reheat, and leaned against the work top, watching the clock and sipping her Médoc. '"Whilst I, my sovereign, watch the clock for you . . ."'

When the buzzer sounded, she opened the oven door and took out the dinner. The sauce had curdled slightly, probably the window cleaner after all, damn. It must be reintegrated. She would have to *faire une liaison* by adding a *beurre manié*. Nope, it was too late now. She couldn't face it. Must go forward, pushing against time.

'*À table*,' she shouted. There was no reply. He never heard the first call, engaged as he was in millennial processes. 'Elliot, darling!' Oh most exasperating of creatures. Mortal enemy. Best of men.

Lydia slipped on her oven gloves, picked up the *Sole dieppoise*, minus shrimp garniture, and took it to the table which had not been set. She hesitated, turned round, and went back to the cooker.

'Elliot, it's ready.' Everything was quiet. The music had stopped. She could hear the clock ticking. It was eleven fifteen. She took the dish once more to the table and stood with it in her hands. Was he coming? She walked back to the cooker. She put down the sole, then picked it up. A horrid skin was forming on the top. Too late to *vanner la sauce*, there were footsteps overhead. She knew she was going to panic, something one must never do in the kitchen where timing is of the essence. And she was well aware of what miracles could be accomplished by keeping one's head and using a small quantity of plain water. But it was too late. Too late for dinner, too late for everything.

'What should I do, being your slave . . . what should I do?'

Lydia took the dish back to the table. Again she hesitated and turned towards the cooker.

'What should I do . . .? What should I do . . .?'

BANANA YOSHIMOTO

# Newlywed

Translated by Megan Backus

*Banana Yoshimoto was born in 1964 and lives in Tokyo. She has won numerous prizes for her work both in Japan and abroad and has sold millions of copies of her novels* Kitchen, Tugumi *and* NP *worldwide. She does not speak English and refuses to give interviews, so little is known about the author other than her work. Her story 'Newlywed' was first published on billboards on the Tokyo underground railway.*

Once, just once, I met the most incredible person on the train. That was a while ago, but I still remember it vividly.

At the time, I was twenty-eight years old, and had been married to Atsuko for about one month.

I had spent the evening downing whisky at a bar with my buddies and was totally smashed by the time I got on the train to head home. For some reason, when I heard them announce my stop, I stayed put, frozen in my seat.

It was very late, and I looked around and saw that there were only three other passengers in the car. I wasn't so far gone that I didn't realize what I'd done. I had stayed on the train because I didn't really feel like going home.

In my drunken haze, I watched as the familiar platform of my station drew near. The train slowed down, and came to a stop. As the doors slid open, I could feel a blast of cool night air rush into the car, and then the doors again closed so firmly that I thought they had been sealed for all eternity. The train started to move, and I could see the neon signs of my neighbourhood stores flash by outside the train window. I sat quietly and watched them fade into the distance.

A few stations later, the man got on. He looked like an old homeless guy, with ragged clothes, long, matted hair, and a beard – plus he smelled really strange. As if on cue, the other three passengers stood up and moved to neighbouring cars, but I missed my chance to escape, and instead stayed where I was, seated right in the middle of the car. I didn't have a problem with the guy anyway, and even felt a trace of contempt for the other passengers, who had been so obvious about avoiding him.

Oddly enough, the old man came and sat right next to me. I held my breath and resisted the urge to look in his direction. I could see our reflections in the window facing us: the image of two men sitting side by side superimposed over the dazzling city lights and the dark of the night. I almost felt like laughing when I saw how anxious I looked there in the window.

'I suppose there's some good reason why you don't want to go home,' the man announced in a loud, scratchy voice.

At first, I didn't realize that he was talking to me, maybe because I was feeling so oppressed by the stench emanating from his body. I closed my eyes and pretended to be asleep, and then I heard him whisper, directly into my left ear, 'Would you like to tell me why you're feeling so reluctant about going home?'

There was no longer any mystery about whom he was addressing, so I screwed my eyes shut even more firmly. The rhythmical sound of the train's wheels clicking along the tracks filled my ears.

'I wonder if you'll change your mind when you see me like this,' he said.

Or I thought that's what he said, but the voice changed radically, and zipped up into a much higher pitch, as if someone had fast-forwarded a tape. This sent my head reeling, and everything around me seemed to rush into a different space, as the stench of the man's body disappeared, only to be replaced by the light, floral scent of perfume. My eyes still closed, I recognized a range of new smells: the warm fragrance of a woman's skin, mingled with fresh summer blossoms.

I couldn't resist; I had to take a look. Slowly, slowly, I opened my eyes, and what I saw almost gave me a heart attack. Inexplicably, there was a woman seated where the homeless guy had been, and the man was no-where to be seen.

Frantic, I looked around to see if anyone else had witnessed this amazing transformation, but the passengers in the neighbouring cars seemed miles away, in a totally different space, separated by a transparent wall, all looking just as tired as they had moments before, indifferent to my surprise. I glanced over at the woman again, and wondered what exactly had happened. She sat primly beside me, staring straight ahead.

I couldn't even tell what country she was from. She had long brown hair, gray eyes, gorgeous legs, and wore a black dress and black patent-leather heels. I definitely knew that face from somewhere – like maybe she was my favourite actress, or my first girlfriend, or a cousin, or my mother, or an older woman I'd lusted after – her face looked very familiar. And she wore a corsage of fresh flowers, right over her ample breasts.

I bet she's on her way home from a party, I thought, but then it occurred to me again that the old guy had disappeared. Where had he gone, anyway?

'You still don't feel like going home, do you?' she said, so sweetly that I could almost smell it. I tried convincing myself that this was nothing more than a drunken nightmare. That's what it was, an ugly-duckling dream, a transformation from bum to beauty. I didn't understand what was happening, but I knew what I saw.

'I certainly don't, with you by my side.'

I was surprised at my own boldness. I had let her know exactly what I had on my mind. Even though the train had pulled in to another station and people were straggling on to the neighbouring cars, not one single person boarded ours. No one so much as glanced our way, probably because they were too tired and preoccupied. I wondered if they wanted to keep riding and riding, as I did.

'You're a strange one,' the woman said to me.

'Don't jump to conclusions,' I replied.

'Why not?'

She looked me straight in the eye. The flowers on her breast trembled. She had incredibly thick eyelashes, and big, round eyes, deep and distant, which reminded me of the ceiling of the first planetarium I ever saw as a child: an entire universe enclosed in a small space.

*

'A minute ago, you were a filthy old bum.'

'But even when I look like this, I'm pretty scary, aren't I?' she said. 'Tell me about your wife.'

'She's petite.'

I felt as if I were watching myself from far away. What are you doing, talking to a stranger on a train? What is this, true confessions?

'She's short, and slender, and has long hair. And her eyes are real narrow, so she looks like she's smiling, even when she's angry.'

Then I'm sure she asked me, 'What does she do when you get home at night?'

'She comes down to meet me with a nice smile, as if she were on a divine mission. She'll have a vase of flowers on the table, or some sweets, and the television is usually on. I can tell that she's been knitting. She never forgets to put a fresh bowl of rice on the family altar every day. When I wake up on Sunday mornings, she'll be doing laundry, or vacuuming, or chatting with the lady next door. Every day, she puts out food for the neighbourhood cats, and she cries when she watches mushy TV shows.

'Let's see, what else can I tell you about Atsuko? She sings in the bath, and she talks to her stuffed animals when she's dusting them. On the phone with her friends, she laughs hard at anything they say, and, if it's one of her old pals from high school, they'll go on for hours. Thanks to Atsuko's ways, we have a happy home. In fact, sometimes it's so much fun at home that it makes me want to puke.'

After this grand speech of mine, she turned and nodded compassionately.

'I can picture it,' she said.

I replied, 'How could you? What do you know about these things?' at which she smiled broadly. Her smile was nothing like Atsuko's, but still it seemed awfully familiar to me. At that moment, a childhood memory flitted through my head: I'm walking to school with a friend, and we're still just little kids, so we're wearing the kind of school uniforms with shorts, instead of long pants. It's the dead of winter, and our legs are absolutely freezing, and we look at each other, about to complain about the cold, but then we just start laughing instead, because we both know that griping isn't going to make us any warmer. Scenes like that – smiles of mutual understanding – kept flashing through my mind, and I actually started having a good time on my little train bench.

Then I heard her saying, 'How long have you been down here in Tokyo?'

Her question struck me as terribly odd. Why had she said it like that, 'down here in Tokyo'?

I asked her, 'Hey, are you speaking Japanese? What language are you using?'

She nodded again, and replied, 'It's not any language from any one country. They're just words that only you and I can understand. You know, like words you only use with certain people, like with your wife, or an old girlfriend, or your dad, or a friend. You know what I mean, a special type of language that only you and they can comprehend.'

'But what if more than two people are talking to one another?'

'Then there'll be a language that just the three of you can understand, and the words will change again if another person joins the conversation. I've been watching this city long enough to know that it's full of people like you, who left their hometowns and came here by themselves. When I meet people who are transplants from other places, I know that I have to use the language of people who never feel quite at home in this big city. Did you know that people who've lived all their lives in Tokyo can't understand that special language? If I run into an older woman who lives alone, and seems reserved, I speak to her in the language of solitude. For men who are out whoring, I use the language of lust. Does that make sense to you?'

'I guess so, but what if the old lady, the horny guy, you, and I all tried to have a conversation?'

'You don't miss anything, do you? If that were to happen, then the four of us would find the threads that tie us together, a common register just for us.'

'I get the idea.'

'To get back to my original question, how long have you been in Tokyo?'

'I came here when I was eighteen, right after my mother died, and I've been here ever since.'

'And your life with Atsuko, how's it been?'

'Well, actually, sometimes I feel like we live in totally different worlds, especially when she goes on and on about the minutiae of our daily lives, anything and everything, and a lot of it's meaningless to me. I mean, what's the big deal? Sometimes I feel like I'm living with the quintessential housewife. I mean, all she talks about is our home.'

A cluster of sharply delineated images floated into my mind: the sound of my mother's slippers pattering by my bed when I was very young, the trembling shoulders of my little cousin, who sat sobbing after her favourite cat died. I felt connected to them, despite their otherness, and found solace in the thought of their physical proximity.

'That's how it feels?'

'And how about you? Where are you headed?' I asked.

'Oh, I just ride around and observe. To me, trains are like a straight line with no end, so I just go on and on, you know. I'm sure that most people think of trains as safe little boxes that transport them back and forth between their homes and offices. They've got their commuter passes, and they get on and get off each day, but not me. That's how you think of trains, right?'

'As a safe box that takes me where I need to go, and then home?' I said. 'Sure I do, or I'd be too scared to get on the train in the morning – I'd never know where I'd end up.'

She nodded, and said, 'Of course, and I'm not saying that you should feel the way I do. If you – or anyone on this train, for that matter – thought of life as a kind of train, instead of worrying only about your usual destinations, you'd be surprised how far you could go, just with the money you have in your wallet right now.'

'I'm sure you're right.'

'That's the kind of thing I have on my mind when I'm on the train.'

'I wish I had that kind of time on my hands.'

'As long as you're on this train, you're sharing the same space with lots of different people. Some people spend the time reading, others look at the ads, and still others listen to music. I myself contemplate the potential of the train itself.'

'But I still don't understand what this transformation's all about.'

'I decided to do it because you didn't get off at your usual station and I wanted to find out why. What better way to catch your eye?'

My head was swimming. Who was this being, anyway? What were we talking about? Our train kept stopping and starting, slipping through the black of the night. And there I was, surrounded by the darkness, being carried farther and farther from my home.

This being sitting next to me felt somehow familiar, like the scent of a place, before I was born, where all the primal emotions, love and hate, blended in the air. I also could sense that I would be in danger if I got too close. Deep inside, I felt timid, even scared, not about my own drunkenness or fear that my mind was playing tricks on me, but the more basic sensation of encountering something much larger than myself, and feeling immeasurably small and insignificant by comparison. Like a wild animal would when confronted by a larger beast, I felt the urge to flee for my life.

In my stupor, I could hear her saying, 'You never have to go back to that station again, if you don't want to. That's one option.'

I guess she's right, I thought, but continued to sit there in silence. Rocked by the motion of the train and soothed by the rhythm of the wheels below, I closed my eyes and pondered the situation. I tried to imagine the station near my house and how it looked when I came home in the late afternoon. I recalled the masses of red and yellow flowers whose names I didn't know out in the plaza in front of the station. The bookstore across the way was always packed with people flipping through paperbacks and magazines. All I could ever see was their backs – at least, when I walked past from the direction of the station.

The delicious smell of soup wafted from the Chinese restaurant, and people lined up in front of the bakery, waiting to buy the special cakes they make there. A group of high-school girls in their uniforms talk loudly and giggle as they walk ever so slowly across the plaza. It's weird that they're moving at such a leisurely pace. A burst of laughter rises from the group, and some teenage boys tense up as they walk past. One of the boys, though, doesn't even seem to notice the girls, and walks on calmly. He's a nice-looking guy, and I'd guess that he's popular with the girls. A perfectly made-up secretary passes by, yawning as she walks. She isn't carrying anything, so I imagine that she's on the way back to the office from an errand. I can tell that she doesn't want to go back to work; the weather's too nice for that. A businessman gulping down some vitamin beverage by the kiosk, other people waiting for friends. Some of them are reading paperbacks, others are people watching as they wait.

One finally catches sight of the friend she's been waiting for and runs to greet him. The elderly lady who walks slowly into my field of vision; the line of yellow and green and white taxis at the taxi stand that roar away from the station, one after another. The solid, weathered buildings nearby and the areas flanking the broad avenue.

And when I began to wonder what would happen if I never went back to that station, the whole image in my mind took on the quality of a haunting scene from an old movie, one fraught with meaning. All the living beings there suddenly became objects of my affection. Some day when I die, and only my soul exists, and my spirit comes home on a summer evening during the Bon Buddhist festival, that's probably what the world will look like to me.

And then Atsuko appears, walking slowly towards the station in the summer heat. She has her hair pulled back in a tight bun, even though I've told her that it makes her look dowdy. Her eyelids are so heavy that I wonder whether she can actually see anything, plus she's squinting now because of the glaring sun and her eyes have narrowed down to practically nothing. She's carrying a big bag instead of a shopping basket. She looks hungrily at the stuffed waffles in the little stall by the station, and even pauses for a moment as if she were going to stop and buy one, but then she changes her mind and walks into the drugstore instead. She stands for a long while in front of the shampoo section.

Come on, Atsuko, they're all the same. Just pick one. You look so serious! Shampoo is not something worth wasting time on. But she can't decide and keeps standing there, until a man rushing through the store bumps into her. Atsuko stumbles and then says she's sorry to the man. He bumped into you! You're not the one who should apologize. You should be as hard on him as you are on me.

Finally, Atsuko finds the perfect shampoo, and she takes it up to the cash register, where she starts chatting with the cashier. She's smiling sweetly. She leaves the store, a slender figure of a woman, becoming a mere black line as she recedes into the distance. A tiny black line. But I can tell that she's walking lightly, though slowly, and drinking in the air of this small town.

Our house is Atsuko's universe, and she fills it with small objects, all of her own choosing. She picks each of them as carefully as she did that bottle of shampoo. And then Atsuko comes to be someone who is neither a mother nor a wife, but an entirely different being.

For me, the beautiful, all-encompassing web spun by this creature is at once so polluted yet so pure that I feel compelled to grab on to it. I am terrified by it but find myself unable to hide from it. At some point I have been caught up in the magical power she has.

'That's the way it is when you first get married.' Her words brought me back to my senses. 'It's scary to think of the day when you'll move beyond the honeymoon stage.'

'Yeah, but there's no point dwelling on it now. I'm still young. Thinking about it just makes me nervous. I'm going home. I'll get off at the next station. At least I've sobered up a bit.'

'I had a good time,' she said.

'Me too,' I replied, nodding.

The train sped forward, unstoppable, like the grains of sand in an hourglass timing some precious event. A voice came booming out of the loudspeaker, announcing the next stop. We both sat there, not saying a word. It was hard for me to leave her. I felt as if we'd been together a very long time.

It seemed as if we had toured Tokyo from every possible angle, visiting each building, observing every person, and every situation. It was the incredible sensation of encountering a life force that enveloped everything, including the station near my house, the slight feeling of alienation I feel towards my marriage and work and life in general, and Atsuko's lovely profile. This town breathes in all the universes that people in this city have in their heads.

Intending to say a few more words, I turned in her direction, only to find the dirty bum sleeping peacefully by my side. Our conversation had come to an end. The train sailed into the station, slowly, quietly, like a ship. I heard the door slide open, and I stood up.

Incredible man, farewell.

# Games at Twilight

For Dada

*Anita Desai was born in 1937; her father was Bengali, her mother German, and she was educated in Delhi. Her published work includes* Clear Light of Day, *which was shortlisted for the 1980 Booker Prize,* Fire on the Mountain, *for which she won the Winifred Holtby Memorial Prize,* Baumgartner's Bombay, The Village by the Sea *and* In Custody, *which was shortlisted for the 1984 Booker Prize. She has also written several books for children. She is married, has four children of her own and lives in India.*

It was still too hot to play outdoors. They had had their tea, they had been washed and had their hair brushed, and after the long day of confinement in the house that was not cool but at least a protection from the sun, the children strained to get out. Their faces were red and bloated with the effort, but their mother would not open the door, everything was still curtained and shuttered in a way that stifled the children, made them feel that their lungs were stuffed with cotton wool and their noses with dust and if they didn't burst out into the light and see the sun and feel the air, they would choke.

'Please, ma, please,' they begged. 'We'll play in the veranda and porch – we won't go a step out of the porch.'

'You will, I know you will, and then –'

'No – we won't, we won't,' they wailed so horrendously that she actually let down the bolt of the front door so that they burst out like seeds from a crackling, over-ripe pod into the veranda, with such wild, maniacal yells that she retreated to her bath and the shower of talcum powder and the fresh sari that were to help her face the summer evening.

\*

They faced the afternoon. It was too hot. Too bright. The white walls of the veranda glared stridently in the sun. The bougainvillaea hung about it, purple and magenta, in livid balloons. The garden outside was like a tray made of beaten brass, flattened out on the red gravel and the stony soil in all shades of metal – aluminium, tin, copper and brass. No life stirred at this arid time of day – the birds still drooped, like dead fruit, in the papery tents of the trees; some squirrels lay limp on the wet earth under the garden tap. The outdoor dog lay stretched as if dead on the veranda mat, his paws and ears and tail all reaching out like dying travellers in search of water. He rolled his eyes at the children – two white marbles rolling in the purple sockets, begging for sympathy – and attempted to lift his tail in a wag but could not. It only twitched and lay still.

Then, perhaps roused by the shrieks of the children, a band of parrots suddenly fell out of the eucalyptus tree, tumbled frantically in the still, sizzling air, then sorted themselves out into battle formation and streaked away across the white sky.

The children, too, felt released. They too began tumbling, shoving, pushing against each other, frantic to start. Start what? Start their business. The business of the children's day which is – play.

'Let's play hide-and-seek.'

'Who'll be It?'

'You be It.'

'Why should I? You be –'

'You're the eldest –'

'That doesn't mean –'

The shoves became harder. Some kicked out. The motherly Mira intervened. She pulled the boys roughly apart. There was a tearing sound of cloth but it was lost in the heavy panting and angry grumbling and no one paid attention to the small sleeve hanging loosely off a shoulder.

'Make a circle, make a circle!' she shouted, firmly pulling and pushing till a kind of vague circle was formed. 'Now clap!' she roared and, clapping, they all chanted in melancholy unison: 'Dip, dip, dip – my blue ship –' and every now and then one or the other saw he was safe by the way his hands fell at the crucial moment – palm on palm, or back of hand on palm – and dropped out of the circle with a yell and a jump of relief and jubilation.

Raghu was It. He started to protest, to cry, 'You cheated – Mira cheated – Anu cheated –' but it was too late, the others had already streaked away. There was no one to hear when he called out, 'Only in the veranda – the porch – Ma said – Ma *said* to stay in the porch!' No one had stopped to listen, all he saw were their brown legs flashing through the dusty shrubs, scrambling up brick walls, leaping over compost heaps and hedges, and then the porch stood empty in the purple shade of the bougainvillaea and the garden was as empty as before; even the limp squirrels had whisked away, leaving everything gleaming, brassy and bare.

Only small Manu suddenly reappeared, as if he had dropped out of an invisible cloud or from a bird's claws, and stood for a moment in the centre of the yellow lawn, chewing his finger and near to tears as he heard Raghu shouting, with his head pressed against the veranda wall, 'Eighty-three, eighty-five, eighty-nine, ninety . . .' and then made off in a panic, half of him wanting to fly north, the other half counselling south. Raghu turned just in time to see the flash of his white shorts and the uncertain skittering of his red sandals, and charged after him with such a blood-curdling yell that Manu stumbled over the hosepipe, fell into its rubber coils and lay there weeping, 'I won't be It – you have to find them all – all – all!'

'I know I have to, idiot,' Raghu said, superciliously kicking him with his toe. 'You're dead,' he said with satisfaction, licking the beads of perspiration off his upper lip, and then stalked off in search of worthier prey, whistling spiritedly so that the hiders should hear and tremble.

Ravi heard the whistling and picked his nose in a panic, trying to find comfort by burrowing the finger deep-deep into that soft tunnel. He felt himself too exposed, sitting on an upturned flowerpot behind the garage. Where could he burrow? He could run around the garage if he heard Raghu come – around and around and around – but he hadn't much faith in his short legs when matched against Raghu's long, hefty, hairy foot-baller legs. Ravi had a frightening glimpse of them as Raghu combed the hedge of crotons and hibiscus, trampling delicate ferns underfoot as he did so. Ravi looked about him desperately, swallowing a small ball of snot in his fear.

The garage was locked with a great heavy lock to which the driver had the key in his room, hanging from a nail on the wall under his work-shirt. Ravi had peeped in and seen him still sprawling on his string-cot in his vest and striped underpants, the hair on his chest and the hair in his nose shaking with the vibrations of his phlegm-obstructed snores. Ravi had wished he were tall enough, big enough, to reach the key on the nail, but it was impossible, beyond his reach for years to come. He had sidled away and sat dejectedly on the flowerpot. That at least was cut to his own size.

But next to the garage was another shed with a big green door. Also locked. No one even knew who had the key to the lock. That shed wasn't opened more than once a year when Ma turned out all the old broken bits of furniture and rolls of matting and leaking buckets, and the white ant hills were broken and swept away and Flit sprayed into the spider webs and rat holes so that the whole operation was like the looting of a poor, ruined and conquered city. The green leaves of the door sagged. They were nearly off their rusty hinges. The hinges were large and made a small gap between the door and the walls – only just large enough for rats, dogs and, possibly, Ravi to slip through.

Ravi had never cared to enter such a dark and depressing mortuary of defunct household goods seething with such unspeakable and alarming animal life but, as Raghu's whistling grew angrier and sharper and his crashing and storming in the hedge wilder, Ravi suddenly slipped off the flowerpot and through the crack and was gone. He chuckled aloud with astonishment at his own temerity so that Raghu came out of the hedge, stood silent with his hands on his hips, listening, and finally shouted, 'I heard you! I'm coming! *Got* you –' and came charging round the garage only to find the upturned flowerpot, the yellow dust, the crawling of white ants in a mud-hill against the closed shed door – nothing. Snarling, he bent to pick up a stick and went off, whacking it against the garage and shed walls as if to beat out his prey.

Ravi shook, then shivered with delight, with self-congratulation. Also with fear. It was dark, spooky in the shed. It had a muffled smell, as of graves. Ravi had once got locked into the linen cupboard and sat there weeping for half an hour before he was rescued. But at least that had been a familiar place, and even smelt pleasantly of starch, laundry and, reassuringly, of his mother. But the shed smelt of rats, ant hills, dust and spider webs. Also of less definable, less recognizable, horrors. And it was dark. Except for the white-hot cracks along the door, there was no light. The roof was very low. Although Ravi was small, he felt as if he could reach up and touch it with his fingertips. But he didn't stretch. He hunched himself into a ball so as not to bump into anything, touch or feel anything. What might there not be to touch him and feel him as he stood there, trying to see in the dark? Something cold, or slimy – like a snake. Snakes! He leapt up as Raghu whacked the wall with his stick – then, quickly realizing what it was, felt almost relieved to hear Raghu, hear his stick. It made him feel protected.

But Raghu soon moved away. There wasn't a sound once his footsteps had gone around the garage and disappeared. Ravi stood frozen inside the shed. Then he shivered all over. Something had tickled the back of his neck. It took him a while to pick up the courage to lift his hand and explore. It was an insect – perhaps a spider – exploring *him*. He squashed it and wondered how many more creatures were watching him, waiting to reach out and touch him, the stranger.

There was nothing now. After standing in that position – his hand still on his neck, feeling the wet splodge of the squashed spider gradually dry – for minutes, hours, his legs began to tremble with the effort, the inaction. By now he could see enough in the dark to make out the large solid shapes of old wardrobes, broken buckets and bedsteads piled on top of each other around him. He recognized an old bathtub – patches of enamel glimmered at him and at last he lowered himself on to its edge.

He contemplated slipping out of the shed and into the fray. He wondered if it would not be better to be captured by Raghu and be returned to the milling crowd as long as he could be in the sun, the light, the free spaces of the garden and the familiarity of his brothers, sisters and cousins. It would be evening soon. Their games would become legitimate. The parents would sit out on the lawn on cane basket chairs and watch them as they tore around the garden or gathered in knots to share a loot of mulberries or black, teeth-splitting *jamun* from the garden trees. The gardener would fix the hosepipe to the water tap and water would fall

lavishly through the air to the ground, soaking the dry yellow grass and
the red gravel and arousing the sweet, the intoxicating, scent of water on
dry earth – that loveliest scent in the world. Ravi sniffed for a whiff of it.
He half-rose from the bathtub, then heard the despairing scream of one
of the girls as Raghu bore down upon her. There was the sound of a
crash, and of rolling about in the bushes, the shrubs, then screams and
accusing sobs of 'I touched the den –' 'You did not –' 'I did –' 'You liar,
you did *not*,' and then a fading away and silence again.

Ravi sat back on the harsh edge of the tub, deciding to hold out a bit
longer. What fun if they were all found and caught – he alone left uncon-
quered! He had never known that sensation. Nothing more wonderful had
ever happened to him than being taken out by an uncle and bought a
whole slab of chocolate all to himself, or being flung into the soda-man's
pony cart and driven up to the gate by the friendly driver with the red
beard and pointed ears. To defeat Raghu – that hirsute, hoarse-voiced
football champion – and to be the winner in a circle of older, bigger,
luckier children – that would be thrilling beyond imagination. He hugged
his knees together and smiled to himself almost shyly at the thought of so
much victory, such laurels.

There he sat smiling, knocking his heels against the bathtub, now and then
getting up and going to the door to put his ear to the broad crack and
listening for sounds of the game, the pursuer and the pursued, and then
returning to his seat with the dogged determination of the true winner, a
breaker of records, a champion.

It grew darker in the shed as the light at the door grew softer, fuzzier,
turned to a kind of crumbling yellow pollen that turned to yellow fur,
blue fur, grey fur. Evening. Twilight. The sound of water gushing, falling.
The scent of earth receiving water, slaking its thirst in great gulps and
releasing that green scent of freshness, coolness. Through the crack Ravi
saw the long purple shadows of the shed and the garage lying still across
the yard. Beyond that, the white walls of the house. The bougainvillaea had
lost its lividity, hung in dark bundles that quaked and twittered and
seethed with masses of homing sparrows. The lawn was shut off from his
view. Could he hear the children's voices? It seemed to him that he could.
It seemed to him that he could hear them chanting, singing, laughing. But

what about the game? What had happened? Could it be over? How could it when he was still not found?

It then occurred to him that he could have slipped out long ago, dashed across the yard to the veranda and touched the den. It was necessary to do that to win. He had forgotten. He had only remembered the part of hiding and trying to elude the seeker. He had done that so successfully, his success had occupied him so wholly, that he had quite forgotten that success had to be clinched by that final dash to victory and the ringing cry of 'Den!'

With a whimper he burst through the crack, fell on his knees, got up and stumbled on stiff, benumbed legs across the shadowy yard, crying heartily by the time he reached the veranda so that when he flung himself at the white pillar and bawled, 'Den! Den! Den!' his voice broke with rage and pity at the disgrace of it all and he felt himself flooded with tears and misery.

Out on the lawn, the children stopped chanting. They all turned to stare at him in amazement. Their faces were pale and triangular in the dusk. The trees and bushes around them stood inky and sepulchral, spilling long shadows across them. They stared, wondering at his reappearance, his passion, his wild animal howling. Their mother rose from her basket chair and came towards him, worried, annoyed, saying, 'Stop it, stop it, Ravi. Don't be a baby. Have you hurt yourself?' Seeing him attended to, the children went back to clasping their hands and chanting 'The grass is green, the rose is red . . .'

But Ravi would not let them. He tore himself out of his mother's grasp and pounded across the lawn into their midst, charging at them with his head lowered so that they scattered in surprise. 'I won, I won, I won,' he bawled, shaking his head so that the big tears flew. 'Raghu didn't find me. I won, I won –'

It took them a minute to grasp what he was saying, even who he was. They had quite forgotten him. Raghu had found all the others long ago. There had been a fight about who was to be It next. It had been so fierce that their mother had emerged from her bath and made them change to another game. Then they had played another and another. Broken mulberries from the tree and eaten them. Helped the driver wash the car when their father returned from work. Helped the gardener water the beds till he roared at them and swore he would complain to their parents. The parents had come out, taken up their positions on the cane chairs. They had begun to play again, sing and chant. All this time no one had remembered Ravi. Having disappeared from the scene, he had disappeared from their minds. Clean.

'Don't be a fool,' Raghu said roughly, pushing him aside, and even Mira said, 'Stop howling, Ravi. If you want to play, you can stand at the end of the line,' and she put him there very firmly.

The game proceeded. Two pairs of arms reached up and met in an arc. The children trooped under it again and again in a lugubrious circle, ducking their heads and intoning,

> 'The grass is green, the rose is red;
> Remember me when I am dead, dead, dead, dead . . .'

And the arc of thin arms trembled in the twilight, and the heads were bowed so sadly, and their feet tramped to that melancholy refrain so mournfully, so helplessly, that Ravi could not bear it. He would not follow them, he would not be included in this funereal game. He had wanted victory and triumph – not a funeral. But he had been forgotten, left out and he would not join them now. The ignominy of being forgotten – how could he face it? He felt his heart go heavy and ache inside him unbearably. He lay down full length on the damp grass, crushing his face into it, no longer crying, silenced by a terrible sense of his insignificance.

# Two Words

Translated by Margaret Sayers Peden

*Isabel Allende was born in Peru and spent her early years in Chile until shortly after the fall of her uncle Salvador Allende's government. She then moved with her family to Caracas, Venezuela, and worked as a journalist. She turned to writing fiction in 1981, and the result was the international bestseller* The House of the Spirits *– a family saga spanning the twentieth century in Chile. She then published* Of Love and Shadows *and a collection of short stories,* Eva Luna. *Her latest book,* Paula, *is a moving account of the death of her twenty-eight-year-old daughter. 'Belisa' is an anagram of the author's name.*

She went by the name of Belisa Crepusculario, not because she had been baptized with that name or given it by her mother, but because she herself had searched until she found the poetry of 'beauty' and 'twilight' and cloaked herself in it. She made her living selling words. She journeyed through the country from the high cold mountains to the burning coasts, stopping at fairs and in markets where she set up four poles covered by a canvas awning under which she took refuge from the sun and rain to minister to her customers. She did not have to peddle her merchandise because from having wandered far and near, everyone knew who she was. Some people waited for her from one year to the next, and when she appeared in the village with her bundle beneath her arm, they would form a line in front of her stall. Her prices were fair. For five *centavos* she delivered verses from memory; for seven she improved the quality of dreams; for nine she wrote love letters; for twelve she invented insults for irreconcilable enemies. She also sold stories, not fantasies but long, true stories she recited at one telling, never skipping a word. This is how she

carried the news from one town to another. People paid her to add a line
or two: our son was born; so and so died; our children got married; the
crops burned in the field. Wherever she went a small crowd gathered
around to listen as she began to speak, and that was how they learned
about each other's doings, about distant relatives, about what was going
on in the civil war. To anyone who paid her fifty *centavos* in trade, she gave
the gift of a secret word to drive away melancholy. It was not the same
word for everyone, naturally, because that would have been collective
deceit. Each person received his or her own word, with the assurance that
no one else would use it that way in this universe or the beyond.

Belisa Crepusculario had been born into a family so poor they did not
even have names to give their children. She came into the world and grew
up in an inhospitable land where some years the rains became avalanches
of water that bore everything away before them and others when not a
drop fell from the sky and the sun swelled to fill the horizon and the
world became a desert. Until she was twelve, Belisa had no occupation or
virtue other than having withstood hunger and the exhaustion of centuries. During one interminable drought, it fell to her to bury four younger
brothers and sisters; when she realized that her turn was next, she decided
to set out across the plains in the direction of the sea, in hopes that she
might trick death along the way. The land was eroded, split with deep
cracks, strewn with rocks, fossils of trees and thorny bushes, and skel-
etons of animals bleached by the sun. From time to time she ran into
families who, like her, were heading south, following the mirage of water.
Some had begun the march carrying their belongings on their back or in
small carts, but they could barely move their own bones, and after a while
they had to abandon their possessions. They dragged themselves along
painfully, their skin turned to lizard hide and their eyes burned by the
reverberating glare. Belisa greeted them with a wave as she passed, but she
did not stop, because she had no strength to waste in acts of compassion.
Many people fell by the wayside, but she was so stubborn that she sur-
vived to cross through that hell and at long last reach the first trickles of
water, fine, almost invisible threads that fed spindly vegetation and farther
down widened into small streams and marshes.

Belisa Crepusculario saved her life and in the process accidentally discovered writing. In a village near the coast, the wind blew a page of

newspaper at her feet. She picked up the brittle yellow paper and stood a long while looking at it, unable to determine its purpose, until curiosity overcame her shyness. She walked over to a man who was washing his horse in the muddy pool where she had quenched her thirst.

'What is this?' she asked.

'The sports page of the newspaper,' the man replied, concealing his surprise at her ignorance.

The answer astounded the girl, but she did not want to seem rude so she merely inquired about the significance of the fly tracks scattered across the page.

'Those are words, child. Here it says that Fulgencio Barba knocked out El Negro Tiznao in the third round.'

That was the day Belisa Crepusculario found out that words make their way in the world without a master, and that anyone with a little cleverness can appropriate them and do business with them. She made a quick assessment of her situation and concluded that aside from becoming a prostitute or working as a servant in the kitchens of the rich there were few occupations she was qualified for. It seemed to her that selling words would be an honourable alternative. From that moment on, she worked at that profession, and was never tempted by any other. At the beginning, she offered her merchandise unaware that words could be written outside of newspapers. When she learned otherwise, she calculated the infinite possibilities of her trade and with her savings paid a priest twenty *pesos* to teach her to read and write; with her three remaining coins she bought a dictionary. She pored over it from A to Z and then threw it into the sea, because it was not her intention to defraud her customers with packaged words.

One August morning several years later, Belisa Crepusculario was sitting in her tent in the middle of a plaza, surrounded by the uproar of market day, selling legal arguments to an old man who had been trying for sixteen years to get his pension. Suddenly she heard yelling and thudding hoofbeats. She looked up from her writing and saw, first, a cloud of dust, and then a band of horsemen come galloping into the plaza. They were the Colonel's men, sent under orders of El Mulato, a giant known throughout the land for the speed of his knife and his loyalty to his chief. Both the Colonel and El Mulato had spent their lives fighting in the civil war, and their names were ineradicably linked to devastation and calamity. The rebels swept into town like a stampeding herd, wrapped in noise, bathed in sweat, and leaving a hurricane of fear in their trail. Chickens took wing, dogs ran for their lives, women and children scurried out of sight, until the only living soul left in the market was Belisa Crepusculario. She had never seen El Mulato and was surprised to see him walking towards her.

'I'm looking for you,' he shouted, pointing his coiled whip at her; even before the words were out, two men rushed her – knocking over her canopy and shattering her inkwell – bound her hand and foot, and threw her like a duffel bag across the rump of El Mulato's mount. Then they thundered off towards the hills.

Hours later, just as Belisa Crepusculario was near death, her heart ground to sand by the pounding of the horse, they stopped, and four strong hands set her down. She tried to stand on her feet and hold her head high, but her strength failed her and she slumped to the ground, sinking into a confused dream. She awakened several hours later to the murmur of night in the camp, but before she had time to sort out the sounds, she opened her eyes and found herself staring into the impatient glare of El Mulato, kneeling beside her.

'Well, woman, at last you have come to,' he said. To speed her to her senses, he tipped his canteen and offered her a sip of liquor laced with gunpowder.

She demanded to know the reason for such rough treatment, and El Mulato explained that the Colonel needed her services. He allowed her to splash water on her face, and then led her to the far end of the camp where the most feared man in all the land was lazing in a hammock strung between two trees. She could not see his face, because he lay in the deceptive shadow of the leaves and the indelible shadow of all his years as a bandit, but she imagined from the way his gigantic aide addressed him with such humility that he must have a very menacing expression. She was surprised by the Colonel's voice, as soft and well modulated as a professor's.

'Are you the woman who sells words?' he asked.

'At your service,' she stammered, peering into the dark and trying to see him better.

The Colonel stood up, and turned straight towards her. She saw dark skin and the eyes of a ferocious puma, and she knew immediately that she was standing before the loneliest man in the world.

'I want to be President,' he announced.

The Colonel was weary of riding across that Godforsaken land, waging useless wars and suffering defeats that no subterfuge could transform into victories. For years he had been sleeping in the open air, bitten by mosquitoes, eating iguanas and snake soup, but those minor inconveniences were not why he wanted to change his destiny. What truly troubled him was the terror he saw in people's eyes. He longed to ride into a town beneath a triumphal arch with bright flags and flowers everywhere; he wanted to be cheered, and be given newly laid eggs and freshly baked bread. Men fled at the sight of him, children trembled, and women miscarried from fright; he had had enough, and so he had decided to become President. El Mulato had suggested that they ride to the capital, gallop up to the Palace and take over the government, the way they had taken so many other things without anyone's permission. The Colonel, however, did not want to be just another tyrant; there had been enough of those before him and, besides, if he did that, he would never win people's hearts. It was his aspiration to win the popular vote in the December elections.

'To do that, I have to talk like a candidate. Can you sell me the words for a speech?' the Colonel asked Belisa Crepusculario.

She had accepted many assignments, but none like this. She did not dare refuse, fearing that El Mulato would shoot her between the eyes, or worse still, that the Colonel would burst into tears. There was more to it than that, however; she felt the urge to help him because she felt a throbbing warmth beneath her skin, a powerful desire to touch that man, to fondle him, to clasp him in her arms.

All night and a good part of the following day, Belisa Crepusculario searched her repertory for words adequate for a presidential speech, closely watched by El Mulato, who could not take his eyes from her firm wanderer's legs and virginal breasts. She discarded harsh, cold words, words that were too flowery, words worn from abuse, words that offered improbable promises, untruthful and confusing words, until all she had left were words sure to touch the minds of men and women's intuition. Calling upon the knowledge she had purchased from the priest for twenty *pesos*, she wrote the speech on a sheet of paper and then signalled El Mulato to untie the rope that bound her ankles to a tree. He led her once more to the Colonel, and again she felt the throbbing anxiety that had seized her when she first saw him. She handed him the paper and waited while he looked at it, holding it gingerly between thumbs and fingertips.

'What the shit does this say?' he asked finally.

'Don't you know how to read?'

'War's what I know,' he replied.

She read the speech aloud. She read it three times, so her client could engrave it on his memory. When she finished, she saw the emotion in the faces of the soldiers who had gathered round to listen, and saw that the Colonel's eyes glittered with enthusiasm, convinced that with those words the presidential chair would be his.

'If after they've heard it three times, the boys are still standing there with their mouths hanging open, it must mean the thing's damn good, Colonel,' was El Mulato's approval.

'All right, woman. How much do I owe you?' the leader asked.

'One *peso*, Colonel.'

'That's not much,' he said, opening the purse he wore at his belt, heavy with proceeds from the last foray.

'The *peso* entitles you to a bonus. I'm going to give you two secret words,' said Belisa Crepusculario.

'What for?'

She explained that for every fifty *centavos* a client paid, she gave him the gift of a word for his exclusive use. The Colonel shrugged. He had no interest at all in her offer, but he did not want to be impolite to someone who had served him so well. She walked slowly to the leather stool where he was sitting, and bent down to give him her gift. The man smelled the scent of a mountain cat issuing from the woman, a fiery heat radiating from her hips, he heard the terrible whisper of her hair, and a breath of sweet mint murmured into his ear the two secret words that were his alone.

'They are yours, Colonel,' she said as she stepped back. 'You may use them as much as you please.'

El Mulato accompanied Belisa to the roadside, his eyes as entreating as a stray dog's, but when he reached out to touch her, he was stopped by an avalanche of words he had never heard before; believing them to be an irrevocable curse, the flame of his desire was extinguished.

During the months of September, October and November, the Colonel delivered his speech so many times that had it not been crafted from glowing and durable words, it would have turned to ash as he spoke. He travelled up and down and across the country, riding into cities with a triumphal air, stopping in even the most forgotten villages where only the dump heap betrayed a human presence, to convince his fellow citizens to vote for him. While he spoke from a platform erected in the middle of the plaza, El Mulato and his men handed out sweets and painted his name on all the walls in gold frost. No one paid the least attention to those advertising ploys; they were dazzled by the clarity of the Colonel's proposals and the poetic lucidity of his arguments, infected by his powerful wish to right the wrongs of history, happy for the first time in their lives. When the Candidate had finished his speech, his soldiers would fire their pistols into the air and set off firecrackers, and when finally they rode off, they left behind a wake of hope that lingered for days on the air, like the splendid memory of a comet's tail. Soon the Colonel was the favourite. No one had ever witnessed such a phenomenon: a man who surfaced from the civil war, covered with scars and speaking like a professor, a man whose fame spread to every corner of the land and captured the nation's heart. The press focused their attention on him. Newspapermen came from far away to interview him and repeat his phrases, and the number of his followers and enemies continued to grow.

'We're doing great, Colonel,' said El Mulato, after twelve successful weeks of campaigning.

But the Candidate did not hear. He was repeating his secret words, as he did more and more obsessively. He said them when he was mellow with nostalgia; he murmured them in his sleep; he carried them with him on horseback; he thought them before delivering his famous speech; and he caught himself savouring them in his leisure time. And every time he thought of those two words, he thought of Belisa Crepusculario, and his senses were inflamed with the memory of her feral scent, her fiery heat, the whisper of her hair and her sweet mint breath in his ear, until he began to go around like a sleepwalker, and his men realized that he might die before he ever sat in the presidential chair.

'What's got hold of you, Colonel,' El Mulato asked so often that finally one day his chief broke down and told him the source of his befuddlement: those two words that were buried like two daggers in his gut.

'Tell me what they are and maybe they'll lose their magic,' his faithful aide suggested.

'I can't tell them, they're for me alone,' the Colonel replied.

Saddened by watching his chief decline like a man with a death sentence on his head, El Mulato slung his rifle over his shoulder and set out to find Belisa Crepusculario. He followed her trail through all that vast country, until he found her in a village in the far south, sitting under her tent reciting her rosary of news. He planted himself, straddle-legged, before her, weapon in hand.

'You! You're coming with me,' he ordered.

She had been waiting. She picked up her inkwell, folded the canvas of her small stall, arranged her shawl around her shoulders, and without a word took her place behind El Mulato's saddle. They did not exchange so much as a word in all the trip; El Mulato's desire for her had turned into rage, and only his fear of her tongue prevented his cutting her to shreds with his whip. Nor was he inclined to tell her that the Colonel was in a fog, and that a spell whispered into his ear had done what years of battle had not been able to do. Three days later they arrived at the encampment, and immediately, in view of all the troops, El Mulato led his prisoner before the Candidate.

'I brought this witch here so you can give her back her words, Colonel,' El Mulato said, pointing the barrel of his rifle at the woman's head. 'And then she can give you back your manhood.'

The Colonel and Belisa Crepusculario stared at each other, measuring one another from a distance. The men knew then that their leader would never undo the witchcraft of those two accursed words, because the whole world could see the voracious puma's eyes soften as the woman walked to him and took his hand in hers.

# Before

Translated by Christine Donougher

*Annie Saumont has published six novels and twelve collections of short stories. She was awarded the Prix Goncourt de la Nouvelle in 1981 for* Quelquefois dans les cérémonies *and in 1990 she received the Grand Prix de la Nouvelle de la Société des Gens de Lettres for* Je ne suis pas un camion, *which has been translated into English (*I'm No Truck). *She has translated many works in English into French, including novels by John Fowles, Tom Sharpe, V. S. Naipaul and Nadine Gordimer. She lives in Paris.*

Mist on the river. Like a ribbon of gauze. Through it you can see the water rippling. You can see currents forming. Gentle currents.

The water slowly makes its way to the sea.

But first the river flows alongside the meadow and other meadows, alongside vegetable gardens and then under a stone bridge with arches that are green with moss.

There are dragonflies in the air streaking through the blueness of a cool morning, at the dawn of their lives, a day for a human being. The men are not angry. The men are pleasant and cheerful, on leave from all toil for the span of a dragonfly's life.

When is the bird pecking at the grain scattered around the earthenware jars at the entrance to the corn loft going to have eaten its fill? Scarcely does it start to shiver and hop about than a breeze makes the ladder creak.

A breeze. Then stillness. The cloud above has gold in its lining.

That was before. It was Sunday. The grown-ups were back from church. Not having insisted on everyone getting up early to go with them. Now at about eleven Mama said, What lovely weather for a picnic. Danilo, help me pack the basket.

On the table there's bread and cheese. Fruit and slices of dried meat. Danilo, pass me the knife, Danilo, stop daydreaming, open the pot of lard, don't wipe your fingers on your trousers. Here, you can also give me – And we'll take –

Papa said, Let's see how strong you are, young man. And the basket was heavy with food and our hearts were light.

Walking along the riverbank, they hear some rustling in the underwood, a titter of ill-contained laughter, and some whispered words. Mama says, It's Wara with the long hair who lives in the grey house by the lock. Papa says, And he comes from the other side, it's Terzine, the tobacconist's son. Mama says, Let's move away from here. Quietly so as not to disturb them. Papa says, That would teach them to behave more correctly in public places. Mama protests, the riverbank isn't a public place. She's right, it's a realm that doesn't belong to anybody and yet everyone secretly owns. Mama says, Let's go a bit further, there's room for everybody in this country.

Danilo wouldn't mind going further but the basket's too heavy. Danilo frets and complains. Papa takes him under the armpits, lifts him very high, and sets him on his shoulders. Papa's big brown hand grips the handle of the basket. Mama says, Wait, I've lost my sandal.

It's Sunday. This is before. At school during the week Danilo sits next to Mirela who comes from across the river. One evening after school Danilo tells white-haired Moumcha, who's Mama's mother, he tells her, and he can't keep still – stop it, you're making me dizzy – that Terzine has his Wara, OK, and they kiss each other in secret, OK, so it's not surprising then if Danilo has his Mirela, that's life, that's normal. When they're a little older Danilo and Mirela will go and kiss on the riverbank. Just to think of it makes you feel hot all over, makes you feel scary. Moumcha says, Don't think about it, sit down and eat your soup. You'll have your pudding afterwards. No, not an apple from the orchard. Something special, a surprise. I knew it was, Moumcha, says Danilo; and he's so glad he's still a little boy.

Mama carries her sandals in her hand and walks barefoot through the meadow. Papa says how foolish. He says it's crawling with snakes.

Danilo can't believe that the snakes would dare to attack Mama's pretty foot on such a bright and cheerful morning. Danilo sings to himself and pulls Papa's hair. Ouch, says Papa, tomorrow I'm going to be like Poupcha, as bald as an egg.

Again, they hear the stifled laughter of another Wara in the tall grass beyond the copse, and the higher-pitched whistling of another Terzine who has now stood up. They watch him approach the riverbank and he shouts, Hey, for no reason, to nobody. To someone on the other side within hearing distance.

A clump of trees. A fragrant hedge. With the path rising to the bridge and at the end of the path, on a slight slope, a field of thick clover, and Mama declares, No need to look any further. Setting down both Danilo and the basket, Papa says, Soon I shan't be able to carry you on my back any more, you're nearly a man now. Mama has already spread out a big linen cloth in the shade of a bush.

That was before.

Before, when the sky was blue and the river quiet, when the picnic basket was well stocked and they emptied it in the knowledge that the following week they'd have what they needed to fill it again.

When Wara waited for Terzine and Terzine came over the bridge and Mama would smile. Look how much in love the pair of them are. Moumcha announced gaily that she hoped to live long enough to go and dance to the sound of the violins with all the young people in their Sunday best when the lock-keeper's daughter got married to the tobacconist's son.

One day – before – a Sunday, Papa said something that he certainly shouldn't have, because Mama got cross, with furrowed brow and thin lips; with thunder in her eyes. Ordinarily calm and gentle Mama. He said that on the other side it wasn't the same as here. They weren't the same people. Mama protested. What kind of nonsense is that? Didn't Poupcha's grandfather come from across the river, and also, from what she said, one of Moumcha's distant ancestors? Papa shrugged his shoulders. Papa said, Sure. He said, Yes.

But when there was the rally in the square in front of the church and those speeches were made accusing the people opposite of behaving like barbarians, Papa again said yes. Mama and Moumcha stayed at home. Papa had decided that none of this was really any of the women's concern. Poupcha stayed behind too, so as not to miss his little afternoon nap. Papa had given orders, And as for you, Danilo, now you get yourself into the vegetable garden and thin out the radish bed for me.

Danilo ate three radishes, then jumped over the fence and walked through the streets to the square. In the square he saw men getting themselves worked up, looking red-faced and furious. Papa was the reddest and most furious of all, shaking his fist in the direction of the people opposite.

Yet that was before.

When Terzine used to cross the river to come and see Wara. When Terzine was so eager to clasp Wara in his arms that he would race madly along the parapet. She would go towards him, meeting him half-way. Wara with her long legs, and still light on her feet, would run as fast as her young man or else it was Terzine that had chosen to slow down a bit, so as to place their meeting under the protection of the angel with outspread wings that stood midway across the bridge. And the two lovers destined to be married wrapped themselves in an endless embrace. Passers-by laughed. Passers-by passed by and lowered their eyes or looked elsewhere.

That was before.

The rally broke up everything. The words that were said split in two the country that had never really been divided by the river. Since there was a bridge. And people on the one side used to cultivate on the other wheat, friendships, love. The words of the rally were words of hatred and anger. Never used until now on either side, words that before were only to be found in books, and suddenly the words had been spoken, hurled, yelled, and everyone knew that nothing was the same as it had been.

Yet that was before.

Before the rifles appeared. And then the machine-guns. And the cannons. Before a shell levelled the fountain, and bullets pitted the walls and façades. Papa kept saying, I told you. Those people over there have always been savages.

Mama says that Papa has no right to make such remarks. That it's adding fat to the fire. Or fire to the fat, everyone's getting muddled. In word and mind. It's on account of the war that makes so much noise. There are empty desks in the classroom, the ones that belong to the children who came from across the river when the bridge wasn't yet under crossfire from the two sides. Mirela doesn't come to school any more. Danilo has told this to Mama, and that Mirela was his girlfriend. Mama says that Danilo will see her again, promise, when the war's over. Mama smiles but it looks like a smile that's meant only to hold back the tears. And any tears that come, she sniffs. Moumcha has her own little cry, while peeling the vegetables. And then she rubs her eyes with the tea-towel.

Mama says that Wara can't see Terzine any more. The soldiers aim at the bridge and the boats day and night, and Terzine and Wara now have to exchange signs from afar. At first they tried to shout endearments at each other so loudly it sounded as if they were quarrelling. Wara doesn't talk any more. Or sometimes her lips move but not the least sound comes out.

Danilo would like to tell Mirela that he's been fishing for tadpoles in the pools left by the rainstorm in the bottom of the quarry-pits, they're full of the little creatures. He catches some and puts them in a jar. When Mirela comes back the tadpoles will have grown into frogs. They'll make a frog-size ladder for them out of twigs. The frogs will bring the warm weather.

Tomorrow was to be their wedding-day. Terzine and Wara's. Mama said, Those two had better be married without delay. She said to Papa, What's to be done? Have you seen Wara's belly?

Moumcha is knitting, with her head bowed. Danilo goes up and asks, Has Papa seen Wara's belly? Moumcha frowns, and drops a stitch, she picks it up again and mutters, Don't ask silly questions.

Wara used to sing, while wringing the sheets at the wash-house by the river under the shelter among the reeds. Wara used to laugh. That was before.

The junipers smell like mint. No, says Mama, they have their own juniper smell, their own smell intensified by the warmth of June. Danilo is adamant, It smells like the mint that grows on the opposite riverbank. Moumcha has turned away and says that he's dreaming, that he's imagining things.

Wara doesn't do her laundry in the river any more. Neither she nor any of the other women on this side, nor the women who used to come across the bridge, behind a donkey loaded with bundles of washing, kneeling-box, and beetle. Mama tells Danilo, No walking by the river. Moumcha says, Don't wander off. I'll tell you a story. Poupcha clears his throat and sighs. Papa says, Those bastards opposite. Mama says, They were our friends.

Wara stares straight ahead of her. Wara becomes very peculiar, her face has shrunk above her big-bellied body. Wara never laughs at all now. At school there's still no one on the bench beside Danilo where Mirela used to sit. At home Danilo has taken the lid off the gherkin jar and let the frogs go free. Mama said that they would die if they were kept prisoner.

There are people that have died. The ones that tried to cross the river. There's a bridge over the river that serves no purpose any more. There are people lying in the grass and the mud along the riverbank. Dead bodies that the people living here and the people living over there will come and fetch during the night.

There's Wara's belly, covered with blood. Mama says that Wara came down the path to the river to shout across to Terzine that the baby was about to be born. And Terzine should be there to hold it in his hands and name it. Wara said the baby would be called Danilo. Like you, says Mama. Danilo, a name she liked. Terzine didn't answer. Wara stayed a little too long by the wash-house. A shell exploded among the junipers.

The place where Wara is buried with the baby still in her belly is at the bottom of the meadow where Mama lost her sandal one Sunday, when we went for a picnic. They had to be put there because shells keep pounding the cemetery, rupturing the ground, opening up the graves. Mama said, These are bad times for our country. Papa said, Tears won't change anything. Danilo asked when Mirela would come back, and Papa replied, When pigs fly, when the world grows honest, when the barber doesn't charge for a shave, when we've killed all the traitors. Mama shouted, Oh, aren't you ashamed of yourself! Then he calmed down and mumbled sullenly, Maybe one day. In a very long time.

Poupcha was asleep, seated at the table, with his forehead cupped in his hands. Moumcha put aside her knitting. She closed the window overlooking the river. She wiped her eyes on the white curtain.

BHARATI MUKHERJEE

# A Wife's Story

*Bharati Mukherjee was born and educated in Calcutta and received her Ph.D. from the University of Iowa. She has taught creative writing at Columbia University and City University in New York and is now a distinguished professor at the University of California at Berkeley. Her novels include* Wife, The Tiger's Daughter *and* Jasmine. *She has published two works of non-fiction,* Days and Nights in Calcutta *and* The Sorrow and the Terror, *and two collections of short stories,* Darkness, *which* The New York Times Book Review *named as one of the best books of the year, and* The Middleman and Other Stories, *which won the 1988 National Book Critics' Circle Award.*

Imre says forget it, but I'm going to write David Mamet. So Patels are hard to sell real estate to. You buy them a beer, whisper Glengarry Glen Ross, and they smell swamp instead of sun and surf. They work hard, eat cheap, live ten to a room, stash their savings under futons in Queens, and before you know it they own half of Hoboken. You say, where's the sweet gullibility that made this nation great?

Polish jokes, Patel jokes: that's not why I want to write Mamet.

*Seen their women?*

Everybody laughs. Imre laughs. The dozing fat man with the Barnes & Noble sack between his legs, the woman next to him, the usher, everybody. The theater isn't so dark that they can't see me. In my red silk sari I'm conspicuous. Plump, gold paisleys sparkle on my chest.

The actor is just warming up. *Seen their women?* He plays a salesman, he's had a bad day and now he's in a Chinese restaurant trying to loosen up. His face is pink. His wool-blend slacks are creased at the crotch. We bought our tickets at half-price, we're sitting in the front row, but at the edge, and we see things we shouldn't be seeing. At least I do, or think I do. Spittle, actors goosing each other, little winks, streaks of make-up.

Maybe they're improvising dialogue too. Maybe Mamet's provided them with insult kits, Thursdays for Chinese, Wednesdays for Hispanics, today for Indians. Maybe they get together before curtain time, see an Indian woman settling in the front row off to the side, and say to each other: 'Hey, forget Friday. Let's get *her* today. See if she cries. See if she walks out.' Maybe, like the salesmen they play, they have a little bet on.

Maybe I shouldn't feel betrayed.

*Their women*, he goes again. *They look like they've just been fucked by a dead cat.*

The fat man hoots so hard he nudges my elbow off our shared armrest.

'Imre. I'm going home.' But Imre's hunched so far forward he doesn't hear. English isn't his best language. A refugee from Budapest, he has to listen hard. 'I didn't pay eighteen dollars to be insulted.'

I don't hate Mamet. It's the tyranny of the American dream that scares me. First, you don't exist. Then you're invisible. Then you're funny. Then you're disgusting. Insult, my American friends will tell me, is a kind of acceptance. No instant dignity here. A play like this, back home, would cause riots. Communal, racist, and antisocial. The actors wouldn't make it off-stage. This play, and all these awful feelings, would be safely locked up.

I long, at times, for clear-cut answers. Offer me instant dignity, today, and I'll take it.

'What?' Imre moves toward me without taking his eyes off the actor. 'Come again?'

Tears come. I want to stand, scream, make an awful scene. I long for ugly, nasty rage.

The actor is ranting, flinging spittle. *Give me a chance. I'm not finished, I can get back on the board. I tell that asshole, give me a real lead. And what does that asshole give me? Patels. Nothing but Patels.*

This time Imre works an arm around my shoulders. 'Panna, what is Patel? Why are you taking it all so personally?'

I shrink from his touch, but I don't walk out. Expensive girls' schools in Lausanne and Bombay have trained me to behave well. My manners are exquisite, my feelings are delicate, my gestures refined, my moods undetectable. They have seen me through riots, uprootings, separation, my son's death.

'I'm not taking it personally.'

The fat man looks at us. The woman looks too, and shushes.

I stare back at the two of them. Then I stare, mean and cool, at the man's elbow. Under the bright-blue polyester Hawaiian shirt sleeve, the elbow looks soft and runny. 'Excuse me,' I say. My voice has the effortless meanness of well-bred displaced Third World women, though my rhetoric has been learned elsewhere. 'You're exploiting my space.'

Startled, the man snatches his arm away from me. He cradles it against his breast. By the time he's ready with come-backs, I've turned my back on him. I've probably ruined the first act for him. I know I've ruined it for Imre.

It's not my fault; it's the *situation*. Old colonies wear down. Patels – the new pioneers – have to be suspicious. Idi Amin's lesson is permanent. AT&T wires move good advice from continent to continent. Keep all assets liquid. Get into 7-11s, get out of condos and motels. I know how both sides feel, that's the trouble. The Patel sniffing out scams, the sad salesmen on the stage: post-colonialism has made me their referee. It's hate I long for; simple, brutish, partisan hate.

After the show Imre and I make our way toward Broadway. Sometimes he holds my hand; it doesn't mean anything more than that crazies and drunks are crouched in doorways. Imre's been here over two years, but he's stayed very old-world, very courtly, openly protective of women. I met him in a seminar on special ed. last semester. His wife is a nurse somewhere in the Hungarian countryside. There are two sons, and miles of petitions for their emigration. My husband manages a mill two hundred miles north of Bombay. There are no children.

'You make things tough on yourself,' Imre says. He assumed Patel was a Jewish name or maybe Hispanic; everything makes equal sense to him. He found the play tasteless, he worried about the effect of vulgar language on my sensitive ears. 'You have to let go a bit.' And as though to show me how to let go, he breaks away from me, bounds ahead with his head ducked tight, then dances on amazingly jerky legs. He's a Magyar, he often tells me, and deep down, he's an Asian too. I catch glimpses of it, knife-blade Attila cheekbones, despite the blondish hair. In his faded jeans and leather jacket, he's a rock-video star. I watch MTV for hours in the apartment when Charity's working the evening shift at Macy's. I listen to WPLJ on Charity's earphones. Why should I be ashamed? Television in India is so uplifting.

Imre stops as suddenly as he started. People walk around us. The summer sidewalk is full of theatergoers in seersucker suits; Imre's year-round jacket is out of place. European. Cops in twos and threes huddle, lightly tap their thighs with night sticks and smile at me with benevolence. I want to wink at them, get us all in trouble, tell them the crazy dancing man is from the Warsaw Pact. I'm too shy to break into dance on Broadway. So I hug Imre instead.

The hug takes him by surprise. He wants me to let go, but he doesn't really expect me to let go. He staggers, though I weigh no more than 104 pounds and, with him, I pitch forward slightly. Then he catches me, and we walk arm in arm to the bus stop. My husband would never dance or hug a woman on Broadway. Nor would my brothers. They aren't stuffy people, but they went to Anglican boarding schools and they have a well-developed sense of what's silly.

'Imre.' I squeeze his big, rough hand. 'I'm sorry I ruined the evening for you.'

'You did nothing of the kind.' He sounds tired. 'Let's not wait for the bus. Let's splurge and take a cab instead.'

Imre always has unexpected funds. The Network, he calls it, Class of '56.

In the back of the cab, without even trying, I feel light, almost free. Memories of Indian destitutes mix with the hordes of New York street people, and they float free, like astronauts, inside my head. I've made it. I'm making something of my life. I've left home, my husband, to get a Ph.D. in special ed. I have a multiple-entry visa and a small scholarship for two years. After that, we'll see. My mother was beaten by her mother-in-law, my grandmother, when she registered for French lessons at the Alliance Française. My grandmother, the eldest daughter of a rich *zamindar*, was illiterate.

Imre and the cabdriver talk away in Russian. I keep my eyes closed. That way I can feel the floaters better. I'll write Mamet tonight. I feel strong, reckless. Maybe I'll write Steven Spielberg too; tell him that Indians don't eat monkey brains.

We've made it. Patels must have made it. Mamet, Spielberg: they're not condescending to us. Maybe they're a little bit afraid.

Charity Chin, my roommate, is sitting on the floor drinking Chablis out of a plastic wineglass. She is five foot six, three inches taller than me, but weighs a kilo and a half less than I do. She is a 'hands' model. Orientals are supposed to have a monopoly in the hands-modelling business, she says. She had her eyes fixed eight or nine months ago and out of gratitude sleeps with her plastic surgeon every third Wednesday.

'Oh, good,' Charity says. 'I'm glad you're back early. I need to talk.'

She's been writing checks. MCI, Con Ed, Bonwit Teller. Envelopes, already stamped and sealed, form a pyramid between her shapely, knee-socked legs. The checkbook's cover is brown plastic, grained to look like cowhide. Each time Charity flips back the cover, white geese fly over sky-colored checks. She makes good money, but she's extravagant. The difference adds up to this shared, rent-controlled Chelsea one-bedroom.

'All right. Talk.'

When I first moved in, she was seeing an analyst. Now she sees a nutritionist.

'Eric called. From Oregon.'

'What did he want?'

'He wants me to pay half the rent on his loft for last spring. He asked me to move back, remember? He *begged* me.'

Eric is Charity's estranged husband.

'What does your nutritionist say?' Eric now wears a red jumpsuit and tills the soil in Rajneeshpuram.

'You think Phil's a creep too, don't you? What else can he be when creeps are all I attract?'

Phil is a flutist with thinning hair. He's very touchy on the subject of *flautists* versus *flutists*. He's touchy on every subject, from music to books to foods to clothes. He teaches at a small college upstate, and Charity bought a used blue Datsun ('Nissan,' Phil insists) last month so she could spend weekends with him. She returns every Sunday night, exhausted and exasperated. Phil and I don't have much to say to each other – he's the only musician I know; the men in my family are lawyers, engineers, or in business – but I like him. Around me, he loosens up. When he visits, he bakes us loaves of pumpernickel bread. He waxes our kitchen floor. Like many men in this country, he seems to me a displaced child, or even a woman, looking for something that passed him by, or for something that he can never have. If he thinks I'm not looking, he sneaks his hands under Charity's sweater, but there isn't too much there. Here, she's a model with high ambitions. In India, she'd be a flat-chested old maid.

I'm shy in front of the lovers. A darkness comes over me when I see them horsing around.

'It isn't the money,' Charity says. Oh? I think. 'He says he still loves me. Then he turns around and asks me for five hundred.'

What's so strange about that, I want to ask. She still loves Eric, and Eric, red jump suit and all, is smart enough to know it. Love is a commodity, hoarded like any other. Mamet knows. But I say, 'I'm not the person to ask about love.' Charity knows that mine was a traditional Hindu marriage. My parents, with the help of a marriage broker, who was my mother's cousin, picked out a groom. All I had to do was get to know his taste in food.

It'll be a long evening, I'm afraid. Charity likes to confess. I unpleat my silk sari – it no longer looks too showy – wrap it in muslin cloth and put it away in a dresser drawer. Saris are hard to have laundered in Manhattan, though there's a good man in Jackson Heights. My next step will be to brew us a pot of chrysanthemum tea. It's a very special tea from the mainland. Charity's uncle gave it to us. I like him. He's a humpbacked, awkward, terrified man. He runs a gift store on Mott Street, and though he doesn't speak much English, he seems to have done well. Once upon a time he worked for the railways in Chengdu, Szechwan Province, and during the Wuchang Uprising, he was shot at. When I'm down, when I'm lonely for my husband, when I think of our son, or when I need to be held, I think of Charity's uncle. If I hadn't left home, I'd never have heard of the Wuchang Uprising. I've broadened my horizons.

Very late that night my husband calls me from Ahmadabad, a town of textile mills north of Bombay. My husband is a vice-president at Lakshmi Cotton Mills. Lakshmi is the goddess of wealth, but LCM (Priv.), Ltd, is doing poorly. Lock-outs, strikes, rock-throwings. My husband lives on digitalis, which he calls the food for our *yuga* of discontent.

'We had a bad mishap at the mill today.' Then he says nothing for seconds.

The operator comes on. 'Do you have the right party, sir? We're trying to reach Mrs Butt.'

'Bhatt,' I insist. '*B* for Bombay, *H* for Haryana, *A* for Ahmadabad, double *T* for Tamil Nadu.' It's a litany. 'This is she.'

'One of our lorries was fire-bombed today. Resulting in three deaths. The driver, old Karamchand, and his two children.'

I know how my husband's eyes look this minute, how the eye rims sag and the yellow corneas shine and bulge with pain. He is not an emotional man – the Ahmadabad Institute of Management has trained him to cut losses, to look on the bright side of economic catastrophes – but tonight he's feeling low. I try to remember a driver named Karamchand, but can't. That part of my life is over, the way *trucks* have replaced *lorries* in my vocabulary, the way Charity Chin and her lurid love life have replaced inherited notions of marital duty. Tomorrow he'll come out of it. Soon he'll be eating again. He'll sleep like a baby. He's been trained to believe in turnovers. Every morning he rubs his scalp with cantharidine oil so his hair will grow back again.

'It could be your car next.' Affection, love. Who can tell the difference in a traditional marriage in which a wife still doesn't call her husband by his first name?

'No. They know I'm a flunky, just like them. Well paid, maybe. No need for undue anxiety, please.'

Then his voice breaks. He says he needs me, he misses me, he wants me to come to him damp from my evening shower, smelling of sandalwood soap, my braid decorated with jasmines.

'I need you too.'

'Not to worry, please,' he says. 'I am coming in a fortnight's time. I have already made arrangements.'

Outside my window, fire trucks whine, up Eighth Avenue. I wonder if he can hear them, what he thinks of a life like mine, led amid disorder.

'I am thinking it'll be like a honeymoon. More or less.'

When I was in college, waiting to be married, I imagined honeymoons were only for the more fashionable girls, the girls who came from slightly racy families, smoked Sobranies in the dorm lavatories and put up posters of Kabir Bedi, who was supposed to have made it as a big star in the West. My husband wants us to go to Niagara. I'm not to worry about foreign exchange. He's arranged for extra dollars through the Gujarati Network, with a cousin in San Jose. And he's bought four hundred more on the black market. 'Tell me you need me. Panna, please tell me again.'

I change out of the cotton pants and shirt I've been wearing all day and put on a sari to meet my husband at JFK. I don't forget the jewelry; the marriage necklace of *mangalsutra*, gold drop earrings, heavy gold bangles. I don't wear them every day. In this borough of vice and greed, who knows when, or whom, desire will overwhelm.

My husband spots me in the crowd and waves. He has lost weight, and changed his glasses. The arm, uplifted in a cheery wave, is bony, frail, almost opalescent.

In the Carey Coach, we hold hands. He strokes my fingers one by one. 'How come you aren't wearing my mother's ring?'

'Because muggers know about Indian women,' I say. They know with us it's 24-karat. His mother's ring is showy, in ghastly taste anywhere but India: a blood-red Burma ruby set in a gold frame of floral sprays. My mother-in-law got her guru to bless the ring before I left for the States.

He looks disconcerted. He's used to a different role. He's the knowing, suspicious one in the family. He seems to be sulking, and finally he comes out with it. 'You've said nothing about my new glasses.' I compliment him on the glasses, how chic and Western-executive they make him look. But I can't help the other things, necessities until he learns the ropes. I handle the money, buy the tickets. I don't know if this makes me unhappy.

Charity drives her Nissan upstate, so for two weeks we are to have the apartment to ourselves. This is more privacy than we ever had in India. No parents, no servants, to keep us modest. We play at housekeeping. Imre has lent us a hibachi, and I grill saffron chicken breasts. My husband marvels at the size of the Perdue hens. 'They're big like peacocks, no? These Americans, they're really something!' He tries out pizzas, burgers, McNuggets. He chews. He explores. He judges. He loves it all, fears nothing, feels at home in the summer odors, the clutter of Manhattan streets. Since he thinks that the American palate is bland, he carries a bottle of red peppers in his pocket. I wheel a shopping cart down the aisles of the neighborhood Grand Union, and he follows, swiftly, greedily. He picks up hair rinses and high-protein diet powders. There's so much I already take for granted.

One night, Imre stops by. He wants us to go with him to a movie. In his work shirt and red leather tie, he looks arty or strung out. It's only been a week, but I feel as though I am really seeing him for the first time. The yellow hair worn very short at the sides, the wide, narrow lips. He's a good-looking man, but self-conscious, almost arrogant. He's picked the movie we should see. He always tells me what to see, what to read. He buys the *Voice*. He's a natural avant-gardist. For tonight he's chosen *Numéro Deux*.

'Is it a musical?' my husband asks. The Radio City Music Hall is on his list of sights to see. He's read up on the history of the Rockettes. He doesn't catch Imre's sympathetic wink.

Guilt, shame, loyalty. I long to be ungracious, not ingratiate myself with both men.

That night my husband calculates in rupees the money we've wasted on Godard. 'The refugee fellow, Nagy, must have a screw loose in his head. I paid very steep price for dollars on the black market.'

Some afternoons we go shopping. Back home we hated shopping, but now it is a lovers' project. My husband's shopping list startles me. I feel I am just getting to know him. Maybe, like Imre, freed from the dignities of old-world culture, he too could get drunk and squirt Cheez Whiz on a guest. I watch him dart into stores in his gleaming leather shoes. Jockey shorts on sale in outdoor bins on Broadway entrance him. White tube socks with different bands of color delight him. He looks for micro-cassettes, for anything small and electronic and smuggleable. He needs a garment bag. He calls it a 'wardrobe', and I have to translate.

'All of New York is having sales, no?'

My heart speeds watching him this happy. It's the third week in August, almost the end of summer, and the city smells ripe, it cannot bear more heat, more money, more energy.

'This is so smashing! The prices are so excellent!' Recklessly, my prudent husband signs away traveller's cheques. How he intends to smuggle it all back I don't dare ask. With a microwave, he calculates, we could get rid of our cook.

This has to be love, I think. Charity, Eric, Phil: they may be experts on sex. My husband doesn't chase me around the sofa, but he pushes me down on Charity's battered cushions, and the man who has never entered the kitchen of our Ahmadabad house now comes toward me with a dish tub of steamy water to massage away the pavement heat.

Ten days into his vacation my husband checks out brochures for sight-seeing tours. Shortline, Grayline, Crossroads: his new vinyl briefcase is full of schedules and pamphlets. While I make pancakes out of a mix, he comparison-shops. Tour number one costs $10.95 and will give us the World Trade Center, Chinatown, and the United Nations. Tour number three would take us both uptown *and* downtown for $14.95, but my husband is absolutely sure he doesn't want to see Harlem. We settle for tour number four: Downtown and the Dame. It's offered by a new tour company with a small, dirty office at Eighth and Forty-eighth.

The sidewalk outside the office is colorful with tourists. My husband sends me in to buy the tickets because he has come to feel Americans don't understand his accent.

The dark man, Lebanese probably, behind the counter comes on too friendly. 'Come on, doll, make my day!' He won't say which tour is his. 'Number four? Honey, no! Look, you've wrecked me! Say you'll change your mind.' He takes two twenties and gives back change. He holds the tickets, forcing me to pull. He leans closer. 'I'm off after lunch.'

My husband must have been watching me from the sidewalk. 'What was the chap saying?' he demands. 'I told you not to wear pants. He thinks you are Puerto Rican. He thinks he can treat you with disrespect.'

The bus is crowded and we have to sit across the aisle from each other. The tour guide begins his patter on Forty-sixth. He looks like an actor, his hair bleached and blow-dried. Up close he must look middle-aged, but from where I sit his skin is smooth and his cheeks faintly red.

'Welcome to the Big Apple, folks.' The guide uses a microphone. 'Big Apple. That's what we native Manhattan degenerates call our city. Today we have guests from fifteen foreign countries and six states from this U.S.

of A. That makes the Tourist Bureau real happy. And let me assure you that while we may be the richest city in the richest country in the world, it's okay to tip your charming and talented attendant.' He laughs. Then he swings his hip out into the aisle and sings a song.

'And it's mighty fancy on old Delancey Street, you know . . .'

My husband looks irritable. The guide is, as expected, a good singer. 'The bloody man should be giving us histories of buildings we are passing, no?' I pat his hand, the mood passes. He cranes his neck. Our window seats have both gone to Japanese. It's the tour of his life. Next to this, the quick business trips to Manchester and Glasgow pale.

'And tell me what street compares to Mott Street in July . . .'

The guide wants applause. He manages a derisive laugh from the Americans up front. He's working the aisles now. 'I coulda been somebody, right? I coulda been a star!' Two or three of us smile, those of us who recognize the parody. He catches my smile. The sun is on his harsh, bleached hair. 'Right, your highness? Look, we gotta maharani with us! Couldn't I have been a star?'

'Right!' I say, my voice coming out a squeal. I've been trained to adapt; what else can I say?

We drive through traffic past landmark office buildings and churches. The guide flips his hands. 'Art Deco,' he keeps saying. I hear him confide to one of the Americans: 'Beats me. I went to a cheap guide's school.' My husband wants to know more about this Art Deco, but the guide sings another song.

'We made a foolish choice,' my husband grumbles. 'We are sitting in the bus only. We're not going into famous buildings.' He scrutinizes the pamphlets in his jacket pocket. I think, at least it's air-conditioned in here. I could sit here in the cool shadows of the city forever.

Only five of us appear to have opted for the 'Downtown and the Dame' tour. The others will ride back uptown past the United Nations after we've been dropped off at the pier for the ferry to the Statue of Liberty.

An elderly European pulls a camera out of his wife's designer tote bag. He takes pictures of the boats in the harbor, the Japanese in kimonos eating popcorn, scavenging pigeons, me. Then, pushing his wife ahead of him, he climbs back on the bus and waves to us. For a second I feel terribly lost. I wish we were on the bus going back to the apartment. I know I'll not be able to describe any of this to Charity, or to Imre. I'm too proud to admit I went on a guided tour.

The view of the city from the Circle Line ferry is seductive, unreal. The skyline wavers out of reach, but never quite vanishes. The summer sun pushes through fluffy clouds and dapples the glass of office towers. My husband looks thrilled, even more than he had on the shopping trips down Broadway. Tourists and dreamers, we have spent our life's savings to see this skyline, this statue.

'Quick, take a picture of me!' my husband yells as he moves toward a gap of railings. A Japanese matron has given up her position in order to change film. 'Before the Twin Towers disappear!'

I focus, I wait for a large Oriental family to walk out of my range. My husband holds his pose tight against the railing. He wants to look relaxed, an international businessman at home in all the financial markets.

A bearded man slides across the bench toward me. 'Like this,' he says and helps me get my husband in focus. 'You want me to take the photo for you?' His name, he says, is Goran. He is Goran from Yugoslavia, as though that were enough for tracking him down. Imre from Hungary. Panna from India. He pulls the old Leica out of my hand, signalling the Orientals to beat it, and clicks away. 'I'm a photographer,' he says. He could have been a camera thief. That's what my husband would have assumed. Somehow, I trusted. 'Get you a beer?' he asks.

'I don't. Drink, I mean. Thank you very much.' I say those last words very loud, for everyone's benefit. The odd bottles of Soave with Imre don't count.

'Too bad.' Goran gives back the camera.

'Take one more!' my husband shouts from the railing. 'Just to be sure!'

The island itself disappoints. The Lady has brutal scaffolding holding her in. The museum is closed. The snack bar is dirty and expensive. My husband reads out the prices to me. He orders two french fries and two Cokes. We sit at picnic tables and wait for the ferry to take us back.

'What was that hippie chap saying?'

As if I could say. A day-care center has brought its kids, at least forty of them, to the island for the day. The kids, all wearing name tags, run around us. I can't help noticing how many are Indian. Even a Patel, probably a Bhatt if I looked hard enough. They toss hamburger bits at pigeons. They kick styrofoam cups. The pigeons are slow, greedy, persistent. I have to shoo one off the table top. I don't think my husband thinks about our son.

'What hippie?'

'The one on the boat. With the beard and the hair.'

My husband doesn't look at me. He shakes out his paper napkin and tries to protect his french fries from pigeon feathers.

'Oh, him. He said he was from Dubrovnik.' It isn't true, but I don't want trouble.

'What did he say about Dubrovnik?'

I know enough about Dubrovnik to get by. Imre's told me about it. And about Mostar and Zagreb. In Mostar white Muslims sing the call to prayer. I would like to see that before I die: white Muslims. Whole peoples have moved before me; they've adapted. The night Imre told me about Mostar was also the night I saw my first snow in Manhattan. We'd walked down to Chelsea from Columbia. We'd walked and talked and I hadn't felt tired at all.

'You're too innocent,' my husband says. He reaches for my hand. 'Panna,' he cries with pain in his voice, and I am brought back from perfect, floating memories of snow, 'I've come to take you back. I have seen how men watch you.'

'What?'

'Come back, now. I have tickets. We have all the things we will ever need. I can't live without you.'

A little girl with wiry braids kicks a bottle cap at his shoes. The pigeons wheel and scuttle around us. My husband covers his fries with spread-out fingers. 'No kicking,' he tells the girl. Her name, Beulah, is printed in green ink on a heart-shaped name tag. He forces a smile, and Beulah smiles back. Then she starts to flap her arms. She flaps, she hops. The pigeons go crazy for fries and scraps.

'Special ed. course is two years,' I remind him. 'I can't go back.'

My husband picks up our trays and throws them into the garbage before I can stop him. He's carried disposability a little too far. 'We've been taken,' he says, moving toward the dock, though the ferry will not arrive for another twenty minutes. 'The ferry costs only two dollars round-trip per person. We should have chosen tour number one for $10.95 instead of tour number four for $14.95.'

With my Lebanese friend, I think. 'But this way we don't have to worry about cabs. The bus will pick us up at the pier and take us back to midtown. Then we can walk home.'

'New York is full of cheats and whatnot. Just like Bombay.' He is not accusing me of infidelity. I feel dread all the same.

That night, after we've gone to bed, the phone rings. My husband listens, then hands the phone to me. 'What is this woman saying?' He turns on the pink Macy's lamp by the bed. 'I am not understanding these Negro people's accents.'

The operator repeats the message. It's a cable from one of the directors of Lakshmi Cotton Mills. 'Massive violent labor confrontation anticipated. Stop. Return posthaste. Stop. Cable flight details. Signed Kantilal Shah.'

'It's not your factory,' I say. 'You're supposed to be on vacation.'

'So, you are worrying about me? Yes? You reject my heartfelt wishes but you worry about me?' He pulls me close, slips the straps of my nightdress off my shoulders. 'Wait a minute.'

I wait, unclothed, for my husband to come back to me. The water is running in the bathroom. In the ten days he has been here he has learned American rites: deodorants, fragrances. Tomorrow morning he'll call Air India; tomorrow evening he'll be on his way back to Bombay. Tonight I should make up to him for my years away, the gutted trucks, the degree I'll never use in India. I want to pretend with him that nothing has changed.

In the mirror that hangs on the bathroom door, I watch my naked body turn, the breasts, the thighs glow. The body's beauty amazes. I stand here shameless, in ways he has never seen me. I am free, afloat, watching somebody else.

ELIZABETH JOLLEY

# *Little Lewis Has Had a Lovely Sleep*

*Elizabeth Jolley was born in England and moved to Australia with her husband and three children in 1959. She has written three collections of short stories and ten novels, including* Cabin Fever, *her last novel, which was published in 1991. Her fiction is sharp, battily original and frequently funny and has prompted Angela Carter to write, 'In the present efflorescence of Australian fiction, Elizabeth Jolley is one of the most pungently scented, most enigmatic, most magical blooms.'*

There's blood showing under the door of the bathroom. Under the door of the room they call the little bathroom. Part of the nursery suite in this house. I'm babysitting. This isn't the only place I go to but Mrs Porter at the agency mostly sends me here. There's never been blood here or in any place before. The sight of blood upsets me. It isn't anything you expect when you're babysitting, is it?

This has been a long night. It is a long night I should say. It isn't over yet. I keep hoping Little Lewis is all right. He's Little Lewis because of his father being called Lewis. Big Lewis. I don't call any of the family by their first names except for Little Lewis, naturally. Dr Barnett I always say, and Mrs Barnett. They are both very nice people and that's why what's hap-pened is so much worse. Mrs Barnett is against nuclear war and she's all for animal rights. She's in favour of subsidized sterilization but it worries her, she says, because animals aren't in a position to choose. That's a bit like I am now. I've got no choice just now about sitting here on this chair out here on the balcony when just inside the playroom is the nice bed Mrs Barnett made for me on the divan. From here I can see Little Lewis's bedroom door and I can see the door of the little bathroom and the blood.

I'd rather be in bed. Before they went out Dr Barnett wheeled the TV in from their own bedroom across the passage.

'Some culture for you, Miss Vales,' he said smiling down at me. He brought in a whole pile of magazines too. New glossies, they cost a fortune. I've hardly had a chance to look at them because of what's happened. Just before they went downstairs Mrs Barnett suddenly remembered the calamine.

'Little Lewis,' she said to me, 'Little Lewis has a touch of prickly heat. Could you dab his rash before he goes to bed. It's medicated,' she said, 'and soothing.' Mrs Barnett has a lovely smile especially when she's happy about going out.

I'm to be here all night. It's an all-night party they've gone to. A slumber party, they call it. Mrs Barnett laughed about it. She said she'd always thought slumber parties are what schoolgirls have. It's not my business but I can't help wondering what those well-off people will get up to during the night. It's drugs as well as sex and alcohol Mrs Porter at the agency always says. These days she says things is different from what they were. Little Lewis, in my opinion, is well out of it here with me. Or should I say *was* to all intents and purposes well out of it.

'Shall you be nervous, Miss Vales, dear?' Mrs Barnett asked when she said they would be out all night. 'Suburbs aren't the quiet places they used to be,' she said. I told her I wouldn't be at all nervous. I told her I always felt very safe in her house.

'I'm afraid the main road is terribly noisy,' she says then. She always apologizes and I always tell her that I like the main road. The sound of the traffic is company, I tell her.

'The people next door,' Mrs Barnett said, 'are away – so you are very much on your own tonight.' She made me promise to phone her if I felt nervous. The house, she said, was well locked up. She said she had put a phone number on a bit of paper for me.

Mrs Barnett and Dr Barnett are two such nice people and Little Lewis, though I never tell him this of course, is the sweetest little boy I ever knew. When Mrs Porter at the agency first sent me to babysit here she said that Little Lewis might be a trouble.

'Don't you take no nonsense, Emily Vales,' Mrs Porter said to me that first time. 'Where you're going is one of the wealthiest houses this side of Christendom, and rich people's children is used to having their own way.

It's a big house, right on the main road. It's got trees all along in front and there's a brass plate set in the wall. A doctor plate. You'll find it easy. That child,' Mrs Porter said, 'that child's used to having everything he wants. As you know, he's *gifted*! Just you don't take no nonsense!' 'I won't Mrs Porter, dear, never you worry,' I told her.

I've been pretending that Dr Barnett's a bone surgeon on account of bone surgeons having muscles. I do hope they'll be home soon. It's getting lighter every minute. They should be home soon.

I suppose the little bathroom's all spoilt. There must be blood all over it. But that's the least of it all. Mrs Porter says some people put all their money into their bathrooms. You know, His and Hers. A nice bathroom's a nice bathroom, but when all's said and done you don't live in the bathroom, that's what Mrs Porter says, though I will say this, matching towels do give a bit of class. At the agency, where I live, the bathroom's really old. It's got a wood floor and there's a tree outside growing in at the window even though it's upstairs. Mrs Porter says there's better things to do with money than put it in the bathroom. I mean, she *likes* her old brass and porcelain.

I wish I could tell Mrs Barnett and Dr Barnett that there's a gun on the piano downstairs. They'll be surprised. I'd like them to get it, the gun, before someone else does. I know this seems silly of me but I did think for a while that Mr Right had come around the corner for me at last. Mrs Porter always says that for every pot there's always a lid. She reads the tea leaves. She's always seeing a tall dark handsome stranger, Mr Right, in my cup. I've been at the agency, living there I mean, boarding for some years. Mrs Porter says the pension cheques help cover the rents and the rates. She's helping Mr Treadaway, the new gentleman, put in his application. Mr Treadaway's an old man. A bit of a giggle. Not Mr *Right*. No way!

It's like this. After Dr Barnett and Mrs Barnett have gone downstairs Lewis and I go out on the balcony to wave as the car comes down the drive and into the street. It's a wide leafy avenue leading into Perth. The houses here cost a fortune.

'Wave, Lewis,' I say, 'there's Mother's hand. See Mother's hand, Lewis? Wave to Mother, Lewis. That's a good boy!' We lean over the parapet to watch the big shiny car glide away. 'Your mother's a lovely person,' I tell Lewis. I tell him that I'd do anything in the whole world for her. 'Did you see her hand,' I ask him, 'and her beautiful lacy glove?'

'Yes,' he says. 'Now let's play the game,' he says as soon as the car has disappeared down there in the long line of cars heading for the city. 'It's too hot for bed.'

We're right up high in the tops of the street trees. Lovely and cool. While Little Lewis finds the things we need for the game I listen to the parrots. They squabble, hidden in the trees, and the cicadas keep on and on. I don't mind them. They're good company. It's the mosquitoes I don't like, so I have a smoke to keep them away. Gorgeous up here. Really nice.

'Here's your paper and pencil.' Lewis pulls one of the chairs up to the parapet.

'No leaning over!' I say. 'I don't want you falling over.' He is an obedient little boy so I haven't any worries really. 'Right,' I say. 'I'll take everything from the left and you do the right. Okay! Here's a taxi coming my side. A taxi. It's gone in next door. How many points for a taxi?'

'Two,' Lewis says. 'You've a bus your side, that's four plus two gives you six.'

'There's a bike your side,' I tell him. 'You don't get many bikes on this road. Six for a bike, isn't it?'

'Six all!' Lewis says. He's so grown-up sometimes. 'Look!' he says. 'There's a man *walking*!'

'Where? Don't often see anyone walking these days. Not along here you don't.'

'There he is. He's got red hair. You'll see him in a minute, down there under the trees. He's yours. You get ten for him. Look! There he is. He walks in a funny way.'

'That makes me sixteen,' I say. I ask if there are extra points for a limp. Lewis really laughs at that. He doesn't laugh often, being a serious child and dedicated to his music. Mrs Porter and I watched him on TV not so long ago playing his little violin. Ever so nicely dressed, and the way he bowed! Ever so sweet he was. I'll never forget it.

'He's turning back! He's coming back.' Lewis is excited. 'I'll get ten points as well if he keeps coming back.'

'Mind you don't go over the edge! Sit down!' I have another smoke. Keeps the mossies away.

'He *is* coming all the way back. Thanks, Mr Man, for my ten points. Sixteen all!' Lewis prints his score.

'Listen! A police siren. And an ambulance.' We listen.

'They're yours.' Lewis sounds disappointed. 'They're yours,' he says with perfect manners, just like his mother and father. I can't help seeing him, in my mind, in his little velvet suit with the white ruffles round his neck. 'Five points each,' he says, 'makes you twenty-six.'

'They'll be back,' I say. 'The hospital's this way. You'll get them on the way back.'

'Look! Look!' he shouts. 'That man's coming back. You've got him your side, that's thirty-six for you. He's looking at the houses. P'raps he's lost. He's really staring at our house!'

'Sit back, Lewis.' I'm uneasy. 'We don't want to be stared at as if we're in the zoo.'

'He's looking straight up here now. He's got funny eyes.' Lewis is laughing.

'Forget him!' I say. 'Here's a car my side. Must say you've got good eyesight. That's two for the car, for me.'

'Makes you thirty-eight, Miss Vales,' Lewis says. 'You're winning.'

I'm thinking about the taxi. It's still next door. I feel indignant. Why should anyone keep a taxi waiting that long. 'The driver must be a relative,' I say.

'Girls,' Lewis says, 'girls live there. Schoolgirls.'

'Ah, well,' I say, 'perhaps the driver's their uncle. An uncle would wait.' It's just like this well-to-do posh neighbourhood. I can't help thinking that schoolgirls these days have everything their own way. Like Mrs Porter at the agency says, all they think about is sex, food and money. 'Mind you!' she says, pointing her pencil at Mr Treadaway and me. 'Mind you! Not always in that order. I'd say money then sex and food more often than not.' Miss Mallow, the retired lady teacher who has Mrs Porter's downstairs front room, comes in just then and is quite upset and says that not all schoolgirls are as Mrs Porter is saying they are. And Mrs Porter says to Miss Mallow, 'And how would you know, dear, you having been shut away such a long time?' That really makes me wonder about Miss Mallow.

'When that taxi comes out,' Lewis says, 'I might get the points. They've all gone away next door, he's sure to realize his mistake and come out soon.'

I'm wondering now if it was a taxi that went in there. And then I see the man, he's still down there, looking up.

'There he is. Our man.' I try to laugh as if he's funny. 'What a mop of red hair!' I feel uneasy again. My mother used to say something about red-headed men. What was it, beware red hair – something about a limp and a squint.

'Miss Vales! Miss Vales!' Lewis is excited. 'The sirens. They are coming back. You said they would. My side. Ten points. That makes me twenty-six and ten, thirty-six, but you get two for the taxi and ten makes – you got two for the car . . .'

'There's the clock striking seven, Lewis,' I say, 'and you yawning fit to swallow the whole street!'

I usually sing him to sleep. Even though he's quite big now, going on seven, I always hold him on my lap while I sing.

I think at first it's the east wind. I left the balcony doors open because of the heat. I think it must be the east wind raising the curtain and knocking a potted plant down. When the curtain lifts again I see a leg over the parapet and a hand grasping the back of one of the little wrought-iron chairs out there. I'm sitting here in bed with the TV really soft and I'm scared stiff. Whoever's out there is swearing to himself, keeping his voice very low. He knocks another plant over. I'm wishing I'd closed the balcony doors and locked them.

'Who are you?' I say, hardly able to make my voice sound. 'What d'you want? How did you get up here? You can't come in here. Get out!' He's saying something but I can't hear him because he's got a knitted cardigan wrapped round his head.

'I can't hear a word of what you're saying,' I say. 'Take that thing off your head.'

'Where's the boy?' He moves the jumper a bit to free his mouth. His eyeholes move then and he has to pull the jumper back.

'In bed of course,' I say, 'where everyone should be this time of night. Fancy you cutting into that lovely cable stitch! A flour bag with holes for the eyes would have been better. Look out!' I say. 'You're going to crash straight into the TV.'

'Where's the boy?' He stumbles over the furniture. 'The boy, the kid. I've come for the kid.'

'I've just told you, you stupid robot,' I tell him, 'Lewis is in his bed,' and I tell him he's the very devil if he's woken up in the night. 'He screams for hours,' I say, 'and what's more, he *bites*.'

I'm shaking all over wondering if it's safer in bed or out of bed. I mean for rape, you see. 'Dr Barnett'll be home any minute now,' I say. I tell him I wouldn't like to be in his shoes when Dr Barnett comes in, and then I see he's got bare feet. Isn't that just like the thing!

I try to laugh off the bare feet. But he keeps insisting that he wants the boy. And I tell him about Lewis's daddy being called Big Lewis and that he made all the furniture because he's an orthopaedic surgeon, a bone doctor who saws and chops through bones. 'He'll just twist you into a little knot,' I say. 'He'll knock you into next week.'

It's then he tells me, would you believe, that he's the uncle and that Lewis loves him very much.

'No one said anything about a relative,' I say. 'What sort of relative? Uncle monkey,' I say, 'coming up the street and over the balcony?' He says he's full of surprises. He can't help it, he says. Jokes and surprises. He's hidden the car next door, he says. So that's it, I say, the taxi, we saw it. 'Uncle, I *don't* think!'

'All you gotta do,' he says, 'is get the kiddie ready. I don't want no nonsense. Haven't all day.'

'You mean night,' I quip, but he doesn't get the joke. He keeps on that he's seen the TV show and the pictures in the paper. 'I want that little egghead,' he says. 'He's a wonder child. A prodigy. Just what I need. And here's the ransom letter.' With that he slaps an envelope on the table.

'You'll not touch him.' I'm really angry. 'Not put one finger on him and that's final. Get out! And take that filthy envelope with you. It's disgusting!'

'It'll be the worse for you if you don't cooperate.'

'Oh my! We do use big words!' I tell him his cardigan's slipping.

Then he tells me to get dressed and to get Lewis up and dressed. 'You're no dumb blonde!' he says. 'Get dressed. I won't look. And pack his little duds. You'll have to come too. He can bite you 'stead of me. Bring some of his toys,' he says, 'make him more at home.' He goes on about Little Lewis being spoilt rotten and tells me to put his toothbrush in as he might be stopping for a few days.

I tell him I'm not coming and neither is Little Lewis. I tell him to just wait till Mrs Porter at the agency hears about this, and the police. I tell him I'd know his red hair any place and the old woolly is not hiding a thing. 'Mrs Porter'll get the police on to you straight away.'

'Listen,' he says, 'any trouble and I'll shoot!' He says he doesn't like violence and I'm not to think for one minute that he likes doing what he's doing. Then he goes on about what he calls inequality, about the rich getting richer and the poor getting nothing at all, getting poorer.

'Lady!' he says, changing his voice, just like in a movie, could be right out of *Gone with the Wind*. 'Lady,' he says, 'dissyeah's ain't no chile lover. Ah doan dig chillun, not one bit, specially eggheads. Ah doan dig but Ah gotta hev dis lid chile.' And then, believe you me, he's all fruitcake just like Mr Treadaway. Robin Hood here, talking just like Mr Treadaway does because he can't help it, says, 'I'd prefer, actually, to do this whole thing without violence of any kind.' And then he goes on telling me he's very tenderhearted.

'Oh my! Little Red Robin Hood! Robin Redhead!' I try to work up a bit of a giggle and I tell him straight he'd frighten the pants off any child. I mean, can he be *serious*!

He says then he'll have a mosey round and see if there's anything he ought to get his mitts on.

'That's my bag, if you don't mind, my handbag.' I try to get the bag off him but he holds it up high. I tell him that if he goes away, right now, he can have my purse, my pension cheque, library cards and all.

'Great!' he says and smashes Little Lewis's piggy bank, carrying on about one-cent bits, and grannies and aunties too mean to fill the pig with decent money. 'Pore lil honey chile!' he says. 'Ahm disgusted, Ah reely em!'

I'm thinking of slipping into the Barnetts' bedroom to the phone but he's wise to this and puts himself in the doorway. I tell him it's so hot and I feel faint and why doesn't he take that woolly right off his head and why don't we both go and get ourselves a nice cool drink.

'Too right!' he says. And all this time the traffic is pouring along down there on the main road unconcerned. There's no way I can cooee a car or anything.

'*À votre* Sandy — oops! I made a boo-boo.' I correct myself. 'Should be *à votre santé*.'

'Come again?' He's got the hiccups. He's got a nice laugh I tell him.

'Ditto,' he says, very gracious for all he's an intruder.

'Oops. You drink too fast. Your very good health.' I make my voice posh. 'Down the hatch!' Just like Mr Treadaway.

He doesn't drink, he tells me. Neither do I, I tell him, but this is an occasion, isn't it? He's very particular about not drinking, he says. But he says what I am pouring for him is very refreshing.

'A pleasant combination,' he says. 'Never had it before,' he says. 'Gin, vodka and orange, you say?'

'There's a first time for everything,' I tell him. 'Have a drop more,' I say. 'You haven't tried the port and lemon yet.'

We're getting a bit noisy, the two of us. It's lucky Lewis sleeps sound. We've been down to the kitchen and fetched up apple pie and cheese and mustard pickle. Mrs Barnett, I tell him, always says to help myself if I'm hungry. That's the kind of person she is. I show him the lovely magazines and I nearly let on that Dr Barnett is a sweet kind man but catch myself in time. My nerves are shot to pieces, practically.

'He's a real wolf in sheep's clothing,' I say. 'He's a terrible man. His family and his friends are scared stiff of him.'

'Come again? I beg yours?' His mouth's full.

'Let me top you up.' I tell him that Dr Barnett appears to be gentle but he is really very violent and quick-tempered. 'He killed a man at a party once, would you believe, so Mrs Barnett told me.' I explain that the reason he's not put away for the crime was because of self-defence. 'It was an intruder,' I tell him. 'A bit like yourself, if you don't mind my saying so. Dr Barnett, quick as a flash, lost his temper, grabbed him, and pressed him in all the fatal places — being a doctor he knows the human body very well — and killed him in seconds. Mrs Porter says that kind of death is more painful than any other.'

He's not all that impressed so I offer him more food and drink. 'There's plenty more pie,' I say.

'Lady,' he says, 'lady, I never pass up a piece of pie.' I tell him his accent is perfect and that he should be in a movie. He agrees with that. I tell him about Mrs Barnett and how when Little Lewis had earache one night she had me round for ten minutes to sing him to sleep and then paid me the four hours' flat rate and for taxis each way. 'That's what Mrs Barnett's like,' I tell him. 'The only song I know is "Short'nin' Bread", perhaps you know it?' I explain that Little Lewis likes me to sing it as if I was a black mammy, 'Mama's little baby loves short'nin' bread – I only know that line of the song,' I say, 'but it's enough for Little Lewis. Though he's going on seven he just loves to sit on my lap while I sing.' When I've finished telling, he's crying, would you believe, so I change the subject.

'When's your birthday?' I ask him. 'Don't tell me,' I say. 'Let me guess. It's at Christmas. I bet you came like little Baby Jesus on Christmas Eve . . .'

He doesn't seem to hear me. He's busy with his gun. Tapping it and holding it up. I'm dead scared, I can tell you.

'Having trouble with your gun?' My voice is all silly and shaky. 'I'd put it away if it's for real.'

'June,' he says, 'beginning of June. It's for real, this gun.' He taps it some more and holds it level with my head.

I grab at the June birthday and carry on quick as I can about us being Gemini. 'Join the club,' I say. I tell him we're the youngest of the zodiac. I tell him that we really liked being children and never wanted to grow up. I tell him that Mrs Porter at the agency has told me that Gemini people are supposed to be devious and that a Gemini should, if possible, marry a Leo and that us both being Gemini was bad luck because two Geminis should not marry. 'Little Lewis,' I say, 'is Virgo, makes him pernickety, a bit pernickety. Nothing too bad. He does have to have special food. Mrs Porter,' I go on, 'makes a point of knowing the birth signs of the children. She won't let us babysit when there's a full moon. Only in pairs. The pay's the same. The clients pay double. Mrs Porter says it's better to be safe than sorry.' He's still messing about with the gun. I try to think of something else to say.

'Gemini men are really nice,' I say, 'even when they're putting on an act. Did you know,' I ask him, 'did you know you're supposed to be agile and lively *and* amusing in bed? I hope you don't mind my saying that.'

'I can't sit here all night,' he says suddenly, his voice all rough. 'I've listened to enough nonsense. Now get the kid up like I told you before.'

'Don't point that thing at me,' I say, 'it's dangerous to point a gun like that.' Then I have the idea of taking him in to have a teeny peek at Little Lewis to see if he really has a fancy for him.

'Doesn't matter if I like him or not,' he shouts. 'He's only the means to an end. So shut up, will ya! Belt up! Dress up and pack up!'

I start on then about Little Lewis's pyjamas. 'You should just see his little pyjamas,' I say. 'Paisley pattern, all colours, he's got tartan ones too, the Gordons and the Hunting Stewarts and one with little racing cars all over, bows and arrows too –'

'Who cares?' he yells and he tells me it's the boy he wants and not his pyjamas. He starts on then telling me that Lewis has everything. Every child should have the same advantages. 'Look at all those expensive toys, that train set and those remote-control trucks and that cubby-house and the chiming musical clock,' he says, his voice going towards a scream. 'You name it, he's got it. This whole house full, all of it, represents food and shelter for other people who need both. The kid's coming with me!'

I tell him to keep his voice down. I tell him I'm every inch of the way with him. I couldn't agree more. 'That's how the world is,' I say. 'Ask Mrs Porter,' I say. 'She knows some families who only think of getting bigger and bigger houses. Their daughters – still at school, mind you! – all have their own cars and new clothes and shoes every day of the week. As for their weddings, Mrs Porter says she's never seen so much waste. You name it, she says, they'll have it. But,' I say, 'Your taking Little Lewis isn't going to help. Scaring Little Lewis to death and killing his mommy and daddy with grief won't solve anything. You'll get caught,' I say. 'Red hair, a limp, and a squint. You'll get picked up straight off. Anyway, I don't believe you!' Suddenly I'm saying things I never thought I would say. 'You want money for *stuff*, don't you,' I say. 'Mrs Porter says thousands of people steal to get *stuff*. And we just don't know about it.'

'Oh, shut up and rack off,' he says. 'You shouldn't criticize a person for something he can't help. I'm an educated man and I'm into doing something for my fellow human beings, I . . .'

'Listen Little Red Hood,' I say. 'Admit you're *hooked*. Admit you want a fix. If you're really educated, you'll know that if you didn't have a griev-ance you'd have no reason to exist.'

'Oh la-di-da!' He's really angry. 'Where'd you get that from?'

'I can read you like a book,' I say. 'I'm Gemini same as you are. P'raps you don't know this but you and I have this gift of changing,' and here I change to Mr Treadaway's voice. Mr Treadaway, before his misfortune, Mrs Porter told me, was one of *them*, a pansy ironmonger with a flair for the arts. He wore loose English shorts, body shirts, all colours, and had his hair permed. He wore spectacles and still does. I change to Mr Treada-way's voice. 'You and I,' I say, 'have this gift of changing our flexible personalities to suit all occasions.'

'Another of Mrs Porter's earth-shattering gems,' he says. And before he can say anything else I remember Lewis's calamine lotion. I'm remember-ing, that is, something I forgot.

I give a great gasp. 'Come on, lover boy!' I say. 'Come and hold the torch and the bottle. I've forgotten to do Little Lewis's chest.'

'What's the matter with the kid?' He's worried.

I peel down the sheet. 'Shine the light,' I say in a whisper and I un-button Lewis's ducky little pyjamas.

'What's that? What's that on his chest?' He backs off still holding the torch and the bottle. I'm dabbing Lewis lightly with the cotton wool. Of course I explain it's a terrible infection he has and it comes out worse in adults.

Back in the playroom he's mad. He starts smashing things, the clock and the chairs. 'Temper! Temper!' I say, pulling Lewis's door closed quickly.

'You've made me waste my whole night.' He's practically weeping with rage.

'What about *my* night?' I say. 'I've lost my beauty sleep.'

Downstairs I show him the knives and forks. 'There's little tiny knives too,' I say, 'with porcelain handles, very old and valuable. There's pure silver spoons and all these really nice arntray dishes, all silver.' I tell him I'll help him load his car. There's famous paintings, I tell him, in Dr Barnett's collection and I suggest he have a pick over Mrs Barnett's rings and jewels. 'She's got some lovely things,' I say. 'I hate to see you disap-pointed,' I say. 'You'll need a wall.'

'Come again?'

'A wall, you *know*,' I say, 'a fence I should say.'

'Oh!' he says. 'I'm not that kind. This isn't my line at all. As a matter of fact, if you must know, if you must know . . .' His voice is thick with all the spirits he's had and he's near tears. He's shivering too. 'If you must know,' he says, 'all I've got to go home to is a dark house and a wife I detest, well, no – it's she who detests me. Perhaps that explains things a bit. I don't know.'

I feel sorry for him. I don't know why because he's awful really. And feeling sorry for him is my big mistake, or nearly is.

'We'll toss,' he says. 'All this or him. Heads I get him. Tails, all this stuff and the paintings, the Hans Heysens and the Tom Robertses. And any others we can get in the car,' he says.

'All righty then,' I say. 'But I'm warning you Little Lewis is a terrible crybaby. Temperamental. You'll have no end of trouble!'

'I know. I know,' he says, 'seen him on TV. You don't have to tell me.' He's strolling zigzag in the gallery like he owns the place. 'Not bad,' he says as he pauses in front of the pictures. 'That a grand piano over there in the alcove?' He's over there like a shot. Smart aleck, I'm thinking, doesn't miss a trick. Drop dead! I'm wishing.

'Yes, it is, yes,' I say all friendly and chatty, 'and next to it, covered up, is the harp. Pure gold.' I'm talking too fast. 'Harps,' I say, 'are so delicate, aren't they? *I took my harp to a party, but nobody asked me to play.*' I keep on humming and laughing. 'Remember Gracie Fields?' I say. He doesn't. But who would now. Only from a record on the radio. I sing some more. Humming, laughing, chatting and laughing, I'm getting on my own nerves. 'You like the piano?' I say.

'Oh yes.' Nonchalantly he runs his fingers over the keys. 'It's in very good condition,' he says. He plays some chords.

'That's nice,' I say. 'Why don't you have a go? Be my guest. I thought you had nice hands. Mrs Porter would say with hands like those you'd have to be a piano player or a thief. Sit down to it,' I say. 'I'll not run away. You can pop your gun up here, out of the way.'

We're dancing. I don't think I've ever enjoyed myself as much as I am just now. He plays really well and is a beautiful dancer. When he's dancing he doesn't seem to limp at all. I've never been held like this before. It's heaven!

'The floor's perfect,' he says. Before we started to dance we had *Drink to Me Only with Thine Eyes*. I told him it was my mother's favourite song, 'and Mrs Porter loves it,' I said. He played a piano piece, a sort of march. And then I found the records. A samba with vocals, the old 'Tango Bolero' and 'Jealousy' and heaps of others. We're dancing and laughing our heads off. Up the gallery and back.

'Wonderful!' I say. 'Makes me forget I'm the wrong side of forty.' I've hardly any breath left.

'You're not exactly Helen of Troy,' he says to me then, 'but has anyone ever told you you're beautiful?' He's purring close to my ear, taking me once more round the floor after the record's finished. I always feel this is the sign of a true gentleman. To go on with the dance.

'Mrs Porter always says,' I say, 'that true beauty can only be revealed – wait for it,' I say, laughing, 'in an X-ray!' I'm laughing that much I can hardly speak. 'Mrs Porter,' I say, 'can see into the future. She says Mr Right is just around the corner and will turn up for me *unexpectedly* . . .' I can see at once I've done what I always do. I always say too much. I've put my foot right in it. Saying too much. I've no head for drink. That's part of the trouble.

'Yeah?' His voice suddenly changes. 'Now,' he says, 'what about that toss? Thought I'd forgotten it, did you? I'm not leaving without the kid. Get that straight!'

'You haven't won yet,' I say. To be perfectly honest I'm shocked at the sudden change in him. Perhaps in a stupid way I actually was thinking we were on the way to a happy ending with Little Lewis safely asleep in his bed till the morning. Me! Wishing for a happy ending. What a laugh! As if anyone would ever come my way!

'Yeah?' he says again. 'Get him up. Have yourselves dressed and ready to leave right away.'

Up in the playroom he sits down on the one good chair and kicks a broken one. He groans and puts his head down. 'My head, it's splitting,' he says.

'I'll go for some aspirin,' I say, thinking of the phone.

'You'll not go anywhere.' He groans again. 'I'm sick.'

'I'll make a nice cup of tea,' I tell him, 'here in the playroom. You go into Mrs Barnett's little cupboard, her side of the bed. She's got everything in there. You go and get some tablets, pick your choice.' He doesn't move. I try once more. God! I'm trying. I don't know how, but I'm trying.

He groans, terrible groaning it is. 'My bloody head! Shit! You've poisoned me. Bloody hell you'll pay for this!'

'Language!' I say. 'Temper! Watch your language in the presence of a lady. Listen,' I say, 'come on out and get some air on the balcony. You'll feel better directly. Look! I'll pull the curtains back. It's getting light.'

All he does is groan and hold his head.

'Listen,' I tell him, 'Mrs Porter always says never mix your drinks. We've made a little mistake, that's all.' I try to be as soothing as I can. 'You'll be better soon.'

For a while he ferrets around in Mrs Barnett's cupboard. He makes me go there with him and he chooses a whole heap of pills and all the time I'm telling him about the game and how it's better than the toss. He swallows his pills. I'm too scared to see what they are.

'Not too many,' I say. I'm anxious, suppose he dies, it'll be my fault.

'Shut your face!' he says.

I'm a dill. That's what I am. Why am I such a dill! I've taken the wrong side. He's stacking up the points, he's up to eighty-seven already. He's got the side with everything heading for the city, all the cars and buses in the early-morning rat race. I could kill myself for being the biggest dill there ever was. First to get a hundred wins and he's up to eighty-seven and what have I got? Twelve. I've got twelve. Nothing's coming my way. I'm praying for a cycling club or some bush walkers. They would be leaving town early, on my side.

'No one walks these days,' he says just as if he can read my mind. But I tell him earlier that there's more points for people walking. 'I'm winning.' He pauses, letting the stream of traffic below go uncounted. 'I'll have the kid, like I said, like we arranged. Once I've got the money I'll have a place in the country. Open space and trees, paddocks, a little house not too far from the road, an orchard, a few sheep, banks of grass by a quiet river, the smell of hay . . .' He stops talking and in a leisurely way adds six to his eighty-seven.

'Ninety-four,' he says dreamily. 'I like this game.'

'Ninety-three,' I say. He's looking uneasy. 'You made a mistake,' I say, 'gave yourself one too many.'

'Er, I'll have to use the bathroom,' he says.

'Be my guest,' I say. 'We'll suspend play at ninety-three to twelve.'

'I'll have to tie you up,' he says. 'Ninety-four.'

'Feel free,' I say. I'm desperate. 'Any rope?' I say. 'Ninety-*three* it is. Suspended.'

He's got the rope he came up on. He says he left it for when he makes his getaway.

'Stupid,' I say. 'If you're in the house, you can leave by the front door. How stupid can you be!'

I tell him the rope's dirty and he's to put it round some newspaper. 'I don't want that filthy thing next to my skin,' I say. 'And not too tight either. I bruise easy. And I've told you I'll not go anywhere. I promise I'll just sit here.'

I tell him where the little bathroom is. 'If you want to be more deluxe,' I call after him, 'the en sooitt's off the master bedroom across the passage.'

He goes. That's the last I see of him. I call out now and then. I think he's taken a tumble in there. I did hear a noise like someone falling and now there's this blood showing under the door. The sight of blood upsets me. I feel sick. There's more blood. He must have hit his head, perhaps on the corner of the basin. I'm wishing the Barnetts, Dr Barnett and Mrs Barnett, would come home now, this very minute, even though it's early. I wish they would walk in right now so that I could tell them Little Lewis has had a lovely sleep and there's a gentleman bleeding in the bathroom.

# Distant View of a Minaret

Translated by Denys Johnson-Davies

*Alifa Rifaat has spent most of her adult life in the Egyptian countryside, and it is from there that she draws the material for many of her short stories. She is the widow of a police officer and now lives in Cairo with her three children.*

Through half-closed eyes she looked at her husband. Lying on his right side, his body was intertwined with hers and his head bent over her right shoulder. As usual at such times she felt that he inhabited a world utterly different from hers, a world from which she had been excluded. Only half-aware of the movements of his body, she turned her head to one side and stared up at the ceiling, where she noticed a spider's web. She told herself she'd have to get out the long broom and brush it down.

When they were first married she had tried to will her husband into sensing the desire that burned within her and so continuing the act longer; she had been too shy and conscious of the conventions to express such wishes openly. Later on, feeling herself sometimes to be on the brink of the experience some of her married women friends talked of in hushed terms, she had found the courage to be explicit about what she wanted. At such moments it had seemed to her that all she needed was just one more movement and her body and soul would be quenched, that once achieved they would between them know how to repeat the experience. But on each occasion, when breathlessly imploring him to continue, he would – as though purposely to deprive her – quicken his movements and bring the act to an abrupt end. Sometimes she had tried in vain to maintain the rhythmic movements a little longer, but always he would stop her. The last time she had made such an attempt, so desperate was she at this critical moment, that she had dug her fingernails into his back, compelling him to remain inside her. He had given a shout as he pushed her away and slipped from her:

'Are you mad, woman? Do you want to kill me?'

It was as though he had made an indelible tattoo mark of shame deep inside her, so that whenever she thought of the incident she felt a flush coming to her face. Thenceforth she had submitted to her passive role, sometimes asking herself: 'Perhaps it's me who's at fault. Perhaps I'm unreasonable in my demands and don't know how to react to him properly.'

There had been occasions when he had indicated that he had had relationships with other women, and sometimes she had suspicions that maybe he still had affairs, and she was surprised that the idea no longer upset her.

She was suddenly aroused from her thoughts by his more urgent movements. She turned to him and watched him struggling in the world he occupied on his own. His eyes were tight closed, his lips drawn down in an ugly contortion, and the veins in his neck stood out. She felt his hand on her leg, seizing it above the knee and thrusting it sideways as his movements became more frenzied. She stared up at her foot that now pointed towards the spider's web and noted her toenails needed cutting.

As often happened at this moment she heard the call to afternoon prayers filtering through the shutters of the closed window and bringing her back to reality. With a groan he let go of her thigh and immediately withdrew. He took a small towel from under the pillow, wrapped it round himself, turned his back to her and went to sleep.

She rose and hobbled to the bathroom where she seated herself on the bidet and washed herself. No longer did she feel any desire to complete the act with herself as she used to do in the first years of marriage. Under the shower she gave her right side to the warm water, then her left, repeating the formula of faith as the water coursed down her body. She wrapped her soaking hair in a towel and wound a large second one under her armpits. Returning to the bedroom, she put on a long house-gown, then took up the prayer carpet from on top of the wardrobe and shut the door behind her.

As she passed through the living-room, the sounds of pop music came to her from the room of her son Mahmoud. She smiled as she imagined him stretched out on his bed, a school book held in front of him; she was amazed at his ability to concentrate in the face of such noise. She closed the living-room door, spread the rug and began her prayers. When she had performed the four *rak'as* she seated herself on the edge of the prayer carpet and counted off her glorifications of the almighty, three at a time on the joints of each finger. It was late autumn and the time for the sunset prayer would soon come and she enjoyed the thought that she would soon be praying again. Her five daily prayers were like punctuation marks that divided up and gave meaning to her life. Each prayer had for her a distinct quality, just as different foods had their own flavours. She folded up the carpet and went out on to the small balcony.

Dusting off the cane chair that stood there, she seated herself and looked down at the street from the sixth floor. She was assailed by the din of buses, the hooting of cars, the cries of street vendors and the raucous noise of competing radios from nearby flats. Clouds of smoke rose up from the outpourings of car exhausts veiling the view of the tall solitary minaret that could be seen between two towering blocks of flats. This single minaret, one of the twin minarets of the Mosque of Sultan Hasan, with above it a thin slice of the Citadel, was all that was now left of the panoramic view she had once had of old Cairo, with its countless mosques and minarets against a background of the Mokattam Hills and Mohamed Ali's Citadel.

Before marriage she had dreamed of having a house with a small garden in a quiet suburb such as Maadi or Helwan. On finding that it would be a long journey for her husband to his work in the centre of the city, she had settled for this flat because of its views. But with the passing of the years, buildings had risen on all sides, gradually narrowing the view. In time this single minaret would also be obscured by some new building.

Aware of the approach of the call to sunset prayers, she left the balcony and went to the kitchen to prepare her husband's coffee. She filled the brass *kanaka* with water and added a spoonful of coffee and a spoonful of sugar. Just as it was about to boil over she removed it from the stove and placed it on the tray with the coffee cup, for he liked to have the coffee poured out in front of him. She expected to find him sitting up in bed smoking a cigarette. The strange way his body was twisted immediately told her that something was wrong. She approached the bed and looked into the eyes that stared into space and suddenly she was aware of the odour of death in the room. She left and placed the tray in the living-room before passing through to her son's room. He looked up as she entered and immediately switched off the radio and stood up:

'What's wrong, mother?'

'It's your father . . .'

'He's had another attack?'

She nodded. 'Go downstairs to the neighbours and ring Dr Ramzi. Ask him to come right away.'

She returned to the living room and poured out the coffee for herself. She was surprised at how calm she was.

# *Hairball*

*Margaret Atwood was born in Ottawa in 1939 and brought up in the northern reaches of Quebec and Ontario. After studying English literature at Toronto University she started writing fiction and has written over twenty books, including poetry, short stories, novels and literary criticism. Her novel* The Handmaid's Tale *sold over a million copies in the USA and held a place in* The New York Times*'s bestseller list for twenty-three weeks. It was shortlisted for the Booker Prize in 1986 and in 1990 was made into a film with a screenplay by Harold Pinter. Her work has been translated into more than twenty languages and has been published in over twenty-five countries. She lives in Toronto with the novelist Graeme Gibson and their daughter.*

On the thirteenth of November, day of unluck, month of the dead, Kat went into the Toronto General Hospital for an operation. It was for an ovarian cyst, a large one.

Many women had them, the doctor told her. Nobody knew why. There wasn't any way of finding out whether the thing was malignant, whether it contained, already, the spores of death. Not before they went in. He spoke of 'going in' the way she'd heard old veterans in TV documentaries speak of assaults on enemy territory. There was the same tensing of the jaw, the same fierce gritting of the teeth, the same grim enjoyment. Except that what he would be going into was her body. Counting down, waiting for the anaesthetic, Kat too gritted her teeth fiercely. She was terrified, but also she was curious. Curiosity has got her through a lot.

She'd made the doctor promise to save the thing for her, whatever it was, so she could have a look. She was intensely interested in her own body, in anything it might choose to do or produce; although when flaky

Dania, who did layout at the magazine, told her this growth was a message to her from her body and she ought to sleep with an amethyst under her pillow to calm her vibrations, Kat told her to stuff it.

The cyst turned out to be a benign tumour. Kat liked that use of *benign*, as if the thing had a soul and wished her well. It was big as a grapefruit, the doctor said. 'Big as a coconut,' said Kat. Other people had grapefruits. 'Coconut' was better. It conveyed the hardness of it, and the hairiness, too.

The hair in it was red – long strands of it wound round and round inside, like a ball of wet wool gone berserk or like the guck you pulled out of a clogged bathroom-sink drain. There were little bones in it too, or fragments of bone; bird bones, the bones of a sparrow crushed by a car. There was a scattering of nails, toe or finger. There were five perfectly formed teeth.

'Is this abnormal?' Kat asked the doctor, who smiled. Now that he had gone in and come out again, unscathed, he was less clenched.

'Abnormal? No,' he said carefully, as if breaking the news to a mother about a freakish accident to her newborn. 'Let's say it's fairly common.' Kat was a little disappointed. She would have preferred uniqueness.

She asked for a bottle of formaldehyde, and put the cut-open tumour into it. It was hers, it was benign, it did not deserve to be thrown away. She took it back to her apartment and stuck it on the mantelpiece. She named it Hairball. It isn't that different from having a stuffed bear's head or a preserved ex-pet or anything else with fur and teeth looming over your fireplace; or she pretends it isn't. Anyway, it certainly makes an impression.

Ger doesn't like it. Despite his supposed yen for the new and outré, he is a squeamish man. The first time he comes around (sneaks around, creeps around) after the operation, he tells Kat to throw Hairball out. He calls it 'disgusting'. Kat refuses point-blank, and says she'd rather have Hairball in a bottle on her mantelpiece than the soppy dead flowers he's brought her, which will anyway rot a lot sooner than Hairball will. As a mantelpiece ornament, Hairball is far superior. Ger says Kat has a tendency to push things to extremes, to go over the edge, merely from a juvenile desire to shock, which is hardly a substitute for wit. One of these days, he says, she will go way too far. Too far for him, is what he means.

'That's why you hired me, isn't it?' she says. 'Because I go way too far.'
But he's in one of his analysing moods. He can see these tendencies of
hers reflected in her work on the magazine, he says. All that leather and
those grotesque and tortured-looking poses are heading down a track he
and others are not at all sure they should continue to follow. Does she see
what he means, does she take his point? It's a point that's been made
before. She shakes her head slightly, says nothing. She knows how that
translates: there have been complaints from the advertisers. *Too bizarre, too
kinky*. Tough.

'Want to see my scar?' she says. 'Don't make me laugh, though, you'll
crack it open.' Stuff like that makes him dizzy: anything with a hint of blood,
anything gynaecological. He almost threw up in the delivery room when his
wife had a baby two years ago. He'd told her that with pride. Kat thinks
about sticking a cigarette into the side of her mouth, as in a black-and-white
movie of the Forties. She thinks about blowing the smoke into his face.

Her insolence used to excite him, during their arguments. Then there
would be a grab of her upper arms, a smouldering, violent kiss. He kisses
her as if he thinks someone else is watching him, judging the image they
make together. Kissing the latest thing, hard and shiny, purple-mouthed,
crop-headed; kissing a girl, a woman, a girl, in a little crotch-hugger skirt
and skin-tight leggings. He likes mirrors.

But he isn't excited now. And she can't decoy him into bed; she isn't
ready for that yet, she isn't healed. He has a drink, which he doesn't finish,
holds her hand as an afterthought, gives her a couple of avuncular pats on
the off-white outsized alpaca shoulder, leaves too quickly.

'Goodbye, Gerald,' she says. She pronounces the name with mockery.
It's a negation of him, an abolishment of him, like ripping a medal off his
chest. It's a warning.

He'd been Gerald when they first met. It was she who transformed
him, first to Gerry, then to Ger. (Rhymed with *flair*, rhymed with *dare*.) She
made him get rid of those sucky pursed-mouth ties, told him what shoes
to wear, got him to buy a loose-cut Italian suit, redid his hair. A lot of his
current tastes – in food, in drink, in recreational drugs, in women's enter-
tainment underwear – were once hers. In his new phase, with his new,
hard, stripped-down name ending on the sharpened note of *r*, he is her
creation.

As she is her own. During her childhood she was a romanticized Katherine, dressed by her misty-eyed, fussy mother in dresses that looked like ruffled pillowcases. By high school she'd shed the frills and emerged as a bouncy, round-faced Kathy, with gleaming freshly washed hair and enviable teeth, eager to please and no more interesting than a health-food ad. At university she was Kath, blunt and no-bullshit in her Take-Back-the-Night jeans and checked shirt and her bricklayer-style striped-denim peaked hat. When she ran away to England, she sliced herself down to Kat. It was economical, street-feline, and pointed as a nail. It was also unusual. In England you had to do something to get their attention, especially if you weren't English. Safe in this incarnation, she Ramboed through the Eighties.

It was the name, she still thinks, that got her the interview and then the job. The job with an avant-garde magazine, the kind that was printed on matte stock in black and white, with overexposed close-ups of women with hair blowing over their eyes, one nostril prominent: *the razor's edge*, it was called. Haircuts as art, some real art, film reviews, a little stardust, wardrobes of ideas that were clothes and of clothes that were ideas – the metaphysical shoulder pad. She learned her trade well, hands-on. She learned what worked.

She made her way up the ladder, from layout to design, then to the supervision of whole spreads, and then whole issues. It wasn't easy, but it was worth it. She had become a creator; she created total looks. After a while she could walk down the street in Soho or stand in the lobby at openings and witness her handiwork incarnate, strolling around in outfits she'd put together, spouting her warmed-over pronouncements. It was like being God, only God had never got around to off-the-rack lines.

By that time her face had lost its roundness, though the teeth of course remained: there was something to be said for North American dentistry. She'd shaved off most of her hair, worked on the drop-dead stare, perfected a certain turn of the neck that conveyed an aloof inner authority. What you had to make them believe was that you knew something they didn't know yet. What you also had to make them believe was that they too could know this thing, this thing that would give them eminence and power and sexual allure, that would attract envy to them – but for a price.

The price of the magazine. What they could never get through their heads was that it was done entirely with cameras. Frozen light, frozen time. Given the angle, she could make any woman look ugly. Any man as well. She could make anyone look beautiful, or at least interesting. It was all photography, it was all iconography. It was all in the choosing eye. This was the thing that could never be bought, no matter how much of your pitiful monthly wage you blew on snakeskin.

Despite the status, *the razor's edge* was fairly low-paying. Kat herself could not afford many of the things she contextualized so well. The grottiness and expense of London began to get to her; she got tired of gorging on the canapés at literary launches in order to scrimp on groceries, tired of the fuggy smell of cigarettes ground into the red-and-maroon carpeting of pubs, tired of the pipes bursting every time it froze in winter, and of the Clarissas and Melissas and Penelopes at the magazine rabbiting on about how they had been literally, absolutely, totally freezing all night, and how it literally, absolutely, totally, usually never got that cold. It always got that cold. The pipes always burst. Nobody thought of putting in real pipes, ones that would not burst next time. Burst pipes were an English tradition, like so many others.

Like, for instance, English men. Charm the knickers off you with their mellow vowels and frivolous verbiage, and then, once they'd got them off, panic and run. Or else stay and whinge. The English called it *whinging* instead of whining. It was better, really. Like a creaking hinge. It was a traditional compliment to be whinged at by an Englishman. It was his way of saying he trusted you, he was conferring upon you the privilege of getting to know the real him. The inner, whinging him. That was how they thought of women, secretly: whinge receptacles. Kat could play it, but that didn't mean she liked it.

She had an advantage over the English women, though: she was of no class. She had no class. She was in a class of her own. She could roll around among the English men, all different kinds of them, secure in the knowledge that she was not being measured against the class yardsticks and accent-detectors they carried around in their back pockets, was not subject to the petty snobberies and resentments that lent such richness to their inner lives. The flip side of this freedom was that she was beyond the pale. She was a colonial – how fresh, how vital, how anonymous, how finally of no consequence. Like a hole in the wall, she could be told all secrets and then be abandoned with no guilt.

She was too smart, of course. The English men were very competitive; they liked to win. Several times it hurt. Twice she had abortions, because the men in question were not up for the alternative. She learned to say that she didn't want children anyway, that if she longed for a rug-rat she would buy a gerbil. Her life began to seem long. Her adrenalin was running out. Soon she would be thirty, and all she could see ahead was more of the same.

This was how things were when Gerald turned up. 'You're terrific,' he said, and she was ready to hear it, even from him, even though *terrific* was a word that had probably gone out with Fifties crew-cuts. She was ready for his voice by that time too: the flat, metallic nasal tone of the Great Lakes, with its clear hard *r*s and its absence of theatricality. Dull normal. The speech of her people. It came to her suddenly that she was an exile.

Gerald was scouting, Gerald was recruiting. He'd heard about her, looked at her work, sought her out. One of the big companies back in Toronto was launching a new fashion-oriented magazine, he said: up-market, international in its coverage, of course, but with some Canadian fashion in it too, and with lists of stores where the items portrayed could actually be bought. In that respect they felt they'd have it all over the competition, those American magazines that assumed you could only get Gucci in New York or Los Angeles. Heck, times had changed, you could get it in Edmonton! You could get it in Winnipeg!

Kat had been away too long. There was Canadian fashion now? The English quip would be to say that 'Canadian fashion' was an oxymoron. She refrained from making it, lit a cigarette with her cyanide-green Covent Garden-boutique leather-covered lighter (as featured in the May issue of *the razor's edge*), looked Gerald in the eye. 'London is a lot to give up,' she said levelly. She glanced around the see-me-here Mayfair restaurant where they were finishing lunch, a restaurant she'd chosen because she'd known he was paying. She'd never spend that kind of money on food otherwise. 'Where would I eat?'

Gerald assured her that Toronto was now the restaurant capital of Canada. He himself would be happy to be her guide. There was a great

Chinatown, there was world-class Italian. Then he paused, took a breath. 'I've been meaning to ask you,' he said. 'About the name. Is that Kat as in Krazy?' He thought this was suggestive. She'd heard it before.

'No,' she said. 'It's Kat as in KitKat. That's a chocolate bar. Melts in your mouth.' She gave him her stare, quirked her mouth, just a twitch.

Gerald became flustered, but he pushed on. They wanted her, they needed her, they loved her, he said in essence. Someone with her fresh, innovative approach and her experience would be worth a lot of money to them, relatively speaking. But there were rewards other than the money. She would be in on the initial concept, she would have a formative influence, she would have a free hand. He named a sum that made her gasp, inaudibly of course. By now she knew better than to betray desire.

So she made the journey back, did her three months of culture shock, tried the world-class Italian and the great Chinese, and seduced Gerald at the first opportunity, right in his junior vice-presidential office. It was the first time Gerald had been seduced in such a location, or perhaps ever. Even though it was after hours, the danger frenzied him. It was the idea of it. The daring. The image of Kat kneeling on the broadloom, in a legendary bra that until now he'd seen only in the lingerie ads of the Sunday *New York Times*, unzipping him in full view of the silver-framed engagement portrait of his wife that complemented the impossible ball-point pen set on his desk. At that time he was so straight he felt compelled to take off his wedding ring and place it carefully in the ashtray first. The next day he brought her a box of David Wood Food Shop chocolate truffles. They were the best, he told her, anxious that she should recognize their quality. She found the gesture banal, but also sweet. The banality, the sweetness, the hunger to impress: that was Gerald.

Gerald was the kind of man she wouldn't have bothered with in London. He was not funny, he was not knowledgeable, he had little verbal charm. But he was eager, he was tractable, he was blank paper. Although he was eight years older than she was, he seemed much younger. She took pleasure from his furtive, boyish delight in his own wickedness. And he was so grateful. 'I can hardly believe this is happening,' he said, more frequently than was necessary and usually in bed.

His wife, whom Kat encountered (and still encounters) at many tedious company events, helped to explain his gratitude. The wife was a priss. Her name was Cheryl. Her hair looked as if she still used big rollers and embalm-your-hairdo spray; her mind was room-by-room Laura Ashley wallpaper: tiny, unopened pastel buds arranged in straight rows. She probably put on rubber gloves to make love, and checked it off on a list afterwards. One more messy household chore. She looked at Kat as if she'd like to spritz her with air deodorizer. Kat revenged herself by picturing Cheryl's bathrooms: hand towels embroidered with lilies, fuzzy covers on the toilet seats.

The magazine itself got off to a rocky start. Although Kat had lots of lovely money to play with, and although it was a challenge to be working in colour, she did not have the free hand Gerald had promised her. She had to contend with the company board of directors, who were all men, who were all accountants or indistinguishable from them, who were cautious and slow as moles.

'It's simple,' Kat told them. 'You bombard them with images of what they ought to be, and you make them feel grotty for being the way they are. You're working with the gap between reality and perception. That's why you have to hit them with something new, something they've never seen before, something they aren't. Nothing sells like anxiety.'

The board, on the other hand, felt that the readership should simply be offered more of what they already had. More fur, more sumptuous leather, more cashmere. More established names. The board had no sense of improvisation, no wish to take risks; no sporting instincts, no desire to put one over on the readers just for the hell of it. 'Fashion is like hunting,' Kat told them, hoping to appeal to their male hormones, if any. 'It's playful, it's intense, it's predatory. It's blood and guts. It's erotic.' But to them it was about good taste. They wanted Dress-for-Success. Kat wanted scattergun ambush.

Everything became a compromise. Kat had wanted to call the magazine *All the Rage*, but the board was put off by the vibrations of anger in the word 'rage'. They thought it was too feminist, of all things. 'It's a *Forties* sound,' Kat said. 'Forties is *back*. Don't you get it?' But they didn't. They wanted to call it *Or*. French for *gold*, and blatant enough in its values, but without any base note, as Kat told them. They sawed off at *Felice*, which had qualities each side wanted. It was vaguely French-sounding, it meant 'happy' (so much less threatening than rage), and, although you couldn't expect the others to notice, for Kat it had a feline bouquet which counteracted the laciness. She had it done in hot-pink lipstick-scrawl, which helped some. She could live with it, but it had not been her first love.

This battle has been fought and refought over every innovation in design, every new angle Kat has tried to bring in, every innocuous bit of semi-kink. There was a big row over a spread that did lingerie, half pulled off and with broken glass perfume bottles strewn on the floor. There was an uproar over the two nouveau-stockinged legs, one tied to a chair with a third, different-coloured stocking. They had not understood the man's three-hundred-dollar leather gloves positioned ambiguously around a neck.

And so it has gone on, for five years.

After Gerald has left, Kat paces her living-room. Pace, pace. Her stitches pull. She's not looking forward to her solitary dinner of microwaved leftovers. She's not sure now why she came back here, to this flat burg beside the polluted inland sea. Was it Ger? Ludicrous thought but no longer out of the question. Is he the reason she stays, despite her growing impatience with him?

He's no longer fully rewarding. They've learned each other too well, they take short-cuts now; their time together has shrunk from whole stolen rolling and sensuous afternoons to a few hours snatched between work and dinner-time. She no longer knows what she wants from him. She tells herself she's worth more, she should branch out; but she doesn't see other men, she can't, somehow. She's tried once or twice but it didn't work. Sometimes she goes out to dinner or a flick with one of the gay designers. She likes the gossip.

Maybe she misses London. She feels caged, in this country, in this city, in this room. She could start with the room, she could open a window. It's too stuffy in here. There's an undertone of formaldehyde, from Hairball's bottle. The flowers she got for the operation are mostly wilted, all except Gerald's from today. Come to think of it, why didn't he send her any at the hospital? Did he forget, or was it a message?

'Hairball,' she says, 'I wish you could talk. I could have a more intelligent conversation with you than with most of the losers in this turkey farm.' Hairball's baby teeth glint in the light; it looks as if it's about to speak.

Kat feels her own forehead. She wonders if she's running a temperature. Something ominous is going on, behind her back. There haven't been enough phone calls from the magazine; they've been able to muddle on without her, which is bad news. Reigning queens should never go on vacation, or have operations either. Uneasy lies the head. She has a sixth sense about these things, she's been involved in enough palace coups to know the signs, she has sensitive antennae for the footfalls of impending treachery.

The next morning she pulls herself together, downs an espresso from her mini-machine, picks out an aggressive touch-me-if-you-dare suede outfit in armour grey, and drags herself to the office, although she isn't due in till next week. Surprise, surprise. Whispering knots break up in the corridors, greet her with false welcome as she limps past. She settles herself at her minimalist desk, checks her mail. Her head is pounding, her stitches hurt. Ger gets wind of her arrival; he wants to see her a.s.a.p., and not for lunch.

He awaits her in his newly done wheat-on-white office, with the eighteenth-century desk they chose together, the Victorian inkstand, the framed blow-ups from the magazine, the hands in maroon leather, wrists manacled with pearls, the Hermès scarf twisted into a blindfold, the model's mouth blossoming lusciously beneath it. Some of her best stuff. He's beautifully done up, in a lick-my-neck silk shirt open at the throat, an eat-your-heart-out Italian silk-and-wool loose-knit sweater. Oh, cool insouciance. Oh, eyebrow language. He's a money man who lusted after art, and now he's got some, now he is some. Body art. Her art. She's done her job well; he's finally sexy.

He's smooth as lacquer. 'I didn't want to break this to you until next week,' he says. He breaks it to her. It's the board of directors. They think she's too bizarre, they think she goes way too far. Nothing he could do about it, although naturally he tried.

Naturally. Betrayal. The monster has turned on its own mad scientist. 'I gave you life!' she wants to scream at him.

She isn't in good shape. She can hardly stand. She stands, despite his offer of a chair. She sees now what she's wanted, what she's been missing.

Gerald is what she's been missing – the stable, unfashionable, previous, tight-assed Gerald. Not Ger, not the one she's made in her own image. The other one, before he got ruined. The Gerald with a house and a small child and a picture of his wife in a silver frame on his desk. She wants to be in that silver frame. She wants the child. She's been robbed.

'And who is my lucky replacement?' she says. She needs a cigarette, but does not want to reveal her shaking hands.

'Actually, it's me,' he says, trying for modesty.

This is too absurd. Gerald couldn't edit a phone book. 'You?' she says faintly. She has the good sense not to laugh.

'I've always wanted to get out of the money end of things here,' he says, 'into the creative area. I knew you'd understand, since it can't be you at any rate. I knew you'd prefer someone who could, well, sort of build on your foundations.' Pompous asshole. She looks at his neck. She longs for him, hates herself for it, and is powerless.

The room wavers. He slides towards her across the wheat-coloured broadloom, takes her by the grey suede upper arms. 'I'll write you a good reference,' he says. 'Don't worry about that. Of course, we can still see one another. I'd miss our afternoons.'

'Of course,' she says. He kisses her, a voluptuous kiss, or it would look like one to a third party, and she lets him. *In a pig's ear.*

She makes it home in a taxi. The driver is rude to her and gets away with it; she doesn't have the energy. In her mailbox is an engraved invitation: Ger and Cheryl are having a drinks party, tomorrow evening. Post-marked five days ago. Cheryl is behind the times.

Kat undresses, runs a shallow bath. There's not much to drink around here, there's nothing to sniff or smoke. What an oversight; she's stuck with herself. There are other jobs. There are other men, or that's the theory. Still, something's been ripped out of her. How could this have happened, to her? When knives were slated for backs, she'd always done the stabbing. Any headed her way she's seen coming in time, and thwarted. Maybe she's losing her edge.

She stares into the bathroom mirror, assesses her face in the misted glass. A face of the Eighties, a mask face, a bottom-line face; push the weak to the wall and grab what you can. But now it's the Nineties. Is she out of style, so soon? She's only thirty-five, and she's already losing track of what people ten years younger are thinking. That could be fatal. As time goes by she'll have to race faster and faster to keep up, and for what? Part of the life she should have had is just a gap, it isn't there, it's nothing. What can be salvaged from it, what can be redone, what can be done at all?

When she climbs out of the tub after her sponge bath, she almost falls. She has a fever, no doubt about it. Inside her something is leaking, or else festering; she can hear it, like a dripping tap. A running sore, a sore from running so hard. She should go to the emergency ward at some hospital, get herself shot up with antibiotics. Instead she lurches into the living-room, takes Hairball down from the mantelpiece in its bottle, places it on the coffee table. She sits cross-legged, listens. Filaments wave. She can hear a kind of buzz, like bees at work.

She'd asked the doctor if it could have started as a child, a fertilized egg that escaped somehow and got into the wrong place. No, said the doctor. Some people thought this kind of tumour was present in seedling form from birth, or before it. It might be the woman's undeveloped twin. What they really were was unknown. They had many kinds of tissue, though. Even brain tissue. Though of course all of these tissues lack structure.

Still, sitting here on the rug looking in at it, she pictures it as a child. It has come out of her, after all. It is flesh of her flesh. Her child with Gerald, her thwarted child, not allowed to grow normally. Her warped child, taking its revenge.

'Hairball,' she says. 'You're so ugly. Only a mother could love you.' She feels sorry for it. She feels loss. Tears run down her face. Crying is not something she does, not normally, not lately.

Hairball speaks to her, without words. It is irreducible, it has the texture of reality, it is not an image. What it tells her is everything she's never wanted to hear about herself. This is new knowledge, dark and precious and necessary. It cuts.

She shakes her head. What are you doing, sitting on the floor and talking to a hairball? You are sick, she tells herself. Take a Tylenol and go to bed.

The next day she feels a little better. Dania from layout calls her and makes dove-like, sympathetic coos at her, and wants to drop by during lunch hour to take a look at her aura. Kat tells her to come off it. Dania gets huffy, and says that Kat's losing her job is a price for immoral behaviour in a previous life. Kat tells her to stuff it; anyway, she's done enough immoral behaviour in this life to account for the whole thing. 'Why are you so full of hate?' asks Dania. She doesn't say it like a point she's making, she sounds truly baffled.

'I don't know,' says Kat. It's a straight answer.

After she hangs up she paces the floor. She's crackling inside, like hot fat under the broiler. What she's thinking about is Cheryl, bustling about her cosy house, preparing for the party. Cheryl fiddles with her freeze-framed hair, positions an overloaded vase of flowers, fusses about the caterers. Gerald comes in, kisses her lightly on the cheek. A connubial scene. His conscience is nicely washed. The witch is dead, his foot is on the body, the trophy; he's had his dirty fling, he's ready now for the rest of his life.

Kat takes a taxi to the David Wood Food Shop and buys two dozen chocolate truffles. She has them put into an oversized box, then into an oversized bag with the store logo on it. Then she goes home and takes Hairball out of its bottle. She drains it in the kitchen strainer and pats it damp-dry, tenderly, with paper towels. She sprinkles it with powdered cocoa, which forms a brown pasty crust. It still smells like formaldehyde, so she wraps it in Saran Wrap and then in tinfoil, and then in pink tissue paper, which she ties with a mauve bow. She places it in the David Wood box in a bed of shredded tissue, with the truffles nestled around. She closes the box, tapes it, puts it into the bag, stuffs several sheets of pink paper on top. It's her gift, valuable and dangerous. It's her messenger, but the message it will deliver is its own. It will tell the truth, to whoever asks. It's right that Gerald should have it; after all, it's his child too.

She prints on the card, 'Gerald, Sorry I couldn't be with you. This is all the rage. Love, K.'

When evening has fallen and the party must be in full swing, she calls a delivery taxi. Cheryl will not distrust anything that arrives in such an expensive bag. She will open it in public, in front of everyone. There will be distress, there will be questions. Secrets will be unearthed. There will be pain. After that, everything will go way too far.

She is not well; her heart is pounding, space is wavering once more. But outside the window it's snowing, the soft, damp, windless flakes of her childhood. She puts on her coat and goes out, foolishly. She intends to walk just to the corner, but when she reaches the corner she goes on. The snow melts against her face like small fingers touching. She has done an outrageous thing, but she doesn't feel guilty. She feels light and peaceful and filled with charity, and temporarily without a name.

LUISA VALENZUELA

# *Blue Water-man*

Translated by Evelyn Picon Garfield

*Luisa Valenzuela was born in Argentina in 1938 and has become the most frequently translated contemporary woman author from Latin America. She has worked as a journalist for major Argentinian newspapers and received a Guggenheim Fellowship. She has taught creative writing at New York University and now lives in Buenos Aires. Her work is often surreal, dream-like, and often parodies political and social conventions. It has prompted Carlos Fuentes to call her the 'heiress of Latin American fiction': 'She wears an opulent crown, but her feet are naked.'*

They pointed him out to me; he's the water-man. I approached him because I like the sound of that word, not because of what that title means around here: the right to distribute rationed water according to whim. But I wasn't the one who lit the wick. Even though I got pretty close and even managed to touch him, as some say (there are witnesses for everything, there's always someone unscrupulous enough to tell the truth: imagination is withering away and nothing's left for the poor).

Water-man and all, it seems I managed to touch him, so the witnesses say. But I insist that I wasn't the one to light the wick. The idea of the uproar didn't even enter my mind.

Water-man. In appearance a respectable man, someone worthy of living in this village so full of respect for fallen leaves, for starving dogs, for what's already dying and also patiently awaiting its end: the human being.

(The cemetery has colored tombstones. The houses in this part of the world are made of clay; while we're above earth it's best that we blend into it.)

The water-man, on the other hand, was the only dustless one in this village; that's rather insulting.

Stone, dust and stone, all the streets climb up to the patch of light we call the market. Up there, the clean water-man shines with his white shirt, golden teeth and mustache. Below we walk around carrying water buckets from the river that's already drying up.

This happened a week ago on Sunday.

I didn't light the wick and I wasn't part of the uproar either.

He was super-clean standing in the atrium to the ancient convent and I, as dirty as ever, dusty, with fingertips of a fresh, indigo blue that I'd been painting on the walls (my house is adobe like everyone else's; I was slowly painting it blue to tone it down: I wanted a bit of blue to imitate water). (And if more than one witness says I touched him well I probably did. Even though I felt that they were his hands on my body and not the unthinkable opposite.)

To be more exact it was Palm Sunday and he was in the atrium calculating profits. An infamous water-man, no doubt: for one hundred *pesos* he allowed the rich man's water tank to overflow, and let the neighbors go to hell. He was the spider in the web of pipes, god in the subterranean world of sewers.

(And to think that just by moving a finger, just by removing the cloak of greed and generously opening up the valves, he could have quenched the thirst of the entire village.)

A blue patch remained on his chest that Sunday – Palm Sunday – almost hidden beneath the white shirt, that's all.

And a week went by:

Monday –

I won't tell you where I got the ten *pesos* I brought him, but enough water flowed from my own spout so that my three turkeys and my neighbor's sow wouldn't die from thirst.

Tuesday –

The tourists left and I didn't even get one *peso*. But because of human nature (weak, weak, weak!!) I got him to let more water flow. I washed my underpants.

Wednesday –

In complete silence, I continued painting the front of my house blue. At nightfall I went to see him for a while. Both of the water-man's arms, his chest and part of his back were already blue.

Holy Thursday –

In vain we waited in the atrium for the performance of the Last Supper. Would there be no water even for this humble re-enactment? It wasn't my idea: the man who dismounted in front of the door said: Even if it's the last one, after this supper, we have to wash the dishes. Where's the water? The show's over, brothers, you can go home.

Good Friday –

Logically it was everyone's Via Crucis, with a procession, prayers, dry lips and cracked skin. (The rich from the houses on high pass by and exchange hidden smiles with our water-man. His pockets are brimming and the rich have full pools, all the water they want. For us there's not even a drop of humidity left for tears.)

Holy Saturday –

All's calm in the village and in my life. Just the water-man's left hand, face and one testicle are still flesh color. The rest of him is indigo, I can't imagine why. Only children are walking around the village today, and dogs, like dried-up skins staked out on four legs.

From my window I saw the truck arrive with the Judas figures – red devils with horns – and I confess that I said to myself: our Judas is blue, we're more afraid of him, he's not made of papier-mâché, nor is he hollow inside; he's evil.

Without much effort, I also saw how they stuck firecrackers inside each figure's belly, hung a string of firecrackers around the neck and left the wicks in the horns. (But it's one thing to see and a very different thing to think of applying what you've seen.)

(They all saw it, for four centuries now they've known much better than me, for even though I come from so far away, I'm on their side. I swear it wasn't me, don't make the usual mistake, don't single out the stranger even as a blessing.)

(Your house's color, they told me afterward, and I shrugged my shoulders, is the color of his tombstone.)

And at eleven o'clock at night rattles called us to mass.
Easter Sunday –
At midnight, bells were clanging away. As if the village still had such spirit. At one o'clock they shot off flares and at two thirty the first rains let loose, putting an end to the long months of drought. What a welcome sight, what an oasis! At last we didn't need him . . . (It rained all night and morning until eleven o'clock mass and the people in the convent thanked the heavens for that solitary offering. And they prayed on their knees proudly showing the mud-covered soles of their feet.)

At noon the sun reappeared unaware of the bliss. And can they think that in the mist's suffocating web I could have summoned up enough strength to concoct the idea? In the midst of infernal heat and firecracker blasts? In the market square the papier-mâché Judas exploded into a thousand pieces, evil was disintegrating, the people knew it and rejoiced.
At five o'clock as the firecrackers piled up, the celebration began. I ran to the marketplace to see the men in the village dancing around heaps of bananas and mangoes, watermelon stands and clay pots. Dazzling colors sparkled like the trees' leaves washed by the rain. I was going to dance in line with the villagers dressed up as fine folk; velvet tunics, embroidered hats, lace and tinsel, white men's masks with pointed beards, white gloves. I wanted to participate in the celebration, become part of the brass music. Communion with the people, until I saw the water-man there (that son of a bitch).
Standing over the fountain in the middle of the market. His back turned to me, looking around (searching for me, I bet), already dressed in blue all over. The water-man, blue atop the dry fountain. That was too much, so even though my job wasn't finished – the left hand, the face and one testicle – I couldn't stop myself and fled, terrified. Seeing me run

away, the inexpressive faces of the masks with eyes (what an idea!) followed my flight. And he was so indigo, so very irreverent.

I bought white paint with my last *pesos* (the house is more demanding than the stomach: I didn't want a house the color of the water-man, I wanted a pure home).

The Judas burst open in the square as I painted to the rhythm of the firecrackers. My electric-blue house began to lose its energy and turned transparent, sky-blue. I had almost repainted one whole wall when I heard the blast of a giant firecracker.

There was a pregnant pause, suspense in the air, when they arrived breathless with the news:

He had been the great Judas, almost like the real one. When I reached the square the dancing had stopped and the masks' inhuman eyes were watching. There was the blue water-man, disemboweled, stuck on the fountain's highest point.

(Was there a stick of dynamite in his fly or a handful of firecrackers in his navel?)

But listen here, *I wasn't the one who lit the wick* as you can verify just by reading my statement carefully.

It was strange that his face and also one of his hands, palm up, were my transparent, sky-blue color. Besides, I could swear that one testicle had turned sky-blue, but it flew off with his guts and they never found it (the guts splattered the people from the houses on high who were at arm's length, seated right there at the only tables with nice tablecloths in the middle of the square, in the dancers' way, sipping their drinks in a dignified manner, showing off their embroidered shirts or their long dresses. It only splattered them a little but they stood up in disgust and took their golden children away from the ill-fated spectacle).

I, on the other hand, remained there to await the miracle: from the riddled belly of this Judas figure, water would forever flow.

The village natives, as often happens, didn't expect that much. Blood flowed from the pierced belly, to the surprise of none and the joy of all.

And the masked ones stuck their white-gloved hands in that blood and washed the perfectly white masks that covered their faces.

Water-man's blood: symbol of water. Perfect ablution.

Later they tried to treat me with too much consideration. They loved me and hated me and shouted my name. And I was so undeserving, so forsaken, while the blue water-man was gradually turning red so that even his color didn't belong to me anymore.

JANET FRAME

# *The Reservoir*

*Janet Frame is best known for her three volumes of autobiography,* To the Island,
An Angel at My Table *and* The Envoy from Mirror City, *which have been made
into an acclaimed film directed by Jane Campion. She has also written many novels,
including* Faces in the Water, Scented Gardens for the Blind, Owls Do Cry
*and* The Blue Lagoon. *She has been a Burns Scholar and a Sargeson Fellow, has
won the New Zealand Scholarship in Letters and was awarded the CBE in 1983.*

It was said to be four or five miles along the gully, past orchards and
farms, paddocks filled with cattle, sheep, wheat, gorse, and the squatters
of the land who were the rabbits eating like modern sculpture into the
hills, though how could we know anything of modern sculpture, we knew
nothing but the Warrior in the main street with his wreaths of poppies on
Anzac Day, the gnomes weeping in the Gardens because the seagulls
perched on their green caps and showed no respect, and how important it
was for birds, animals and people, especially children, to show respect!

And that is why for so long we obeyed the command of the grown-ups
and never walked as far as the forbidden Reservoir, but were content to
return 'tired but happy' (as we wrote in our school compositions), answering the question 'Where did you walk today?' with a suspicion of
blackmail, 'Oh, nearly, nearly to the Reservoir!'

The Reservoir was the end of the world; beyond it, you fell; beyond it
were paddocks of thorns, strange cattle, strange farms, legendary people
whom we would never know or recognize even if they walked among us
on a Friday night downtown when we went to follow the boys and listen
to the Salvation Army Band and buy a milk shake in the milk bar and then

return home to find that everything was all right and safe, that our Mother
had not run away and caught the night train to the North Island, that our
Father had not shot himself with worrying over the bills, but had in fact
been downtown himself and had bought the usual Friday-night treat,
a bag of liquorice allsorts and a bag of chocolate roughs, from
Woolworth's.

The Reservoir haunted our lives. We never knew one until we came to
this town; we had used pump water. But here, in our new house, the water
ran from the taps as soon as we turned them on, and if we were careless
and left them on, our Father would shout, as if the affair were his personal concern, 'Do you want the Reservoir to run dry?'

That frightened us. What should we do if the Reservoir ran dry? Would
we die of thirst like Burke and Wills in the desert?

'The Reservoir,' our Mother said, 'gives pure water, water safe to drink
without boiling it.'

The water was in a different class, then, from the creek which flowed
through the gully; yet the creek had its source in the Reservoir. Why had it
not received the pampering attention of officialdom which strained weed
and earth, cockabullies and trout and eels, from our tap water? Surely the
Reservoir was not entirely pure?

'Oh, no,' they said, when we inquired. We learned that the water from
the Reservoir had been 'treated'. We supposed this to mean that during
the night men in light-blue uniforms with sacks over their shoulders
crept beyond the circle of pine trees which enclosed the Reservoir, and
emptied the contents of the sacks into the water, to dissolve dead bodies
and prevent the decay of teeth.

Then, at times, there would be news in the paper, discussed by my
Mother with the neighbours over the back fence. Children had been
drowned in the Reservoir.

'No child,' the neighbour would say, 'ought to be allowed near the
Reservoir.'

'I tell mine to keep strictly away,' my Mother would reply.

And for so long we obeyed our Mother's command, on our favourite
walks along the gully simply following the untreated cast-off creek
which we loved and which flowed day and night in our heads in all its
detail – the wild sweet peas, boiled-lolly pink, and the mint growing along

the banks; the exact spot in the water where the latest dead sheep could be found, and the stink of its bloated flesh and floating wool, an allowable earthy stink which we accepted with pleasant revulsion and which did not prompt the 'inky-pinky, I smell Stinkie' rhyme which referred to offensive human beings only. We knew where the water was shallow and could be paddled in, where forts could be made from the rocks; we knew the frightening deep places where the eels lurked and the weeds were tangled in gruesome shapes; we knew the jumping places, the mossy stones with their dangers, limitations, and advantages; the sparkling places where the sun trickled beside the water, upon the stones; the bogs made by roaming cattle, trapping some of them to death; their gaunt telltale bones; the little valleys with their new growth of lush grass where the creek had 'changed its course', and no longer flowed.

'The creek has changed its course,' our Mother would say, in a tone which implied terror and a sense of strangeness, as if a tragedy had been enacted.

We knew the moods of the creek, its levels of low-flow, half-high-flow, high-flow which all seemed to relate to interference at its source – the Reservoir. If one morning the water turned the colour of clay and crowds of bubbles were passengers on every suddenly swift wave hurrying by, we would look at one another and remark with the fatality and reverence which attends a visitation or prophecy, 'The creek's going on high-flow. They must be doing something at the Reservoir.'

By afternoon the creek would be on high-flow, turbulent, muddy, unable to be jumped across or paddled in or fished in, concealing beneath a swelling fluid darkness whatever evil which 'they', the authorities, had decided to purge so swiftly and secretly from the Reservoir.

For so long, then, we obeyed our parents, and never walked as far as the Reservoir. Other things concerned us, other curiosities, fears, challenges. The school year ended. I got a prize, a large yellow book the colour of cat's mess. Inside it were editions of newspapers, *The Worms' Weekly*, supposedly written by worms, snails, spiders. For the first part of the holidays we spent the time sitting in the long grass of our front lawn nibbling the stalks of shamrock and reading insect newspapers and relating their items to the lives of those living on our front lawn down among the summer-dry roots of the couch, tinkertailor, daisy, dandelion, shamrock, clover, and ordinary 'grass'. High summer came. The blowzy old red roses shed their petals to the regretful refrain uttered by our Mother year after year at the same time, 'I should have made potpourri, I have a wonderful recipe for potpourri in Dr Chase's Book.'

Our Mother never made the potpourri. She merely quarrelled with our Father over how to pronounce it.

The days became unbearably long and hot. Our Christmas presents were broken or too boring to care about. Celluloid dolls had loose arms and legs and rifts in their bright pink bodies; the invisible ink had poured itself out in secret messages; diaries frustrating in their smallness (two lines to a day) had been filled in for the whole of the coming year . . . Days at the beach were tedious, with no room in the bathing sheds so that we were forced to undress in their common room downstairs with its floor patched with wet and trailed with footmarks and sand in its tiny barred window (which made me believe that I was living in the French Revolution).

Rumours circled the burning world. The sea was drying up, soon you could paddle or walk to Australia. Sharks had been seen swimming inside the breakwater; one shark attacked a little boy and bit off his you-know-what.

We swam. We wore bathing togs all day. We gave up cowboys and ranches; and baseball and sledding; and 'those games' where we mimicked grown-up life, loving and divorcing each other, kissing and slapping, taking secret paramours when our husband was working out of town. Everything exhausted us. Cracks appeared in the earth; the grass was bled yellow; the ground was littered with beetle shells and snail shells; flies came in from the unofficial rubbish-dump at the back of the house; the twisting flypapers hung from the ceiling; a frantic buzzing filled the room as the flypapers became crowded. Even the cat put out her tiny tongue, panting in the heat.

We realized, and were glad, that school would soon reopen. What was school like? It seemed so long ago, it seemed as if we had never been to school, surely we had forgotten everything we had learned, how frightening, thrilling and strange it would all seem! Where would we go on the first day, who would teach us, what were the names on the new books?

Who would sit beside us, who would be our best friend?

The earth crackled in early-autumn haze and still the February sun dried the world; even at night the rusty sheet of roofing-iron outside by the cellar stayed warm, but with rows of sweat-marks on it; the days were still long, with night face to face with morning and almost nothing in between but a snatch of turning sleep with the blankets on the floor and the windows wide open to moths with their bulging lamplit eyes moving through the dark and their grandfather bodies knocking, knocking upon the walls.

Day after day the sun still waited to pounce. We were tired, our skin itched, our sunburn had peeled and peeled again, the skin on our feet was hard, there was dust in our hair, our bodies clung with the salt of sea-bathing and sweat, the towels were harsh with salt.

School soon, we said again, and were glad; for lessons gave shade to rooms and corridors; cloakrooms were cold and sunless. Then, swiftly, suddenly, disease came to the town. Infantile paralysis. Black headlines in the paper, listing the number of cases, the number of deaths. Children everywhere, out in the country, up north, down south, two streets away.

The schools did not reopen. Our lessons came by post, in smudged print on rough white paper; they seemed makeshift and false, they inspired distrust, they could not compete with the lure of the sun still shining, swelling, the world would go up in cinders, the days were too long, there was nothing to do, there was nothing to do; the lessons were dull; in the front room with the navy-blue blind half down the window and the tiny splits of light showing through, and the lesson papers sometimes covered with unexplained blots of ink as if the machine which had printed them had broken down or rebelled, the lessons were even more dull.

Ancient Egypt and the flooding of the Nile!

The Nile, when we possessed a creek of our own with individual flooding!

'Well, let's go along the gully, along by the creek,' we would say, tired with all these.

Then one day when our restlessness was at its height, when the flies buzzed like bees in the flypapers, and the warped wood of the house cracked its knuckles out of boredom, the need for something to do in the heat, we found once again the only solution to our unrest.

Someone said, 'What's the creek on?'

'Half-high flow.'

'Good.'

So we set out, in our bathing suits, and carrying switches of willow.

'Keep your sun hats on!' our Mother called.

All right. We knew. Sunstroke when the sun clipped you over the back of the head, striking you flat on the ground. Sunstroke. Lightning. Even tidal waves were threatening us on this southern coast. The world was full of alarm.

'And don't go as far as the Reservoir!'

We dismissed the warning. There was enough to occupy us along the gully without our visiting the Reservoir. First, the couples. We liked to find a courting couple and follow them and when, as we knew they must do because they were tired or for other reasons, they found a place in the grass and lay down together, we liked to make jokes about them, amongst ourselves. 'Just wait for him to kiss her,' we would say. 'Watch. There. A beaut. Smack.'

Often we giggled and lingered even after the couple had observed us. We were waiting for them to do it. Every man and woman did it, we knew that for a fact. We speculated about technical details. Would he wear a frenchie? If he didn't wear a frenchie, then she would start having a baby and be forced to get rid of it by drinking gin. Frenchies, by the way, were for sale in Woolworth's. Some said they were fingerstalls, but we knew they were frenchies and sometimes we would go downtown and into Woolworth's just to look at the frenchies for sale. We hung around the counter, sniggering. Sometimes we nearly died laughing, it was so funny.

After we tired of spying on the couples we would shout after them as we went our way,

> *'Pound, shillings and pence,*
> *a man fell over the fence,*
> *he fell on a lady,*
> *and squashed out a baby,*
> *pound, shillings and pence!'*

Sometimes a slight fear struck us – what if a man fell on us like that and squashed out a chain of babies?

Our other pastime along the gully was robbing the orchards, but this summer day the apples were small, green, hard and hidden by leaves. There were no couples either. We had the gully to ourselves. We followed the creek, whacking our sticks, gossiping and singing, but we stopped, immediately silent, when someone – sister or brother – said, 'Let's go to the Reservoir!'

A feeling of dread seized us. We knew, as surely as we knew our names and our address, Thirty-three Stour Street Ohau Otago South Island New Zealand Southern Hemisphere The World, that we would some day visit the Reservoir, but the time seemed almost as far away as leaving school, getting a job, marrying.

And then there was the agony of deciding the right time – how did one decide these things?

'We've been told not to, you know,' one of us said timidly.

That was me. Eating bread and syrup for tea had made my hair red, my skin too, so that I blushed easily, and the grown-ups guessed if I told a lie.

'It's a long way,' said my little sister.

'Coward!'

But it *was* a long way, and perhaps it would take all day and night, perhaps we would have to sleep there among the pine trees with the owls hooting and the old needle-filled warrens which now reached to the centre of the earth where pools of molten lead bubbled, waiting to seize us if we tripped and then there was the crying sound made by the trees, a sound of speech at its loneliest level where the meaning is felt but never explained, and it goes on and on in a kind of despair, trying to reach a point of understanding.

We knew that pine trees spoke in this way. We were lonely listening to them because we knew we could never help them to say it, whatever they were trying to say, for if the wind who was so close to them could not help them, how could we?

Oh, no, we could not spend the night at the Reservoir among the pine trees.

'Billy Whittaker and his gang have been to the Reservoir, Billy Whittaker and the Green Feather gang, one afternoon.'

'Did he say what it was like?'

'No, he never said,'

'He's been in an iron lung.'

That was true. Only a day or two ago our Mother had been reminding us in an ominous voice of the fact which roused our envy just as much as our dread, 'Billy Whittaker was in an iron lung two years ago. Infantile paralysis.'

Some people were lucky. None of us dared to hope that we would ever be surrounded by the glamour of an iron lung; we would have to be content all our lives with paltry flesh lungs.

'Well, are we going to the Reservoir or not?'

That was someone trying to sound bossy like our Father, 'Well, am I to have salmon sandwiches or not, am I to have lunch at all today or not?'

We struck our sticks in the air. They made a whistling sound. They were supple and young. We had tried to make musical instruments out of them, time after time we hacked at the willow and the elder to make pipes to blow our music, but no sound came but our own voices. And why did two sticks rubbed together not make fire? Why couldn't we ever *make* anything out of the bits of the world lying about us?

An airplane passed in the sky. We craned our necks to read the writing on the underwing, for we collected airplane numbers.

The plane was gone, in a glint of sun.

'Are we?' someone said.

'If there's an eclipse you can't see at all. The birds stop singing and go to bed.'

'Well, are we?'

Certainly we were. We had not quelled all our misgivings, but we set out to follow the creek to the Reservoir.

What is it? I wondered. They said it was a lake. I thought it was a bundle of darkness and great wheels which peeled and sliced you like an apple and drew you toward them with demonic force, in the same way that you were drawn beneath the wheels of a train if you stood too near the edge of the platform. That was the terrible danger when the Limited came rushing in and you had to approach to kiss arriving aunts.

We walked on and on, past wild sweet peas, clumps of cutty grass, horse mushrooms, ragwort, gorse, cabbage trees; and then, at the end of the gully, we came to strange territory, fences we did not know, with the barbed wire tearing at our skin and at our skirts put on over our bathing suits because we felt cold though the sun stayed in the sky.

We passed huge trees that lived with their heads in the sky, with their great arms and joints creaking with age and the burden of being trees, and their mazed and linked roots rubbed bare of earth, like bones with the flesh cleaned from them. There were strange gates to be opened or climbed over, new directions to be argued and plotted, notices which said TRESPASSERS WILL BE PROSECUTED BY ORDER. And there was the remote immovable sun shedding without gentleness its influence of burning upon us and upon the town, looking down from its heavens and considering our infantile-paralysis epidemic, and the children tired of holidays and wanting to go back to school with the new stiff books with their crackling pages, the scrubbed ruler with the sun rising on one side amidst the twelfths, tenths, millimetres, the new pencils to be sharpened with the pencil shavings flying in long pickets and light-brown curls scalloped with red or blue; the brown school, the bare floors, the clump clump in the corridors on wet days.

We came to a strange paddock, a bull-paddock with its occupant planted deep in the long grass, near the gate, a jersey bull polished like a wardrobe, burnished like copper, heavy beams creaking in the wave and flow of the grass.

'Has it got a ring through its nose? Is it a real bull or a steer?'

Its nose was ringed which meant that its savagery was tamed, or so we thought; it could be tethered and led; even so, it had once been savage and it kept its pride, unlike the steers who pranced and huddled together and ran like water through the paddocks, made no impression, quarried no massive shape against the sky.

The bull stood alone.

Had not Mr Bennet been gored by a bull, his own tame bull, and been rushed to Glenham Hospital for thirty-three stitches? Remembering Mr Bennet we crept cautiously close to the paddock fence, ready to escape.

Someone said, 'Look, it's pawing the ground!'

A bull which pawed the ground was preparing for a charge. We escaped quickly through the fence. Then, plucking up courage, we skirted the bushes on the far side of the paddock, climbed through the fence, and continued our walk to the Reservoir.

We had lost the creek between deep banks. We saw it now before us, and hailed it with more relief than we felt, for in its hidden course through the bull-paddock it had undergone change, it had adopted the shape, depth, mood of foreign water, foaming in a way we did not recognize as belonging to our special creek, giving no hint of its depth. It seemed to flow close to its concealed bed, not wishing any more to communicate with us. We realized with dismay that we had suddenly lost possession of our creek. Who had taken it? Why did it not belong to us any more? We hit our sticks in the air and forgot our dismay. We grew cheerful.

Till someone said that it was getting late, and we reminded one another that during the day the sun doesn't seem to move, it just remains pinned with a drawing pin against the sky, and then, while you are not looking, it suddenly slides down quick as the chopped-off head of a golden eel, into the sea, making everything in the world go dark.

'That's only in the tropics!'

We were not in the tropics. The divisions of the world in the atlas, the different coloured cubicles of latitude and longitude fascinated us.

'The sand freezes in the desert at night. Ladies wear bits of sand . . .'

'grains . . .'

'grains or bits of sand as necklaces, and the camels . . .'

'with necks like snails . . .'

'with horns, do they have horns?'

'Minnie Stocks goes with boys . . .'

'I know who your boy is, I know who your boy is . . .'

> *Waiting by the garden gate,*
> *Waiting by the garden gate . . .*

'We'll never get to the Reservoir!'

'Whose idea was it?'

'I've strained my ankle!'

Someone began to cry. We stopped walking.

'I've strained my ankle!'

There was an argument.

'It's not strained, it's sprained.'

'strained.'

'sprained.'

'All right, sprained then. I'll have to wear a bandage, I'll have to walk on crutches . . .'

'I had crutches once. Look. I've got a scar where I fell off my stilts. It's a white scar, like a centipede. It's on my shins.'

'Shins! Isn't it a funny word? Shins. Have you ever been kicked in the shins?'

'shins, funnybone . . .'

'it's humerus . . .'

'knuckles . . .'

'a sprained ankle . . .'

'a strained ankle . . .'

'a whitlow, an ingrown toenail the roots of my hair warts spinal meningitis infantile paralysis . . .'

'Infantile paralysis, infantile paralysis, you have to be wheeled in a chair and wear irons on your legs and your knees knock together . . .'

'Once you're in an iron lung you can't get out, they lock it, like a cage . . .'

'You go in the amberlance . . .'

'*ambulance* . . .'

'amberlance . . .'

'amberlance to the hostible . . .'

'the *hospital*, an *amberlance to the hospital* . . .'

'Infantile paralysis . . .'

'Friar's Balsam! Friar's Balsam!'

'Baxter's Lung Preserver, Baxter's Lung Preserver!'

'Syrup of Figs, California Syrup of Figs!'

'The creek's going on high-flow!'

Yes, there were bubbles on the surface, and the water was turning muddy. Our doubts were dispelled. It was the same old creek, and there, suddenly, just ahead, was a plantation of pine trees, and already the sighing sound of it reached our ears and troubled us. We approached it, staying close to the banks of our newly claimed creek, until once again the creek deserted us, flowing its own private course where we could not follow, and we found ourselves among the pine trees, a narrow strip of them, and beyond lay a vast surface of sparkling water, dazzling our eyes, its centre chopped by tiny grey waves. Not a lake, nor a river, nor a sea.

'The Reservoir!'

The damp smell of the pine needles caught in our breath. There were no birds, only the constant sighing of the trees. We could see the water clearly now; it lay, except for the waves beyond the shore, in an almost perfect calm which we knew to be deceptive – else why were people so afraid of the Reservoir? The fringe of young pines on the edge, like toy trees, subjected to the wind, sighed and told us their sad secrets. In the Reservoir there was an appearance of neatness which concealed a disarray too frightening to be acknowledged except, without any defence, in moments of deep sleep and dreaming. The little sparkling innocent waves shone now green, now grey, petticoats, lettuce leaves; the trees sighed, and told us to be quiet, hush-sh, as if something were sleeping and should not be disturbed – perhaps that was what the trees were always telling us, to hush-sh in case we disturbed something which must never ever be awakened?

What was it? Was it sleeping in the Reservoir? Was that why people were afraid of the Reservoir?

Well, we were not afraid of it, oh no, it was only the Reservoir, it was nothing to be afraid of, it was just a flat Reservoir with a fence around it, and trees, and on the far side a little house (with wheels inside?) and nothing to be afraid of.

'The Reservoir! The Reservoir!'

A noticeboard said DANGER: RESERVOIR.

Overcome with sudden glee we climbed through the fence and swung over the lower branches of the trees, shouting at intervals, gazing possessively and delightedly at the sheet of water with its wonderful calm and menace.

'The Reservoir! The Reservoir! The Reservoir!'

We quarrelled again about how to pronounce and spell the word.

Then it seemed to be getting dark – or was it that the trees were stealing the sunlight and keeping it above their heads? One of us began to run. We all ran, suddenly, wildly, not caring about our strained or sprained ankles, through the trees out into the sun where the creek, but it was our creek no longer, waited for us. We wished it were our creek, how we wished it were our creek! We had lost all account of time. Was it nearly night? Would darkness overtake us, would we have to sleep on the banks of the creek that did not belong to us any more, among the wild sweet peas and the tussocks and the dead sheep? And would the eels come up out of the creek, as people said they did, and on their travels through the paddocks would they change into people who would threaten us and bar our way, TRESPASSERS WILL BE PROSECUTED, standing arm in arm in their black glossy coats, swaying, their mouths open, ready to swallow us? Would they ever let us go home, past the orchards, along the gully? Perhaps they would give us infantile paralysis, perhaps we would never be able to walk home, and no one would know where we were, to bring us an iron lung with its own special key!

We arrived home, panting and scratched. How strange! The sun was still in the same place in the sky!

The question troubled us, 'Should we tell?'

The answer was decided for us. Our Mother greeted us as we went in the door with, 'You haven't been long away, kiddies. Where have you been? I hope you didn't go anywhere near the Reservoir.'

Our Father looked up from reading his newspapers.

'Don't let me catch you going near the Reservoir!'

We said nothing. How out of date they were! They were actually afraid!

# Fat People

*Alison Lurie is Professor of English at Cornell University. She won the Pulitzer Prize for her novel* Foreign Affairs*; her other novels include* Love and Friendship, Imaginary Friends, The War Between the Tates *and* The Truth About Lorin Jones. *Like the works of Anthony Powell, a writer whom Lurie greatly admires, all of her novels follow a closely related group of characters over the years. Secondary characters in one novel reappear, sometimes in more major roles, in another. Her non-fiction titles include* The Language of Clothes *and a collection of essays on children's literature,* Don't Tell the Grown-ups. *'Fat People' comes from her first collection of short stories,* Women and Ghosts.

I never ran into any spooks in sheets, no headless horsemen, haunted mansions, nothing like that. But there was something weird once –

It was a while ago, when Scott went to India on that research grant. The first thing that happened was, I began noticing fat people. I saw them snatching the shrimps and stuffed eggs at parties; I saw them strolling along Cayuga Street with the swaying sailor's gait of the obese, and pawing through the queen-size housecoats in J. C. Penney. They were buying tubs of popcorn at the flicks, ahead of me in line at the post office and the bank, and pumping self-serve gas into their pick-up trucks when I went to the garage.

I didn't pay much attention at first; I figured that since I was dieting I was more aware of people who should be doing the same. My idea was to lose fifteen pounds while Scott was away – twenty if possible, because of what he'd said just before he left.

We were at the county airport on a cold weepy day in March, waiting for Scott's plane and trying to keep up a conversation, repeating things we'd already said. I'd seen Scott off on trips before; but this time he'd be gone over three months. He was saying he wished I were coming, and promising to wire from Delhi and write twice a week, and telling me he loved me and reminding me again to check the oil on the Honda. I said I would, and was there anything else I should do while he was away?

Then the flight was announced and we grabbed each other. But we were both wearing heavy down jackets, and it didn't feel real. It was like two bundles of clothes embracing, I said, all choked up. And Scott said, 'Well, there is one thing we could both do while I'm gone, Ellie; we could lose a few pounds.' He was kissing my face and I was trying not to break down and howl.

Then Scott was through the x-ray scanner into the boarding lounge, and then he was crossing the wet Tarmac with his carry-on bag, getting smaller and smaller, and climbing the steps. It wasn't till I'd gone back to the main waiting-room and was standing inside the teary steamed-up window watching his plane shrink and blur into fog that I really registered his last remark.

I drove back to Pine Grove Apartments and dragged off my fat coat and looked at myself in the mirror on the back of the closet door. I knew I was a big girl, at the top of the range for my height, but it had never bothered me before. And as far as I knew it hadn't bothered Scott, who was hefty himself. Maybe when he suggested we lost a few pounds he was just kidding. But it was the last thing I'd hear him say for three months. Or possibly forever, I thought, because India was so far away and full of riots and diseases, and maybe in one of the villages he was going to they wouldn't want to change their thousand-year-old agricultural methods, and they would murder Scott with long wavy decorated knives or serve him curry with thousand-year-old undetectable poisons in it.

I knew it was bad luck to think that way, Scott had said so himself. I looked back at the mirror again, turning sideways. Usually I was pleased by what I saw there, but now I noticed that when I didn't breathe in, my tummy stuck out as far as my breasts.

Maybe I had put on some extra pounds that winter, I thought. Well, it should be pretty easy to take them off. It could be a project, something to do while Scott was gone. I wouldn't write him about it, I'd save it for a surprise when he got back. 'Wow, Ellie,' he would say, 'you look great.'

Only it turned out not to be as easy as all that. After two weeks, I weighed exactly the same. One problem was that all our friends kept asking me over and serving meals it would have been a shame to refuse, not to mention rude. And when I didn't have anywhere to go in the evening I started wandering around the apartment and usually ended up wandering into the kitchen and opening the fridge, just for something to do.

It was about then that I began to notice how many fat people there were in town. All sorts and all ages: overweight country-club types easing themselves out of overweight cars; street people shoving rusted grocery carts jammed with bottles and bundles. Fat old men like off-duty Santa Clauses waddling through the shopping mall, fat teenagers with acne, and babies so plump they could hardly get their thumbs into their mouths.

Of course I'd seen types like this before occasionally, but now they seemed to be everywhere. At first I put it down to coincidence, plus having the subject on my mind. It didn't bother me; in a way it was reassuring. When some bulgy high-school senior came for an interview at the college, and tried to fit their rear end on to the chair by my desk, I would think as I smiled nicely and asked the standard questions, well, at least I don't look like that.

My folks knew I was trying to lose weight, and wanted to help, but they only made it worse. Every time I went over to the house for Sunday dinner Dad would ask first if I'd heard from Scott. It got to be over three weeks, and I still had to say, 'No, nothing since the telegram,' and remind them that we'd been warned about how bad the mails were.

Then we'd sit down to the table and Mom would pass my plate, and there'd be this measly thin slice of chicken on it, and a bushel of cooked greens, as if I was in some kind of concentration camp for fatties. The salads all started to have sour low-cal dressing, and there was never anything but fruit for dessert: watery melon, or oranges cut up with a few shreds of dry coconut on top, like little undernourished white worms.

All through the meal Mom and Dad wouldn't mention Scott again, so as not to upset me. There was nothing in the dining-room to remind anybody of Scott either, and of course there wasn't any place set for him at the table. It was as if he'd disappeared or maybe had never even existed. By the time dinner was over I'd be so low in my mind I'd have to stop on the way home for a pint of chocolate marshmallow.

I'd hang up my coat and turn on the television and measure out exactly half a cup of ice cream, 105 calories, less than a bagel. I'd put the rest in the freezer and feel virtuous. But when the next commercial came on I'd open the freezer and have a few more spoonfuls. And then the whole process would repeat, like a commercial, until the carton was scraped clean down to the wax.

It got to be four weeks since Scott had left, and I still didn't weigh any less, even when I shifted my feet on the scale to make the needle wobble downwards. I'd never tried to lose weight before; I'd always thought it was ridiculous the way some people went into agonies over diets. I'd even been kind of shocked when one of my married friends made more fuss about taking a second slice of peach pie than she did about taking a lover. Displaced guilt, I used to think.

Now I was as hysterical about food as any of them. I brooded all afternoon over a fudge brownie I hadn't had for lunch; and if I broke down and ordered one I made up excuses for hours afterwards. 'I didn't promise Scott I'd lose weight,' I would tell myself, or 'It's not fair asking someone to give up both food and love at the same time.'

I started to read all the articles on losing weight that I used to skip before, and I took books out of the library. Over the next couple of weeks I tried one crazy diet after another: no-carbohydrate, no-fat, grapefruit and cornflakes, chipped beef and bananas and skimmed milk. Only I couldn't stick with any of them. Things went wrong at night when I started thinking about how I'd written nine letters to Scott and hadn't got one back. I'd lie in bed asking myself where the hell he was, what was he doing now? And pretty soon I'd feel hungry, starving.

Another thing I kept asking myself, especially when I chewed through some dried-out salad or shook Sweet 'n' Low into my coffee, was what Scott, assuming he was still alive, was eating over there on the other side of the world. If he wasn't on a diet, what was the point? I would think, watching my hand reach out for the blue-cheese dressing or the half-and-half. He hadn't meant it seriously, I'd tell myself.

But suppose he had meant it? Suppose Scott was becoming slimmer and trimmer every day; what would he think if he knew I hadn't lost a pound in nearly five weeks?

Trying to do it on my own wasn't working. I needed support, and I thought I knew where to find it. There was a young woman in the Admissions Office called Dale. She was only a couple of years older than me, maybe twenty-six, but in two months she'd just about reorganized our files, and she obviously had her life under control. She was a brunette, with a narrow neat little figure and a narrow neat little poodle face; you got the feeling her hair wouldn't dare get itself mussed up, and she'd never weigh one ounce more than she chose to.

I figured that Dale would have ideas about my problem, because she was always talking about interesting new diets. And whenever some really heavy person came in she'd make a yapping noise under her breath and remark later how awful it was for people to let themselves go physically. 'Heaven knows how that hippopotamus is going to fulfil his athletic requirement,' she would say, or 'That girl's mother ought to be in a circus, she hardly looked human.' And I'd think, do I look human to Dale?

So one day when we were alone in the washroom I let on that I was trying to lose some weight. Dale lit up like a fluorescent tube. 'Yes, I think that's a good idea, Ellie,' she said, looking from herself to me, poodle to hippo, in the mirror over the basins. 'And I'd like to help you, okay?'

'Okay, thanks,' I said. I didn't have any idea what I was getting into.

On our way back to the office, Dale explained to me that being overweight was a career handicap. It was a known fact that heavy people didn't get ahead as fast in business. Besides, fat was low-class: the Duchess of Windsor had said you could never be too rich or too thin. When I told her there wasn't much danger of my ever being either one, Dale didn't laugh. She printed her Duchess of Windsor line out in computer-graphic caps, and fastened it on the side of my filing cabinet with two pineapple magnets.

The next thing Dale did was persuade me to see a doctor to make sure I was healthy, the way they tell you to do in the diet books. Then she started organizing my life. She got me enrolled in an aerobics class, and set up a schedule for me to jog every day after work, regardless of the weather. Then she invited herself over to my apartment and cleaned out the cupboards and icebox. Bags of pretzels and fritos, butter and cream cheese and cold cuts, a loaf of cinnamon-raisin bread, most of a pound of Jones bacon – Dale packed everything up, and we hauled it down to the local soup-kitchen. I kind of panicked when I saw all that lovely food disappearing, but I was hopeful too.

The next day Dale brought in a calorie-counter and planned my meals for a week in advance. She kept a chart, and every day she'd ask me how much I'd weighed that morning and write it down.

Only the scale still stuck at the same number. If there was nothing in the apartment, there was always plenty in the grocery. I'd go in for celery and cottage cheese and Ry-Krisp, but when I was pushing the cart down the last aisle it was as if the packages of cookies on the shelves were crying out to me, especially the chocolate-covered grahams and the Mallomars. I could almost hear them squeaking inside their cellophane wrappers, in these little high sugary voices: 'Ellie, Ellie! Here we are, Ellie!'

When I confessed to falling off my diet, Dale didn't lose her cool. 'Never mind, Ellie, that's all right,' she said. 'I know what we'll do. From now on, don't you go near a supermarket alone. I'll shop with you twice a week on the way home.'

So the next day she did. But as soon as she got a little ahead of me in the bakery section, I began drifting towards a tray of apricot crois-sants. Dale looked round and shook her poodle curls and said, 'Naughty, naughty' – which kind of made me feel crazy, because I hadn't done anything naughty yet – and then she grabbed my arm and pulled me along fast.

There'd been several fat people in the A & P that day, the way there always were lately. When we were in line at the check-out with a load of groceries only a rabbit could love, I noticed one of them, a really heavy blonde girl about my own age, leaving the next register. Her cart was full and a couple of plump bakery boxes, a carton of potato chips and a giant bottle of Coke were bulging out of the brown-paper bags. As she came past the fat girl picked up a package of Hershey bars and tore it open, and half-smiled in my direction as if she were saying, 'Come on, Ellie, have one.'

I looked round at Dale, figuring she would make some negative com-ment, but she didn't. Maybe she hadn't seen the fat girl yet. The funny thing was, when I looked back I didn't see her either; she must have been in a big rush to get home. And she was going to have a really good time when she got there, too, I thought.

Another week dragged by full of carrots and diet soda and frozen Weight Watchers dinners, and no news from Scott. My diet wasn't making much progress either. I'd take a couple of pounds off, but then I'd go out to dinner or a party and put some back on. Instead of losing I was gaining.

I was still seeing fat people too, more and more of them. I tried to convince myself it was just because they weren't disguised inside winter clothes any longer. The only problem was, the people I was seeing weren't just heavy, they were gross.

The first time I knew for sure that something strange was going on was one day when I was in the shopping plaza downtown, sitting on the edge of a planter full of sticky purple petunias and listening to a band concert instead of eating lunch, which had been Dale's idea, naturally. I was feeling kind of dizzy and sick, and when I touched my head it seemed to vibrate, as if it wasn't attached to my body too well.

Then I happened to glance across the plaza, and through the window of the Home Bakery I saw two middle-aged women, both of them bulging out of flowered blouses and slacks as if they'd been blown up too full. I couldn't make out their faces well because of the way the light shimmered and slid on the shop window; but I could see that one of them was looking straight at me and pointing to a tray of strawberry tarts: big ones with thick ruby glaze and scallops of whipped cream. It was as if she was saying, 'Come and get it, Ellie.'

Without even intending to I stood up and started to push through the crowd. But when I reached the bakery there weren't any fat women, and I hadn't seen them leave either. There'd been a moment when I was blocked by a twin stroller; but it still didn't make sense, unless maybe the fat women hadn't really been there. Suddenly I started feeling sick to my stomach. I didn't want a strawberry tart any more; I just wanted to go somewhere and lie down, only I was due back in the Admissions Office.

When I got there I said to Dale, making my voice casual, 'You know something funny, I keep seeing all these really fat people around lately.'

'There are a lot of them around, Ellie,' Dale said. 'Americans are terribly overweight.'

'But I'm seeing more. I mean, lots more than I ever did before. I mean, do you think that's weird?'

'You're just noticing them more,' Dale said stapling forms together, bang-bang. 'Most people block out unpleasant sights of that sort. They don't see the disgusting rubbish in the streets, or the way the walls are peeling right in this office.' She pointed with her head to a corner above the swing doors, where the cream-coloured paint was swollen into bubbles and flaking away; I hadn't noticed it before. Somehow that made me feel better.

'I guess you could be right,' I said. I knew that Dale was getting impatient with me. She'd stopped keeping my weight chart, and when we went shopping now she read the labels on things aloud in a cross way, as if she suspected I was cheating on my diet and had a package of shortbread or a box of raisins hidden away at home, which was sometimes true.

It was around that time that eating and sex started to get mixed up in my mind. Sometimes at night I still woke up hot and tense and longing for Scott; but more often I got excited about food. I read articles on cooking and restaurants in a greedy lingering way, and had fantasies about veal paprika with sour cream and baby onions, or lemon meringue pie. Once after I'd suddenly gone up to a pushcart and bought a giant hotdog with ketchup and relish I heard myself saying half aloud, 'I just had to have it.' And that reminded me of the way men talked in tough-guy thrillers. 'I had to have her,' they always said, and they would speak of some woman as if she was a rich dessert and call her a dish or a cupcake and describe parts of her as melons or buns. Scott isn't really a macho type, but he's always liked thrillers; he says they relax him on trips. And when he got on the plane that awful day he'd had one with him.

He'd been gone over six weeks by then, and no news since the telegram from Delhi. Either something really terrible had happened to him or he deliberately wasn't writing. Maybe while I was cheating on my diet, Scott was cheating on me, I thought. Maybe he'd found some Indian cupcake to relax him. As soon as I had that idea I tried to shove it out of my head, but it kept oozing back.

Then one sunny afternoon early in June I came home from work and opened the mailbox, and there among the bills and circulars was a postcard from Scott. There wasn't any apology for not writing, just a couple of lines about a beautiful temple he'd visited, and a scrawled 'love and kisses'. On the other side was a picture of a sexy over-decorated Indian woman and a person or god with the head of an elephant, both of them wearing smug smiles.

As I looked at that postcard something kind of exploded inside me. For weeks I'd been telling myself and everyone, 'If only I knew Scott was all right, I'd feel fine.' Now I knew he was all right, but what I felt was a big rush of suspicion and fury.

Pictures from the coffee-table books on India Scott had borrowed from the library crowded into my mind. I saw sleek prune-eyed exotic beauties draped in shiny silk and jewels, looking at me with hard sly expressions; and plump nearly naked blue gods with bedroom eyes; and close-ups of temple sculptures in pockmarked stone showing one thousand and one positions for sexual intercourse. The idea came to me that at that exact moment Scott was making out in one thousand different positions with some woman who had an elephant's head or was completely blue. I knew that was crazy, but still he had to be doing something he didn't want to tell me about and was ashamed of, or he would have written.

I didn't go on upstairs to the apartment. Instead I got back into the car, not knowing where I was going till the Honda parked of its own volition in front of a gourmet shop and café that I hadn't been near for weeks. There were five other customers there, which wasn't unusual at that time of day. The unusual thing was, all of them were fat; and not just overweight: humongously huge. All of them looked at me in a friendly way when I came in, as if maybe they knew me and had something to tell me.

For a moment I couldn't move. I just stood there stuck to the indoor-outdoor carpeting and wondered if I was going out of my mind. Five out of five; it wasn't reasonable, but there they were, or anyhow I was seeing them.

The fat people knew about Scott, I thought. They'd known all along. That was what they'd been trying to say to me when they smiled and held up cones or candy bars: 'Come on, honey, why should you deny yourself? You can bet your life Scott isn't.'

A huge guy with a grizzly-bear beard left the counter, giving me a big smile, and I placed my order. A pound of assorted butter cookies, a loaf of cinnamon bread, and a date-walnut coffee ring with white sugar icing. As soon as I got in the car I tore open the box and broke off a piece of the coffee ring, and it was fantastic: the sweet flaky yellow pastry and the sugar-glazed walnuts; a lot better than sex with Scott, I told myself.

For the next four days I pigged out. I finished the cookies and coffee ring that same evening, and on Friday afternoon I sneaked over to the grocery without telling Dale and bought everything I'd dreamt about for weeks: bacon and sausages and sliced Virginia ham, butter and sour cream and baking potatoes, pretzels and barbecue potato chips and frozen french fries. And that was just the beginning.

When I went in to work Monday morning with a box of assorted jam doughnuts I let Dale know I was off my diet for good. Dale tried to shove me back on. It didn't really matter about the weekend binge, she yipped. If I skipped lunch all week and cut way down on dinner and jogged two miles a day I'd be back on track.

'I don't want to be on track,' I told her. 'Eight weeks Scott has been gone, and all I've had from him is one disgusting postcard.'

Dale looked pained and started talking about self-respect and self-image, but I wasn't having any. 'Leave me alone, please,' I said. 'I know what I'm doing.'

Two days and a lot of pork chops and baked potatoes and chicken salad and chocolate almond bark and cherry pie later, I walked into my building, steadied a bag of high-calorie groceries against my hip, and opened the mailbox.

Jesus, I practically dropped the bag. The galvanized-metal slot was crammed with fat white and flimsy blue airmail letters from India. Most of them looked as if they'd been opened and read and crumpled up and walked on, and they were covered with stamps and cancellations.

An hour later, sitting on my sofa surrounded by two months' worth of Scott's letters, I faced facts. He was dieting: his second letter said so, mentioning that he didn't want to look overfed when he walked through a village full of hungry people. All right. I had three weeks, which meant – I went into the bathroom and dragged out the scale from the bottom of the cupboard where I'd shoved it on Friday – which meant, oh God, I'd have to lose over two pounds a week just to get back to where I was when Scott left.

It was an awful three weeks. I had cereal and skimmed milk and fruit for breakfast and lunch, to get through work, but otherwise I didn't eat anything much. Pretty soon I was blurred and headachy most of the time, in spite of all the vitamins and minerals I was scarfing down, and too tired to exercise. And I was still behind schedule on losing weight.

What made it worse was the fat people. I was seeing them again everywhere, only now they didn't look happy or friendly. 'You're making a big mistake, Ellie,' they seemed to be telling me at first. Then they began to get angry and disgusted. 'Sure, he wrote you, stupid,' their expressions said. 'That doesn't prove he's not helping himself to some Indian dish right this minute.'

I quit going out after work; I didn't have the energy. Mostly I just stayed home drinking diet soda and re-reading Scott's letters, kind of to prove to myself that he existed, I guess, because there hadn't been any more. Then I'd watch a little television and go to bed early, hoping to forget about food for a while. But for the first time in my life I was having insomnia, jolting awake in the small hours and lying there starving.

The day Scott was due back, I woke up about four a.m. and couldn't doze off again, even with Valium. For what seemed like hours I thrashed around in bed. Finally I got up and opened a can of diet soda and switched on the TV. Only now, on all the channels that were still broadcasting, everybody was overweight: the third-string newscasters, the punk MTV singers, the comics in an old black-and-white film. On the weather channel I could tell that the girl was hiding thighs like hams under the pleated skirt she kept swishing around as she pointed out the tornado areas. Then the picture changed and a soft plump guy smiled from between chipmunk cheeks and told me that airports were fogged in all over Europe and Scott would never get home.

I turned off the television, dragged on some jeans and a T-shirt, and went out. It was a warm June night full of noises: other tenants' air-conditioners and fans, traffic out on the highway, and planes overhead. There was a hard wind blowing, which made me feel kind of dizzy and slapped about, and it was that uneasy time just before dawn when you start to see shapes but can't make out colours. The sky was a pale sick lemon, but everything else was lumps of blurred grey.

Pine Grove Apartments is surrounded on three sides by an access road, and I'd just turned the corner and was starting towards the dead end. That was when I saw them, way down by the trees. There was a huge sexless person with long stringy hair waving its arms and walking slowly towards me out of the woods, and behind it came more angry fat grey people, and then more and more.

I wanted to run, but I knew somehow that if I turned round the fat people would rush after me the way kids do when you play Giant Steps, and they would catch me and, God, I didn't know what. So I just backed up slowly step by step towards the corner of the building, breathing in shallow gasps.

They kept coming out of the woods in the half-light, more and more, maybe ten or twenty or fifty, I didn't know. I thought I recognized the women from the bakery, and the big guy with the beard – and then I realized I could hear them too, kind of mumbling and wailing. I couldn't take it any more, I turned and raced for home, stumbling over the potholes in the drive.

Well, somehow I made it to the apartment, and slammed the door and double-locked it and put on the chain, and leaned up against the wall panting and gulping. For what seemed like hours I stood there, listening to the sounds of the fat people coming after me, crowding up the stairs, all grey and blubbery, and roaring and sobbing and sliding and thumping against the walls and door.

Then the noises started to change. Gradually they turned into the wind in the concrete stairwell and the air-conditioner downstairs and the six-thirty plane to New York flying over the complex and a dog barking somewhere. It was light out now, nearly seven o'clock. I unbolted my door, keeping the chain on, and eased it open a slow inch. The hall was empty.

I still felt completely exhausted and crazy, but I got myself dressed somehow and choked down some coffee and left for work. On the way I took a detour in the Honda round the corner of the building. At first I was afraid to look, even though I was safe inside the locked car. At the edge of the woods where the mob of fat people had been there was nothing but some big old spirea bushes blowing and tossing about.

*

That evening Scott came home, ten pounds overweight. A couple of days later, when he was talking about his trip, he said that Indian food was great, especially the sweets, but the women were hard to talk to and not all that good-looking.

'A lot of Indians are heavy too, you know,' he told me.

'Really?' I asked. I wondered if Scott had had some spooky experience like mine, which I still hadn't mentioned: I didn't want him to think I was going to crack up whenever he left town.

'It's a sign of prosperity, actually. You notice them especially in the cities, much more than in this country. I mean you don't see many fat people around here for instance, do you?'

'No,' I agreed, cutting us both another slice of pineapple upside-down cake. 'Not lately, anyhow.'

# Perpetual Spinach

*Shena Mackay was born in Edinburgh in 1944. She left school at sixteen and worked in odd jobs while writing; she became an overnight literary sensation at twenty when her two novellas,* Dust Falls on Eugene Schlumburger *and* Toddler on the Run, *were published. She married and had three daughters but continued to write, publishing* Music Upstairs *in 1965,* Old Crow *in 1967,* An Advent Calendar, A Bowl of Cherries, Redhill Rococo, *which won the 1987 Fawcett Prize, and, most recently* Dunedin. *She has also published three collections of short stories, which have been collected in one volume by Penguin, and she has edited an anthology of short stories called* Such Devoted Sisters.

Old Cartwright belonged to the snow-shovelling generation. The dread sound of metal scraping the pavement woke his young neighbours and even before they were aware of the strange feathery light in the bedroom they knew it was snowing, and pictured him holding out his spade to catch the first sparse flakes falling from the sky. They groaned at the thought of that old man shovelling their shared path, as he surely would, and pulled the duvet over their heads, burying themselves in goose feathers.

Despite his London ancestry there was something bucolic about Old Cartwright; a sense of warm rabbits dangling from his belt, or a brace of wood-pigeons with rubies of blood on their breasts. He rode a stiff old black woman's bicycle to his urban allotment, pedalling slowly with one corduroy trouser leg, the colour of ploughed fields, caught up in a cycle clip and the other tied up with string. The bicycle, like its owner Miss

Defreitas, his sub-tenant, who lived above Mr Cartwright, was old and stiff and black, and was furnished with wicker baskets front and rear in which he brought back bouquets of carrots, potatoes and beans, frilly dark savoy cabbages, rhubarb and, endlessly, spinach. 'I can see why it's called perpetual spinach,' Olivia had said despairingly, plunging her hands into yet another washing-up bowl full of wet leaves. He set traps of jam jars filled with beer for the slugs and snails and they floundered and drowned, swelling to grotesque bleached alcoholic fungi before he threw them in a jellied heap on the compost. His crops were nourished with blood and bonemeal; the veins of his beetroots ran red above their swollen globes, his tomatoes were solid balls of haemoglobin and under their toxic green umbrellas the sanguineous sticks of his rhubarb were as thick as vultures' legs. Until his retirement he had been a driver on the Southern Region of British Rail, and Miss Defreitas had cleaned trains. She had been one of those women whose dustpan and brush were as much a reproach to commuters, swinging their feet out of the path of the cartons and cups and cigarette butts left by their predecessors, in the guilty knowledge that they would be replacing the rubbish as soon as she had gone, as Old Cartwright's spade was to Nick and Olivia. Miss Defreitas received his vegetables with politeness, although she continued to buy sweet potatoes and other strange tubers and roots which he could not identify, and refused to try. At first, Nick and Olivia had indulged in lewd speculation about the relationship of their elderly neighbours, but apart from Sunday lunch, which they took turns to cook, when Old Cartwright returned from the pub and Miss Defreitas from church, and the occasional sultry evenings when she brought out a kitchen chair and sat fanning herself while he slopped water over the begonias in the bed at the side of the yard, they led separate lives.

'This is ridiculous,' Nick said, hobbling to the window wrapped in the duvet, leaving Olivia exposed on the bed. 'Doesn't he know that if you clear the snow from outside your house you are responsible if anybody slips and breaks a leg?' He banged on the window and shouted at Cartwright to put back their snow. The double glazing muffled his voice and Old Cartwright, looking up with dimmed eyes, perceived him to be wearing an off-the-shoulder ball gown and raised his spade in an old-soldierly salute.

'If this keeps on, we can build a snowman later,' said Olivia.

'Dress it up in one of Old Cartwright's caps and pelt it with snowballs,' agreed Nick coming back to bed. The radio came on and he pressed the snooze button.

'Why do those old fogeys have to get up so early?'

'Because they haven't anything better to do,' Olivia snuggled into him.

Why despite the earthy bundles of produce left on their doorstep, Nick and Olivia sometimes wondered, did they regard him as a horrible old man? True, they had once heard him braying through the fence in mockery of the laughter at one of their parties where the guests spilled into the yard on summer nights, and one of their friends had asked if there was a donkey next door. She was pissed, of course; they all were. 'Only a silly ass,' Nick had replied quick as a flash; it was hilarious, but generally Cartwright was no trouble. They did not know about the slugs and snails, having resisted his invitations to visit the allotment, but taking the grisly titbits suspended from his washing line for the birds as an indication, fantasized a gamekeeper's gibbet of crucified fur and feathers on his tool-shed wall. Before they had learned that he had been a train driver they had decided that he was a ratcatcher. There was an empty rabbit hutch by his back door, mossy-roofed, with wire netting rusted to brittleness. At their firework party, Miss Defreitas had appeared at her window as a floating white nightdress against the blackness. Olivia held out a sparkler to her but a rocket whizzing towards the house made her disappear in a burst of golden stars, leaving the midnight sky and her window darker than before.

'Stupid old cockroach,' Nick had said, but Olivia had been pleased that their youthful pyrotechnics had lighted up her drab life for a minute or two.

'You ought to get yourself an allotment,' Old Cartwright had told Nick, leaning over the wooden fence that separated their back yards. It was broken, pulled down or held in the arms of an old Russian vine, and was, as he was fond of pointing out, their responsibility. 'Keep the missis in fruit and veg. I'll have a word with my committee. There's a waiting list, but a word in the right ear . . .'

He rubbed his own right lobe between an earthy finger and thumb while the thin burned-out cigarette stuck to his lip waggled in complicity.

'I wouldn't have time to look after an allotment,' Nick responded in weak alarm from the lounger where he lay with a book and a pitcher of Pimm's, swiping at a wasp as if warding off a barrage of onions and tomatoes. He swung his legs, still golden from a Turkish holiday, in cut-off denim shorts, to the ground and took refuge in the kitchen, leaving the Pimm's, like one of Cartwright's traps, to entice a variety of winged insects to a sweet and sticky death among the mint and melting ice floes.

'Oh, you've just broken my dream,' Olivia said, when he told her. 'I had a really funny dream last night. Henry was on a bicycle going to the allotments. When I say funny, it wasn't really funny, it was scary for some reason; I can't remember . . .' Henry cycled across her consciousness, his tabby trousers encircled with a bicycle clip and a piece of string, and the image faded.

'Look – he's got earth in his pads! That proves . . .'

'Been scratching in the begonias next door.'

'I suppose so.'

As she put down the food for Henry and his black companion Ruby, she thought for a second that a thin burned-out cigarette stuck from his mouth, but it turned out, to her relief, to be a tiny white feather.

It had been in a summer smelling of basil and tomatoes that they had moved into one of the row of pretty artisan's dwellings, some like the cottage next door still hung with net curtains and others with the coloured rattan and bamboo blinds of *arrivistes* such as themselves. Old Cartwright had occupied his house for sixty years; Nick and Olivia, who intended to remain in theirs for not more than two or three, were shocked by the way he had let his property deteriorate. It looked doubly disreputable beside their repointed brickwork and fresh paint; Miss Defreitas had geraniums in white plastic pots on her front windowsill and there was even a gnome and a stone tortoise in the tiny front garden. One night Nick and Olivia had attached a piece of battered cod from the chip shop to the end of the gnome's fishing rod, but one of their cats had eaten it before morning and spoiled the joke; and their plan to replace the stone reptile with a live one had been thwarted so far by the import ban on tortoises. They had a special loathing of the curtain of coloured plastic strips that hung across the open back door in summer.

'Makes it look like a betting shop,' grumbled Nick to their closest friends Annabel and Mark, as they set up the barbecue.

'If there's a chance of it ever coming on the market,' Mark said, 'we want to be the first to know.'

'That would be brilliant,' sighed Olivia.

'Do they use that old tin bath?' asked Annabel pointing to the thing hanging from a nail on the outside wall.

'Not any more,' said Nick.

'We shall use it,' Mark said, 'in front of the kitchen fire. Annabel can scrub my back when I come off shift at t'pit.'

'Brilliant. Very D. H. Lawrence.' They laughed as sparks flew like fire-flies and the smell of grilled flesh made their mouths water and the cats came crashing over the fence. It was such a lovely evening that it was three o'clock before the last meaty and winey kisses were exchanged and the last goodbyes shouted into the sleeping street and the last car door banged.

In the morning Old Cartwright complained to Olivia that the cats had broken one of his begonias. She reported it to Nick, adding, 'I'm never sure whether I like begonias or not. I can't decide if they are beautiful or obscene.'

'Need one preclude the other?'

'They're like roses but too fleshy – if he didn't plant them so regularly, so far apart, with all that bald earth in between, they might look better . . . anyway, he accused the cats of breaking one.'

'Did they?'

'Mmm. I denied it of course. How pathetic, one measly flower . . .'

'You'd think Miss Defreitas might run to something more exotic. I mean begonias and geraniums in plastic pots – some bougainvillaea or mimosa – a bit of tropical splendour –'

'I don't think Martinique is in the tropics.'

'– the brilliant hues of hummingbirds darting through the frangipani, the flash of a hyacinthine macaw's wing reflecting the waters of a blue lagoon . . .'

'You'd like a hummingbird, wouldn't you?' Olivia seized the black cat, Ruby, and kissed her nose. 'Or a hyacinthine wing ... that's funny, Nick, Ruby smells of perfume ... it's not mine, sort of sickly, and cheap ... I wonder what she's been up to?'

'All cats lead secret lives their owners know nothing about. Have you any idea where Henry goes at night?'

'No, but I wish he'd stay in.'

'She's not very good value, is she, our Miss Defreitas? I mean, remember when we peeked into her church and she was just standing there, in her pink hat, singing a hymn, not flinging herself around, rolling her eyes and waving her hands in the air and shouting, "Hallelujah, yes, Lord, I'se a comin'!" and speaking in tongues. She really ought to make more effort.'

Ruby leapt from Olivia's arms, scratching her shoulder.

Summer seemed far away as Monday morning's cold-chisel broke the lovers' embrace and they, having decided to leave their cars at home, set out to walk to the station. 'Here comes the Green-wellie Brigade,' said Old Cartwright as they passed.

'Boring old f—' Nick started saying and ended in a bellow as Olivia rubbed a cold handful of snow down his neck. The snow exhilarated her; she felt as frisky as a young husky in harness.

'Do you think we'll have a white Christmas, Mr Cartwright?' she called, knowing how he loved to expound weather lore. He looked up at the sky.

'Plenty more where that came from,' he pronounced, 'but it'll all be gone in a couple of days.'

'Why bother to shovel it up then?' asked Nick, rubbing the back of his neck with his scarf. 'Hope you fall and break your leg,' he muttered, as Miss Defreitas came out of the front door with a mug of something steaming. 'What a pair.'

That evening there was a ring at the front door. Annabel answered it, as Nick and Olivia were busy in the kitchen.

'There's a funny old man at the door,' she called, coming into the kitchen. 'I think it might be your next-door neighbour. Something about calor gas ...'

Old Cartwright stood, stamping his feet on the step, in overcoat and gloves letting a current of icy air into the hall. Nick noticed his nose was cross-hatched with red veins with a dewdrop threatening to fall. He was asking Nick to drive him and an empty gas cylinder to the hardware shop in the morning.

'They were supposed to deliver Wednesday, only they never came,' he explained. 'I wouldn't ask, only . . . nice and warm in here, innit? Normally I wouldn't ask, only . . .'

'Oh, all right,' Nick cut him off. 'It'll have to be early. I've got a meeting at ten. It's very inconvenient.'

'Bloody liberty,' he said, when he had got rid of Cartwright. 'I hope he doesn't think I'm going to make a habit of chauffeuring him all over the place.'

He had to send Cartwright back into the house in the morning to get an old blanket to wrap the cylinder in so that it would not damage the car; the thing weighed a ton even when empty. The house was as cold as it was outside, he noticed when he rolled the new cylinder over the doorstep. Miss Defreitas leaned from the banister in her black coat.

'This place is like an icebox,' he told them. 'You ought to get in touch with the council, or somebody, get some double glazing and draught proofing.' Soggy newspaper was wedged round the windows.

Nick and Olivia spent Christmas with Olivia's parents near Godalming. True to Old Cartwright's prediction, it was not white, but simulated snow drifted in the leaded window panes and the porch was picked out in frosted fairy lights and the old cedar tree in the front garden was hung with coloured bulbs. The only fly in the ointment, or mulled wine, for Olivia and Nick, was that they had had to ask Old Cartwright and Miss Defreitas to feed the cats, and from time to time, scratching the heads of Olivia's parents' Jack Russell and hyperactive Red Setter, they wondered how they were getting on.

They let themselves in to their own house to find a brown skeleton of a Christmas tree, like an ancient murdered princess still wearing her jewels, surrounded by a circle of needles. There was no thud of flying feet to greet them, no loud welcoming purring, not even the swish of a resentful tail.

'Ruby, Henry,' called Olivia from the back door. Miss Defreitas appeared silhouetted against an upstairs window, and Old Cartwright poked his head out of the back door. Olivia shut her door quickly. Nick was inspecting the cupboard. He brought out several tins of cat food.

'They haven't been feeding them,' Olivia shrieked. 'They must have starved to death! Oh, Nick, where are they?'

'Don't panic. Don't cry, they'll be around somewhere, hang on, the pilchards have gone, and the salmon for their Christmas dinner – and the cod in cheese and butter sauce have gone from the fridge . . . they can't have starved. They're punishing us for going away – you know what cats are like, they'll turn up at supper time, large as life. You sit down, I'll make a cup of tea.'

'Don't you think it's odd,' Olivia asked as they sat in the kitchen, relieved to have their hands round their familiar mugs of tea, 'that those particular items should have gone?'

'If you're thinking what I think you are, I'm sure cat food would be more to our neighbour's taste – Whiskas and two veg, followed by rhubarb and custard.'

When Olivia had cooked rhubarb according to Old Cartwright's instructions, with no water and a spoonful of strawberry jam, she had had to throw away the pan, one of a set, a wedding present. She, as the rhubarb had done, still seethed at the memory. The cat-flap banged and Henry and Ruby stalked in, tails in the air.

'They're enormous! They must have put on a stone! What on earth have they been feeding them on?'

'Curried goat? Yams? Perpetual spinach?'

'Whatever, they look marvellous. Come on then, pussies, have you missed your mummy then?'

The two cats walked straight past them and into the bedroom. Nick and Olivia had to laugh, they looked so disdainful.

'Shouldn't we go next door and thank them?'

'Tomorrow will do – let's go to bed. I find Godalming somewhat inhibiting.'

'I noticed. Do you think we should have brought them something?'

'I thought you put some bits of turkey in a bag?'

'Old Cartwright and Miss Defreitas, silly, not the cats.'

'They loved looking after them. Gave them something to do, poor old things. Give them the turkey if you like, of course . . .'

'No, it's for the cats.'

They went to bed. The cats leapt on and walked, purring, all over them.

'Ouch. Ruby, delighted as I am to see you, do you mind not sitting on my face?'

'Yuk, Henry absolutely stinks of cigarette smoke. Mind your claws!'

'I suppose they're just pleased to see us – ouch, get off. This is ridiculous. Go and eat your nice turkey.' He pushed the cats off the bed. 'That's better. Oh, God, I didn't mean bring it in here to eat – they're dragging it all over the bed, it's disgusting. Get off! What's the matter with them?'

The cats tore the meat with teeth and claws, purring and chewing simultaneously; their eyes were huge and yellow. Olivia and Nick lay there, under their weight, almost afraid to shoo them off, waiting for them to finish. Then they started to wash; the bed throbbed with their snouting and licking; it seemed they would never finish; they must have swelled to the size of tigers as their tongues rasped vast tracts of fur, licking their own and each other's enormous limbs and backs and faces, slicking paws across great ears, with whiskers rattling like embattled porcupines' quills. At last they decided to sleep, one on either side of Nick and Olivia, pulling the duvet taut across them, weighing it down so that the two humans lay side by side, swaddled like mummies, slick with sweat, unable to turn or move their restless legs, pinioned in misery all the intolerable night.

In the morning the cats resumed their normal size and seemed to be their old selves, except for the fact that Ruby never quite lost the smell of perfume and Henry's coat still reeked of tobacco smoke. Olivia and Nick got out of the way of encouraging them to jump on to their knees, although they would have said they were as fond of them as ever. They kept meaning to go round and thank their neighbours for feeding them, but they kept putting it off, and then it seemed too late. Life went on as before. Old Cartwright cycled to the allotment, when the weather wasn't too bad, to tend his winter and early spring greens; the wing mirror was

ripped off one of the cars, and the radio stolen. Olivia and Nick entertained friends and went to the cinema and restaurants, the fence sagged
and bits broke off as the cats came and went, aconites appeared in the
front garden; Miss Defreitas gave them a reproachful good morning as
she stepped aside in the sound of church bells to let them pass her on the
path with their heavy cartons from the Wine Warehouse.

One Saturday morning in April Annabel and Mark came over. Mark and
Nick were in the front room fortifying themselves before attempting to
mend the fence, standing at the window with glasses in their hands. The
cats were sprawled on the path luxuriating in the dust and sun on their fur.
Down the road Nick saw Old Cartwright pedalling homewards, encounter
Miss Defreitas coming out of the shop, and dismount. He took her shopping bag and hung it from his handlebars. She was carrying a fan of
unripe bananas, bright green against her black coat. They approached the
zebra crossing.

'Don't you worry about them, with that dangerous road?' Mark said,
meaning the cats. Nick was watching Old Cartwright and Miss Defreitas
and misunderstood.

'Oh, they're indestructible. Besides, they always use the crossing.'

As he spoke a lorry slewed across the zebra, hurling Miss Defreitas
and Old Cartwright in an arc of bodies, bicycle and bananas that was
suspended in the air, then came crashing in a blitz of vegetables into the
protective grille on the off-licence window, bounced, and fell in a twisted
heap to the pavement.

Witnessing the accident knocked Nick for six. Both he and Olivia were
surprised at how the accident affected them. Nobody could eat lunch. The
policeman who came to interview Nick and Mark found the four of them
holding a wake, sitting stunned and tear-stained round the kitchen table
heaped with the empty bottles and full ashtrays of the bereaved. It took
the officers some time to convince the mourners that Old Cartwright and
Miss Defreitas had not been killed, but were in hospital, mangled like
the bicycle, critically ill but still alive. The bicycle itself was a write-off.
Olivia and Annabel rushed off to the newsagent's to buy get-well cards;
they found the perfect one for Old Cartwright, a still life of fruit and

vegetables, and a lovely one for Miss Defreitas, with white lilies, that said 'With Deepest Sympathy', that they were sure would be to her taste.

Then they realized that they didn't know where to send the cards. Nick said he would ring the local hospital to inquire but was informed that there was no casualty department there and before he could ask where the nearest one was the phone was put down.

'Yellow Pages,' said Mark.

'Local Thomson's Directory,' suggested Annabel.

'That's the one sponsored by that ghastly cat in a T-shirt, with no trousers, isn't it?' said Olivia, but in the event they couldn't find the directories, which Olivia had forgotten she had pushed under the bed when they were repapering the bedroom. The quartet spent the rest of the day in a subdued game of Trivial Pursuit, and later the girls made some toast and pâté. Nick was sick.

The local paper gave a graphic account of the accident to the two pensioners and said that a court case was pending but did not name the hospital to which the victims had been taken. The cards grew dusty on the mantelpiece. Olivia realized that 'With Deepest Sympathy' was perhaps not suitable after all. They came home from work one day to find a downstairs window in the house next door had been broken. Miss Defreitas's geraniums grew leggy and yellow. The gnome and tortoise were stolen. Olivia kept meaning to ask in the shops if there was any news of their neighbours but as the weeks passed it became too embarrassing to expose her own unneighbourliness in not having visited them. Then one Sunday morning when Nick was buying hot bread for their breakfast the man who served him remarked, 'Shame about old Harry Cartwright.'

'Yes, a great shame. Wonderful old character, old Harry.'

'And her, of course, Miss Whatsername. Pity it wasn't instantaneous really.'

'Yes, it would have saved a great deal of trouble, I suppose – I mean suffering.'

He left with his bread to the pronouncement that something – faulty brakes or drunk drivers – made the shopkeeper's blood boil.

The boards of several rival estate agents were nailed up in the front garden of the house next door. Nick was on the phone to Mark and Annabel at once. They put in a bid, and with a bit of judicious gazumping, their offer was accepted. Olivia and Nick were ecstatic. Summer would be one long spritzer.

Annabel and Mark came over for a celebratory breakfast, a foretaste of the Sundays when they would be neighbours.

'Cheers,' said Mark, raising his glass of Buck's Fizz. 'You'll have to do something about that fence, old man. I believe it's your responsibility.'

A carillon of church bells broke on the summer air like brass confetti, as if in joyful collaboration with the clinking glasses, pealing a benison over the future. At that moment Ruby jumped out of the open window and stalked up the road towards the church, thin and black with her tail at a resolute but pious angle. The cat-flap crashed and Henry strode into the room with something in his jaws. He dropped it in the centre of the circle of friends. Olivia screamed. It was grey and furry and very dead. It could have been a rat or a decaying vegetable. Nobody could bear to touch it.

# Broken Transformers

Translated by Shi Junbao

*Bi Shumin was born in Shandong province, China, and served in the Chinese army after middle school. She then went on to work as a physicist before turning to writing. Most of her work depicts army life and includes* Kunlun Mountains, A Red Carpet for You *and* Flying Northward. *'Broken Transformers' was first published in 1992.*

'Mum, let's go. I don't want a Transformer,' said my ten-year-old son.

We were standing in a newly opened department store. As mother of a low-income family I was used to steering my son firmly away from toy counters; but this store had taken me by surprise; its manager had shrewdly filled the entrance hall with brightly coloured playthings instead of the usual dull array of cosmetics.

I stood in the doorway, debating whether or not to leave. There had been a sign outside saying the store sold wool, and I desperately needed to knit myself a new hat and scarf. Still, wool could be bought elsewhere.

I gripped my son's hand and drew him towards me intending to make up some excuse to get him out of the store, and thus out of temptation's way. Ten was an age, after all, at which innocence gradually begins to give way to questioning, and I didn't want him to become conscious too early of the power of money and thus of our limited supply. At the same time I hated the thought of his disappointment at not being able to have the toy he so adored. I felt like covering his eyes with my palm!

The last thing I expected him to say was, 'Mum, let's leave. I don't want a Transformer.' I was at a loss to know how to express my gratitude.

I hated the monstrous cartoon family which had my son glued to the TV set every Saturday and Sunday night; not only did it prevent me watching the news, but it had so captured the imagination of thousands of children that the toy replicas now pouring into the stores were sucking money from parents like locusts devouring crops.

If we hadn't been in the crowded store I would have bent down and kissed his smooth brow, now covered with beads of salty sweet sweat. But it immediately became clear to me that my sense of relief was premature, for his feet were as though rooted to the spot. His neck twisted towards the counter and he stared, through long dark eyelashes, at the colourful range of robots which stared back at him in disdain.

My heart bled as I looked admiringly at his lithe young neck which, like the branch of a willow tree, seemed able to twist back endlessly without incurring discomfort. Was it only a matter of a hat and a scarf?

A perfect example of the trend towards 'late marriage and late birth' characteristic of the time, I had now passed the age of forty while my son was only ten. I had been through all the turmoil and confusion, whereas his was still to come. My troubles tended to be physical, like the fact that the first northern winter winds had nearly frozen my head off and, worse, I had discovered I was beginning to lose my hair which was, moreover, turning grey. This was not only thoroughly unattractive, but meant I was even less well insulated than before. I considered myself pretty good with my hands; as well as lathing machine parts I could also knit and sew. For some time now I had been planning to knit myself a really good hat and scarf and had even told my husband about it. He had, as a gesture towards financing the project, stubbed out his cigarette. I knew he wouldn't give up permanently, of that I had been convinced from the very first day I met him, no matter what other money-saving hobbies he might dispense with. We also saved by eating less meat at dinner, concentrating our chopsticks on vegetables and hoping our son wouldn't notice the decline.

Despite the fact that since the boy's birth cold winds tended to cause a painful throbbing in my head, I could still do without a hat; my old square scarf would suffice, though no doubt I would look odd, like a solemn Arab woman or Mother Hen from the children's cartoon series. But so what? As long as my son could get his beloved robot.

I glanced at the Transformers. They were so expensive that the price of a hat and scarf would be enough to cover maybe the leg of one of the larger models.

And what would my husband say? He had always maintained that I spoiled the child and warned me that ours was just an ordinary 'blue-collar family' which shouldn't aspire to the same heights of those better-off.

But was it to be the case that no 'blue-collar' worker should ever own a Transformer?

I had enough money with me for one of the smallest models available, and knew I could make up a story about the hat and scarf which would satisfy my husband and indicate that I didn't need them.

It was at this point, just as I had made up my mind to buy it, that my son suddenly turned towards the exit, saying resolutely, 'Mum, let's go. The paper says Transformers are only foreign kids' cast-offs. They move them into China to get our money.'

He tugged my hand with his little damp one and glanced back at the toys as though taking a last look at a corpse. Then he quickened his short legs and made for the door as if fearful the Transformers might otherwise snatch him back.

He sounded like an adult, the logic of his argument certainly exceeded anything I might have come up with and it occurred to me that in comparison with our boy, who was, moreover, a model student at school, my husband and I were selfish.

Spurred by this revelation I strode back to the counter and, without giving a second's thought as to who profited by my action, whether foreigners or Hong Kong Chinese, I impulsively took possession of the smallest Transformer money could buy. Suddenly I no longer cared about the pains I would get in my head and neck. This purchase was a token of appreciation for my son's understanding and an expression of our mutual love.

That evening he skipped dinner in order to play with his robot. He put a black toy pistol into its hand and the creature, with a twist and a turn, obligingly turned into an exquisite streamlined bomber. The thermo-coloured American trademark turned from red to blue and back to red in his warm little hands.

'Convertible Transformer fights for justice and freedom with an iron will . . .' he sang sweetly. It was the theme song from the TV series.

Although my husband had grumbled, I felt the purchase had been a wise one. True, Transformers were expensive, but the moments of happiness they gave were priceless. In the event of my son growing up to be an important public figure, I didn't want to have to read in his autobiography: I liked toys when I was little but my family was too poor to afford them, so I could only watch the other children playing with theirs . . .

Of course he might also simply turn out to be a blue-collar worker; either way I was loath to leave him with any regrets about his childhood. Children are, after all, easy to satisfy: the smallest Transformer intoxicates them.

'Don't neglect your homework now,' I cautioned in an unusually serious, perhaps overcompensatory, tone of voice. He earnestly promised not to.

Over the next few days I carried out spot checks on his homework and was satisfied to find that he had lost none of his willpower; he allowed himself to play with his toy only after finishing his work.

Winter finally arrived with a vengeance.

My husband prolonged his prohibition on cigarettes, and though I tried to reassure him that my old scarf was perfectly adequate, his response was gloomy. 'You should have a pair of warm boots,' he said.

I gave him a grateful smile and made a face indicating that it was indeed cold down there.

One evening I suddenly found my son playing with a different Transformer: this one was yellow, and much larger and fiercer than his own.

'What's this?' I asked, almost severely. All the guidebooks on 'parenting' warned us not to ignore any new tangents a child went off on.

'Transformer Giant,' he answered calmly, as though discussing a close relative.

Thanks to the protracted TV series, I was equipped with basic knowledge of the Transformer family and I knew that the Giant was one of the principal characters.

Be that as it may, its name was not important to me – its owner was. Without softening my voice I demanded to know whose it was. His reply was matter-of-fact. 'One of my classmates',' he said, without registering my suspicion. 'Almost everybody has one and they're all different, so we trade to play.'

Although I felt a slight twinge of guilt about my tone of voice, I couldn't guarantee I wouldn't react in the same way in the future. Dishonesty was above all others the thing I feared most in children and I was constantly on the look-out for it.

The kids were clever. They traded like primitive tribes. It was a new phenomenon, and I wasn't sure whether to oppose or support it. 'Giant or not,' I said to my elated son, 'don't let it ruin your school work, and be careful with other people's toys.'

He nodded his assent. I could always rely on him to listen.

Somebody was tapping at the door.

My son ran over and hospitably pulled it wide open. But the visitor slowly closed it again as if he wished to remain outside. Presently a round head hesitantly pushed its way through the crack. It was my son's classmate, one who seemed to go by the name of Fatty and who regularly dropped by to get my son to help him with his homework. Only this time Fatty hadn't come for help. He neither entered nor retreated but remained hovering on the threshold facing my son and glancing up at me with a miserable expression on his face. Finally he stammered out in embarrassment, 'I'm so sorry . . . I broke your toy . . .'

The blood drained from my son's cheeks. I had never seen such an agonized look pass across his face. He took the dismantled toy from Fatty, held it before his eyes and blew on it softly, as though it were a wounded pigeon.

After the initial shock had subsided, my son looked at me to rescue him. For one bitter moment the sacrificed hat and scarf flashed across my mind, but there was nothing we could do except face it. Trying to avoid my son's eye, I said, 'It's up to you. It's your toy, what do you think we should do?'

Perhaps inhibited by my presence, he remained silent. I therefore discreetly moved into the inner room and listened intently. I could hear Fatty wheezing in the silence and longed to put an end to his misery by running out and saying, 'Fatty, you may leave now.' But the verdict, whatever it was, had to come from my son.

'How did you smash it?' I heard him ask, with anger in his voice.

'I just . . . then, flop . . .' Fatty must have been gesticulating. An exasperated gurgle appeared to be my son's stifled response.

What was I to do? Maybe I should go out and intervene. Transformers cost money, but magnanimity is something that no amount of money can buy; and although I believed my son had absorbed the moral principles I had instilled in him over the years, I nevertheless recognized that to him a small Transformer was the equivalent of a colour TV set or a deluxe camera to an adult. The prolonged silence was agony, for him and for Fatty as well as for me.

Finally he spoke. He seemed to have covered a great deal of mental ground and his voice, though weak, was none the less clear: 'Don't worry . . .'

Fatty grasped the opportunity and fled, as though afraid that my son might otherwise change his mind.

I heaved a long sigh of relief, as if I too had just returned from a long journey. Emerging, I kissed my son's sweaty forehead.

'It's dead,' he said as his eyes filled with tears.

'I'll try and glue it together,' I said comfortingly, though with little hope of success.

I duly went flat out to fix it, drawing on all my resources of skill and ingenuity. After spending a great deal more time and effort on it than I would have spent knitting a hat, it finally became recognizable again as a toy. But though it looked all right, it was too delicate to touch and it could no longer change shapes.

My son, meanwhile, devoted himself to the Giant. A Transformer should change shape, he said, otherwise it was just a trinket. So saying, he deftly changed the shape of the toy he had in his hand. One has to admire the Americans. Who else would come up with the idea of turning the belly of a fighter into a robot's head and then proceed to create a machine that executes the transition so flawlessly?

A good toy attracts both children and grown-ups, but no sooner had I begun to move closer to watch him play than I heard an ominous crash and saw the toy collapse in pieces.

What had happened? We looked at each other in horror.

Unfortunately, though we could hardly believe it, the truth was all too painfully clear: he had broken the Giant.

For a while my son tried to fix it, but only ended up with more pieces than he had started with. Realizing the situation was hopeless, he gathered the pieces together, wrapped them in a sheet of paper and prepared to leave the house.

'Where are you going?' I asked, still in a state of shock.

'To return the toy and apologize,' he said, looking calm and prepared.

'Is it Fatty's?' I asked, with a glimmer of hope.

'No.' He then mentioned a name.

Hers! My heart plunged, then leapt into my throat.

The only impression I had ever been able to gain of this girl was that she was like a delicate flower and had a very arrogant mother. The family was well heeled – my husband would call them 'wealthy' – and it was entirely natural that they should have bought such a large and ferocious-looking toy for their daughter.

'You're going . . . like this?' I stammered.

'Should I take something with me?' he asked, confused.

I looked at his limpid eyes and refrained from further comment.

'OK, mum, I'm off.' He disappeared out the door.

'Come home soon,' I called after him apprehensively.

I knew he wouldn't dawdle, but he didn't return soon, and when he hadn't returned later either my heart began to flutter like fish on a hook.

I should have warned him that people were all different, that he might not be pardoned, even though he himself had forgiven a similar accident. I should have prepared him better for the possibility of an unpleasant scene, otherwise he might cry.

On the other hand things might turn out OK. His classmate might have asked him hospitably to stay a little, while her mother peeled him an orange, which my son would naturally push back politely. He is a lovable boy. They would surely forgive him in the same manner in which we had forgiven little Fatty.

The more I thought about it the more I convinced myself that that could be the only possible outcome. Moreover I congratulated myself now on not having filled his heart with my own cynical suspicions.

But as time passed, no matter how I tried to reassure myself, I grew increasingly concerned.

At last he returned, his footstep so light that, deep in thought as I was, I didn't even notice he was there until he was standing right in front of me.

One look at him was enough to convince me that he had undergone a profound inner trauma. I could also tell that he had been crying and that he had already dried his tears in the cold wind so that I wouldn't notice. A child often reveals more when he is hiding something.

I did not have the heart to get him to go into details; it would have been too painful.

'Mum, they want us . . . to compensate . . .' he said finally, as large, cold teardrops rolled down his cheeks and on to my hand.

I now had to deal not only with a broken toy but with a broken heart.

'It's only natural,' I said, wiping away his tears, 'that they'd want to be compensated for their loss.'

'Then let me go and find Fatty and ask him to compensate me for mine. All he said was "I'm sorry." Next time I go shopping I won't take my money, I'll just say, "I'm sorry." Will that do?' he asked, jumping up to leave.

'Don't go!' I pulled him back. He struggled wildly, suddenly seeming to have acquired the strength of a calf.

'Why, mum? Tell me!' he demanded, lifting his head.

I didn't know how to respond. Sometimes principles are all very well and, like beautiful clothes can be very attractive, but they are not the stuff from which clothes are actually made.

I had to give him an answer. It is a cat's responsibility to teach her kitten how to catch mice. I had to provide my son with an explanation, no matter how impractical it might be.

'The words "I'm sorry" mean you are being courteous. Their value ought not to be counted in terms of money.'

He nodded quietly. I probably sounded like one of his teachers, so he forced himself to listen.

'You forgave Fatty when he broke your Transformer,' I continued, patiently trying to explain things in terms he would understand. 'He was relieved. That was a nice thing to do.'

'But, mum, I haven't been forgiven for a similar mistake!' he protested. His sense of shame seemed to override my reasoned arguments.

'Well, son, there are many ways of solving a problem. Problems are like Transformers: they can either be a robot, a plane or a car . . . Understand?'

'Yeah.' He nodded reluctantly. I knew he was unconvinced, and just wanted to placate me.

I let go of his hand, exhausted.

He relaxed and stood aside.

The large broken toy was going to involve a hideous amount of money, and though we hadn't yet reached the stage where we needed to go to the pawn shop – which our street didn't have anyway – we were still pretty broke.

Sitting on the bad news, we waited for my husband to come home. My son looked at me pitifully. Was he hoping I would not tell him about the incident at all, or hoping I would do it quickly?

I dreaded the prospect, but knew it had to be done, and despite my inclination to postpone the reckoning I knew it would be better in the long run to get it over and done with immediately.

On hearing the news, my husband managed temporarily to retain his composure.

'Tell me,' he said calmly, 'how did you come to break the thing?' He couldn't bring himself to give it a name.

'I just twisted it, and "flop", it broke . . .' stammered my son, looking at me appealingly for support. I'd seen it happen, certainly, but I couldn't have said how.

But describing how it broke was in any event unimportant. The consequence was that our son would never again be able to play with such a costly toy.

My husband's eyebrows locked and the ferocity of his expression sent my son scurrying behind me for protection. Suddenly he exploded.

'Tell me,' he said, his voice rising in a crescendo, 'did you break it on purpose or deliberately?'

I frankly couldn't see what the difference was between 'on purpose' and 'deliberately', but didn't dare interfere.

'I did it . . . on purpose. No, dad, I did it deliberately . . .' Desperately searching for whichever seemed the less incriminating, he lurched from one to the other, shrinking beneath his father's glare.

'You little wretch! A whole month's salary won't pay for this thing, yet you think you can go around lording it like the master of some grand mansion. I'll give you a hiding you'll never forget.'

With that he raised his arm, and as it came crashing down I lifted my own to intercept the blow. A blinding pain instantly spread from my side down to my fingers. He was a strong man, a labourer, and it was fortunate I had blocked him.

For a few moments my son was stunned, then he let out a sharp cry, as if it had been he who had been hit.

'You've got a nerve to blubber like that!' shouted my husband, breathing heavily. 'That damn thing your mother bought you already cost her her wool hat, and now that! That's our fuel and cabbage for the whole winter gone!' Then he turned to me and added, 'It's your fault for spoiling him.'

I let him rant. As long as he didn't resort to violence again I could cope. My son had never been beaten before.

That winter, on one particularly freezing day when the sun seemed to be emanating blasts of cold air instead of warmth, I arrived home to find that the stove was barely alight. My son was waiting for me, his face burning red and his eyes glittering like stars reflected in a pool. I was afraid he had a fever.

'Close your eyes, mum,' he said. That sweet tone of his voice reassured me that he was not ill.

I closed my eyes quietly. I thought he must have a little surprise for me: a perfect exam paper perhaps, or a toy he might have made out of paper and bottles.

'You can open your eyes now, mum.'

I kept my eyes closed, savouring the happy moment that only a mother can experience.

'Quick, mum!' he urged.

I opened my eyes on to what seemed at first like a meadow in spring-time. It took me a moment to register that what my son was, in fact, holding in front of me was a bundle of green knitting wool.

'Do you like the colour, mum?' he asked, looking at me expectantly.

Green was my favourite.

'Yes, very much! How did you know I like it?'

'You must have forgotten. You've always knitted me green clothes ever since I was little. I would be able to pick out the colour among a thousand others.' He must have wondered how I could even ask such a question.

'Did dad take you there?'

'No, I went by myself,' he said proudly.

'Where did you get the money?' I asked in surprise.

He didn't answer, but stared at me motionlessly.

He could not have stolen it. The very thought of stealing was anathema to my young son. He must have got the money by recycling used paper or toothpaste tubes, but I hadn't noticed him returning home late with blackened fingers. Well, I'd have to ask him again.

'Tell me, where did you get the money?' I persisted, almost pleading with him to give me a satisfactory answer.

'I asked Fatty for it,' he answered clearly.

'You asked who?' I couldn't believe my ears. It was impossible that he could have done something like that. He had always been so obedient.

'Fatty!' he repeated, staring at me resolutely.

A loud buzzing sounded in my head. His bold expression seemed to come from a boy I didn't know.

'How did you get it from him?' I asked in a weak voice.

'The way those other people asked us for it,' he said dismissively, as though I was being pernickety.

He saw my hand rise and, thinking I was about to stroke his head, moved in closer. But I slapped him. Remembering, in the split second before my arm descended, an article I had read somewhere warning parents never to hit their children on the head. But it was too late. My hand slanted at an angle and landed on his neck.

He didn't flinch, but merely looked at me in astonishment.

I had never really hit him before, but now I felt certain that this would not be the last time.

Since then, every time a gust of wind pushes open the front door, I expect to see a little fellow with a round head appear. But Fatty has never been back. He paid for our Transformer and left it with us.

I fixed the big one with glue. Its bold appearance added a sense of wealth to our house.

Now we have two Transformers that do not transform.

My son has never touched them again.

# BARBARA ANDERSON

# *Tuataras*

*Barbara Anderson was born in New Zealand in 1926. She completed a science degree at the University of Otago and, thirty years later, an arts degree at Victoria University in Wellington. She has worked as a schoolteacher and a laboratory technician, and she is married with two sons. She is the author of one collection of short stories,* I Think We Should Go into the Jungle, *and two novels,* Girls High *and* Portrait of the Artist's Wife. *For the latter novel she won the Goodman Fielder Wattie Book Award, New Zealand's most prestigious literary prize, in 1992.*

They fascinated him, the hatching tuataras. Inch-long dragons pecking their way to a wider world. Shells are expected to enclose endearing and vulnerable balls of yellow, grey, or black fluff, but these were different. Leathery, wrinkled like dirty white gloves, the discarded ones resembled something unattractive and crumpled in the bottom of a laundry basket. Each shell had a number written on it with a felt pen. Charles Renshawe opened the inner glass door of the incubator and picked up 18 with care. The occupant had made little progress since his last inspection. The minuscule eyes stared, their sudden blink as startling as a wink from a blank face. They peered at him above a jagged rim, the body still completely enclosed.

Charles despised anthropomorphism in any form. Dogs with parasols teetering on their hind legs, advertisements in which chimpanzees jabbered their delight at cups of tea, made him very angry. 'What happened to the Mesozoic reptiles?' he asked the head.

He replaced the egg quickly, closed the double doors of the incubator, then turned to watch the juveniles which had hatched during the last week.

They were housed in a display case the base of which was covered with a deep layer of dry compost. The tuatara-hatching project was the work of one of his brighter honours students and had been almost too successful. 'We'll have them coming out our ears soon, Doctor,' said Mrs Blume, crooning and pecking at the department's computer in the back room.

Charles relit his pipe yet again and counted them. Still eleven. The juveniles were exact miniatures of the adult forms except that they had no upstanding spines along the midline of their backs. Three of them had red dots between their eyes, the identification system of another student's research. This too pleased Charles. Class distinction among the archaic reptiles.

You hardly ever saw them moving. Their immobility was one of the things which fascinated him. He stared at one which was standing on three legs, willing it to ground the fragment of claw. He thought of the toads he had seen on an overnight stop in Guam on his way to present a paper at a Royal Society conference in Tokyo. They had appeared from this tropical dark, dozens of them, to squat motionless on the floodlit concrete path beneath his host's window. Suddenly one would move. Hop. Hop hop hop. Hop. Hop hop. Then resume its rock-like squat, immobile as a programmed chess piece between moves.

Charles glanced at his watch. He had had his five minutes. He gave a faint sigh, turned off the light and returned through Mrs Blume's office to his own shambles. He sat at the desk which was submerged beneath piles of examination papers and resumed his marking. He worked steadily for an hour, ballpoint in hand, ticking, marking, deciding.

His laugh crashed through the silence of the still building, an explosion of pleasure as he rocked back in his chair. He had used the metaphor 'a dishcover of membrane bones' in an unfortunate attempt at clarification in a second-year lecture. He remembered standing in front of a hundred faces, the Asians and their tape recorders intent in the front rows, the rest a haze, a sea of uninterest. Every one of the papers already marked had chanted back the inane phrase. This candidate wrote with authority about a dishcloth of membrane bones. Charles read on, his heart sinking. You would think they would pick up something. At least have a glimmer. Hopeless. Hopeless.

At two a.m. he gave up. He stretched his arms above his head in capitulation, yawned wide as the goodnight kiwi, marched out of the mess and locked the door.

He lay very still when he woke next morning, then shut his eyes again quickly. Marking, he thought. That's all. Marking. Then he remembered. Last night had been bad. Very bad. So bad that he had picked up a pile of papers and retreated to his office at the university leaving Rhona red-faced and outraged at the table, abandoned among the chop bones and wilting salad. Charles heaved himself up in the bed. His thin hair stood up from his head in a caricature of fright, his myopic eyes searched with his groping fingers for the spectacles on the beside table. No sound. Rhona must have finished in the bathroom. Her knuckles tapped against his door. 'Out,' said his sister, stumping back along the passage to her room.

She was still a good-looking woman. Her fine papery skin lay virtually unlined across the 'good bones' of her face. Her grey hair was puffed and gentle about her face except when Ashley did it too tight. 'Don't worry,' Charles said. 'It'll grow out.' 'All very well for you,' replied Rhona, her eyes snapping. And of course it was all very well for him, it had no effect whatsoever, even if she had had it dyed purple as she'd once threatened to do.

Rhona had been the toast of the town when towns still had toasts. She had appeared frequently among the photographs on the Social Page of slim girls 'escorted' by haunted-looking young men with jug ears. Her face, even in the smudged print, was flawless, her eyes large, the corners of her mouth curving upwards with pleasure. And she was friendly too, and generous. Often she would hiss at one of the young men hovering around her, Go on, go and dance with Leonie. She's been there all night. And the youth would retreat and return to be rewarded by a smile, that smile.

As the years passed the lesser toasts married, their nuptial photographs splashing through the pages of the *Free Lance*. 'Broad acres united', sang the caption beneath the bucolic groom and the hysterical-looking girl clinging to his arm. 'Titan bride' followed 'Twins unite in double cere-mony', and still Rhona was unmarried. Nobody could understand it.

Charles was not interested. He was grateful to his sister for being a success and thus freeing him from responsibilities often hissed upon other young men. 'And look after your sister. Especially the Supper Waltz.' He flatly refused to go to dances. Mrs Renshawe, a strong-minded woman, threatened, cajoled, pleaded. Charles wore her down. 'I am not going to the Combined Dance.' 'I am not going to the Leavers' Dance.' 'I am not going.' Endless scraps of paper bearing such messages haunted Mrs Renshawe in the ball season. They greeted her from every box, container, drawer. They confronted her as she reached for an ivory tip, fluttered from the inside of her rolled napkin, lay beneath the knives in the knife drawer, even, she found once with a slight shock, fell from inside the toilet roll. Defeated, Mrs Renshawe decided that Charles would be better copy as an embryo intellectual. And he was a boy.

Charles fulfilled his mother's predictions. A good student, his interest in zoology was quickened in the sixth form by one of the few effective teachers left behind during the war. Mr Beson was 4F, unfit for active service. He taught science, taught it well, and Charles was hooked. He enrolled at Otago as soon as he left school and majored in chemistry and zoology before going overseas for postgraduate study.

It never occurred to Charles not to go home from Dunedin each holiday. He was quite happy in Hobson Street. He was quite happy anywhere. And besides, he knew he was not staying. He drove his mother about the town, opened the door of the Buick for her as he had been instructed since childhood, stowed her parcels with care, smiled at her when she had finished her shopping and asked with a professional backwards chuck of his head, 'Home, Mum?' He accompanied his father to the club occasionally, but not often. He stood around politely as his father played snooker in the Billiard Room with Neville Frensham, and the light glinted on the bottles in the bar and the tension heightened and Charles thought what a balls-aching waste of time it all was.

Neville Frensham was a stockbroker in the same firm as his father. Younger, but not a great deal. He and Mr Renshawe walked home together after work and his father often asked Frensham in for a drink. Charles remembered the man, relaxed, at his ease in a large chair, the evening sunlight falling on the hand which held a full glass, a 'mixed trough' of dahlias and Michaelmas daisies on the mantelpiece above him. Mrs Renshawe sat smiling at him from a smaller chair. She liked large, decisive men with firm handshakes. Charles and his father sat on the padded window seat with cushions at their backs. Rhona, calm, still, beautiful, was perched on the edge of a spindly unpadded thing. She proffered nuts while Charles poured the drinks, the women's gin and tonics in small cut glasses, the men's whiskies in things twice the size; strong, hefty containers you could get a grip on. He saw Mr Frensham shake his head in rejection at the nuts. He patted his stomach, smiling up at Rhona.

'And do you know what he said?' he asked. Welcomed after toil, Mr Frensham was enjoying himself. Four pairs of eyes watched him, four faces were attentive. The saga concerned a friend of his son's, a lad about seventeen, to whom Mr Frensham had offered a whisky. He had then inquired about diluents. 'And do you know what he said? He asked for ginger ale!' exploded Mr Frensham. He rocked back in his flowery chair, a wary eye on his glass. 'I ask you!' Shock was registered. Excessive from Mr Renshawe, milder from his wife. None from Charles, who was refusing to play. His usual chameleon-like attribute of melding into any social decor seemed to have deserted him. He stared moodily into his beer. Rhona's smile blessed them all.

'Well, you can imagine!' Mr Frensham gave a little kick with both feet in his excitement. 'I'll give you a whisky if you want one,' I said, 'but I'm damned if I'm going to let any callow youth ruin my hard-found whisky with lolly water. I told him! He got short shift from me.'

'Shrift,' said Charles.

The bristling bad-tempered eyebrows leapt at him.

'Pardon?'

'The word's shrift,' said Charles.

He always enjoyed seeing Rhona, who was now more beautiful than ever. Her pale skin seemed to be illuminated from within. He supposed her capillaries must lie close to the surface, but had the wit not to say so. They had the ease together of those who expect and require nothing from each other. She was still rather notably unmarried.

The next day they trailed upstairs after Sunday Lunch, Rhona in front, Charles two steps behind. She stopped and gripped the newel post on the landing.

'Charles,' she said.

'Yes,' he said, his eyes on her hand.

'Come along to my room for a minute.'

'OK.'

It was a pleasant room, low-ceilinged, a small window framed with flowered curtains. He watched the leaves blowing about on the striped lawn below them. His father appeared with the hand mower and began shaving the stripes. Charles pulled the curtain slightly to screen himself, and smiled at Rhona. She took no notice.

'Sit down,' she said, patting the bed beside her. The bedcover was the same flowered pattern of poppies, daisies and cornflowers. A pastoralist's nightmare, he thought, and opened his mouth to say so.

'Charles,' said Rhona.

'Yes?' He sat down beside her and crossed his legs. The bed tipped them towards each other. Charles moved slightly.

'Charles, I want to tell you something.'

'Yes,' said Charles.

She seemed remarkably agitated. She scrambled up on to the pillow and hugged her knees, wrapping the Liberty's skirt tight around them.

'Aren't you going to ask me what it is?' she demanded.

'You'll tell me,' he said.

'Oh!' The gasp was a rasping intake of air.

'I'm having an affair with Neville Frensham,' she said.

'Oh,' said Charles.

'Is that all you've got to say!' Her blue eyes seared him. His skin prickled.

'He's married, isn't he?' said Charles miserably.

'Of course he's married, you clot. That's why it's an affair.'

An affair, thought Charles. Good heavens. And with that sod. He thought of that hand, that stomach.

'Why are you telling me?' he asked.

'God knows,' said Rhona, and burst into tears all over him.

She went overseas soon afterwards. Charles was home when they fare-welled her on the *Rangitoto*. They inspected the cabin she was to share with her friend Penelope, large, fair, a good sort. Rhona's side of the cabin was deep in flowers, hot spikes of gladioli were piled upon her bunk, the tiny inadequate shelves spilled over with pyramid-shaped 'arrangements' in posy bowls. Charles watched his sister's face as she read the card attached to a large bouquet of fleshy white orchids.

'Whoever sent those, dear?' said Mrs Renshawe.

'The girls from the office,' replied Rhona. Charles removed his spectacles, blew on them and wiped them with care. When they left the ship Rhona clung to him, sobbing, hiccuping with the abandoned despair of a lost child. Mrs Renshawe was puzzled.

Rhona did various jobs in London. She was sacked from Harrods for suggesting to a customer who complained of the high price of the handkerchiefs that perhaps she should shop elsewhere. She trained at an exclusive interior-design shop and developed the languid hauteur required. She was hardworking, used her initiative, and they enjoyed her slightly flattened vowels. She lived with English girls which pleased her mother. 'What is the point,' Mrs Renshawe asked her friend Rita, 'of going twelve thousand miles across the world to flat with Penelope Parsons?'

Rhona wrote cheerful letters home which told nothing. Charles read them and was glad she was happy. They exchanged postcards. He collected all the interesting ones, the bottle at Paeroa, the floral clock at Napier, diners with their mouths open stuffing food at the Hermitage. Rhona replied with reproductions of naked male sculptures from the Louvre, the Uffizi, wherever. 'Wish you were here.' Charles liked her.

She came home occasionally. She was now elegant as well as beautiful. She was invited to meals with all her married friends and played on floors with her many godchildren to whom she gave expensive English-type presents. Corals, for example, for the little girls to wear with their party frocks. Large Dinky Toy milk floats and rubbish collection vans which the little boys did not recognize, and which had to be explained and demonstrated by Rhona from England.

She came home when their father died, and two years later when they moved Mrs Renshawe into a home. 'I'm not coming home to look after her,' she said, glaring at Charles. 'Good God, no,' he answered. 'And you can't, can you?' 'No,' said Charles. He had done his best but fortunately it was not enough.

Charles stayed on, rattling around in the Hobson Street house where he had lived since he returned to take up his appointment in Wellington. He gardened, he visited his mother, he invited people for meals. 'Anyone who can read can cook,' he said, though the hard part was having it all ready at the same countdown. He enjoyed his work and was good at it. He was glad his mother had given up on grandchildren.

He and Rhona never discussed Neville Frensham. He wondered whether to tell her when he died, but did nothing. Someone else would and anyway it was forty years ago. Good God.

He was astounded when Rhona's letter arrived. 'I am returning to New Zealand. Presumably it's all right by you if I come to Hobson Street. Mother can't last much longer and I should be there. Anyway, I want to come home. Very odd. Obviously I'll take over the cooking etc. It might be rather fun. Two of us bumbling towards extinction together. Much love, Rhona.'

Charles thought hard, his mind scurrying for solutions. He thought of cabling 'Don't come. Have made alternative arrangements.' Or just plain 'No. Don't.' But how could he? Under the terms of their father's will she had an equal share in the house. And anyway, how could he?

She came. She stayed. She moved into their mother's bedroom, a large room with a fireplace in one corner, a dressing table on which Mrs Renshawe's silver brushes still sat, a high bed covered with a crocheted bedspread and a long box thing covered in flowered cretonne. When he carried Rhona's suitcases up she had touched the box with the tip of her small pointed shoe. 'Good God,' she said, 'the ottoman. What on earth would Zaharis Interior Design say?' She flung her squashy leather bag on the bed and flopped down beside it. She stared up at Charles with something like panic. He was puffing slightly. 'Mr Parkin begged me,' she said. 'They didn't want me to leave, you know.' Then why the hell did you? thought Charles, disliking himself. He put an arm around the padded shoulder of her Italian knit and pressed slightly. She buried her fluffy grey head against his jacket for a moment and sniffed.

'Oh, well,' she said standing up, silver bangles jangling. 'Is there any sherry?'

*

But things got worse. He could have told her. He should have told her.

Charles stumped down the stairs, his right hand touching the wall lightly at intervals in a gesture imitated by his students. He turned left through the hall and padded into the kitchen. Rhona was sitting at the table with her back to the sun in the chair in which he had always sat, reading the paper.

'Good morning,' said Charles.

'Hullo.' She didn't look up.

He lifted the small blue-and-white-striped teapot from the bench. 'Old or new?' he said. She glanced up briefly. 'Old,' she said. Charles opened the window and emptied the teapot on to the rose beneath. He pressed down the red flag of the Russell Hobbs kettle. A plastic bag, its contents weeping and bloody, lay beside it. Charles poked it.

'What's this?'

She glanced up, frowning. 'What?'

He poked again. 'This.'

'Plums,' said Rhona.

'Ah.'

Charles made tea, poured himself a cup and pulled out a chair which raked loudly on the faded green vinyl. A blackbird sang, defining its territory. He glanced out across the sunlit lawn. There it was as usual, singing its proprietorial heart out from the spindly kauri in the next door garden. Charles sat down and helped himself to cornflakes, refolding Rhona's open packet of muesli and placing it on the bench. 'Which is the whole milk?' he asked. Head down, still reading, Rhona handed him a jug embellished with the crowned image of George VI. She had finished her breakfast and was smoking the first of her day's cigarettes. She was a tidy smoker, meticulous in the removal of butts, the emptying of ashtrays. Unlike Charles, whose pipe dottle and matchstick-filled messes overflowed throughout the house. He poured milk on to the cereal and attacked the mush with quick scooping movements of his spoon, herding it into his mouth. He banged a striped cotton napkin at his face and reached for the toast.

'Any chance of a piece of the paper?' he asked.

Rhona swung into action, slapping and tugging at the paper as though it was putting up enormous resistance. Still clutching the overseas news page she handed a crumpled heap to Charles.

'Thank you,' said Charles, smoothing and refolding the thing. They read in bristling silence for a while.

'I heard on the radio that Lange's not going to Paris,' he said, raising a tentative flag of truce.

It was shot to ribbons. 'Would you,' snapped Rhona, 'in the circumstances?'

'Perhaps not,' said Charles.

Rhona snorted, flicking her ash into the small brass ashtray with a quick decisive tap. She finished her cigarette and ground the glowing butt into extinction, then heaved herself up against the unstable plastic table. It rocked, slopping milky tea into Charles's saucer. She emptied the ashtray into the Pelican bag beneath the sink and reclosed the door. She remained planted in front of the sink, a strong white arm clasping the stained blue formica either side of her. Charles, from the corner of his eye, saw her put her head in her hands. Oh, God, he thought dully. A miasma of dread enclosed him, paralysing action, thought, threatening his very existence as a civilized thinking being.

He made an enormous effort. 'What's the matter, Rhona?' he said.

Rhona swung around, her pearls about her plump neck, her hands clasped in agony. 'It's so bloody *awful* here,' she said.

Charles glared at her. Who was she to stand in his familiar old-fashioned kitchen, to breathe its slightly gas-scented air and mouth such antediluvian, anti-colonial crap?

'Are you pining for dear dirty old London?' he asked.

Rhona's eyes blinked with surprise. Charles was surprised himself.

'Yes,' snapped Rhona. 'Yes, I am.'

Charles felt rage thickening in his throat. Stronger even than his interest in the comparative anatomy of vertebrates was his feeling for the land forms, the fauna and flora of the country where he grew up. When he had been a postgraduate student in England many of his New Zealand contemporaries had worked and schemed for the glittering prizes of overseas appointments. Charles, more able than most, had regarded these men (there were no women) as unusual genetic aberrations who could not be blamed for their imperfections. He knew he was going home and did so.

'And you're so *boring*!' continued Rhona, angrily banging her wrists in search of her handkerchief.

Charles breathed out, a liberating puff of relief. 'I've always been boring,' he said.

Rhona slammed back to the table and crashed her behind on to the unstable silly little chair opposite him.

'Don't you care?' she demanded.

'Not in the slightest,' said Charles.

She thumped the table with her closed fist.

'And I suppose you're proud of that! Proud of your Intellectual Honesty!' she cried. Her face, usually a pleasant sight, was mottled, despairing, damp.

'I don't bore me,' said Charles mildly.

To his horror, just when Charles thought he had cushioned the trauma, siphoned off the excess, set things on an even keel again, Rhona for only the third time in his experience, burst into tears.

'You're only half a . . .' She gasped. 'Only half *there*!'

She disintegrated before him. She laid her rounded arms on the plastic table and howled like a – like a what? Charles had never seen anything like it in his life. He stared at her. What should he do? Slap her? God forbid. Ice? Wet towels? He slipped sideways from his skittery little chair and tiptoed from the kitchen.

He felt bad about it. Very bad. Twice in twenty-four hours he had abandoned a suffering human being. Charles was not an uncaring man. He gave to things. Not only to any conservation scheme, however bizarre or impractical, but also to humanity. His donations to the City Mission had been regular and substantial. They had asked him to join the Board but he had declined owing to pressure of work. They quite understood.

He felt miserable all day. He chaired a Scholarship Board meeting with firm detachment. He continued with his marking, refusing as always to count how many papers remained unmarked. He lunched in the staff cafeteria, sitting with his salami and tomato roll, staring across the tossing windblown harbour a thousand miles away. He exchanged pleasantries with Mrs Blume who was suffering from a completely unjustified excess of work, but there you were.

\*

He had not visited the tuataras all day. He finished his last second-year paper and leaned back, reaching out a spatulate-fingered hand for the striped tobacco pouch on his desk. He tamped the tobacco into his Lovat Saddle pipe with a nicotine-stained forefinger, wiped the finger on the carpet, and lit up, puffing his pipe with the catharsis of release. After a few minutes he pushed his chair back and ambled out of his office, through Mrs Blume's room into the small laboratory which housed the tuataras.

His fingers quivered as he opened the inner glass door of the incubator. He had timed it well. Before him the tuatara which last night had been a shell, a half head with eyes, climbed out from the remnants of its shell. With a backwards flick of its fragmentary left rear leg it tossed the shell aside. The movement reminded Charles of a stripper in a Soho dive thirty years ago as she kicked aside the irrelevant sloughed-off garments beneath her feet. Charles clutched the sides of the incubator. He felt weak with pleasure. Infinitely tender, he picked the newly hatched tuatara up from the incubator and enrolled it among its associates in the compost. It did nothing. It just squatted there, planted on its four angled legs, occasionally moving its head very slowly to one side or the other. Charles picked up a piece of waste paper from the bench on which the incubator stood, pulled out his ballpoint and wrote, 'Have removed No. 18 (contents of) from incubator. In display case. C. R.' He slipped the note into the incubator door as he closed it.

He stood back. A transfusion of happiness flowed through him. He had thought of something. He hurried back to his office, giving Mrs Blume no more than a perfunctory nod. He would do something. Show his concern, his love almost. He reached for the telephone and dialled his home number. 'Rhona,' he said into the quacking receiver. 'Would you like to see the juvenile tuataras? The babies?'

# You're Ugly, Too

*Lorrie Moore was born in 1957 in Glen Falls, New York. She worked for two years as a legal assistant, hated it and went to Cornell University to do a Master of Fine Arts degree in writing. In 1976 she won first prize in the* Seventeen *short-story competition and in 1983 was awarded a Granville Hicks Memorial Fellowship at Yaddo. She teaches English at the University of Wisconsin at Madison and is the author of two collections of short stories,* Self Help *and* Like Life, *and two novels,* Anagrams *and* Who Will Run the Frog Hospital?

You had to get out of them occasionally, those Illinois towns with the funny names: Paris, Oblong, Normal. Once, when the Dow-Jones dipped two hundred points, the Paris paper boasted a banner headline: NORMAL MAN MARRIES OBLONG WOMAN. They knew what was important. They did! But you had to get out once in a while, even if it was just across the border to Terre Haute, for a movie.

Outside of Paris, in the middle of a large field, was a scatter of brick buildings, a small liberal-arts college with the improbable name of Hilldale-Versailles. Zoë Hendricks had been teaching American History there for three years. She taught 'The Revolution and Beyond' to freshmen and sophomores, and every third semester she had the Senior Seminar for Majors, and although her student evaluations had been slipping in the last year and a half – *Professor Hendricks is often late for class and usually arrives with a cup of hot chocolate, which she offers the class sips of* – generally the department of nine men was pleased to have her. They felt she added some needed feminine touch to the corridors – that faint trace of Obsession and sweat, the light, fast clicking of heels. Plus they had had a sex-discrimination suit, and the dean had said, well, it was time.

The situation was not easy for her, they knew. Once, at the start of last semester, she had skipped into her lecture hall singing 'Getting to Know You' – both verses. At the request of the dean, the chairman had called her into his office, but did not ask her for an explanation, not really. He asked her how she was and then smiled in an avuncular way. She said, 'Fine,' and he studied the way she said it, her front teeth catching on the inside of her lower lip. She was almost pretty, but her face showed the strain and ambition of always having been close but not quite. There was too much effort with the eyeliner, and her earrings, worn no doubt for the drama her features lacked, were a little frightening, jutting out from the side of her head like antennae.

'I'm going out of my mind,' said Zoë to her younger sister, Evan, in Manhattan. *Professor Hendricks seems to know the entire sound track to* The King and I. *Is this history?* Zoë phoned her every Tuesday.

'You always say that,' said Evan, 'but then you go on your trips and vacations and then you settle back into things and then you're quiet for a while and then you say you're fine, you're busy, and then after a while you say you're going crazy again, and you start all over.' Evan was a part-time food designer for photo shoots. She cooked vegetables in green dye. She propped up beef stew with a bed of marbles and shopped for new kinds of silicone sprays and plastic ice cubes. She thought her life was 'OK'. She was living with her boyfriend of many years, who was independently wealthy and had an amusing little job in book publishing. They were five years out of college, and they lived in a luxury mid-town high-rise with a balcony and access to a pool. 'It's not the same as having your own pool,' Evan was always sighing, as if to let Zoë know that, as with Zoë, there were still things she, Evan, had to do without.

'Illinois. It makes me sarcastic to be here,' said Zoë on the phone. She used to insist it was irony, something gently layered and sophisticated, something alien to the Midwest, but her students kept calling it sarcasm, something they felt qualified to recognize, and now she had to agree. It wasn't irony. *What is your perfume?* a student once asked her. *Room freshener,* she said. She smiled, but he looked at her, unnerved.

Her students were by and large good Midwesterners, spacey with estrogen from large quantities of meat and cheese. They shared their parents' suburban values; their parents had given them things, things, things. They were complacent. They had been purchased. They were armed with a healthy vagueness about anything historical or geographic. They seemed actually to know very little about anything, but they were extremely good-natured about it. 'All those states in the East are so tiny and jagged and bunched up,' complained one of her undergraduates the week she was lecturing on 'The Turning Point of Independence: The Battle at Saratoga'. 'Professor Hendricks, you're from Delaware originally, right?' the student asked her.

'Maryland,' corrected Zoë.

'Aw,' he said, waving his hand dismissively. 'New England.'

Her articles – chapters toward a book called *Hearing the One About: Uses of Humor in the American Presidency* – were generally well received, though they came slowly for her. She liked her pieces to have something from every time of day in them – she didn't trust things written in the morning only – so she reread and rewrote painstakingly. No part of a day, its moods, its light, was allowed to dominate. She hung on to a piece for over a year sometimes, revising at all hours, until the entirety of a day had registered there.

The job she'd had before the one at Hilldale-Versailles had been at a small college in New Geneva, Minnesota, Land of the Dying Shopping Mall. Everyone was so blond there that brunettes were often presumed to be from foreign countries. *Just because Professor Hendricks is from Spain doesn't give her the right to be so negative about our country.* There was a general emphasis on cheerfulness. In New Geneva you weren't supposed to be critical or complain. You weren't supposed to notice that the town had overextended and that its shopping malls were raggedy and going under. You were never to say you weren't fine thank you and yourself. You were supposed to be Heidi. You were supposed to lug goat milk up the hills and not think twice. Heidi did not complain. Heidi did not do things like stand in front of the new IBM photocopier, saying, 'If this fucking Xerox machine breaks on me one more time, I'm going to slit my wrists.'

But now, in her second job, in her fourth year of teaching in the Midwest, Zoë was discovering something she never suspected she had: a crusty edge, brittle and pointed. Once she had pampered her students, singing them songs, letting them call her at home, even, and ask personal questions. Now she was losing sympathy. They were beginning to seem different. They were beginning to seem demanding and spoiled.

'You act,' said one of her Senior Seminar students at a scheduled conference, 'like your opinion is worth more than everybody else's in the class.'

Zoë's eyes widened, 'I *am* the teacher,' she said. 'I *do* get paid to act like that.' She narrowed her gaze at the student, who was wearing a big leather bow in her hair, like a cowgirl in a TV ranch show. 'I mean, otherwise *everybody* in the class would have little offices and office hours.' *Sometimes Professor Hendricks will take up the class's time just talking about movies she's seen.* She stared at the student some more, then added, 'I bet you'd like that.'

'Maybe I sound whiny to you,' said the girl, 'but I simply want my history major to mean something.'

'Well, there's your problem,' said Zoë, and with a smile, she showed the student to the door. 'I like your bow,' she added.

Zoë lived for the mail, for the postman, that handsome blue jay, and when she got a real letter, with a real full-price stamp, from someplace else, she took it to bed with her and read it over and over. She also watched television until all hours and had her set in the bedroom, a bad sign. *Professor Hendricks has said critical things about Fawn Hall, the Catholic religion, and the whole state of Illinois. It is unbelievable.* At Christmastime she gave twenty-dollar tips to the mailman and to Jerry, the only cabbie in town, whom she had gotten to know from all her rides to and from the Terre Haute airport, and who, since he realized such rides were an extravagance, often gave her cut rates.

'I'm flying in to visit you this weekend,' announced Zoë.

'I was hoping you would,' said Evan. 'Charlie and I are having a party for Halloween. It'll be fun.'

'I have a costume already. It's a bonehead. It's this thing that looks like a giant bone going through your head.'

'Great,' said Evan.

'It is, it's great.'

'All I have is my moon mask from last year and the year before. I'll probably end up getting married in it.'

'Are you and Charlie getting *married*?' Foreboding filled her voice.

'Hmmmmmmnnno, not immediately.'

'Don't get married.'

'Why?'

'Just not yet. You're too young.'

'You're only saying that because you're five years older than I am and *you*'re not married.'

'*I*'m not married? Oh, my God,' said Zoë. 'I forgot to get married.'

Zoë had been out with three men since she'd come to Hilldale-Versailles. One of them was a man in the Paris municipal bureaucracy who had fixed a parking ticket she'd brought in to protest and who then asked her to coffee. At first she thought he was amazing – at last, someone who did not want Heidi! But soon she came to realize that all men, deep down, wanted Heidi. Heidi with cleavage. Heidi with outfits. The parking-ticket bureaucrat soon became tired and intermittent. One cool fall day, in his snazzy, impractical convertible, when she asked him what was wrong, he said, 'You would not be ill-served by new clothes, you know.' She wore a lot of gray-green corduroy. She had been under the impression that it brought out her eyes, those shy stars. She flicked an ant from her sleeve.

'Did you have to brush that off in the car?' he said, driving. He glanced down at his own pectorals, giving first the left, then the right, a quick survey. He was wearing a tight shirt.

'Excuse me?'

He slowed down at a yellow light and frowned. 'Couldn't you have picked it up and thrown it outside?'

'The ant? It might have bitten me. I mean, what difference does it make?'

'It might have bitten you! Ha! How ridiculous! Now it's going to lay eggs in my car!'

The second guy was sweeter, lunkier, though not insensitive to certain paintings and songs, but too often, too, things he'd do or say would startle her. Once, in a restaurant, he stole the garnishes off her dinner plate and waited for her to notice. When she didn't, he finally thrust his fist across the table and said, 'Look,' and when he opened it, there was her parsley sprig and her orange slice, crumpled to a wad. Another time he described to her his recent trip to the Louvre. 'And there I was in front of Géricault's *Raft of the Medusa*, and everyone else had wandered off, so I had my own private audience with it, all those painted, drowning bodies splayed in every direction, and there's this motion in that painting that starts at the bottom left, swirling and building, and building, and building, and going up to the right-hand corner, where there's this guy waving a flag, and on the horizon in the distance you could see this teeny tiny boat . . .' He was breathless in the telling. She found this touching and smiled in encouragement. 'A painting like that,' he said, shaking his head. 'It just makes you shit.'

'I have to ask you something,' said Evan. 'I know every woman complains about not meeting men, but really, on my shoots, I meet a lot of men. And they're not all gay, either.' She paused. 'Not anymore.'

'What are you asking?'

The third guy was a political-science professor named Murray Peterson, who liked to go out on double dates with colleagues whose wives he was attracted to. Usually the wives would consent to flirt with him. Under the table sometimes there was footsie, and once there was even kneesie. Zoë and the husband would be left to their food, staring into their water glasses, chewing like goats. 'Oh, Murray,' said one wife, who had never finished her master's in physical therapy and wore great clothes. 'You know, I know everything about you: your birthday, your license plate number. I have everything memorized. But then that's the kind of mind I have. Once at a dinner party I amazed the host by getting up and saying goodbye to every single person there, first *and* last names.'

'I knew a dog who could do that,' said Zoë, with her mouth full. Murray and the wife looked at her with vexed and rebuking expressions, but the husband seemed suddenly twinkling and amused. Zoë swallowed. 'It was a Talking Lab, and after about ten minutes of listening to the dinner conversation this dog knew everyone's name. You could say, "Bring this knife to Murray Peterson," and it would.'

'Really,' said the wife, frowning, and Murray Peterson never called again.

'Are you seeing anyone?' said Evan. 'I'm asking for a particular reason, I'm not just being like mom.'

'I'm seeing my house. I'm tending to it when it wets, when it cries, when it throws up.' Zoë had bought a mint-green ranch house near campus, though now she was thinking that maybe she shouldn't have. It was hard to live in a house. She kept wandering in and out of the rooms, wondering where she had put things. She went downstairs into the basement for no reason at all except that it amused her to own a basement. It also amused her to own a tree. The day she moved in, she had tacked to her tree a small paper sign that said ZOË'S TREE.

Her parents, in Maryland, had been very pleased that one of their children had at last been able to afford real estate, and when she closed on the house they sent her flowers with a congratulations card. Her mother had even UPS'd a box of old decorating magazines saved over the years, photographs of beautiful rooms her mother used to moon over, since there never had been any money to redecorate. It was like getting her mother's pornography, that box, inheriting her drooled-upon fantasies, the endless wish and tease that had been her life. But to her mother it was a rite of passage that pleased her. 'Maybe you will get some ideas from these,' she had written. And when Zoë looked at the photographs, at the bold and beautiful living-rooms, she was filled with longing. Ideas and ideas of longing.

Right now Zoë's house was rather empty. The previous owner had wallpapered around the furniture, leaving strange gaps and silhouettes on the walls, and Zoë hadn't done much about that yet. She had bought furniture, then taken it back, furnishing and unfurnishing, preparing and shedding, like a womb. She had bought several plain pine chests to use as love seats or boot boxes, but they came to look to her more and more like children's coffins, so she returned them. And she had recently bought an Oriental rug for the living-room, with Chinese symbols on it that she didn't understand. The salesgirl had kept saying she was sure they meant *Peace* and *Eternal Life*, but when Zoë got the rug home, she worried. What if they didn't mean *Peace* and *Eternal Life*? What if they meant, say, *Bruce Springsteen*. And the more she thought about it, the more she became convinced she had a rug that said *Bruce Springsteen*, and so she returned that, too.

She had also bought a little baroque mirror for the front entryway, which she had been told, by Murray Peterson, would keep away evil spirits. The mirror, however, tended to frighten *her*, startling her with an image of a woman she never recognized. Sometimes she looked puffier and plainer than she remembered. Sometimes shifty and dark. Most times she just looked vague. *You look like someone I know*, she had been told twice in the last year by strangers in restaurants in Terre Haute. In fact, sometimes she seemed not to have a look of her own, or any look whatsoever, and it began to amaze her that her students and colleagues were able to recognize her at all. How did they know? When she walked into a room, how did she look so that they knew it was her? Like that? Did she look like this? And so she returned the mirror.

'The reason I'm asking is that I know a man I think you should meet,' said Evan. 'He's fun. He's straight. He's single. That's all I'm going to say.'

'I think I'm too old for fun,' said Zoë. She had a dark bristly hair in her chin, and she could feel it now with her finger. Perhaps when you had been without the opposite sex for too long, you began to resemble them. In an act of desperate invention, you began to grow your own. 'I just want to come, wear my bonehead, visit with Charlie's tropical fish, ask you about your food shoots.'

She thought about all the papers on 'Our Constitution: How It Affects Us' she was going to have to correct. She thought about how she was going in for ultrasound tests on Friday, because, according to her doctor and her doctor's assistant, she had a large, mysterious growth in her abdomen. Gallbladder, they kept saying. Or ovaries or colon. 'You guys practice medicine?' asked Zoë, aloud, after they had left the room. Once, as a girl, she brought her dog to a vet, who had told her, 'Well, either your dog has worms or cancer or else it was hit by a car.'

She was looking forward to New York.

'Well, whatever. We'll just play it cool. I can't wait to see you, hon. Don't forget your bonehead,' said Evan.

'A bonehead you don't forget,' said Zoë.

'I suppose,' said Evan.

The ultrasound Zoë was a keeping a secret, even from Evan. 'I feel like I'm dying,' Zoë had hinted just once on the phone.

'You're not dying,' said Evan. 'You're just annoyed.'

'Ultrasound,' Zoë now said jokingly to the technician who put the cold jelly on her bare stomach. 'Does that sound like a really great stereo system, or what?' She had not had anyone make this much fuss over her bare stomach since her boyfriend in graduate school, who had hovered over her whenever she felt ill, waved his arms, pressed his hands upon her navel, and drawled evangelically, 'Heal! Heal for thy Baby Jesus's sake!' Zoë would laugh and they would make love, both secretly hoping she would get pregnant. Later they would worry together, and he would sink a cheek to her belly and ask whether she was late, was she late, was she sure, she might be late, and when after two years she had not gotten pregnant, they took to quarreling and drifted apart.'

'OK,' said the technician absently.

The monitor was in place, and Zoë's insides came on the screen in all their gray and ribbony hollowness. They were marbled in the finest gradations of black and white, like stone in an old church or a picture of the moon. 'Do you suppose,' she babbled at the technician, 'that the rise in infertility among so many couples in this country is due to completely different species trying to reproduce?' The technician moved the scanner around and took more pictures. On one view in particular, on Zoë's right side, the technician became suddenly alert, the machine he was operating clicking away.

Zoë stared at the screen. 'That must be the growth you found there,' suggested Zoë.

'I can't tell you anything,' said the technician rigidly. 'Your doctor will get the radiologist's report this afternoon and will phone you then.'

'I'll be out of town,' said Zoë.

'I'm sorry,' said the technician.

Driving home, Zoë looked in the rearview mirror and decided she looked – well, how would one describe it? A little wan. She thought of the joke about the guy who visits his doctor and the doctor says, 'Well, I'm sorry to say you've got six weeks to live.'

'I want a second opinion,' says the guy. *You act like your opinion is worth more than everyone else's in the class.*

'You want a second opinion? OK,' says the doctor. 'You're ugly, too.' She liked that joke. She thought it was terribly, terribly funny.

She took a cab to the airport, Jerry the cabbie happy to see her.

'Have fun in New York,' he said, getting her bag out of the trunk. He liked her, or at least he always acted as if he did. She called him 'Jare'.

'Thanks, Jare.'

'You know, I'll tell you a secret: I've never been to New York. I'll tell you two secrets: I've never been on a plane.' And he waved at her sadly as she pushed her way in through the terminal door. 'Or an escalator!' he shouted.

The trick to flying safe, Zoë always said, was never to buy a discount ticket and to tell yourself you had nothing to live for anyway, so that when the plane crashed it was no big deal. Then, when it didn't crash, when you had succeeded in keeping it aloft with your own worthlessness, all you had to do was stagger off, locate your luggage, and, by the time a cab arrived, come up with a persuasive reason to go on living.

'*You're here!*' shrieked Evan over the doorbell, before she even opened the door. Then she opened it wide. Zoë set her bags on the hall floor and hugged Evan hard. When she was little, Evan had always been affectionate and devoted. Zoë had always taken care of her, advising, reassuring, until recently, when it seemed Evan had started advising and reassuring *her*. It startled Zoë. She suspected it had something to do with Zoë's being alone. It made people uncomfortable. 'How *are* you?'

'I threw up on the plane. Besides that, I'm OK.'

'Can I get you something? Here, let me take your suitcase. Sick on the plane. Eeeyew.'

'It was into one of those sickness bags,' said Zoë, just in case Evan thought she'd lost it in the aisle. 'I was very quiet.'

The apartment was spacious and bright, with a view all the way downtown along the East Side. There was a balcony and sliding glass doors. 'I keep forgetting how nice this apartment is. Twentieth floor, doorman . . .' Zoë could work her whole life and never have an apartment like this. So could Evan. It was Charlie's apartment. He and Evan lived in it like two kids in a dorm, beer cans and clothes strewn around. Evan put Zoë's bag away from the mess, over by the fish tank. 'I'm so glad you're here,' she said. 'Now what can I get you?'

Evan made them a snack – soup from a can, and saltines.

'I don't know about Charlie,' she said, after they had finished. 'I feel like we've gone all sexless and middle-aged already.'

'Hmmm,' said Zoë. She leaned back into Evan's sofa and stared out the window at the dark tops of the buildings. It seemed a little unnatural to live up in the sky like this, like birds that out of some wrongheaded derring-do had nested too high. She nodded toward the lighted fish tank and giggled. 'I feel like a bird,' she said, 'with my own personal supply of fish.'

Evan sighed. 'He comes home and just sacks out on the sofa, watching fuzzy football. He's wearing the psychic cold cream and curlers, if you know what I mean.'

Zoë sat up, readjusted the sofa cushions. 'What's fuzzy football?'

'We haven't gotten cable yet. Everything comes in fuzzy. Charlie just watches it that way.'

'Hmmm, yeah, that's a little depressing,' Zoë said. She looked at her hands. 'Especially the part about not having cable.'

'This is how he gets into bed at night.' Evan stood up to demonstrate. 'He whips all his clothes off, and when he gets to his underwear, he lets it drop to one ankle. Then he kicks up his leg and flips the underwear in the air and catches it. I, of course, watch from the bed. There's nothing else. There's just that.'

'Maybe you should just get it over with and get married.'

'Really?'

'Yeah. I mean, you guys probably think living together like this is the best of both worlds, but . . .' Zoë tried to sound like an older sister; an older sister was supposed to be the parent you could never have, the hip, cool mom. '. . . I've always found that as soon as you think you've got the best of both worlds' – she thought now of herself, alone in her house; of the toad-faced cicadas that flew around like little caped men at night, landing on her screens, staring; of the size-fourteen shoes she placed at the door-step, to scare off intruders; of the ridiculous inflatable blow-up doll someone had told her to keep propped up at the breakfast table – 'it can suddenly twist and become the worst of both worlds.'

'Really?' Evan was beaming. 'Oh, Zoë. I have something to tell you. Charlie and I *are* getting married.'

'Really.' Zoë felt confused.

'I didn't know how to tell you.'

'Yes, well, I guess the part about fuzzy football misled me a little.'

'I was hoping you'd be my maid of honor,' said Evan, waiting. 'Aren't you happy for me?'

'Yes,' said Zoë, and she began to tell Evan a story about an award-winning violinist at Hilldale-Versailles, how the violinist had come home from a competition in Europe and taken up with a local man, who made her go to all his summer softball games, made her cheer for him from the stands, with the wives, until she later killed herself. But when she got halfway through, to the part about cheering at the softball games, Zoë stopped.

'What?' said Evan. 'So what happened?'

'Actually, nothing,' said Zoë lightly. 'She just really got into softball. I mean, really. You should have seen her.'

Zoe decided to go to a late-afternoon movie, leaving Evan to chores she needed to do before the party – *I have to do them alone*, she'd said, a little tense after the violinist story. Zoë thought about going to an art museum, but women alone in art museums had to look good. They always did. Chic and serious, moving languidly, with a great handbag. Instead, she walked over and down through Kips Bay, past an earring boutique called Stick It in Your Ear, past a beauty salon called Dorian Gray's. That was the funny thing about *beauty*, thought Zoë. Look it up in the yellow pages, and you found a hundred entries, hostile with wit, cutesy with warning. But look up *truth* – ha! There was nothing at all.

Zoë thought about Evan getting married. Would Evan turn into Peter Pumpkin-eater's wife? Mrs Eater? At the wedding would she make Zoë wear some flouncy lavender dress, identical with the other maids'? Zoë hated uniforms, had even, in the first grade, refused to join Elf Girls, because she didn't want to wear the same dress as everyone else. Now she might have to. But maybe she could distinguish it. Hitch it up on one side with a clothespin. Wear surgical gauze at the waist. Clip to her bodice one of those pins that said in loud letters, SHIT HAPPENS.

At the movie – *Death by Number* – she bought strands of red licorice to tug and chew. She took a seat off to one side in the theater. She felt strangely self-conscious sitting alone and hoped for the place to darken fast. When it did, and the coming attractions came on, she reached inside her purse for her glasses. They were in a Baggie. Her Kleenex was also in a Baggie. So were her pen and her aspirin and her mints. Everything was in Baggies. This was what she'd become: *a woman alone at the movies with everything in a Baggie.*

At the Halloween party, there were about two dozen people. There were people with ape heads and large hairy hands. There was someone dressed as a leprechaun. There was someone dressed as a frozen dinner. Some man had brought his two small daughters: a ballerina and a ballerina's sister, also dressed as a ballerina. There was a gaggle of sexy witches – women dressed entirely in black, beautifully made up and jeweled. 'I hate those sexy witches. It's not in the spirit of Halloween,' said Evan. Evan had abandoned the moon mask and dolled herself up as a *Hausfrau*, in curlers and an apron, a decision she now regretted. Charlie, because he liked fish, because he owned fish, collected fish, had decided to go as a fish. He had fins and eyes on the side of his head. 'Zoë! How are you! I'm sorry I wasn't here when you first arrived!' He spent the rest of his time chatting up the sexy witches.

'Isn't there something I can help you with here?' Zoë asked her sister. 'You've been running yourself ragged.' She rubbed her sister's arm, gently, as if she wished they were alone.

'Oh, God, not at all,' said Evan, arranging stuffed mushrooms on a plate. The timer went off, and she pulled another sheetful out of the oven. 'Actually, you know what you can do?'

'What?' Zoë put on her bonehead.

'Meet Earl. He's the guy I had in mind for you. When he gets here, just talk to him a little. He's nice. He's fun. He's going through a divorce.'

'I'll try.' Zoë groaned. 'OK? I'll try.' She looked at her watch.

When Earl arrived, he was dressed as a naked woman, steel wool glued strategically to a body stocking, and large rubber breasts protruding like hams.

'Zoë, this is Earl,' said Evan.

'Good to meet you,' said Earl, circling Evan to shake Zoë's hand. He stared at the top of Zoë's head. 'Great bone.'

Zoë nodded. 'Great tits,' she said. She looked past him, out the window at the city thrown glitteringly up against the sky; people were saying the usual things: how it looked like jewels, like bracelets and necklaces unstrung. You could see Grand Central station, the clock of the Con Ed building, the red-and-gold-capped Empire State, the Chrysler like a rocket ship dreamed up in a depression. Far west you could glimpse the Astor Plaza, its flying white roof like a nun's habit. 'There's beer out on the balcony, Earl – can I get you one?' Zoë asked.

'Sure, uh, I'll come along. Hey, Charlie, how's it going?'

Charlie grinned and whistled. People turned to look. 'Hey, Earl,' someone called, from across the room. 'Va-va-va-voom.'

They squeezed their way past the other guests, past the apes and the sexy witches. The suction of the sliding door gave way in a whoosh, and Zoë and Earl stepped out on to the balcony, a bonehead and a naked woman, the night air roaring and smoky-cool. Another couple was out here, too, murmuring privately. They were not wearing costumes. They smiled at Zoë and Earl. 'Hi,' said Zoë. She found the plastic-foam cooler, dug into it, and retrieved two beers.

'Thanks,' said Earl. His rubber breasts folded inward, dimpled and dented, as he twisted open the bottle.

'Well,' sighed Zoë anxiously. She had to learn not to be afraid of a man, the way, in your childhood, you learned not to be afraid of an earthworm or a bug. Often, when she spoke to men at parties, she rushed things in her mind. As the man politely blathered on, she would fall in love, marry, then find herself in a bitter custody battle with him for the kids and hoping for a reconciliation, so that despite all his betrayals she might no longer despise him, and in the few minutes remaining, learn, perhaps, what his last name was and what he did for a living, though probably there was already too much history between them. She would nod, blush, turn away.

'Evan tells me you're a professor. Where do you teach?'

'Just over the Indiana border into Illinois.'

He looked a little shocked. 'I guess Evan didn't tell me that part.'

'She didn't?'

'No.'

'Well, that's Evan for you. When we were kids we both had speech impediments.'

'That can be tough,' said Earl. One of his breasts was hidden behind his drinking arm, but the other shone low and pink, full as a strawberry moon.

'Yes, well, it wasn't a total loss. We used to go to what we called peach pearapy. For about ten years of my life I had to map out every sentence in my mind, way ahead, before I said it. That was the only way I could get a coherent sentence out.'

Earl drank from his beer. 'How did you do that? I mean, how did you get through?'

'I told a lot of jokes. Jokes you know the lines to already – you can just say them. I love jokes. Jokes and songs.'

Earl smiled. He had on lipstick, a deep shade of red, but it was wearing off from the beer. 'What's your favorite joke?'

'Uh, my favorite joke is probably . . . OK, all right. This guy goes into a doctor's office and –'

'I think I know this one,' interrupted Earl, eagerly. He wanted to tell it himself. 'A guy goes into a doctor's office, and the doctor tells him he's got some good news and some bad news – that one, right?'

'I'm not sure,' said Zoë. 'This might be a different version.'

'So the guy says, "Give me the bad news first," and the doctor says, "OK. You've got three weeks to live." And the guy cries, "Three weeks to live! Doctor, what is the good news?" And the doctor says, "Did you see that secretary out front? I finally fucked her."'

Zoë frowned.

'That's not the one you were thinking of?'

'No.' There was accusation in her voice. 'Mine was different.'

'Oh,' said Earl. He looked away and then back again. 'You teach history, right? What kind of history do you teach?'

'I teach American, mostly – eighteenth and nineteenth century.' In graduate school, at bars, the pick-up line was always: 'So what's your century?'

'Occasionally I teach a special theme course,' she added, 'say, "Humor and Personality in the White House". That's what my book's on.' She thought of something someone once told her about bowerbirds, how they build elaborate structures before mating.

'Your book's on *humor*?'

'Yeah, and, well, when I teach a theme course like that, I do all the centuries.' *So what's your century?*

'All three of them.'

'Pardon?' The breeze glistened her eyes. Traffic revved beneath them. She felt high and puny, like someone lifted into heaven by mistake and then spurned.

'Three. There's only three.'

'Well, four, really.' She was thinking of Jamestown, and of the Pilgrims coming here with buckles and witch hats to say their prayers.

'I'm a photographer,' said Earl. His face was starting to gleam, his rouge smearing in a sunset beneath his eyes.

'Do you like that?'

'Well, actually I'm starting to feel it's a little dangerous.'

'Really?'

'Spending all your time in a darkroom with that red light and all those chemicals. There's links with Parkinson's, you know.'

'No, I didn't.'

'I suppose I should wear rubber gloves, but I don't like to. Unless I'm touching it directly, I don't think of it as real.'

'Hmmm,' said Zoë. Alarm buzzed through her, mildly, like a bee.

'Sometimes, when I have a cut or something, I feel the sting and think, *Shit.* I wash constantly and just hope. I don't like rubber over the skin like that.'

'Really.'

'I mean, the physical contact. That's what you want, or why bother?'

'I guess,' said Zoë. She wished she could think of a joke, something slow and deliberate, with the end in sight. She thought of gorillas, how when they had been kept too long alone in cages, they would smack each other in the head instead of mating.

'Are you . . . in a relationship?' Earl suddenly blurted.

'Now? As we speak?'

'Well, I mean, I'm sure you have a relationship to your *work*.' A smile, a weird one, nestled in his mouth like an egg. She thought of zoos in parks, how when cities were under siege, during world wars, people ate the animals. 'But I mean, with a *man*.'

'No, I'm not in a relationship with a *man*.' She rubbed her chin with her hand and could feel the one bristly hair there. 'But my last relationship was with a very sweet man,' she said. She made something up. 'From Switzerland. He was a botanist – a weed expert. His name was Jerry. I called him "Jare". He was so funny. You'd go to the movies with him and all he would notice were the plants. He would never pay attention to the plot. Once, in a jungle movie, he started rattling off all these Latin names, out loud. It was very exciting for him.' She paused, caught her breath.

'Eventually he went back to Europe to, uh, study the edelweiss.' She looked at Earl. 'Are you involved in a relationship? With a *woman*?'

Earl shifted his weight, and the creases in his body stocking changed, splintering outward like something broken. His pubic hair slid over to one hip, like a corsage on a saloon girl. 'No,' he said, clearing his throat. The steel wool in his underarms was inching toward his biceps. 'I've just gotten out of a marriage that was full of bad dialogue, like "You want more *space*? I'll give you more space!" *Clonk.* Your basic Three Stooges.'

Zoë looked at him sympathetically. 'I suppose it's hard for love to recover after that.'

His eyes lit up. He wanted to talk about love. 'But *I* keep thinking love should be like a tree. You look at trees and they've got bumps and scars from tumors, infestations, what have you, but they're still growing. Despite the bumps and bruises, they're . . . straight.'

'Yeah, well,' said Zoë, 'where I'm from, they're all married or gay. Did you see that movie *Death by Number*?'

Earl looked at her, a little lost. She was getting away from him. 'No,' he said.

One of his breasts had slipped under his arm, tucked there like a baguette. She kept thinking of trees, of gorillas and parks, of people in wartime eating the zebras. She felt a stabbing pain in her abdomen.

'Want some hors d'oeuvres?' Evan came pushing through the sliding door. She was smiling, though her curlers were coming out, hanging bedraggled at the ends of her hair like Christmas decorations, like food put out for the birds. She thrust forward a plate of stuffed mushrooms.

'Are you asking for donations or giving them away?' said Earl, wittily. He liked Evan, and he put his arm around her.

'You know, I'll be right back,' said Zoë.

'Oh,' said Evan, looking concerned.

'Right back. I promise.'

Zoë hurried inside, across the living-room into the bedroom, to the adjoining bath. It was empty; most of the guests were using the half bath near the kitchen. She flicked on the light and closed the door. The pain had stopped and she didn't really have to go to the bathroom, but she stayed there anyway, resting. In the mirror above the sink she looked haggard beneath her bonehead, violet grays showing under the skin like a plucked and pocky bird. She leaned closer, raising her chin a little to find the bristly hair. It was there, at the end of the jaw, sharp and dark as a wire. She opened the medicine cabinet, pawed through it until she found some tweezers. She lifted her head again and poked at her face with the metal tips, grasping and pinching and missing. Outside the door she could hear two people talking low. They had come into the bedroom and were discussing something. They were sitting on the bed. One of them giggled in a false way. She stabbed again at her chin, and it started to bleed a little. She pulled the skin tight along the jawbone, gripped the tweezers hard around what she hoped was the hair, and tugged. A tiny square of skin came away with it, but the hair remained, blood bright at the root of it. Zoë clenched her teeth. 'Come on,' she whispered. The couple outside in the bedroom were now telling stories, softly, and laughing. There was a bounce and squeak of mattress, and the sound of a chair being moved out of the way. Zoë aimed the tweezers carefully, pinched, then pulled gently away, and this time the hair came, too, with a slight twinge of pain and then a great flood of relief. 'Yeah!' breathed Zoë. She grabbed some toilet paper and dabbed at her chin. It came away spotted with blood, and so she tore off some more and pressed hard until it stopped. Then she turned off the light and opened the door, to return to the party. 'Excuse me,' she said to the couple in the bedroom. They were the couple from the balcony, and they looked at her, a bit surprised. They had their arms around each other, and they were eating candy bars.

Earl was still out on the balcony, alone, and Zoë rejoined him there.

'Hi,' she said. He turned around and smiled. He had straightened his costume out a bit, though all the secondary sex characteristics seemed slightly doomed, destined to shift and flip and zap around again any moment.

'Are you OK?' he asked. He had opened another beer and was chugging.

'Oh, yeah. I just had to go to the bathroom.' She paused. 'Actually I have been going to a lot of doctors recently.'

'What's wrong?' asked Earl.

'Oh, probably nothing. But they're putting me through tests.' She sighed. 'I've had sonograms. I've had mammograms. Next week I'm going in for a candygram.' He looked at her worriedly. 'I've had too many gram words,' she said.

'Here, I saved you these.' He held out a napkin with two stuffed mushroom caps. They were cold and leaving oil marks on the napkin.

'Thanks,' said Zoë, and pushed them both in her mouth. 'Watch,' she said, with her mouth full. 'With my luck, it'll be a gallbladder operation.'

Earl made a face. 'So your sister's getting married,' he said, changing the subject. 'Tell me, really, what you think about love.'

'*Love?*' Hadn't they done this already? 'I don't know.' She chewed thoughtfully and swallowed. 'All right. I'll tell you what I think about love. Here is a love story. This friend of mine –'

'You've got something on your chin,' said Earl, and he reached over to touch it.

'*What?*' said Zoë, stepping back. She turned her face away and grabbed at her chin. A piece of toilet paper peeled off it, like tape. 'It's nothing,' she said. 'It's just – it's nothing.'

Earl stared at her.

'At any rate,' she continued, 'this friend of mine was this award-winning violinist. She traveled all over Europe and won competitions; she made records, she gave concerts, she got famous. But she had no social life. So one day she threw herself at the feet of this conductor she had a terrible crush on. He picked her up, scolded her gently, and sent her back to her hotel room. After that she came home from Europe. She went back to her old hometown, stopped playing the violin, and took up with a local boy. This was in Illinois. He took her to some Big Ten bar every night to drink with his buddies from the team. He used to say things like "Katrina here likes to play the violin," and then he'd pinch her cheek. When she once suggested that they go home, he said, "What, you think you're too famous for a place like this? Well, let me tell you something. You may think you're famous, but you're not *famous* famous." Two famouses. "No one here's ever heard of you." Then he went up and bought a round of drinks for everyone but her. She got her coat, went home, and shot a gun through her head.'

Earl was silent.

'That's the end of my love story,' said Zoë.

'You're not at all like your sister,' said Earl.

'Ho, really,' said Zoë. The air had gotten colder, the wind singing minor and thick as a dirge.

'No.' He didn't want to talk about love anymore. 'You know, you should wear a lot of blue – blue and white – around your face. It would bring out your coloring.' He reached an arm out to show her how the blue bracelet he was wearing might look against her skin, but she swatted it away.

'Tell me, Earl. Does the word *fag* mean anything to you?'

He stepped back, away from her. He shook his head in disbelief. 'You know, I just shouldn't try to go out with career women. You're all stricken. A guy can really tell what life has done to you. I do better with women who have part-time jobs.'

'Oh, yes?' said Zoë. She had once read an article entitled 'Professional Women and the Demographics of Grief'. Or no, it was a poem: *If there were a lake, the moonlight would dance across it in conniptions.* She remembered that line. But perhaps the title was 'The Empty House: Aesthetics of Barrenness'. Or maybe 'Space Gypsies: Girls in Academe'. She had forgotten.

Earl turned and leaned on the railing of the balcony. It was getting late. Inside, the party guests were beginning to leave. The sexy witches were already gone. 'Live and learn,' Earl murmured.

'Live and get dumb,' replied Zoë. Beneath them on Lexington there were no cars, just the gold rush of an occasional cab. He leaned hard on his elbows, brooding.

'Look at those few people down there,' he said. 'They look like bugs. You know how bugs are kept under control? They're sprayed with bug hormones, female bug hormones. The male bugs get so crazy in the presence of this hormone, they're screwing everything in sight: trees, rocks – everything but female bugs. Population control. That's what's happening in this country,' he said drunkenly. 'Hormones sprayed around, and now men are screwing rocks. Rocks!'

In the back the Magic Marker line of his buttocks spread wide, a sketchy black on pink like a funnies page. Zoë came up, slow, from behind and gave him a shove. His arms slipped forward, off the railing, out over the street. Beer spilled out of his bottle, raining twenty stories out over the city below.

'Hey, what are you doing?!' he said, whipping around. He stood straight and readied and moved away from the railing, sidestepping Zoë. 'What the *hell* are you doing?'

'Just kidding,' she said. 'I was just kidding.' But he gazed at her, appalled and frightened, his Magic Marker buttocks turned away now toward all of downtown, a naked pseudo-woman with a blue bracelet at the wrist, trapped out on a balcony with – with *what*? '*Really, I was just kidding!*' Zoë shouted. The wind lifted the hair up off her head, skyward in spines behind the bone. If there were a lake, the moonlight would dance across it in conniptions. She smiled at him, and wondered how she looked.

# The Burial

Translated by Evelyn Picon Garfield

*Armonía Somers (whose real name is Armonía Etchepare de Henestrosa) was born in 1920. She worked as a teacher, in the administration of the Museum of Education and in educational documentation in her native Uruguay until she turned to full-time writing in 1972. She has received numerous literary prizes for narratives such as* El Derrumbamiento *(The Cave-in) and* Un Retrato para Dickens *(A Portrait of Dickens), and in 1986 she was honoured at the National Library of Uruguay. She has written five novels and more than two dozen short stories, but her neo-baroque literary style makes translation difficult, and only a few of her works have been translated into English. She lives in the heart of Montevideo.*

Following his initial surprise at the trifling way the man received news of his discharge, the male nurse helped him dress and gather together his few belongings, noticing all along the man's lamentable physical condition, so very different from the festive spirit that never wavered even during his post-operation mumblings under anaesthesia. Barely managing to control his curiosity, the nurse finally returned the flask with 'that thing' in it, a flask the patient had not relinquished until the very moment he was forced to put on his own shoes.

Since the first days of his stay in the clinic, attention was drawn to this patient, to his friends of all stripes concerned with his fate, and to oranges and cigarettes left in his name. One time a kind of anthology of jokes arrived at the reception desk. It was made up of all the comic strips from the weekly newspapers, with a very peculiar dedication: 'To the dead man in Room 2, Honoribaldo Selva, so that by reading this he may be resuscitated. Your seven friends of THE SMALL BOTTLE TAVERN'. So the matter of leaving the hospital carrying off with him his extirpated viscera, a kind of compensatory demand made by the patient upon agreeing to the operation, would prove to be but one more peculiarity of a fellow whose charm had even convinced the surgeons to give him that macabre trophy as a vindication of his unquestionable rights of possession. While wrapping up the flask, he still maintained enough good humour to choose the best page from the newspaper for holding a putrid piece of flesh. Pointing to the headline, he explained to the nurse that it was in keeping with his natural repugnance towards certain human deceits. And of course, accompanied by his most loyal friends awaiting him in the street, he left that morning with the bundle tucked under his arm like a good gentleman, he said, fetching something from the market.

Faced with Selva's announcement some days before that their first outing together would be to the cemetery, one of the men hit upon the idea of renting a car, primarily because of the considerable distance that prudently separated the dead from the living. 'That's the last straw,' commented the cadaverous convalescent with a contagious guffaw. 'I manage to survive under the knives of three doctors with faces covered like bandits from the silent screen, and you think that now I'm going to die because of three meek kilometres stretched out ahead of us beneath the trees. As for risks, some are incomparable, and the way we face them remains to be seen, even if we let them drug us till we're impotent. And now you want to protect me from an innocent stroll between heaven and earth . . .'

Then, without further discussion, he chose to walk down that long road on which tiny pieces of his wit would remain like a great bread of hilarity reduced to crumbs. Midway, because of a depression due to a ford, Honoribaldo had to slow down. Holding on to a branch to support himself, he threw a stone into the narrow stream of water at his side. But neither this first stretch nor the next one managed to daunt his spirits, despite the visible sacrifice that absurd voyage was exacting.

Finally they reached the cemetery and crossed over the chessboard of tombs where the man decided to carry out his plan right there next to the back wall. With great difficulty, he began making a hole in the earth, using the branch that had supported him. No sooner had he finished than he backed away a few steps, aimed at the hole with his package, and quickly threw it right into the centre. Then he returned to the spot looking just as calm as could be, pushed the excavated earth with his foot, and began covering the thing up. He cleared his throat, straightened his tie, and awaited some taunt that never materialized for, what the devil, each of them probably had someone nearby with his mouth full of roots. He coughed, then unfurled his characteristically oblique smile that showed off a dimple in a gaunt cheek, and finally let loose with this mysterious speech:

'Future dinner guests feasting on my remains below, this package is advance payment. Besides, for after-dinner conversation I'm leaving you this newspaper open to the international page, always cheerful and rotten, to tell the truth the more cheerful, the more rotten. Enjoy! As they say here on earth above when they greet each other, until we meet again for that truly promising feast.'

He coughed once more, pressed both hands against the pit of his stomach, and without further ado, rejoined the group, leaning on one of the men instead of on the green branch left poetically beside the grave.

At this point, the group's rowdy mood changed considerably, not only because of the gist of the joke but also because of the friend's calamitous appearance. Each one, shoring up his reserves, decided unanimously to end the day in a certain low-brow bar called the Small Bottle, the only way to recuperate, according to past experience. With Honoribaldo in tow, they went into that place that meant a day off to them any time during the week, and sat down at the usual table. From then on things acquired frantic shapes. It was necessary to celebrate the main character's return to the ring. Wasn't that so? But it was second nature and urgent to take steps against a certain cold lodged in the spine for which the only sure cure was a drink. So much so that even the owner, yielding to the game, decided to medicate himself for free. That was really the beginning of the disaster, marked at the critical moment when someone suggested that the owner shouldn't bother closing the cabinets every time he took out another bottle. What need was there to wear out those beautiful old bronze handles? From then on with the self-service system, the contents began to flow without the miserable container's limitations, as someone said throwing a bottle over his shoulder.

During one late afternoon and the whole night, they finished off everything at hand until the very bottle that symbolized the bar's founding day appeared on the table wrapped in cobwebs. It was so unusual that it provoked a kind of collective panic. It was the small bottle that gave its name to the tavern and was endowed with such a mysterious survival instinct that not even the most unforgettable brawls registered in the bar's annals had succeeded in tearing it from its pedestal. Then, as with all taboos, a kind of possessive anguish broke through the first scruples. How and in the name of which unwritten law was the fascinating mini-ature to be saved? The table was already bristling with arms as if the men to whom they belonged had transmigrated into a kind of Brahman symbol. Immediately following a blow with the fist that made all the nearby shelves tremble, Honoribaldo Selva's voice was heard trying to rise above the group.

'Not this bottle, lads. Don't you see that it looks like an aged Lady Godiva only with ashen-coloured hair?'

'La-dy what, did you say?' stuttered a thirsty fellow stretching out his hand, unsuccessfully.

'You're not going to scare me with stories about old ladies,' added another one bravely. 'Let the old lady show up here, because in needy cases, even a little old lady can warm the body. You can't rob them all from the cradle. Why be turned off by a few white hairs, more or less . . .?'

'You'll open that bottle over my dead body!' shouted Honoribaldo, managing to avoid the kidnappers despite his noticeable fatigue.

Perhaps it was the extreme intervention by the guest of honour de-fending the bottle that made the group come to its senses. Until that moment, no one had recalled either the original episode or the reason for the festivities. And therefore it didn't occur to them to observe the man's pallor, almost fading away from the world, as if squeezed and pressed inwards by an imminent joke that didn't manage to surface because of its sheer weight. That pallor along with the romantic rescue soon turned the collective attention towards Honoribaldo's famous silence that usually pre-ceded some sort of pronouncement. This time it would not be very dignified, however, due to one person who was hiccuping and the rooster crowing outside. No doubt the air was charged with a certain tension, as if the edge of an electrical storm had been touched, or more simply and humbly as if Honoribaldo had decided to die right there and then in front of them, in sweet sight of the small bottle, its virginity intact like an old button on the table. The guest of honour continued sitting there among them, but he was dead. Judging from several details, he had apparently left the hospital with a black passport. One never knows how long the mysterious cord is capable of vibrating in spite of all appearances. But man is only accustomed to calling certain states death, and nothing else.

For a long time they remained hypnotized by the corpse. Finally through the initiative of someone used to such situations or perhaps to avoid Honoribaldo's intense gaze, they decided to lay him down on the floor amid the spittle and the sawdust, the cigarette butts and the broken glasses. One person shut his eyes and mouth, another crossed his hands over his chest. Having nothing else left to offer, the owner put the disputed bottle between Honoribaldo's fingers. His oblique little smile remained fixed on his face; it never failed him, come what may.

Finally they returned to the table. And there, almost without planning it out loud, they decided to put together a coffin with whatever was at hand, bolting in search of materials like nocturnal termites. After using the wood shelving, the most active one spotted the intriguing bronze handles on the glass cases and twisted them off so that the box ended up acquiring an authentic funereal dignity, that subtle touch that was synonymous with 'Don't be confused, it's the real thing.'

It seemed as if everything was finished, when one of the fellows, trying to suppress a sigh, let go with a cracked, drunken cry capable of moving the very heart of the deceased. 'Long live the dead man, long live the dead man, I say!' That was decisive. Those who could stand up lifted the open box, and repeating, 'Long live . . . ,' carried it into the street followed with great effort by the others. They walked down the street in such a frantic state, bothering the sleepy neighbours with that cry that seemed to come from their solar plexus, until they discovered another open bar, like the one they had already sacked. So after depositing the coffin on the sidewalk, they decided to round off the posthumous honours.

'Nothing else . . . in the meantime . . . let the filthy sun . . . old buddy . . . ,' clarified one of them in his circumstantial double-talk. 'If it were still nighttime . . . we'd carry you inside . . . to keep on drinking . . . But the sun is going to come out, brother . . . And by daylight everything must be . . . as ordered, untamed things . . . people wanting everything in order . . . man with woman . . . right shoe and left shoe . . . the living with the living . . . the dead with the dead . . .'

Such words, equally weighted with the absurd and with common sense, seemed to awaken another individual's consciousness. Hiccuping at the same irregular rate as his buddy, as if receiving the hiccups by stealth, he managed to connect with his own ideas.

'And what about the formalities due a deceased human being?' he said. 'Or do you brutes think that a dead man is a contraband bundle that can slip by without being taxed? Let's back up, I know what I'm saying; we have to do other things first . . .'

Formalities with a man who had buried his own entrails, kept on smiling in that box, and even looked better than the rest of them? That must have crossed most of their minds, for the dead man had to remain where he was, adding to the street's solitude like a valise abandoned on a railroad platform.

Burping away, more livid and bearded than when they entered, they left some hours later in broad daylight to find two surprises: a muffled noise like barricades among the clouds, making the structures below tremble as if punished by vibrations, and the robbery of the bronze handles, the coffin's only luxury. One of the staggering group, who seemed not to care about the impending rain, was the first to be terrified by the last fact, as important as a blow to the Achilles tendon, not because of the handles' functionality but because of their sumptuous nature. With his legs as twisted up as his tongue, he managed to crouch down, verifying the disaster, wherein he caught on to the idea of the unlikely guilt of the dead man in this matter.

'You're not going to fool me,' he succeeded in muttering in a mono-tone, as he was about to fall into the box, 'it's you who's playing a joke on us. Now you're really dead; without handles there's no burial. Let's have a look-see. Out with them if you don't want us to take them away by force . . .'

They were just about to carry out the desecration, searching the dead man's pockets, when one of them who'd vomited by a nearby tree man-aged to avoid the disaster, chasing off some flies that had landed on the corpse's mouth and nose. They decided to pick him up and set out again on yesterday's route.

With all this going on, the first drops could be felt, big and round as if fallen from an umbrella's ribs, albeit luckily spaced and slowly. To no advantage, for Honoribaldo Selva, at once remote and present, wasn't all there this time to make the trip seem shorter. And due to their collective drunkenness, he was shifting around in their consciousness like a reflection in the water.

So they travelled halfway to the cemetery when a certain fatalism materialized again, always occurring in duplicate – from the celebration to the death of the guest of honour, from the storm to the robbery in the street: a certain big black bird jumping from tree to tree decided to accompany them just as the downpour also joined the procession.

They had to quicken their pace, first because of the bird that was frightening them and then because of the elements. Furthermore, in spite of their mental fogginess, all of them remembered the existence of a kind of ford and how it usually swelled in such cases. Meanwhile Honoribaldo's body was jerking about up above due to the zig-zagging forced march, weighing more and more from the rain. Setting foot in the flooded road, all of a sudden they realized that a dirty trick had been played on them as usual: not only did the water reach crotch level, but it also stirred up a mean eddy in the middle, making everything dance about as it was dragged along by the water. After a quick and desperate 'Every man for himself', they faced the danger of landing on the lateral wire fencing that marked the current's theoretical bounds, now totally obscured by the water. Flailing about and grabbing on to each other, they had managed to dodge the small but raging whirlpool when they caught sight of the empty box floating behind them. They realized it could be useful to them as a life preserver. Restored to relative sobriety by the dunking, but still fuzzy about the reason for the crossing, they looked at the coffin, almost failing to recognize it. The box went floating along like any one of the many things they clung to with all their might. Then the last man to leave the riverbed behind became Honoribaldo's choice once again to refresh their memory, for Selva was escaping between the fence wires, moving with the current. Face-up, hands crossed over its chest, the corpse rolled over three or four times and followed the current, missing a half-submerged tree, intermittently hitting another head on, but always determined by an urgency to flow on inexorably.

Very little time had transpired since the beginning of this episode. Nevertheless, as is common in this kind of flood, the water was already subsiding. A fiery yellow sun appeared behind the clouds. They looked at each other like strangers, a group of half-drowned men discovered among the driftwood, with stones and pieces of shell caught in their ears and hair, but not such strangers that they were unaware that somehow they ought to remain together, even though the reason, passing from one brain to another, burst like a bubble in the air. In such a poor state of affairs, they didn't even have any cigarettes in their pockets but rather foul mixtures, extricable only by turning the linings inside out. Some time went by before anyone was able to utter a word, at least one that allowed the others to tug on the ball of twine each felt sloshing about inside him along with the dirty water he'd swallowed. One of the men, perhaps tempting fate, abruptly got up from the box that had been converted into a seat and began to examine a dead rat nearby, doubtless taken by surprise despite its usually formidable instincts in such emergencies. He turned it over with his foot, unconvinced that such a nervous, inaccessible, and worldly animal had fallen into the same trap. 'It's a country rat,' he smiled timidly. 'You'd recognize it even on the asphalt sidewalk of a city full of skyscrapers.'

Out of the corner of his eye, he looked at the group that seemed to solidify into a whole, confirmed that it wasn't worth while showing off his command of the subject matter, and ended up sitting down on the ground facing the others. 'So?' he even managed to say, throwing to the wind the most laconic question of all for any occasion.

The adventure of speech still seemed impossible. But as if that word by its very provocative nature had introduced itself into their minds, the most miserable, small, skinny one, plagued by nervous tics, began to let loose a jumble of basic ideas similar to a bunch of tacks that were bothering him inside.

'We came to bury our friend. Isn't that so? We kept him company when he dug that damned hole, then we celebrated his return until the filthy bottle showed up, the one he baptized somehow and insisted on defending to his death. Later we made him this box with our own hands; we shouldered it halfway down the road, all along putting up with that big black bird's squawks . . .'

He looked around hoping in vain that someone would want to relieve him from going on.

'. . . The water tricked us. But who's to blame for that? It's always raining and the water's always carrying off loose stuff. God's that way; he doesn't send the rain when there's a drought, but throws it down in bucketfuls if you're carrying a dead man around. He doesn't pluck out the eye of someone who's had bad luck because he'd keep on staring with the other one anyway . . .'

You could guess by his voice, progressively more choked up and confused, that he was about to do something he'd never dared to do, cry over the inexplicable matters that oppress innocent men like a punishment. When suddenly another in the group, whose worse luck was apparent from his condition, decided to take advantage of the opening left by that weakness, and after throwing up a few slushy mouthfuls, left his place to brusquely confront the others. He looked like a drowned and bearded ghost. Bluish, transparent skin showed through the holes of his shirt torn in various spots.

'If it's so,' he began to say with difficulty, 'he slipped away from us, better yet, he was taken from us. But remember, we were going to bury him in a specific place. So if we're not a bunch of wretches, unworthy of sharing the spit left on his glass, what we have to do now is go on polishing that box as if it were a chair in a waiting room, then hoist it on to our shoulders again and finish the burial where he left his offering, carrying out what we all witnessed, his last wish.'

He was spitting out more dirty water each time, waiting for an answer. Until one of them, like a sort of mentally retarded mongoloid child, looked both ways and asked:

'You said to carry on the burial anyway? How? A funeral, I believe, requires a dead body on a stretcher or something like that. Without a corpse there's no ceremony . . .'

'What do you mean "how"? However we can!' the man shouted, blue from more effort than his mud-filled lungs seemed to allow. He continued, controlling his voice with great sacrifice. 'Honoribaldo always used to say that the most serious matters, the ones that turn out best, aren't thought about a lot but simply surface at the last moment. And if he thought that way, it was for a good reason. I never heard him utter a senseless word. Why do you think we're his friends? Let's see, can someone explain it any other way?'

The little man with the tics began to shout, 'Long live the dead man, long live the dead man! Didn't I say that from the start?' He stood up, arms flailing about.

They had to force him to be seated, holding his legs down and placing a knee on his stomach. The crisis past, the small madman looked at them one by one and calmly chewed them out.

'You animals can't understand the human soul. While you're holding a makeshift funeral, you get to thinking that somebody's crazy just because he's discovered something in life but can't find the words to express it. I have a three-week-old kid, you know, and that's why I have the right to shout, "Long live the dead man," as many times as I like. Because if it hadn't been for something that simply happened without much thought, like Selva used to say, the baby wouldn't be here, and I'd be nothing more than the smut that's left when rain washes off a rear end. We have to look for him,' he shouted, becoming agitated again, 'and if you're still afraid of that big black bird, I'll go by myself. Let go of me, you fags, let go!'

They had to pin him down again. He let them do it after all because, if you think about it, it was important to know just what would happen in the last instance, the one always foreseen by Selva.

'All right, let's carry on,' said the man who pointed out that there's no funeral with an empty coffin. 'But we'll have to throw something in, even though it's that dead rat, to weigh it down and get some flies to follow. Because first it was a box without handles, then without a corpse, but damn it, there have to be flies!'

One fellow tried to argue in a sober voice that the business with the rat was an insult, an offence to human dignity. They were already bending to the usual impulses despite having been schooled in Honoribaldo Selva's influential and captivating immorality. But at that very second, and as if Honoribaldo himself had chosen him as his representative in that tournament, one man joined the polemic with the following thoughts:

'An insult to human dignity, you say? Don't give me that . . . I was once a ship's stoker. What do you think of that? And there's where I saw a lot worse done by the Americans, who are really somebody, you know, because whatever you say, they're important all right . . .'

He was going to reach for his cigarettes but discovered the jacket lining was turned inside out and chose to continue in a suspenseful tone:

'One day an official died on board. A dispatch was sent to his country's embassy in the nearest port. A group of local high officials met on board and the crew gathered to honour him before a coffin just like this one, only draped with a flag. Afterwards, everyone was satisfied. But those of us who were down below knew otherwise; you see the body was really in the cold-storage room, and they had honoured a box full of spare parts. Nevertheless, the dead man was so grateful they hadn't let him rot that he spent the rest of the voyage without one single nighttime trick, like leaving the refrigerator for a minute to stroll around on deck at dawn, as he would have done had he been offended. Because as someone who knows more than me explained, what's symbolic is symbolic and ought to command everyone's respect.'

The anecdote was so clear to everyone that it seemed to convince the group. The man who'd discovered the rat grabbed it by the tail and threw it into the box. They immediately set out again. That stormy late afternoon, a strange sun beat down on their backs, making a sort of cauldron's steam rise from their sopping clothes, chilling their shivering bodies as the clouds again covered the heavens. They finally reached the cemetery. The gravedigger saw the procession arrive shouldering the burden, but because of professional indifference, he didn't even notice their physical state. By chance or mysterious design, they once again took the same route of the day before, though this time sinking ankle-deep into the mire. And luck would have it that the excavated grave was right next to Honoribaldo's buried innards. The stick was still there, oblivious to all and fresh as a kiss in the rain. By some common stroke, all eyes were riveted to that trivial object, a simple green-leafed stick, and not even where they were going to unload their burden. But the gravedigger's knowing glance convinced them the critical moment had arrived. In turn the pallbearers looked about as if asking the others for help. They weren't there to joke around, everyone knew that. The dead man had so rigorously drawn a dividing line between their last minutes together and the grey, empty hours, that each one had a semi-conscious premonition about his imminent future, a sort of sentence to live by, without resorting to Honoribaldo's tender, universal soul. Each lost spirit fighting to stay afloat in his own solitude was becoming a mere shadow of himself, like a tree uprooted from the earth.

Finally coming to their senses, the two who were carrying the box decided to lower it. That's when it was seen for what it was, empty. Not even the rat's corpse lost in one corner served to maintain the lie.

After watching with distrust, the gravedigger looked up at the group, then at the sky which had clouded over again. Finally he observed each man, figuring that somebody's always ready to pull a fast one. So these scoundrels must be pulling his leg, holding the dead man up on his feet between them so that he would strike up a conversation with a corpse. At that very moment, thunder clapped against the stone wall and the gravedigger glanced towards the heavens, inspected the group one by one, then faced the bluish-looking man whose chin was splattered with muddy spittle from his last vomiting spell. The gravedigger grabbed him by his skinny arm, brutally threatening him.

'Hey you, fresh corpse, what do you say we finish this off now? Or are you waiting for it to rain so that you can drown again without being buried?'

As the man, more rigid and blue than ever, lifted his foot to get into the box, the first swollen drops began to fall from the sky, huge and promising like the morning rain. For once and for all, the burial must go on, he thought, feeling his life ebb away.

# *Heavy Weather*

*Helen Simpson was born in Bristol, grew up on the outskirts of London and studied English at Oxford. After winning its talent competition she worked as a staff writer for* Vogue *magazine for five years before going freelance. Her first collection of short stories,* Four Bare Legs in a Bed, *met with rapturous reviews and won her the* Sunday Times *Young Writer of the Year Award, the Somerset Maugham Award and a place on* Granta's *list of twenty best young British novelists. She has also written a novella,* Flesh and Grass; *the libretto for the opera* Good Friday 1663, *which was commissioned by Channel 4; a play,* Pinstripe; *and a second collection of short stories entitled* Dear George. *She is married with two small children and lives in London.*

'You should never have married me.'

'I haven't regretted it for an instant.'

'Not *you*, you fool! *Me!* You shouldn't have got me to marry you if you loved me. Why *did* you, when you knew it would let me in for all *this*. It's not *fair*!'

'I didn't know. I know it's not. But what can I do about it?'

'I'm being mashed up and eaten alive.'

'I know. I'm sorry.'

'It's not your fault. But what can I do?'

'I don't know.'

So the conversation had gone last night in bed, followed by platonic embraces. They were on ice at the moment, so far as anything further was concerned. The smoothness and sweet smell of their children, the baby's densely packed pearly limbs, the freshness of the little girl's breath when she yawned, these combined to accentuate the grossness of their own bodies. They eyed each other's mooching adult bulk with mutual lack of enthusiasm, and fell asleep.

At four in the morning, the baby was punching and shouting in his Moses basket. Frances forced herself awake, lying for the first moments like a flattened boxer in the ring trying to rise while the count was made. She got up and fell over, got up again and scooped Matthew from the basket. He was huffing with eagerness, and scrabbled crazily at her breasts like a drowning man until she lay down with him. A few seconds more and he had abandoned himself to rhythmic gulping. She stroked his soft head and drifted off. When she woke again, it was six o'clock and he was sleeping between her and Jonathan.

For once, nobody was touching her. Like Holland she lay, aware of a heavy ocean at her seawall, its weight poised to race across the low country.

The baby was now three months old, and she had not had more than half an hour alone in the twenty-four since his birthday in February. He was big and hungry and needed her there constantly on tap. Also, his two-year-old sister Lorna was, unwillingly, murderously jealous, which made everything much more difficult. This time round was harder, too, because when one was asleep the other would be awake and vice versa. If only she could get them to nap at the same time, Frances started fretting, then she might be able to sleep for some minutes during the day and that would get her through. But they wouldn't, and she couldn't. She had taken to muttering, I can't bear it, I can't bear it, without realizing she was doing so until she heard Lorna chanting, I can't bear it! I can't bear it! as she skipped along beside the pram, and this made her blush with shame at her own weediness.

Now they were all four in Dorset for a week's holiday. The thought of having to organize all the food, sheets, milk, baths and nappies made her want to vomit.

In her next chunk of sleep came that recent nightmare, where men with knives and scissors advanced on the felled trunk which was her body.

'How would you like it?' she said to Jonathan. 'It's like a doctor saying, now we're just going to snip your scrotum in half, but don't worry, it mends very well down there, we'll stitch you up and you'll be fine.'

It was gone seven by now, and Lorna was leaning on the bars of her cot like Farmer Giles, sucking her thumb in a ruminative pipe-smoking way. The room stank like a lion house. She beamed as her mother came in and lifted her arms up. Frances hoisted her into the bath, stripped her down and detached the dense brown nappy from between her knees. Lorna carolled, 'I can sing a *rain*bow,' raising her faint eyebrows at the high note, graceful and perfect, as her mother sluiced her down with jugs of water.

'Why does everything take so *long*?' moaned Jonathan. 'It only takes *me* five minutes to get ready.'

Frances did not bother to answer. She was sagging with the effortful boredom of assembling the paraphernalia needed for a morning out in the car. Juice. Beaker with screw-on lid. Flannels. Towels. Changes of clothes in case of car sickness. Nappies. Rattle. Clean muslins to catch Matthew's curdy regurgitations. There was more. What was it?

'Oh, come on, Jonathan, think,' she said. 'I'm fed up with having to plan it all.'

'What do you think I've been doing for the last hour?' he shouted. 'Who was it that changed Matthew's nappy just now? Eh?'

'Congratulations,' she said. 'Don't shout or I'll cry.'

Lorna burst into tears.

'Why is everywhere always such a *mess*?' said Jonathan, picking up plastic spiders, dinosaurs, telephones, beads and bears, his grim scowl over the mound of primary colours like a traitor's head on a platter of fruit.

'I *want* dat spider, Daddy!' screamed Lorna. 'Give it to me!'

During the ensuing struggle, Frances pondered her tiredness. Her muscles twitched as though they had been tenderized with a steak bat. There was a bar of iron in the back of her neck, and she felt unpleasantly weightless in the cranium, a gin-drinking side effect without the previous fun. The year following the arrival of the first baby had gone in pure astonishment at the loss of freedom, but second time round it was spinning away in exhaustion. Matthew woke at one a.m. and four a.m., and Lorna at six thirty a.m. During the days, fatigue came at her in concentrated doses, like a series of time bombs.

'Are we ready at last?' said Jonathan, breathing heavily. 'Are we ready to go?'

'Um, nearly,' said Frances. 'Matthew's making noises. I think I'd better feed him, or else I'll end up doing it in a lay-by.'

'Right,' said Jonathan. 'Right.'

Frances picked up the baby. 'What a nice fat parcel you are,' she murmured in his delighted ear. 'Come on, my love.'

'Matthew's not your love,' said Lorna. '*I*'m your love. You say, C'mon, love, to *me*.'

'You're *both* my loves,' said Frances.

The baby was shaking with eagerness, and pouted his mouth as she pulled her shirt up. The little girl sat down beside her, pulled up her own teeshirt and applied a teddy bear to her nipple. She grinned at her mother.

Frances looked down at Matthew's head, which was shaped like a brick or a small wholemeal loaf, and remembered again how it had come down through the middle of her. She was trying very hard to lose her awareness of this fact, but it would keep re-presenting itself.

'D'you know,' said Lorna, her free hand held palm upwards, her hyphen eyebrows lifting, 'd'you know, I was sucking my thumb when I was coming downstairs, mum, mum, then my foot slipped and my thumb came out of my mouth.'

'Well, that's very interesting, Lorna,' said Frances.

Two minutes later, Lorna caught the baby's hand a ringing smack and ran off. Jonathan watched as Frances lunged clumsily after her, the baby jouncing at her breast, her stained and crumpled shirt undone, her hair a bird's nest, her face craggy with fatigue, and found himself dubbing the tableau, Portrait of rural squalor in the manner of William Hogarth. He bent to put on his shoes, stuck his right foot in first then pulled it out as though bitten.

'What's *that*,' he said in tones of profound disgust. He held his shoe in front of Frances's face.

'It looks like baby sick,' she said. 'Don't look at me. It's not my fault.'

'It's all so bloody *basic*,' said Jonathan, breathing hard, hopping off towards the kitchen.

'If you think that's basic, try being me,' muttered Frances. 'You don't know what basic *means*.'

'Daddy put his foot in Matthew's sick,' commented Lorna, laughing heartily.

At Cerne Abbas they stood and stared across at the chalky white outline of the Iron Age giant cut into the green hill.

'It's enormous, isn't it,' said Frances.

'Do you remember when we went to stand on it?' said Jonathan. 'On that holiday in Child Okeford five years ago?'

'Of course,' said Frances. She saw the ghosts of their frisky former selves running around the giant's limbs and up on to his phallus. Nostalgia filled her eyes and stabbed her smartly in the guts.

'The woman riding high above with bright hair flapping free,' quoted Jonathan. 'Will you be able to grow *your* hair again?'

'Yes, yes. Don't look at me like that, though. I know I look like hell.'

A month before this boy was born, Frances had had her hair cut short. Her head had looked like a pea on a drum. It still did. With each pregnancy, her looks had hurtled five years on. She had started using sentences beginning, 'When I was young.' Ah, youth! Idleness! Sleep! How pleasant it had been to play the centre of her own stage. And how disorientating was this overnight demotion from Brünnhilde to spear-carrier.

'What's that,' said Lorna. 'That *thing.*'

'It's a giant,' said Frances.

'Like in Jacknabeanstork?'

'Yes.'

'But what's that *thing.* That thing on the giant.'

'It's the giant's thing.'

'Is it his stick thing?'

'Yes.'

'My baby budder's got a stick thing.'

'Yes.'

'But I haven't got a stick thing.'

'No.'

'Daddy's got a stick thing.'

'Yes.'

'But *Mummy* hasn't got a stick thing. We're the same, Mummy.'

She beamed and put her warm paw in Frances's.

'You can't see round without an appointment,' said the keeper of Hardy's cottage. 'You should have telephoned.'

'We did,' bluffed Jonathan. 'There was no answer.'

'When was that?'

'Twenty to ten this morning.'

'Hmph. I was over sorting out some trouble at Clouds Hill. T. E. Lawrence's place. All right, you can go through. But keep them under control, won't you?'

They moved slowly through the low-ceilinged rooms, whispering to impress the importance of good behaviour on Lorna.

'This is the room where he was born,' said Jonathan, at the head of the stairs.

'Do you remember from when we visited last time?' said Frances slowly. 'It's coming back to me. He was his mother's first child, she nearly died in labour, then the doctor thought the baby was dead and threw him into a basket while he looked after the mother. But the midwife noticed he was breathing.'

'Then he carried on till he was eighty-seven,' said Jonathan.

They clattered across the old chestnut floorboards, on into another little bedroom with deep thick-walled windowseats.

'Which one's your favourite now?' asked Frances.

'Oh, still *Jude the Obscure*, I think,' said Jonathan. 'The tragedy of unfulfilled aims. Same for anyone first-generation at university.'

'Poor Jude, laid low by pregnancy,' said Frances. 'Another victim of biology as destiny.'

'Don't *talk*, you two,' said Lorna.

'At least Sue and Jude aimed for friendship as well as all the other stuff,' said Jonathan.

'Unfortunately, all the other stuff made friendship impossible, didn't it?,' said Frances.

'Don't *talk*!' shouted Lorna.

'Don't shout!' said Jonathan. Lorna fixed him with a calculating blue eye and produced an ear-splitting scream. The baby jerked in his arms and started to howl.

'Hardy didn't have children, did he?' said Jonathan above the din. 'I'll take them outside, I've seen enough. You stay up here a bit longer if you want to.'

Frances stood alone in the luxury of the empty room and shuddered. She moved around the furniture and thought fond savage thoughts of silence in the cloisters of a convent, a blessed place where all was monochrome and non-viscous. Sliding up unprepared to a mirror on the wall she gave a yelp at her reflection. The skin was the colour and texture of pumice stone, the grim jaw set like a lion's muzzle. And the eyes, the eyes far back in the skull were those of a herring three days dead.

Jonathan was sitting with the baby on his lap by a row of lupins and marigolds, reading to Lorna from a newly acquired guide book.

'When Thomas was a little boy he knelt down one day in a field and began eating grass to see what it was like to be a sheep.'

'What did the sheep say?' asked Lorna.

'The sheep said, er, so now you know.'

'And what else?'

'Nothing else.'

'Why?'

'What do you mean, why?'

'*Why?*'

'Look,' he said when he saw Frances. 'I've bought a copy of *Jude the Obscure* too, so we can read to each other when we've got a spare moment.'

'Spare moment!' said Frances. 'But how lovely you look with the children at your knees, the roses round the cottage door. How I would like to be the one coming back from work to find you all bathed and brushed, and a hot meal in the oven and me unwinding with a glass of beer in a hard-earned crusty glow of righteousness.'

'*I* don't get that,' Jonathan reminded her.

'That's because I can't do it properly yet,' said Frances. 'But still, I wish it could be the other way round. Or at least, half and half. And I was thinking, what a cheesy business Eng. Lit. is, all those old men peddling us lies about life and love. They never get as far as this bit, do they?'

'Thomas 1840, Mary 1842, Henry 1851, Kate 1856,' read Jonathan. 'Perhaps we could have two more.'

'I'd kill myself,' said Frances.

'What's the matter with you?' said Jonathan to Matthew, who was grizzling and struggling in his arms.

'I think I'll have to feed him again,' said Frances.

'What, already?'

'It's nearly two hours.'

'Hey, you can't do that here,' said the custodian, appearing at their bench like a bad fairy. 'We have visitors from all over the world here. Particularly from Japan. The Japanese are a very modest people. And they don't come all this way to see *that* sort of thing.'

'It's a perfectly natural function,' said Jonathan.

'So's going to the lavatory!' said the custodian.

'Is it all right if I take him over behind those hollyhocks?' asked Frances. 'Nobody could possibly see me there. It's just, in this heat he won't feed if I try to do it in the car.'

The custodian snorted and stumped back to his lair.

Above the thatched roof the huge and gentle trees rustled hundreds of years' worth of leaves in the pre-storm stir. Frances shrugged, heaved Matthew up so that his socks dangled on her hastily covered breast, and retreated to the hollyhock screen. As he fed, she observed the green-tinged light in the garden, the crouching cat over in a bed of limp snapdragons, and registered the way things look before an onslaught, defenceless and excited, tense and passive. She thought of Bathsheba Everdene at bay, crouching in the bed of ferns.

When would she be able to read a book again? In life before the children, she had read books on the bus, in the bathroom, in bed, while eating, through television, under radio noise, in cafés. Now, if she picked one up, Lorna shouted, 'Stop reading, Mummy,' and pulled her by the nose until she was looking into her small cross face.

Jonathan meandered among the flowerbeds flicking through *Jude the Obscure*, Lorna snapping and shouting at his heels. He was ignoring her, and Frances could see he had already bought a tantrum since Lorna was now entered into one of the stretches of the day when her self-control flagged and fled. She sighed like Cassandra but didn't have the energy to nag as he came towards her.

'Listen to this,' Jonathan said, reading from *Jude the Obscure*. '"Time and circumstance, which enlarge the views of most men, narrow the views of women almost invariably." '

'Is it any bloody wonder,' said Frances.

'I want you to *play* with me, Daddy,' whined Lorna.

'Bit of a sexist remark, though, eh?' said Jonathan.

'Bit of a sexist process, you twit,' said Frances.

Lorna gave Matthew a tug which almost had him on the ground. Torn from his milky trance, he quavered, horror-struck, for a moment, then, as Frances braced herself, squared his mouth and started to bellow.

Jonathan seized Lorna, who became as rigid as a steel girder, and swung her high up above his head. The air was split with screams.

'Give her to me,' mouthed Frances across the awe-inspiring noise.

'She's a noise terrorist,' shouted Jonathan.

'Oh, please let me have her,' said Frances.

'You shouldn't give in to her,' said po-faced Jonathan, handing over the flailing parcel of limbs.

'Lorna, sweetheart, look at me,' said Frances.

'Naaoow!' screamed Lorna.

'Shshush,' said Frances. 'Tell me what's the matter.'

Lorna poured out a flood of incomprehensible complaint, raving like a chimpanzee. At one point, Frances deciphered, 'You always feed *Matthew*.'

'You should *love* your baby brother,' interposed Jonathan.

'You can't tell her she *ought* to love anybody,' snapped Frances. 'You can tell her she must behave properly, but you can't tell her what to feel. Look, Lorna,' she continued, exercising her favourite distraction technique. 'The old man is coming back. He's cross with us. Let's run away.'

Lorna turned her streaming eyes and nose in the direction of the custodian, who was indeed hot-footing it across the lawn towards them, and tugged her mother's hand. The two of them lurched off, Frances buttoning herself up as she went.

They found themselves corralled into a cement area at the back of the Smuggler's Arms, a separate space where young family pariahs like themselves could bicker over fish fingers. Waiting at the bar, Jonathan observed the comfortable tables inside, with their noisy laughing groups of the energetic elderly tucking into plates of gammon and plaice and profiteroles.

'Just look at them,' said the crumpled man beside him, who was paying for a tray load of Fanta and baked beans. 'Skipped the war. Nil unemployment, home in time for tea.' He took a great gulp of lager. 'Left us to scream in our prams, screwed us up good and proper. When our kids come along, what happens? You don't see the grandparents for dust, that's what happens. They're all off out enjoying themselves, kicking the prams out the way with their Hush Puppies, spending the money like there's no tomorrow.'

Jonathan grunted uneasily. He still could not get used to the way he found himself involved in intricate conversations with complete strangers, incisive, frank, frequently desperate, whenever he was out with Frances and the children. It used to be only women who talked like that, but now, among parents of young children, it seemed to have spread across the board.

Frances was trying to allow the baby to finish his recent interrupted feed as discreetly as she could, while watching Lorna move inquisitively among the various family groups. She saw her go up to a haggard woman changing a nappy beside a trough of geraniums.

'Your baby's got a stick thing like my baby budder.' Lorna's piercing voice soared above the babble. 'I haven't got a stick thing cos I'm a little gel. My mummy's got fur on her potim.'

Frances abandoned their table and made her way over to the geranium trough.

'Sorry if she's been getting in your way,' she said to the woman.

'Chatty, isn't she?' commented the woman unenthusiastically. 'How many have you got?'

'Two. I'm shattered.'

'The third's the killer.'

'Dat's my baby budder,' said Lorna, pointing at Matthew.

'He's a big boy,' said the woman. 'What did he weigh when he came out?'

'Ten pounds.'

'Just like a turkey,' she said, disgustingly, and added, 'Mine were whoppers too. They all had to be cut out of me, one way or the other.'

*

By the time they returned to the cottage, the air was weighing on them like blankets. Each little room was an envelope of pressure. Jonathan watched Frances collapse into a chair with children all over her. Before babies, they had been well matched. Then, with the arrival of their first child, it had been a case of Woman Overboard. He'd watched, ineffectual but sympathetic, trying to keep her cheerful as she clung on to the edge of the raft, holding out weevil-free biscuits for her to nibble, and all the time she gazed at him with appalled eyes. Just as they had grown used to this state, difficult but tenable, and were even managing to start hauling her on board again an inch at a time, just as she had her elbows up on the raft and they were congratulating themselves with a kiss, well, along came the second baby in a great slap of a wave that drove her off the raft altogether. Now she was out there in the sea while he bobbed up and down, forlorn but more or less dry, and watched her face between its two satellites dwindling to the size of a fist, then to a plum, and at last to a mere speck of plankton. He dismissed it from his mind.

'I'll see if I can get the shopping before the rain starts,' he said, dashing out to the car again, knee-deep in cow parsley.

'You really should keep an eye on how much bread we've got left,' he called earnestly as he unlocked the car. 'It won't be *my* fault if I'm struck by lightning.'

There was the crumpling noise of thunder, and silver cracked the sky. Frances stood in the doorway holding the baby, while Lorna clawed and clamoured at her to be held in her free arm.

'Oh, Lorna,' said Frances, hit by a wave of bone-aching fatigue. 'You're too heavy, my sweet.' She closed the cottage door as Lorna started to scream, and stood looking down at her with something like fear. She saw a miniature fee-fi-fo-fum creature working its way through a pack of adults, chewing them up and spitting their bones out.

'Come into the back room, Lorna, and I'll read you a book while I feed Matthew.'

'I don't want to.'

'Why don't you want to?'

'I just don't want to.'

'Can't you tell me why?'

'Do you know, I just don't WANT to!'

'All right, *dear*. I'll feed him on my own then.'

'NO!' screamed Lorna. 'PUT HIM IN DA BIN! HE'S RUBBISH!'

'Don't scream, you little beast,' said Frances hopelessly, while the baby squared his mouth and joined in the noise.

Lorna turned the volume up and waited for her to crack. Frances walked off to the kitchen with the baby and quickly closed the door. Lorna gave a howl of rage from the other side and started to smash at it with fists and toys. Children were petal-skinned ogres, Frances realized, callous and whimsical, holding autocratic sway over lower, larger vassals like herself.

There followed a punishing stint of ricochet work, where Frances let the baby cry while she comforted Lorna; let Lorna shriek while she soothed the baby; put Lorna down for her nap and was called back three times before she gave up and let her follow her destructively around; bathed the baby after he had sprayed himself, Lorna and the bathroom with urine during the nappy-changing process; sat on the closed lavatory seat and fed the baby while Lorna chattered in the bath which she had demanded in the wake of the baby's bath.

She stared at Lorna's slim silver body, exquisite in the water, graceful as a Renaissance statuette.

'Shall we see if you'd like a little nap after your bath?' she suggested hopelessly, for only if Lorna rested would she be able to rest, and then only if Matthew was asleep or at least not ready for a feed.

'No,' said Lorna, off-hand but firm.

'Oh, thank God,' said Frances as she heard the car door slam outside. Jonathan was back. It was like the arrival of the cavalry. She wrapped Lorna in a towel and they scrambled downstairs. Jonathan stood puffing on the doormat. Outside was a mid-afternoon twilight, the rain as thick as turf and drenching so that it seemed to leave no room for air between its stalks.

'You're wet, Daddy,' said Lorna, fascinated.

'There were lumps of ice coming down like tennis balls,' he marvelled.

'Here, have this towel,' said Frances, and Lorna spun off naked as a sprite from its folds to dance among the chairs and tables while thunder crashed in the sky with the cumbersomeness of heavy furniture falling down uncarpeted stairs.

'*S'il vous plaît*,' said Frances to Jonathan, '*Dancez, jouez avec le petit diable, cette fille. Il faut que je* get Matthew down for a nap, she just wouldn't let me. *Je suis tellement* shattered.'

'Mummymummymummy,' Lorna chanted as she caught some inkling of this, but Jonathan threw the towel over her and they started to play ghosts.

'My little fat boy,' she whispered at last, squeezing his strong thighs. '*Hey*, fatty boomboom, *sweet* sugar dumpling. It's not fair, is it? I'm never alone with you. You're getting the rough end of the stick just now, aren't you?'

She punctuated this speech with growling kisses, and his hands and feet waved like warm pink roses. She sat him up and stroked the fine duck tail of hair on his baby bull neck. Whenever she tried to fix his essence, he wriggled off into mixed metaphor. And so she clapped his cloud cheeks and revelled in his nest of smiles; she blew raspberries into the crease of his neck and on to his astounded hardening stomach, forcing lion-deep chuckles from him.

She was dismayed at how she had to treat him like some sort of fancy man to spare her daughter's feelings, affecting nonchalance when Lorna was around. She would fall on him for a quick mad embrace if the little girl left the room for a moment, only to spring apart guiltily at the sound of the returning Startrites.

The serrated teeth of remorse bit into her. In late pregnancy she had been so sandbagged that she had had barely enough energy to crawl through the day, let alone reciprocate Lorna's incandescent two-year-old passion.

'She thought I'd come back to her as before once the baby arrived,' she said aloud. 'But I haven't.'

The baby was making the wrangling noise which led to unconsciousness. Then he fell asleep like a door closing. She carried him carefully to his basket, a limp solid parcel against her bosom, the lashes long and wet on his cheeks, lower lip out in a soft semicircle. She put him down and he lay, limbs thrown wide, spatchcocked.

*

After the holiday, Jonathan would be back at the office with his broad quiet desk and filter coffee while she, she would have to submit to a fate worse than death, drudging round the flat to Lorna's screams and the baby's regurgitations and her own sore eyes and body aching to the throb of next door's heavy metal.

The trouble with prolonged sleep deprivation was, that it produced the same coarsening side effects as alcoholism. She was rotten with self-pity, swarming with irritability and despair.

When she heard Jonathan's step on the stairs, she realized that he must have coaxed Lorna to sleep at last. She looked forward to his face, but when he came into the room and she opened her mouth to speak, all that came out were toads and vipers.

'I'm smashed up,' she said. 'I'm never alone. The baby guzzles me and Lorna eats me up. I can't ever go out because I've always got to be there for the children, but you flit in and out like a humming bird. You need me to be always there, to peck at and pull at and answer the door. I even have to feed the cat.'

'I take them out for a walk on Sunday afternoons,' he protested.

'But it's like a favour, and it's only a couple of hours, and I can't use the time to read, I always have to change the sheets or make a meatloaf.'

'For pity's sake. I'm tired too.'

'Sorry,' she muttered. 'Sorry. Sorry. But I don't feel like me any more. I've turned into some sort of oven.'

They lay on the bed and held each other.

'Did you know what Hardy called *Jude the Obscure* to begin with?' he whispered in her ear. '*The Simpletons*. And the Bishop of Wakefield burnt it on a bonfire when it was published.'

'You've been reading!' said Frances accusingly. '*When* did you read!'

'I just pulled in by the side of the road for five minutes. Only for five minutes. It's such a good book. I'd completely forgotten that Jude had three children.'

'*Three?*' said Frances. 'Are you sure?'

'Don't you remember Jude's little boy who comes back from Australia?' said Jonathan. 'Don't you remember little Father Time?'

'Yes,' said Frances. 'Something very nasty happens to him, doesn't it?'

She took the book and flicked through until she reached the page where Father Time and his siblings are discovered by their mother hanging from a hook inside a cupboard door, the note at their feet reading, 'Done because we are too menny.'

'What a wicked old man Hardy was!' she said, incredulous. 'How *dare* he!' She started to cry.

'You're too close to them,' murmured Jonathan. 'You should cut off from them a bit.'

'How *can* I?' sniffed Frances. '*Somebody's* got to be devoted to them. And it's not going to be you because you know I'll do it for you.'

'They're yours, though, aren't they, because of that,' said Jonathan. 'They'll love you best.'

'They're *not* mine. They belong to themselves. But I'm not allowed to belong to *my*self any more.'

'It's not easy for me either.'

'I know it isn't, sweetheart. But at least you're still allowed to be your own man.'

They fell on each other's necks and mingled maudlin tears.

'It's so awful,' sniffed Frances. 'We may never have another.'

They fell asleep.


When they awoke, the landscape was quite different. Not only had the rain stopped, but it had rinsed the air free of oppression. Drops of water hung like lively glass on every leaf and blade. On their way down to the beach, the path was hedged with wet hawthorn, the fiercely spiked branches glittering with green-white flowers.

The late sun was surprisingly strong. It turned the distant moving strokes of the waves to gold bars, and dried salt patterns on to the semi-precious stones which littered the shore. As Frances unbuckled Lorna's sandals, she pointed out to her translucent pieces of chrysoprase and rose quartz in amongst the more ordinary egg-shaped pebbles. Then she kicked off her own shoes and walked wincingly to the water's edge. The sea was casting lacy white shawls on to the stones, and drawing them back with a sigh.

She looked behind her and saw Lorna building a pile of pebbles while Jonathan made the baby more comfortable in his pushchair. A little way ahead was a dinghy, and she could see the flickering gold veins on its white shell thrown up by the sun through moving seawater, and the man standing in it stripped to the waist. She walked towards it, then past it, and as she walked on, she looked out to sea and was aware of her eyeballs making internal adjustments to the new distance which was being demanded of them, as though they had forgotten how to focus on a long view. She felt an excited bubble of pleasure expanding her ribcage, so that she had to take little sighs of breath, warm and fresh and salted, and prevent herself from laughing aloud.

After some while she reached the far end of the beach. Slowly she wheeled like a hero on the cusp of anagnorisis, narrowing her eyes to make out the little group round the pushchair. Of course it was satisfying and delightful to see Jonathan – she supposed it *was* Jonathan? – lying with the fat mild baby on his stomach while their slender elf of a daughter skipped around him. It was part of it. But not the point of it. The concentrated delight was there to start with. She had not needed babies and their pleased-to-be-alive-ness to tell her this.

She started to walk back, this time higher up the beach in the shade of cliffs which held prehistoric snails and traces of dinosaur. I've done it, she thought, and I'm still alive. She took her time, dawdling with deliberate pleasure, as though she were carrying a full glass of milk and might not spill a drop.

'I thought you'd done a Sergeant Troy,' said Jonathan. 'Disappeared out to sea and abandoned us.'

'Would I do a thing like that,' she said, and kissed him lightly beside his mouth.

Matthew reached up from his arms and tugged her hair.

'When I saw you over there by the rock pools you looked just as you used to,' said Jonathan. 'Just the same girl.'

'I am not just as I was, however,' said Frances. 'I am no longer the same girl.'

The sky, which had been growing more dramatic by the minute, was now a florid stagy empyrean, the sea a soundless blaze beneath it. Frances glanced at the baby, and saw how the sun made an electric fleece of the down on his head. She touched it lightly with the flat of her hand as though it might burn her.

'Isn't it mind-boggling,' said Jonathan, 'isn't it impossible to take in that when we were last on this beach, these two were thin air? Or less. They're so solid now that I almost can't believe there was a time before them, and it's only been a couple of years.'

'What?' said Lorna. '*What* did you say?'

'Daddy was just commenting on the mystery of human existence,' said Frances, scooping her up and letting her perch on her hip. She felt the internal chassis, her skeleton and musculature, adjust to the extra weight with practised efficiency. To think, she marvelled routinely, to think that this great heavy child grew in the centre of my body. But the surprise of the idea had started to grow blunt, worn down by its own regular self-contemplation.

'Look, Lorna,' she said. 'Do you see how the sun is making our faces orange?'

In the flood of flame-coloured light their flesh turned to coral.

MARÍA ELENA LLANO

# In the Family

Translated by Beatriz Teleki

*María Elena Llano was born in Cuba in 1936. She works as a journalist for the cultural section of* La Habana*'s news agency* Latin Press*, and she has written for radio and television.* La Reja*, a volume of her short stories, was published in 1966, and she has also published a collection of poetry.*

When my mother found out that the large mirror in the living-room was inhabited, we all gradually went from disbelief to astonishment, and from this to a state of contemplation, ending up by accepting it as an everyday thing.

The fact that the old, spotted mirror reflected the dear departed in the family was not enough to upset our life style. Following the old saying of 'Let the house burn as long as no one sees the smoke', we kept the secret to ourselves since, after all, it was nobody else's business.

At any rate, some time went by before each one of us would feel absolutely comfortable about sitting down in our favourite chair and learning that, in the mirror, that same chair was occupied by somebody else. For example, it could be Aurelia, my grandmother's sister (1939), and even if cousin Natalie would be on my side of the room, across from her would be the almost forgotten Uncle Nicholas (1927). As could have been expected, our departed reflected in the mirror presented the image of a family gathering almost identical to our own, since nothing, absolutely nothing in the living-room – the furniture and its arrangement, the light, etc. – was changed in the mirror. The only difference was that on the other side it was them instead of us.

I don't know about the others, but I sometimes felt that, more than a vision in the mirror, I was watching an old worn-out movie, already clouded. The deceaseds' efforts to copy our gestures were slower, restrained, as if the mirror were not truly showing a direct image but the reflection of some other reflection.

From the very beginning I knew that everything would get more complicated as soon as my cousin Clara got back from vacation. Because of her boldness and determination, Clara had long given me the impression that she had blundered into our family by mistake. This suspicion had been somewhat bolstered by her being one of the first women dentists in the country. However, the idea that she might have been with us by mistake went away as soon as my cousin hung up her diploma and started to embroider sheets beside my grandmother, aunts and other cousins, waiting for a suitor who actually did show up but was found lacking in one respect or another – nobody ever really found out why.

Once she graduated, Clara became the family oracle, even though she never practised her profession. She would prescribe painkillers and was the arbiter of fashion; she would choose the theatre shows and rule on whether the punch had the right amount of liquor at each social gathering. In view of all this, it was fitting that she take one month off every year to go to the beach.

That summer when Clara returned from her vacation and learned about my mother's discovery, she remained pensive for a while, as if weighing the symptoms before issuing a diagnosis. Afterwards, without batting an eye, she leaned over the mirror, saw for herself that it was true, and then tossed her head, seemingly accepting the situation. She immediately sat by the bookcase and craned her neck to see who was sitting in the chair on the other side. 'Gosh, look at Gus,' was all she said. There in the very same chair the mirror showed us Gus, some sort of godson of Dad, who after a flood in his home town came to live with us and had remained there in the somewhat ambiguous character of adoptive poor relation. Clara greeted him amiably with a wave of the hand, but he seemed busy, for the moment, with something like a radio tube and did not pay attention to her. Undoubtedly, the mirror people weren't going out of their way to be sociable. This must have wounded Clara's self-esteem, although she did not let on.

Naturally, the idea of moving the mirror to the dining-room was hers.

And so was its sequel: to bring the mirror near the big table, so we could all sit together for meals.

In spite of my mother's fears that the mirror people would run away or get annoyed because of the fuss, everything went fine. I must admit it was comforting to sit every day at the table and see so many familiar faces, although some of those from the other side were distant relatives, and others, due to their lengthy – although unintentional – absence, were almost strangers. There were about twenty of us sitting at the table every day, and even if their gestures and movements seemed more remote than ours and their meals a little washed-out, we generally gave the impression of being a large family that got along well.

At the boundary between the real table and the other one, on this side, sat Clara and her brother Julius. On the other side was Eulalia (1949), the second wife of Uncle Daniel, aloof and indolent in life, and now the most distant of anyone on the other side. Across from her sat my godfather Sylvester (1952), who even though he was not a blood relative was always a soul relation. I was sad to see that Sylvester had lost his ruddiness, for he now looked like a faded mannequin, although his full face seemed to suggest perfect health. This pallor did not suit the robust Asturian, who undoubtedly felt a bit ridiculous in these circumstances.

For a while we ate all together, without further incidents or problems. We mustn't forget Clara, however, whom we had allowed to sit at the frontier between the two tables, the equator separating what was from what was not. Although we paid no attention to the situation, we should have. Compounding our regrettable oversight was the fact that lethargic Eulalia sat across from her so that one night, with the same cordiality with which she had addressed Gus, Clara asked Eulalia to pass the salad. Eulalia affected the haughty disdain of offended royalty as she passed the spectral salad bowl, filled with dull lettuce and greyish semi-transparent tomatoes which Clara gobbled up, smiling mischievously at the novelty of it all. She watched us with the same defiance in her eyes that she had on the day she enrolled in a man's subject. There was no time to act. We just watched her grow pale, then her smile faded away until finally Clara collapsed against the mirror.

Once the funeral business was over and we sat back down at the table again, we saw that Clara had taken a place on the other side. She was between cousin Baltazar (1940) and a great-uncle whom we simply called 'Ito'.

This *faux pas* dampened our conviviality somewhat. In a way, we felt betrayed; we felt that they had grievously abused our hospitality. However, we ended up divided over the question of who was really whose guest. It was also plain that our carelessness and Clara's irrepressible inquisitiveness had contributed to the mishap. In fact, a short time later we realized that there wasn't a great deal of difference between what Clara did before and what she was doing now, and so we decided to overlook the incident and get on with things. Nevertheless, each day we became less and less sure about which side was life and which its reflection, and as one bad step leads to another, I ended up taking Clara's empty place.

I am now much closer to them. I can almost hear the distant rustle of the folding and unfolding of napkins, the slight clinking of glasses and cutlery, the movement of chairs. The fact is that I can't tell if these sounds come from them or from us. I'm obviously not worried about clearing that up. What really troubles me, though, is that Clara doesn't seem to behave properly, with either the solemnity or with the opacity owed to her new position; I don't know how to put it. Even worse, the problem is that I – more than anybody else in the family – may become the target of Clara's machinations, since we were always joined by a very special affection, perhaps because we were the same age and had shared the same children's games and the first anxieties of adolescence . . .

As it happens, she is doing her best to get my attention, and ever since last Monday she has been waiting for me to slip up so she can pass me a pineapple this big, admittedly a little bleached-out, but just right for making juice and also a bit sour, just as she knows I like it.

# A Gift from Somewhere

*Ama Ata Aidoo was born in the Gold Coast (Ghana) in 1942. She produced her first play,* Dilemma of a Ghost, *at the University of Ghana in 1964. This successful debut was followed in 1969 by a second play,* Anowa, *which focuses on the rejection by traditional society of an independent, gifted woman who dares to flout convention and follow her own heart and mind. Her short-story collection* No Sweetness Here *was published in 1970; she has also written two novels,* Our Sister Killjoy: Reflections from a Black-eyed Squint *and* Changes, *as well as a collection of poetry.*

The Mallam had been to the village once. A long time ago. A long time ago, he had come to do these parts with Ahmadu. That had been his first time. He did not remember what had actually happened except that Ahmadu had died one night during the trip. Allah, the things that can happen to us in our exile and wanderings!

Now the village was quiet. But these people. How can they leave their villages so empty every day like this? Any time you come to a village in these parts in the afternoon, you only find the too young, the too old, the maimed and the dying, or else goats and chickens, never men and women. They don't have any cause for alarm. There is no fighting here, no marauding.

He entered several compounds which were completely deserted. Then he came to this one and saw the woman. Pointing to her stomach, he said, 'Mami Fanti, there is something there.' The woman started shivering. He was embarrassed.

Something told him that there was nothing wrong with the woman herself. Perhaps there was a baby? Oh, Allah, one always has to make such violent guesses. He looked round for a stool. When he saw one lying by the wall, he ran to pick it up. He returned with it to where the woman was sitting, placed it right opposite her, and sat down.

Then he said, 'Mami, by Allah, by his holy prophet Mohamet, let your heart rest quiet in your breast. This little one, this child, he will live . . .'

And she lifted her head which until then was so bent her chin touched her breasts, and raised her eyes to the face of the Mallam for the first time, and asked, 'Papa Kramo, is that true?'

'Ah Mami Fanti,' the Mallam rejoined. 'Mm . . . mm,' shaking awhile the forefinger of his right hand. This movement accompanied simultaneously as it was by his turbanned head and face, made him look very knowing indeed.

'Mm . . . mm, and why must you yourself be asking me if it is true? Have I myself lied to you before, eh, Mami Fanti?'

'Hmmmm . . .' sighed she of the anxious heart. 'It is just that I cannot find it possible to believe that he will live. That is why I asked you that.'

His eyes glittered with the pleasure of his first victory and her heart did a little somersault.

'Mami Fanti, I myself, me, I am telling you. The little one, he will live. Now today he may not look good, perhaps not today. Perhaps even after eight days he will not be good but I tell you, Mami, one moon, he will be good . . . good . . . good,' and he drew up his arms, bent them, contracted his shoulders and shook up the upper part of his body to indicate how well and strong he thought the child would be. It was a beautiful sight and for an instant a smile passed over her face. But the smile was not able to stay. It was chased away by the anxiety that seemed to have come to occupy her face forever.

'Papa Kramo, if you say that, I believe you. But you will give me something to protect him from the witches?'

'Mami Fanti, you yourself you are in too much hurry, and why? Have I got up to go?'

She shook her head and said, 'No,' with a voice that quaked with fear.

'Aha . . . so you yourself you must be patient. I myself will do every-thing . . . everything . . . Allah is present and Mohamet his holy prophet is here too. I will do everything for you. You hear?'

She breathed deeply and loudly in reply.

'Now bring to me the child.' She stood up, and unwound the other cloth with which she had so far covered up her bruised soul and tied it around her waist. She turned in her step and knocked over the stool. The clanging noise did not attract her attention in the least. Slowly, she walked towards the door. The Mallam's eyes followed her while his left hand groped through the folds of his *boubou* in search of his last piece of cola. Then he remembered that his sack was still on his shoulder. He removed it, placed it on the floor and now with both his hands free, he fished out the cola. He popped it into his mouth and his tongue received the bitter piece of fruit with the eagerness of a lover.

The stillness of the afternoon was yet to be broken. In the hearth, a piece of coal yielded its tiny ash to the naughty breeze, blinked with its last spark and folded itself up in death. Above, a lonely cloud passed over the Mallam's turban, on its way to join camp in the south. And as if the Mallam had felt the motion of the cloud, he looked up and scanned the sky.

Perhaps it shall rain tonight? I must hurry up with this woman so that I can reach the next village before nightfall.

'Papa Kramo-e-e –!'

This single cry pierced through the dark interior of the room in which the child was lying, hit the aluminium utensils in the outer room, gathered itself together, cut through the silence of that noon, and echoed in the several corners of the village. The Mallam sprang up. 'What is it, Mami Fanti?' And the two collided at the door to her rooms. But neither of them saw how she managed to throw the baby on him and how he came to himself sufficiently to catch it. But the world is a wonderful place and such things happen in it daily. The Mallam caught the baby before it fell.

'Look, look, Papa Kramo, look! Look and see if this baby is not dead. See if this baby too is not dead. Just look – O – O Papa Kramo, look!' And she started running up and down, jumping, wringing her hands and undoing the threads in her hair. Was she immediately mad? Perhaps. The only way to tell that a possessed woman of this kind is not completely out of her senses is that she does not unclothe herself to nakedness. The Mallam was bewildered.

'Mami Fanti, *hei*, Mami Fanti,' he called unheeded. Then he looked down at the child in his arms.

Allah, tch, tch, tch. Now, O holy Allah. Now only you can rescue me from this trouble, since my steps found this house guided by the Prophet, but Allah, this baby is dead.

And he looked down again at it to confirm his suspicion.

Allah, the child is breathing but what kind of breath is this? I must hurry up and leave. Ah . . . what a bad day this is. But I will surely not want the baby to grow still in my arms! At all . . . for that will be bad luck, big bad luck . . . And now where is its mother? This is not good. I am so hungry now. I thought at least I was going to earn some four pennies so I could eat. I do not like to go without food when it is not Ramaddan. Now look – And I can almost count its ribs! One, two, three, four, five . . . And, Allah, it is pale. I could swear this is a Fulani child only its face does not show that it is. If this is the pallor of sickness . . . O Mohamet! Now I must think up something quickly to comfort the mother with.

'*Hei*, Mami Fanti, Mami Fanti!'

'Papaa!'

'Come.'

She danced in from the doorway still wringing her hands and sucking in the air through her mouth like one who had swallowed a mouthful of scalding-hot porridge.

'It is dead, is it not?' she asked with the courtesy of the insane.

'Mami, sit down.'

She sat.

'Mami, what is it yourself you are doing? Yourself you make plenty noise. It is not good. Eh, what is it for yourself you do that?'

Not knowing how to answer the questions, she kept quiet. 'Yourself, look well.' She craned her neck as though she were looking for an object in a distance. She saw his breath flutter.

'Yourself you see he is not dead?'

'Yes,' she replied without conviction. It was too faint a breath to build any hopes on, but she did not say this to the Mallam.

'Now listen, Mami,' he said, and he proceeded to spit on the child: once on his forehead and then on his navel. Then he spat into his right palm and with this spittle started massaging the child very hard on his joints, the neck, shoulder blades, ankles and wrists. You could see he was straining himself very hard. You would have thought the child's skin would peel off any time. And the woman could not bear to look on.

If the child had any life in him, surely, he could have yelled at least once more? She sank her chin deeper into her breast.

'Now, Mami, I myself say, you yourself, you must listen.'

'Papa, I am listening.'

'Mami, I myself say, this child will live. Now himself he is too small. Yourself you must not eat meat. You must not eat fish from the sea, Friday, Sunday. You hear?' She nodded in reply. 'He himself, if he is about ten years,' and he counted ten by flicking the five fingers of his left hand twice over, 'if he is about ten, tell him he must not eat meat and fish from the sea, Friday, Sunday. If he himself he does not eat, you Mami Fanti, you can eat. You hear?'

She nodded again.

'Now, the child he will live, yourself you must stop weeping. If you do that it is not good. Now you have the blue dye for washing?'

'Yes,' she murmured.

'And a piece of white cloth?'

'Yes, but it is not big. Just about a yard and a quarter.'

'That does not matter. Yourself, find those things for me and I will do something and your child he shall be good.'

She did not say anything.

'Did you yourself hear me, Mami Fanti?'

'Yes.'

'Now take the child, put him in the room. Come back, go and find all the things.'

She took the thing which might once have been a human child but now was certainly looking like something else and went back with it to the room.

And she was thinking.

Who does the Mallam think he is deceiving? This is the third child to die. The others never looked half this sick. No! In fact the last one was fat . . . I had been playing with it. After the evening meal I had laid him down on the mat to go and take a quick bath. Nothing strange in that. When I returned to the house later, I powdered myself and finished up the last bits of my toilet . . . When I eventually went in to pick up my baby, he was dead.

. . . O my Lord, my Mighty God, who does the Mallam think he is deceiving?

And he was thinking.

Allah just look, I cannot remain here. It will be bad of me to ask the woman for so much as a penny when I know this child will die. Allah, look, the day has come a long way and I have still not eaten.

He rose up, picked up his bag from the ground and with a quietness and swiftness of which only a nomad is capable, he vanished from the house. When the woman had laid the child down, she returned to the courtyard.

'Papa Kramo, Papa Kramo,' she called. A goat who had been lying nearby chewing the cud got up and went out quietly too.

'Kramo, Kramo,' only her own voice echoed in her brain. She sat down again on the stool. If she was surprised at all, it was only at the neatness of his escape. So he too had seen death.

Should any of my friends hear me moaning, they will say I am behaving like one who has not lost a baby before, like a fresh bride who sees her first baby dying. Now all I must do is to try and prepare myself for another pregnancy, for it seems this is the reason why I was created . . . to be pregnant for nine of the twelve months of every year . . . Or is there a way out of it at all? And where does this road lie? I shall have to get used to it . . . It is the pattern set for my life. For the moment, I must be quiet until the mothers come back in the evening to bury him.

Then rewrapping the other cloth around her shoulders, she put her chin in her breast and she sat, as though the Mallam had never been there.

But do you know, this child did not die. It is wonderful but this child did not die. Mmm . . . This strange world always has something to surprise us with . . . Kweku Nyamekye. Somehow, he did not die. To his day name Kweku, I have added Nyamekye. Kweku Nyamekye. For, was he not a gift from God through the Mallam of the Bound Mouth? And he, the Mallam of the Bound Mouth, had not taken from me a penny, not a single penny that ever bore a hole. And the way he had vanished! Or it was perhaps the god who yielded me to my mother who came to my aid at last? As he had promised her he would? I remember Maame telling me that when I was only a baby the god of Mbemu from whom I came had promised never to desert me and that he would come to me once in my life when I needed him most. And was it not him who had come in the person of the Mallam? . . . But was it not strange, the way he disappeared without asking for a penny? He had not even waited for me to buy the things he had prescribed. He was going to make a charm. It is good that he did not, for how can a scholar go through life wearing something like that? Looking at the others of the Bound Mouth, sometimes you can spot familiar faces, but my Mallam has never been here again.

Nyamekye, hmm, and after him I have not lost any more children. Let me touch wood. In this world, it is true, there is always something somewhere, covered with leaves. Nyamekye lived. I thought his breathing would have stopped by the time the old woman returned in the evening. But it did not. Towards nightfall his colour changed completely. He did not feel so hot. His breathing improved and from then, he grew stronger every day. But if ever I come upon the Mallam, I will just fall down before him, wipe his tired feet with a silk *kente*, and then spread it before him and ask him to walk on it. If I do not do that then no one should call me Abena Gyaawa again.

When he started recovering, I took up the taboo as the Mallam had instructed. He is now going to be eleven years old I think. Eleven years, and I have never, since I took it up, missed observing it any Friday or Sunday. Not once. Sometimes I wonder why he chose these two days and not others. If my eyes had not been scattered about me that afternoon, I would have asked him to explain the reason behind this choice to me. And now I shall never know.

Yes, eleven years. But it has been difficult. Oh, it is true I do not think that I am one of these women with a sweet tooth for fish and meats. But if you say that you are going to eat soup, then soup you are going to eat. Perhaps no meat or fish may actually hit your teeth but how can you say any broth has soul when it does not contain anything at all? It is true that like everyone else, I liked *kontomire*. But like everyone else too, I ate it only when my throat ached for it or when I was on the farm. But since I took up the taboo, I have had to eat it at least twice two days of the week, Sunday and Friday. I have come to hate its deep-green look. My only relief came with the season of snails and mushrooms. But everyone knows that these days they are getting rarer because it does not rain as often as it used to. Then after about five years of this strict observance, someone who knew about these things advised me. He said that since the Mallam had mentioned the sea, at least I could eat freshwater fish or prawns and crabs. I did not like the idea of eating fish at all. Who can tell which minnow has paid a visit to the ocean? So I began eating freshwater prawns and crabs – but, of course, only when I could get them. Normally, you do not get these things unless you have a grown-up son who would go trapping in the river for you.

But I do not mind these difficulties. If the Mallam came back to tell me that I must stop eating fish and meat altogether so that Nyamekye and the others would live, I would do it. I would. After all, he had told me that I could explain the taboo to Nyamekye when he was old enough to understand, so he could take it up himself. But I have not done it and I do not think I shall ever do it. How can a schoolboy – and who knows, one day he may become a real scholar – how can he go through life dragging this type of taboo along with him? I have never heard any scholar doing it, and my son is not going to be first to do it. No. I myself will go on observing it until I die. For, how could I have gone on living with my two empty hands? I swear by everything, I do not understand people who complain that I am spoiling them, especially him. And anyway, is it any business of theirs? Even if I daily anointed them with shea-butter and placed them in the sun, whom would I hurt? Who else should be concerned apart from me?

But the person whose misunderstanding hurts me is their father. I do not know what to do. Something tells me it's his people and his wives who prevent him from having good thoughts about me and mine. I was his first wife and if you knew how at the outset of our lives death haunted us, hmmm. Neither of us had a head to think in. And if things were what they should be, should he be behaving in this way? In fact, I swear by everything, he hates Nyamekye. Or how could what happened last week have happened?

It was a Friday and they had not gone to school. It was a holiday for them. I do not know what this one was for but it was one of those days they do not go. When the time came for us to leave for the farm, I showed him where food was and asked him to look after himself and his younger brother and sisters. Well, my tongue was still moving when his father came in with his face shut down, the way it is when he is angry. He came up to us and asked '*Hei*, Nyamekye, are you not following your mother to the farm?' Oh, I was hurt. Is this the way to talk to a ten-year-old child? If he had been any other father, he would have said, 'Nyamekye, since you are not going to school today, pick up your knife and come with me to the farm.'

Would that not have been beautiful?

'Nyamekye, are you not following your mother to the farm?' As if I am the boy's only parent. But he is stuck with this habit, especially where I and my little ones are concerned.

'Gyaawa, your child is crying . . . Gyaawa, your child is going to fall off the terrace if you do not pay more attention to him . . . Gyaawa, your child this, and your child that!'

Anyway, that morning I was hurt and when I opened up my mouth, all the words which came to my lips were, 'I thought this boy was going to be a scholar and not a farm-goer. What was the use in sending him to school if I knew he was going to follow me to the farm?'

This had made him more angry. 'I did not know that if you go to school, your skin must not touch a leaf!'

I did not say anything. What had I to say? We went to the farm, leaving Nyamekye with the children. I returned home earlier than his father did. Nyamekye was not in the house. I asked his brother and sisters if they knew where he had gone. But they had not seen him since they finished eating earlier in the afternoon. When he had not come home by five o'clock, I started getting worried. Then his father was too returned from the farm. He learned immediately that he was missing. He clouded up. After he had had his bath, he went to sit in his chair, dark as a rainy sky. Then he got up to go by the chicken coop. I did not know that he was going to fetch a cane. Just as he was sitting in the chair again, Nyamekye appeared.

'*Hei*, Kweku Nyamekye, come here.'

Nyamekye was holding the little bucket and I knew where he had been to. He moved slowly up to his father.

'Papa, I went to the river to visit my trap, because today is Friday.'

'Have I asked you for anything? And your traps! Is that what you go to school to learn?'

And then he pulled out the cane and fell on the child. The bucket dropped and a few little prawns fell out. Something tells me it was the sight of those prawns which finished his father. He poured those blows on him as though he were made of wood. I had made up my mind never to interfere in any manner he chose to punish the children, for, after all, they are his too. But this time I thought he was going too far. I rushed out to rescue Nyamekye and then it came, wham! The sharpest blow I have ever received in my life caught me on the inside of my arm. Blood gushed out. When he saw what had happened, he was ashamed. He went away into his room. That evening he did not eat the *fufu* I served him.

Slowly, I picked up the bucket and the prawns. Nyamekye followed me to my room, where I wept.

The scar healed quickly but the scar is of the type which rises so anyone can see it. Nyamekye's father's attitude has changed towards us. He is worse. He is angry all the time. He is angry with shame.

But I do not even care. I have my little ones. And I am sure someone is wishing she were me. I have Nyamekye. And for this, I do not even know whom to thank.

Do I thank you, O Mallam of the Bound Mouth?

Or you, Nana Mbemu, since I think you came in the person of the Mallam?

Or Mighty Jehovah-after-whom-there-is-none-other, to you alone should I give my thanks?

But why should I let this worry me? I thank you all. Oh, I thank you all. And you, our ancestral spirits, if you are looking after me, then look after the Mallam too. Remember him at meals, for he is a kinsman.

And as for this scar, I am glad it is not on Nyamekye. Any time I see it I only recall one afternoon when I sat with my chin in my breast before a Mallam came in, and after a Mallam went out.

# The Bloody Chamber

*Angela Carter was born in 1940. She read English at Bristol, spent two years living in Japan and from 1976 to 1978 was a Fellow in Creative Writing at Sheffield University. Her first novel,* Shadowdance, *was published in 1965, followed by* The Magic Toyshop, *which won the 1967 John Llewellyn Rhys Prize,* Several Percep-tions, *which won the 1968 Somerset Maugham Award,* Heroes and Villains, Love, The Passion of the New Eve, Nights at the Circus *and* Wise Children. *She also published two collections of short stories,* Fireworks *and* The Bloody Cham-ber, *and two works of non-fiction,* The Sadeian Woman: An Exercise in Cul-tural History *and* Nothing Sacred, *a collection of her journalism. She died of lung cancer in February 1992.*

I remember how, that night, I lay awake in the *wagon-lit* in a tender, delicious ecstasy of excitement, my burning cheek pressed against the impeccable linen of the pillow and the pounding of my heart mimicking that of the great pistons ceaselessly thrusting the train that bore me through the night, away from Paris, away from girlhood, away from the white, enclosed quietude of my mother's apartment, into the unguessable country of marriage.

And I remember I tenderly imagined how, at this very moment, my mother would be moving slowly about the narrow bedroom I had left behind for ever, folding up and putting away all my little relics, the tum-bled garments I would not need any more, the scores for which there had been no room in my trunks, the concert programmes I'd abandoned; she would linger over this torn ribbon and that faded photograph with all the half-joyous, half-sorrowful emotions of a woman on her daughter's wedding day. And, in the midst of my bridal triumph, I felt a pang of loss as if, when he put the gold band on my finger, I had, in some way, ceased to be her child in becoming his wife.

Are you sure, she'd said when they delivered the gigantic box that held the wedding dress he'd bought me, wrapped up in tissue paper and red ribbon like a Christmas gift of crystallized fruit. Are you sure you love him? There was a dress for her, too; black silk, with the dull, prismatic sheen of oil on water, finer than anything she'd worn since that adventurous girlhood in Indo-China, daughter of a rich tea-planter. My eagle-featured, indomitable mother; what other student at the Conservatoire could boast that her mother had outfaced a junkful of Chinese pirates, nursed a village through a visitation of the plague, shot a man-eating tiger with her own hand and all before she was as old as I?

'Are you sure you love him?'

'I'm sure I want to marry him,' I said.

And would say no more. She sighed, as if it was with reluctance that she might at last banish the spectre of poverty from its habitual place at our meagre table. For my mother herself had gladly, scandalously, defiantly beggared herself for love; and, one fine day, her gallant soldier never returned from the wars, leaving his wife and child a legacy of tears that never quite dried, a cigar box full of medals and the antique service revolver that my mother, grown magnificently eccentric in hardship, kept always in her reticule, in case – how I teased her – she was surprised by footpads on her way home from the grocer's shop.

Now and then a starburst of lights spattered the drawn blinds as if the railway company had lit up all the stations through which we passed in celebration of the bride. My satin nightdress had just been shaken from its wrappings; it had slipped over my young girl's pointed breasts and shoulders, supple as a garment of heavy water, and now teasingly caressed me, egregious, insinuating, nudging between my thighs as I shifted restlessly in my narrow berth. His kiss, his kiss with tongue and teeth in it and a rasp of beard, had hinted to me, though with the same exquisite tact as this nightdress he'd given me, of the wedding night, which would be voluptuously deferred until we lay in his great ancestral bed in the sea-girt, pinnacled domain that lay, still, beyond the grasp of my imagination . . . that magic place, the fairy castle whose walls were made of foam, that legendary habitation in which he had been born. To which, one day, I might bear an heir. Our destination, my destiny.

Above the syncopated roar of the train, I could hear his even, steady breathing. Only the communicating door kept me from my husband and it stood open. If I rose up on my elbow, I could see the dark, leonine shape of his head and my nostrils caught a whiff of the opulent male scent of leather and spices that always accompanied him and sometimes, during his courtship, had been the only hint he gave me that he had come into my mother's sitting-room, for, though he was a big man, he moved as softly as if all his shoes had soles of velvet, as if his footfall turned the carpet into snow.

He had loved to surprise me in my abstracted solitude at the piano. He would tell them not to announce him, then soundlessly open the door and softly creep up behind me with his bouquet of hot-house flowers or his box of *marrons glacés*, lay his offering upon the keys and clasp his hands over my eyes as I was lost in a Debussy prelude. But that perfume of spiced leather always betrayed him; after my first shock, I was forced always to mimic surprise, so that he would not be disappointed.

He was older than I. He was much older than I; there were streaks of pure silver in his dark mane. But his strange, heavy, almost waxen face was not lined by experience. Rather, experience seemed to have washed it perfectly smooth, like a stone on a beach whose fissures have been eroded by successive tides. And sometimes that face, in stillness when he listened to me playing, with the heavy eyelids folded over eyes that always disturbed me by their absolute absence of light, seemed to me like a mask, as if his real face, the face that truly reflected all the life he had led in the world before he met me, before, even, I was born, as though that face lay underneath this mask. Or else, elsewhere. As though he had laid by the face in which he had lived for so long in order to offer my youth a face unsigned by the years.

And, elsewhere, I might see him plain. Elsewhere. But, where?

In, perhaps, that castle to which the train now took us, that marvellous castle in which he had been born.

Even when he asked me to marry him, and I said, 'Yes,' still he did not lose that heavy, fleshy composure of his. I know it must seem a curious analogy, a man with a flower, but sometimes he seemed to me like a lily.

Yes. A lily. Possessed of that strange, ominous calm of a sentient veget-able, like one of those cobra-headed, funeral lilies whose white sheaths are curled out of a flesh as thick and tensely yielding to the touch as vellum. When I said that I would marry him, not one muscle in his face stirred, but he let out a long, extinguished sigh. I thought: Oh! how he must want me! And it was as though the imponderable weight of his desire was a force I might not withstand, not by virtue of its violence but because of its very gravity.

He had the ring ready in a leather box lined with crimson velvet, a fire opal the size of a pigeon's egg set in a complicated circle of dark antique gold. My old nurse, who still lived with my mother and me, squinted at the ring askance: opals are bad luck, she said. But this opal had been his own mother's ring, and his grandmother's, and her moth-er's before that, given to an ancestor by Catherine de' Medici ... Every bride that came to the castle wore it, time out of mind. And did he give it to his other wives and have it back from them? asked the old woman rudely; yet she was a snob. She hid her incredulous joy at my marital coup – her little *marquise* – behind a façade of fault-finding. But, here, she touched me. I shrugged and turned my back pettishly on her. I did not want to remember how he had loved other women before me, but the knowledge often teased me in the threadbare self-confidence of the small hours.

I was seventeen and knew nothing of the world; my *marquis* had been married before, more than once, and I remained a little bemused that, after those others, he should now have chosen me. Indeed, was he not still in mourning for his last wife? Tsk, tsk, went my old nurse. And even my mother had been reluctant to see her girl whisked off by a man so recently bereaved. A Romanian countess, a lady of high fashion. Dead just three short months before I met him, a boating accident, at his home, in Brittany. They never found her body, but I rummaged through the back copies of the society magazines my old nanny kept in a trunk under her bed and tracked down her photograph. The sharp muzzle of a pretty, witty, naughty monkey; such potent and bizarre charm, of a dark, bright, wild yet worldly thing whose natural habitat must have been some lux-urious interior decorator's jungle filled with potted palms and tame, squawking parakeets.

Before that? *Her* face is common property; everyone painted her but the Redon engraving I liked best, *The Evening Star Walking on the Rim of Night.* To see her skeletal, enigmatic grace, you would never think she had been a barmaid in a café in Montmartre until Puvis de Chavannes saw her and had her expose her flat breasts and elongated thighs to his brush. And yet it was the absinthe doomed her, or so they said.

The first of all his ladies? That sumptuous diva; I had heard her sing Isolde, precociously musical child that I was, taken to the opera for a birthday treat. My first opera; I had heard her sing Isolde. With what white-hot passion had she burned from the stage! So that you could tell she would die young. We sat high up, halfway to heaven in the gods, yet she half-blinded me. And my father, still alive (oh, so long ago), took hold of my sticky little hand, to comfort me, in the last act, yet all I heard was the glory of her voice.

Married three times within my own brief lifetime to three different graces, now, as if to demonstrate the eclecticism of his taste, he had invited me to join this gallery of beautiful women, I, the poor widow's child with my mouse-coloured hair that still bore the kinks of the plaits from which it had so recently been freed, my bony hips, my nervous, pianist's fingers.

He was rich as Croesus. The night before our wedding – a simple affair, at the Mairie, because his countess was so recently gone – he took my mother and me, curious coincidence, to see *Tristan.* And, do you know, my heart swelled and ached so during the *Liebestod* that I thought I must truly love him. Yes. I did. On his arm, all eyes were upon me. The whispering crowd in the foyer parted like the Red Sea to let us through. My skin crisped at his touch.

How my circumstances had changed since the first time I heard those voluptuous chords that carry such a charge of deathly passion in them! Now, we sat in a loge, in red velvet armchairs, and a braided, bewigged flunkey brought us a silver bucket of iced champagne in the interval. The froth spilled over the rim of my glass and drenched my hands, I thought: My cup runneth over. And I had on a Poiret dress. He had prevailed upon my reluctant mother to let him buy my trousseau; what would I have gone to him in, otherwise? Twice-darned underwear, faded gingham, serge skirts, hand-me-downs. So, for the opera, I wore a sinuous shift of white muslin tied with a silk string under the breasts. And everyone stared at me. And at his wedding gift.

His wedding gift, clasped round my throat. A choker of rubies, two inches wide, like an extraordinarily precious slit throat.

After the Terror, in the early days of the Directory, the aristos who'd escaped the guillotine had an ironic fad of tying a red ribbon round their necks at just the point where the blade would have sliced it through, a red ribbon like the memory of a wound. And his grandmother, taken with the notion, had her ribbon made up in rubies; such a gesture of luxurious defiance! That night at the opera comes back to me even now . . . the white dress; the frail child within it; and the flashing crimson jewels round her throat, bright as arterial blood.

I saw him watching me in the gilded mirrors with the assessing eye of a connoisseur inspecting horseflesh, or even of a housewife in the market, inspecting cuts on the slab. I'd never seen, or else had never acknowledged, that regard of his before, the sheer carnal avarice of it; and it was strangely magnified by the monocle lodged in his left eye. When I saw him look at me with lust, I dropped my eyes but, in glancing away from him, I caught sight of myself in the mirror. And I saw myself, suddenly, as he saw me, my pale face, the way the muscles in my neck stuck out like thin wire. I saw how much that cruel necklace became me. And, for the first time in my innocent and confined life, I sensed in myself a potentiality for corruption that took my breath away.

The next day, we were married.

The train slowed, shuddered to a halt. Lights; clank of metal; a voice declaring the name of an unknown, never-to-be visited station; silence of the night; the rhythm of his breathing, that I should sleep with, now, for the rest of my life. And I could not sleep. I stealthily sat up, raised the blind a little and huddled against the cold window that misted over with the warmth of my breathing, gazing out at the dark platform towards those rectangles of domestic lamplight that promised warmth, company, a supper of sausages hissing in a pan on the stove for the station master, his children tucked up in bed asleep in the brick house with the painted shutters . . . all the paraphernalia of the everyday world from which I, with my stunning marriage, had exiled myself.

Into marriage, into exile; I sensed it, I knew it – that, henceforth, I would always be lonely. Yet that was part of the already familiar weight of the fire opal that glimmered like a gypsy's magic ball, so that I could not take my eyes off it when I played the piano. This ring, the bloody bandage of rubies, the wardrobe of clothes from Poiret and Worth, his scent of Russian leather – all had conspired to seduce me so utterly that I could not say I felt one single twinge of regret for the world of *tartines* and *maman* that now receded from me as if drawn away on a string, like a child's toy, as the train began to throb again as if in delighted anticipation of the distance it would take me.

The first grey streamers of the dawn now flew in the sky and an eldritch half-light seeped into the railway carriage. I heard no change in his breathing but my heightened, excited senses told me he was awake and gazing at me. A huge man, an enormous man, and his eyes, dark and motionless as those eyes the ancient Egyptians painted upon their sarcophagi, fixed upon me. I felt a certain tension in the pit of my stomach, to be so watched, in such silence. A match struck. He was igniting a Romeo y Julieta fat as a baby's arm.

'Soon,' he said in his resonant voice that was like the tolling of a bell and I felt, all at once, a sharp premonition of dread that lasted only as long as the match flared and I could see his white broad face as if it were hovering, disembodied, above the sheets, illuminated from below like a grotesque carnival head. Then the flame died, the cigar glowed and filled the compartment with a remembered fragrance that made me think of my father, how he would hug me in a warm fug of Havana, when I was a little girl, before he kissed me and left me and died.

As soon as my husband handed me down from the high step of the train, I smelled the amniotic salinity of the ocean. It was November; the trees, stunted by the Atlantic gales, were bare and the lonely halt was deserted but for his leather-gaitered chauffeur waiting meekly beside the sleek black motor car. It was cold; I drew my furs about me, a wrap of white and black, broad stripes of ermine and sable, with a collar from which my head rose like the calyx of a wildflower. (I swear to you, I had never been vain until I met him.) The bell clanged; the straining train leapt its leash and left us at that lonely wayside halt where only he and I had descended. Oh, the wonder of it; how all that might of iron and steam had paused only to suit his convenience. The richest man in France.

'*Madame.*'

The chauffeur eyed me; was he comparing me, invidiously, to the countess, the artist's model, the opera singer? I hid behind my furs as if they were a system of soft shields. My husband liked me to wear my opal over my kid glove, a showy, theatrical trick – but the moment the ironic chauffeur glimpsed its simmering flash he smiled, as though it was proof positive I was his master's wife. And we drove towards the widening dawn, that now streaked half the sky with a wintry bouquet of pink of roses, orange of tiger-lilies, as if my husband had ordered me a sky from a florist. The day broke around me like a cool dream.

Sea; sand; a sky that melts into the sea – a landscape of misty pastels with a look about it of being continuously on the point of melting. A landscape with all the deliquescent harmonies of Debussy, of the études I played for him, the reverie I'd been playing that afternoon in the salon of the princess where I'd first met him, among the teacups and the little cakes, I, the orphan, hired out of charity to give them their digestive of music.

And, ah! his castle. The faery solitude of the place; with its turrets of misty blue, its courtyard, its spiked gate, his castle that lay on the very bosom of the sea with seabirds mewing about its attics, the casements opening on to the green and purple, evanescent departures of the ocean, cut off by the tide from land for half a day . . . that castle, at home neither on the land nor on the water, a mysterious, amphibious place, contravening the materiality of both earth and the waves, with the melancholy of a mermaiden who perches on her rock and waits, endlessly, for a lover who had drowned far away, long ago. That lovely, sad, sea-siren of a place!

The tide was low; at this hour, so early in the morning, the causeway rose up out of the sea. As the car turned on to the wet cobbles between the slow margins of water, he reached out for my hand that had his sultry, witchy ring on it, pressed my fingers, kissed my palm with extraordinary tenderness. His face was as still as ever I'd seen it, still as a pond iced thickly over, yet his lips, that always looked so strangely red and naked between the black fringes of his beard, now curved a little. He smiled; he welcomed his bride home.

No room, no corridor that did not rustle with the sound of the sea and all the ceilings, the walls on which his ancestors in the stern regalia of rank lined up with their dark eyes and white faces, were stippled with refracted light from the waves which were always in motion; that luminous, murmurous castle of which I was the châtelaine, I, the little music student whose mother had sold all her jewellery, even her wedding ring, to pay the fees at the Conservatoire.

First of all, there was the small ordeal of my initial interview with the housekeeper, who kept this extraordinary machine, this anchored, castellated ocean liner, in smooth running order no matter who stood on the bridge; how tenuous, I thought, might be my authority here! She had a bland, pale, impassive, dislikeable face beneath the impeccably starched white linen headdress of the region. Her greeting, correct but lifeless, chilled me; daydreaming, I dared presume too much on my status . . . briefly wondered how I might install my old nurse, so much loved, however cosily incompetent, in her place. Ill-considered schemings! He told me this one had been his foster mother; was bound to his family in the utmost feudal complicity, 'as much part of the house as I am, my dear'. Now her thin lips offered me a proud little smile. She would be my ally as long as I was his. And with that, I must be content.

But, here, it would be easy to be content. In the turret suite he had given me for my very own, I could gaze out over the tumultuous Atlantic and imagine myself the Queen of the Sea. There was a Bechstein for me in the music room and, on the wall, another wedding present – an early Flemish primitive of St Cecilia at her celestial organ. In the prim charm of this saint, with her plump, sallow cheeks and crinkled brown hair, I saw myself as I could have wished to be. I warmed to a loving sensitivity I had not hitherto suspected in him. Then he led me up a delicate spiral staircase to my bedroom; before she discreetly vanished, the housekeeper set him chuckling with some, I dare say, lewd blessing for newlyweds in her native Breton. That I did not understand. That he, smiling, refused to interpret.

And there lay the grand, hereditary matrimonial bed, itself the size, almost, of my little room at home, with the gargoyles carved on its surfaces of ebony, vermilion lacquer, gold leaf; and its white gauze curtains, billowing in the sea breeze. Our bed. And surrounded by so many mirrors! Mirrors on all the walls, in stately frames of contorted gold, that reflected more white lilies than I'd ever seen in my life before. He'd filled the room with them, to greet the bride, the young bride. The young bride, who had become that multitude of girls I saw in the mirrors, identical in their chic navy-blue tailor-mades, for travelling, *madame*, or walking. A maid had dealt with the furs. Henceforth, a maid would deal with everything.

'See,' he said, gesturing towards those elegant girls. 'I have acquired a whole harem for myself!'

I found that I was trembling. My breath came thickly. I could not meet his eye and turned my head away, out of pride, out of shyness, and watched a dozen husbands approach me in a dozen mirrors and slowly, methodically, teasingly, unfasten the buttons of my jacket and slip it from my shoulders. Enough! No; more! Off comes the skirt; and, next, the blouse of apricot linen that cost more than the dress I had for first communion. The play of the waves outside in the cold sun glittered on his monocle; his movements seemed to me deliberately coarse, vulgar. The blood rushed to my face again, and stayed there.

And yet, you see, I guessed it might be so — that we should have a formal disrobing of the bride, a ritual from the brothel. Sheltered as my life had been, how could I have failed, even in the world of prim bohemia in which I lived, to have heard hints of *his* world?

He stripped me, gourmand that he was, as if he were stripping the leaves off an artichoke — but do not imagine much finesse about it; this artichoke was no particular treat for the diner nor was he yet in any greedy haste. He approached his familiar treat with a weary appetite. And when nothing but my scarlet, palpitating core remained, I saw, in the mirror, the living image of an etching by Rops from the collection he had shown me when our engagement permitted us to be alone together . . . the child with her sticklike limbs, naked but for her button boots, her gloves, shielding her face with her hand as though her face were the last repository of her modesty; and the old, monocled lecher who examined her, limb by limb. He in his London tailoring; she, bare as a lamb chop. Most pornographic of all confrontations. And so my purchaser unwrapped his bargain. And, as at the opera, when I had first seen my flesh in his eyes, I was aghast to feel myself stirring.

At once he closed my legs like a book and I saw again the rare move-ment of his lips that meant he smiled.

Not yet. Later. Anticipation is the greater part of pleasure, my little love.

And I began to shudder, like a racehorse before a race, yet also with a kind of fear, for I felt both a strange, impersonal arousal at the thought of love and at the same time a repugnance I could not stifle for his white, heavy flesh that had too much in common with the armfuls of arum lilies that filled my bedroom in great glass jars, those undertakers' lilies with the heavy pollen that powders your fingers as if you had dipped them in turmeric. The lilies I always associate with him; that are white. And stain you.

This scene from a voluptuary's life was now abruptly terminated. It turns out he has a business to attend to; his estates, his companies – even on your honeymoon? Even then, said the red lips that kissed me before he left me alone with my bewildered senses – a wet, silken brush from his beard; a hint of the pointed tip of the tongue. Disgruntled, I wrapped a négligé of antique lace around me to sip the little breakfast of hot choco-late the maid brought me; after that, since it was second nature to me, there was nowhere to go but the music room and soon I settled down at my piano.

Yet only a series of subtle discords flowed from beneath my fingers: out of tune . . . only a little out of tune; but I'd been blessed with perfect pitch and could not bear to play any more. Sea breezes are bad for pianos; we shall need a resident piano-tuner on the premises if I'm to continue with my studies! I flung down the lid in a little fury of disappointment; what should I do now, how shall I pass the long, sea-lit hours until my husband beds me?

I shivered to think of *that*.

His library seemed the source of his habitual odour of Russian leather. Row upon row of calf-bound volumes, brown and olive, with gilt lettering on their spines, the octavo in brilliant scarlet morocco. A deep-buttoned leather sofa to recline on. A lectern, carved like a spread eagle, that held open upon it an edition of Huysmans's *Là-bas*, from some over-exquisite private press; it had been bound like a missal, in brass, with gems of coloured glass. The rugs on the floor, deep, pulsing blues of heaven and red of the heart's dearest blood, came from Isfahan and Bokhara; the dark panelling gleamed; there was the lulling music of the sea and a fire of apple logs. The flames flickered along the spines inside a glass-fronted case that held books still crisp and new. Eliphas Levy; the name meant nothing to me. I squinted at a title or two: *The Initiation*, *The Key of Mysteries*, *The Secret of Pandora's Box*, and yawned. Nothing, here, to detain a seventeen-year-old girl waiting for her first embrace. I should have liked, best of all, a novel in yellow paper; I wanted to curl up on the rug before the blazing fire, lose myself in a cheap novel, munch sticky liqueur chocolates. If I rang for them, a maid would bring me chocolates.

Nevertheless, I opened the doors of that bookcase idly to browse. And I think I knew, I knew by some tingling of the fingertips, even before I opened that slim volume with no title at all on the spine, what I should find inside it. When he showed me the Rops, newly bought, dearly prized, had he not hinted that he was a connoisseur of such things? Yet I had not bargained for this, the girl with tears hanging on her cheeks like stuck pearls, her cunt a split fig below the great globes of her buttocks on which the knotted tails of the cat were about to descend, while a man in a black mask fingered with his free hand his prick, that curved upwards like the scimitar he held. The picture had a caption: 'Reproof of curiosity'. My mother, with all the precision of her eccentricity, had told me what it was that lovers did; I was innocent but not naïve. *The Adventures of Eulalie at the Harem of the Grand Turk* had been printed, according to the flyleaf, in Amsterdam in 1748, a rare collector's piece. Had some ancestor brought it back himself from that northern city? Or had my husband bought it for himself, from one of those dusty little bookshops on the Left Bank where an old man peers at you through spectacles an inch thick, daring you to inspect his wares . . .? I turned the pages in the anticipation of fear; the print was rusty. Here was another steel engraving: 'Immolation of the wives of the Sultan'. I knew enough for what I saw in that book to make me gasp.

There was a pungent intensification of the odour of leather that suffused his library; his shadow fell across the massacre.

'My little nun has found the prayerbooks, has she?' he demanded, with a curious mixture of mockery and relish; then, seeing my painful, furious bewilderment, he laughed at me aloud, snatched the book from my hands and put it down on the sofa.

'Have the nasty pictures scared Baby? Baby mustn't play with grown-ups' toys until she's learned how to handle them, must she?'

Then he kissed me. And with, this time, no reticence. He kissed me and laid his hand imperatively upon my breast, beneath the sheath of ancient lace. I stumbled on the winding stair that led to the bedroom, to the carved, gilded bed on which he had been conceived. I stammered fool-ishly: We've not taken luncheon yet; and, besides, it is broad daylight . . .

All the better to see you.

He made me put on my choker, the family heirloom of one woman who had escaped the blade. With trembling fingers, I fastened the thing about my neck. It was cold as ice and chilled me. He twined my hair into a rope and lifted it off my shoulders so that he could the better kiss the downy furrows below my ears; that made me shudder. And he kissed those blazing rubies, too. He kissed them before he kissed my mouth. Rapt, he intoned: 'Of her apparel she retains / Only her sonorous jewellery.'

A dozen husbands impaled a dozen brides while the mewing gulls swung on invisible trapezes in the empty air outside.

I was brought to my senses by the insistent shrilling of the telephone. He lay beside me, felled like an oak, breathing stertorously, as if he had been fighting with me. In the course of that one-sided struggle, I had seen his deathly composure shatter like a porcelain vase flung against a wall; I had heard him shriek and blaspheme at the orgasm; I had bled. And perhaps I had seen his face without its mask; and perhaps I had not. Yet I had been infinitely dishevelled by the loss of my virginity.

I gathered myself together, reached into the cloisonné cupboard beside the bed that concealed the telephone and addressed the mouthpiece. His agent in New York. Urgent.

I shook him awake and rolled over on my side, cradling my spent body in my arms. His voice buzzed like a hive of distant bees. My husband. My husband, who, with so much love, filled my bedroom with lilies until it looked like an embalming parlour. Those somnolent lilies, that wave their heavy heads, distributing their lush, insolent incense reminiscent of pam-pered flesh.

When he'd finished with the agent, he turned to me and stroked the ruby necklace that bit into my neck, but with such tenderness now, that I ceased flinching and he caressed my breasts. My dear one, my little love, my child, did it hurt her? He's so sorry for it, such impetuousness, he could not help himself; you see, he loves her so . . . and this lover's recitative of his brought my tears in a flood. I clung to him as though only the one who had inflicted the pain could comfort me for suffering it. For a while, he murmured to me in a voice I'd never heard before, a voice like the soft consolations of the sea. But then he unwound the tendrils of my hair from the buttons of his smoking jacket, kissed my cheek briskly and told me the agent from New York had called with such urgent business that he must leave as soon as the tide was low enough. Leave the castle? Leave France! And would be away for at least six weeks.

'But it is our honeymoon!'

A deal, an enterprise of hazard and chance involving several millions, lay in the balance, he said. He drew away from me into that waxworks stillness of his; I was only a little girl, I did not understand. And, he said unspoken to my wounded vanity, I have had too many honeymoons to find them in the least pressing commitments. I know quite well that this child I've bought with a handful of coloured stones and the pelts of dead beasts won't run away. But, after he'd called his Paris agent to book a passage for the States next day – just one tiny call, my little one – we should have time for dinner together.

And I had to be content with that.

A Mexican dish of pheasant with hazelnuts and chocolate; salad; white, voluptuous cheese; a sorbet of muscat grapes and Asti spumante. A celebration of Krug exploded festively. And then acrid black coffee in precious little cups so fine it shadowed the birds with which they were painted. I had cointreau, he had cognac in the library, with the purple velvet curtains drawn against the night, where he took me to perch on his knee in a leather armchair beside the flickering log fire. He had made me change into that chaste little Poiret shift of white muslin; he seemed especially fond of it, my breasts showed through the flimsy stuff, he said, like little soft white doves that sleep, each one, with a pink eye open. But he would not let me take off my ruby choker, although it was growing very uncomfortable, nor fasten up my descending hair, the sign of a virginity so recently ruptured that still remained a wounded presence between us. He twined his fingers in my hair until I winced; I said I remember, very little.

'The maid will have changed our sheets already,' he said. 'We do not hang the bloody sheets out of the window to prove to the whole of Brittany you are a virgin, not in these civilized times. But I should tell you it would have been the first time in all my married lives I could have shown my interested tenants such a flag.'

Then I realized, with a shock of surprise, how it must have been my innocence that captivated him – the silent music, he said, of my unknowingness, like *La Terrasse des audiences au clair de lune* played upon a piano with keys of ether. You must remember how ill at ease I was in that luxurious place, how unease had been my constant companion during the whole length of my courtship by this grave satyr who now gently martyrized my hair. To know that my naïvety gave him some pleasure made me take heart. Courage! I shall act the fine lady to the manner born one day, if only by virtue of default.

Then, slowly yet teasingly, as if he were giving a child a great, mysterious treat, he took out a bunch of keys from some interior hidey-hole in his jacket – key after key, a key, he said, for every lock in the house. Keys of all kinds – huge, ancient things of black iron; others slender, delicate, almost baroque; wafer-thin Yale keys for safes and boxes. And, during his absence, it was I who must take care of them all.

I eyed the heavy bunch with circumspection. Until that moment, I had not given a single thought to the practical aspects of marriage with a great house, great wealth, a great man, whose key ring was as crowded as that of a prison warder. Here were the clumsy and archaic keys for the dungeons, for dungeons we had in plenty although they had been converted to cellars for his wines; the dusty bottles inhabited in racks all those deep holes of pain in the rock on which the castle was built. These are the keys to the kitchens, this is the key to the picture gallery, a treasure house filled by five centuries of avid collectors – ah! he foresaw I would spend hours there.

He had amply indulged his taste for the Symbolists, he told me with a glint of greed. There was Moreau's great portrait of his first wife, the famous *Sacrificial Victim* with the imprint of the lacelike chains on her pellucid skin. Did I know the story of the painting of that picture? How, when she took off her clothes for him for the first time, she fresh from her bar in Montmartre, she had robed herself involuntarily in a blush that reddened her breasts, her shoulders, her arms, her whole body? He had thought of that story, of that dear girl, when first he had undressed me . . . Ensor, the great Ensor, his monolithic canvas: *The Foolish Virgins.* Two or three late Gauguins, his special favourite the one of the tranced brown girl in the deserted house which was called *Out of the Night We Come, Into the Night We Go.* And, besides the additions he had made himself, his marvellous inheritance of Watteaus, Poussins and a pair of very special Fragonards, commissioned for a licentious ancestor who, it was said, had posed for the master's brush himself with his own two daughters . . . He broke off his catalogue of treasures abruptly.

Your thin white face, *chérie,* he said, as if he saw it for the first time. Your thin white face, with its promise of debauchery only a connoisseur could detect.

A log fell in the fire, instigating a shower of sparks; the opal on my finger spurted green flame. I felt as giddy as if I were on the edge of a precipice; I was afraid, not so much of him, of his monstrous presence, heavy as if he had been gifted at birth with more specific *gravity* than the rest of us, the presence that, even when I thought myself most in love with him, always subtly oppressed me . . . No. I was not afraid of him; but of myself. I seemed reborn in his unreflective eyes, reborn in unfamiliar shapes. I hardly recognized myself from his descriptions of me and yet, and yet – might there not be a grain of beastly truth in them? And, in the red firelight, I blushed again, unnoticed, to think he might have chosen me because, in my innocence, he sensed a rare talent for corruption.

Here is the key to the china cabinet – don't laugh, my darling; there's a king's ransom in Sèvres in that closet, and a queen's ransom in Limoges. And a key to the locked, barred room where five generations of plate were kept.

Keys, keys, keys. He would trust me with the keys to his office, although I was only a baby; and the keys to his safes, where he kept the jewels I should wear, he promised me, when we returned to Paris. Such jewels! Why, I would be able to change my earrings and necklaces three times a day, just as the Empress Josephine used to change her underwear.

He doubted, he said, with that hollow, knocking sound that served him for a chuckle, I would be quite so interested in his share certificates although they, of course, were worth infinitely more.

Outside our firelit privacy, I could hear the sound of the tide drawing back from the pebbles of the foreshore; it was nearly time for him to leave me. One single key remained unaccounted for on the ring and he hesitated over it; for a moment, I thought he was going to unfasten it from its brothers, slip it back into his pocket and take it away with him.

'What is *that* key?' I demanded, for his chaffing had made me bold. 'The key to your heart? Give it me!'

He dangled the key tantalizingly above my head, out of reach of my straining fingers; those bare red lips of his cracked sidelong in a smile.

'Ah, no,' he said. 'Not the key to my heart. Rather, the key to my *enfer*.'

He left it on the ring, fastened the ring together, shook it musically, like a carillon. Then threw the keys in a jingling heap in my lap. I could feel the cold metal chilling my thighs through my thin muslin frock. He bent over me to drop a beard-masked kiss on my forehead.

'Every man must have one secret, even if only one, from his wife,' he said. 'Promise me this, my whey-faced piano-player; promise me you'll use all the keys on the ring except that last little one I showed you. Play with anything you find, jewels, silver plate; make toy boats of my share certificates, if it pleases you, and send them sailing off to America after me. All is yours, everywhere is open to you – except the lock that this single key fits. Yet all it is is the key to a little room at the foot of the west tower, behind the still-room, at the end of a dark little corridor full of horrid cobwebs that would get into your hair and frighten you if you ventured there. Oh, and you'd find it such a dull little room! But you must promise me, if you love me, to leave it well alone. It is only a private study, a hideaway, a 'den', as the English say, where I can go, sometimes, on those infrequent yet inevitable occasions when the yoke of marriage seems to weigh too heavily on my shoulders. There I can go, you understand, to savour the rare pleasure of imagining myself wifeless.'

There was a little thin starlight in the courtyard as, wrapped in my furs, I saw him to his car. His last words were, that he had telephoned the mainland and taken a piano-tuner on to the staff; this man would arrive to take up his duties the next day. He pressed me to his vicuña breast, once, and then drove away.

I had drowsed away that afternoon and now I could not sleep. I lay tossing and turning in his ancestral bed until another daybreak discoloured the dozen mirrors that were iridescent with the reflections of the sea. The perfume of the lilies weighed on my senses; when I thought that, henceforth, I would always share these sheets with a man whose skin, as theirs did, contained that toad-like, clammy hint of moisture, I felt a vague desolation that within me, now my female wound had healed, there had awoken a certain queasy craving like the cravings of pregnant women for the taste of coal or chalk or tainted food, for the renewal of his caresses. Had he not hinted to me, in his flesh as in his speech and looks, of the thousand, thousand baroque intersections of flesh upon flesh? I lay in our wide bed accompanied by a sleepless companion, my dark newborn curiosity.

I lay in bed alone. And I longed for him. And he disgusted me.

Were there jewels enough in all his safes to recompense me for this predicament? Did all that castle hold enough riches to recompense me for the company of the libertine with whom I must share it? And what, precisely, was the nature of my desirous dread for this mysterious being who, to show his mastery over me, had abandoned me on my wedding night?

Then I sat straight up in bed, under the sardonic masks of the gargoyles carved above me, riven by a wild surmise. Might he have left me, not for Wall Street but for an importunate mistress tucked away God knows where who knew how to pleasure him far better than a girl whose fingers had been exercised, hitherto, only by the practice of scales and arpeggios? And, slowly, soothed, I sank back on to the heaping pillows; I acknowledged that the jealous scare I'd just given myself was not unmixed with a little tincture of relief.

At last I drifted into slumber, as daylight filled the room and chased bad dreams away. But the last thing I remembered, before I slept, was the tall jar of lilies beside the bed, how the thick glass distorted their fat stems so they looked like arms, dismembered arms, drifting drowned in greenish water.

Coffee and croissants to console this bridal, solitary waking. Delicious.

Honey, too, in a section of comb on a glass saucer. The maid squeezed the aromatic juice from an orange into a chilled goblet while I watched her as I lay in the lazy, midday bed of the rich. Yet nothing, this morning, gave me more than a fleeting pleasure except to hear that the piano-tuner had been at work already. When the maid told me that, I sprang out of bed and pulled on my old serge skirt and flannel blouse, costume of a student, in which I felt far more at ease with myself than in any of my fine new clothes.

After my three hours of practice, I called the piano-tuner in, to thank him. He was blind, of course; but young, with a gentle mouth and grey eyes that fixed upon me although they could not see me. He was a blacksmith's son from the village across the causeway; a chorister in the church whom the good priest had taught a trade so that he could make a living. All most satisfactory. Yes. He thought he would be happy here. And if, he added shyly, he might sometimes be allowed to hear me play . . . for, you see, he loved music. Yes. Of course, I said. Certainly. He seemed to know that I had smiled.

After I dismissed him, even though I'd woken so late, it was still barely time for my 'five o'clock'. The housekeeper, who, thoughtfully forewarned by my husband, had restrained herself from interrupting my music, now made me a solemn visitation with a lengthy menu for a late luncheon. When I told her I did not need it, she looked at me obliquely, along her nose. I understood at once that one of my principal functions as châtelaine was to provide work for the staff. But, all the same, I asserted myself and said I would wait until dinner-time, although I looked forward nervously to the solitary meal. Then I found I had to tell her what I would like to have prepared for me; my imagination, still that of a schoolgirl, ran riot. A fowl in cream – or should I anticipate Christmas with a varnished turkey? No; I have decided. Avocado and shrimp, lots of it, followed by no entrée at all. But surprise me for dessert with every ice-cream in the ice-box. She noted all down but sniffed; I'd shocked her. Such tastes! Child that I was, I giggled when she left me.

But, now . . . what shall I do, now?

I could have spent a happy hour unpacking the trunks that contained my trousseau but the maid had done that already, the dresses, the tailor-mades hung in the wardrobe in my dressing-room, the hats on wooden heads to keep their shape, the shoes on wooden feet as if all these inanimate objects were imitating the appearance of life, to mock me. I did not like to linger in my overcrowded dressing-room, nor in my lugubriously lily-scented bedroom. How shall I pass the time?

I shall take a bath in my own bathroom! And found the taps were little dolphins made of gold, with chips of turquoise for eyes. And there was a tank of goldfish, who swam in and out of moving fronds of weeds, as bored, I thought, as I was. How I wished he had not left me. How I wished it were possible to chat with, say, a maid; or, the piano-tuner . . . but I knew already my new rank forbade overtures of friendship to the staff.

I had been hoping to defer the call as long as I could, so that I should have something to look forward to in the dead waste of time I foresaw before me, after my dinner was done with, but, at a quarter before seven, when darkness already surrounded the castle, I could contain myself no longer. I telephoned my mother. And astonished myself by bursting into tears when I heard her voice.

No, nothing was the matter. Mother, I have gold bath taps.

I said, gold bath taps!

No; I suppose that's nothing to cry about, Mother.

The line was bad, I could hardly make out her congratulations, her questions, her concern, but I was a little comforted when I put the receiver down.

Yet there still remained one whole hour to dinner and the whole, unimaginable desert of the rest of the evening.

The bunch of keys lay, where he had left them, on the rug before the library fire which had warmed their metal so that they no longer felt cold to the touch but warm, almost, as my own skin. How careless I was; a maid, tending the logs, eyed me reproachfully as if I'd set a trap for her as I picked up the clinking bundle of keys, the keys to the interior doors of this lovely prison of which I was both the inmate and the mistress and had scarcely seen. When I remembered that, I felt the exhilaration of the explorer.

Lights! More lights!

At the touch of a switch, the dreaming library was brilliantly illuminated. I ran crazily about the castle, switching on every light I could find – I ordered the servants to light up all their quarters, too, so the castle would shine like a seaborne birthday cake lit with a thousand candles, one for every year of its life, and everybody on shore would wonder at it. When everything was lit as brightly as the café in the Gare du Nord, the significance of the possessions implied by that bunch of keys no longer intimidated me, for I was determined, now, to search through them all for evidence of my husband's true nature.

His office first, evidently.

A mahogany desk half a mile wide, with an impeccable blotter and a bank of telephones. I allowed myself the luxury of opening the safe that contained the jewellery and delved sufficiently among the leather boxes to find out how my marriage had given me access to a jinn's treasury – parures, bracelets, rings . . . While I was thus surrounded by diamonds, a maid knocked on the door and entered before I spoke; a subtle discourtesy. I would speak to my husband about it. She eyed my serge skirt superciliously; did *madame* plan to dress for dinner?

She made a moue of disdain when I laughed to hear that, she was far more the lady than I. But, imagine – to dress up in one of my Poiret extravaganzas, with the jewelled turban and aigrette on my head, roped with pearl to the navel, to sit down all alone in the baronial dining-hall at the head of that massive board at which King Mark was reputed to have fed his knights . . . I grew calmer under the cold eye of her disapproval. I adopted the crisp inflections of an officer's daughter. No, I would not dress for dinner. Furthermore, I was not hungry enough for dinner itself. She must tell the housekeeper to cancel the dormitory feast I'd ordered. Could they leave me sandwiches and a flask of coffee in my music room? And would they all dismiss for the night?

*Mais oui, madame.*

I knew by her bereft intonation I had let them down again but I did not care; I was armed against them by the brilliance of his hoard. But I could not find his heart amongst the glittering stones; as soon as she had gone, I began a systematic search of the drawers of his desk.

All was in order, so I found nothing. Not a random doodle on an old envelope, nor the faded photograph of a woman. Only the files of business correspondence, the bills from the home farms, the invoices from tailors, the billets-doux from international financiers. Nothing. And this absence of the evidence of his real life began to impress me strangely;

there must, I thought, be a great deal to conceal if he takes such pains to hide it.

His office was a singularly impersonal room, facing inwards, on to the courtyard, as though he wanted to turn his back on the siren sea in order to keep a clear head while he bankrupted a small businessman in Amsterdam or – I noticed with a thrill of distaste – engaged in some business in Laos that must, from certain cryptic references to his amateur botanist's enthusiasm for rare poppies, be to do with opium. Was he not rich enough to do without crime? Or was the crime itself his profit? And yet I saw enough to appreciate his zeal for secrecy.

Now I had ransacked his desk, I must spend a cool-headed quarter of an hour putting every last letter back where I had found it, and, as I covered the traces of my visit, by some chance, as I reached inside a little drawer that had stuck fast, I must have touched a hidden spring, for a secret drawer flew open within that drawer itself; and this secret drawer contained – at last! – a file marked: *Personal.*

I was alone, but for my reflection in the uncurtained window.

I had the brief notion that his heart, pressed flat as a flower, crimson and thin as tissue paper, lay in this file. It was a very thin one.

I could have wished, perhaps, I had not found that touching, ill-spelt note, on a paper napkin marked *La Coupole*, that began: 'My darling, I cannot wait for the moment when you may make me yours completely.' The diva had sent him a page of the score of *Tristan*, the *Liebestod*, with the single, cryptic word: 'Until . . .' scrawled across it. But the strangest of all these love letters was a postcard with a view of a village graveyard, among mountains, where some black-coated ghoul enthusiastically dug at a grave; this little scene, executed with the lurid exuberance of Grand Guignol, was captioned: 'Typical Transylvanian Scene – Midnight, All Hallows'. And, on the other side, the message: 'On the occasion of this marriage to the descendant of Dracula – always remember, "the supreme and unique pleasure of love is the certainty that one is doing evil." *Toutes amitiés*, C.'

A joke. A joke in the worst possible taste; for had he not been married to a Romanian countess? And then I remembered her pretty, witty face, and her name – Carmilla. My most recent predecessor in this castle had been, it would seem, the most sophisticated.

I put away the file, sobered. Nothing in my life of family love and music had prepared me for these grown-up games and yet these were clues to his self that showed me, at least, how much he had been loved, even if they did not reveal any good reason for it. But I wanted to know still more; and, as I closed the office door and locked it, the means to discover more fell in my way.

Fell, indeed; and with the clatter of a dropped canteen of cutlery, for, as I turned the slick Yale lock, I contrived, somehow, to open up the key ring itself, so that all the keys tumbled loose on the floor. And the very first key I picked out of the pile was, as luck or ill fortune had it, the key to the room he had forbidden me, the room he would keep for his own so that he could go there when he wished to feel himself once more a bachelor.

I made my decision to explore it before I felt a faint resurgence of my ill-defined fear of his waxen stillness. Perhaps I half-imagined, then, that I might find his real self in his den, waiting there to see if indeed I had obeyed him; that he had sent a moving figure of himself to New York, the enigmatic, self-sustaining carapace of his public person, while the real man, whose face I had glimpsed in the storm of orgasm, occupied himself with pressing private business in the study at the foot of the west tower, behind the still-room. Yet, if that were so, it was imperative that I should find him, should know him; and I was too deluded by his apparent taste for me to think my disobedience might truly offend him.

I took the forbidden key from the heap and left the others lying there.

It was now very late and the castle was adrift, as far as it could go from the land, in the middle of the silent ocean where, at my orders, it floated, like a garland of light. And all silent, all still, but for the murmuring of the waves.

I felt no fear, no intimation of dread. Now I walked as firmly as I had done in my mother's house.

Not a narrow, dusty little passage at all; why had he lied to me? But an ill-lit one, certainly; the electricity, for some reason, did not extend here, so I retreated to the still-room and found a bundle of waxed tapers in a cupboard, stored there with matches to light the oak board at grand dinners. I put a match to my little taper and advanced with it in my hand, like a penitent along the corridor hung with heavy, I think Venetian, tapestries. The flame picked out, here, the head of a man, there, the ripe breast of a woman spilling through a rent in her dress – the Rape of the Sabines, perhaps? The naked swords and immolated horses suggested some grisly mythological subject. The corridor wound downwards; there was an almost imperceptible ramp to the thickly carpeted floor. The heavy hangings on the wall muffled my footsteps, even my breathing. For some reason, it grew very warm; the sweat sprang out in beads on my brow. I could no longer hear the sound of the sea.

A long, a winding corridor, as if I were in the viscera of the castle; and this corridor led to a door of worm-eaten oak, low, round-topped, barred with black iron.

And still I felt no fear, no raising of the hairs on the back of the neck, no pricking of the thumbs.

The key slid into the new lock as easily as a hot knife into butter.

No fear; but a hesitation, a holding of the spiritual breath.

If I had found some traces of his heart in a file marked: *Personal*, perhaps, here, in his subterranean privacy, I might find a little of his soul. It was the consciousness of the possibility of such a discovery, of its possible strangeness, that kept me for a moment motionless, before, in the foolhardiness of my already subtly tainted innocence, I turned the key and the door creaked slowly back.

'There is a striking resemblance between the act of love and the ministrations of a torturer,' opined my husband's favourite poet; I had learned something of the nature of that similarity on my marriage bed. And now my taper showed me the outlines of a rack. There was also a great wheel, like the ones I had seen in woodcuts of the martyrdoms of the saints, in my old nurse's little store of holy books. And – just one glimpse of it before my little flame caved in and I was left in absolute darkness – a metal figure, hinged at the side, which I knew to be spiked on the inside and to have the name: the Iron Maiden.

Absolute darkness. And, about me, the instruments of mutilation.

Until that moment, this spoiled child did not know she had inherited nerves and a will from the mother who had defied the yellow outlaws of Indo-China. My mother's spirit drove me on, into that dreadful place, in a cold ecstasy to know the very worst. I fumbled for the matches in my pocket; what a dim, lugubrious light they gave! And yet, enough, oh, more than enough, to see a room designed for desecration and some dark night of unimaginable lovers whose embraces were annihilation.

The walls of this stark torture chamber were the naked rock; they gleamed as if they were sweating with fright. At the four corners of the room were funerary urns, of great antiquity, Etruscan, perhaps, and, on three-legged ebony stands, the bowls of incense he had left burning which filled the room with a sacerdotal reek. Wheel, rack and Iron Maiden were, I saw, displayed as grandly as if they were items of statuary and I was almost consoled, then, and almost persuaded myself that I might have stumbled only upon a little museum of his perversity, that he had installed these monstrous items here only for contemplation.

Yet at the centre of the room lay a catafalque, a doomed ominous bier of Renaissance workmanship, surrounded by long white candles and, at its foot, an armful of the same lilies with which he had filled my bedroom, stowed in a four-foot-high jar glazed with a sombre Chinese red. I scarcely dared examine this catafalque and its occupant more closely; yet I knew I must.

Each time I struck a match to light those candles round her bed, it seemed a garment of that innocence of mine for which he had lusted fell away from me.

The opera singer lay, quite naked, under a thin sheet of very rare and precious linen, such as the princes of Italy used to shroud those whom they had poisoned. I touched her, very gently, on the white breast; she was cool, he had embalmed her. On her throat I could see the blue imprint of his strangler's fingers. The cool, sad flame of the candles flickered on her white, closed eyelids. The worst thing was, the dead lips smiled.

Beyond the catafalque, in the middle of the shadows, a white, nacreous glimmer; as my eyes accustomed themselves to the gathering darkness, I at last – oh, horrors! – made out a skull; yes, a skull, so utterly denuded, now, of flesh, that it scarcely seemed possible the stark bone had once been richly upholstered with life. And this skull was strung up by a system of unseen cords, so that it appeared to hang, disembodied, in the still, heavy air, and it had been crowned with a wreath of white roses, and a veil of lace, the final image of his bride.

Yet the skull was still so beautiful, had shaped with its sheer planes so imperiously the face that had once existed above it, that I recognized her the moment I saw her; face of the evening star walking on the rim of night. One false step, oh, my poor, dear girl, next in the fated sisterhood of his wives; one false step and into the abyss of the dark you stumbled.

And where was she, the latest dead, the Romanian countess who might have thought her blood would survive his depredations? I knew she must be here, in the place that had wound me through the castle towards it on a spool of inexorability. But, at first, I could see no sign of her. Then, for some reason – perhaps some change of atmosphere wrought by my presence – the metal shell of the Iron Maiden emitted a ghostly twang; my feverish imagination might have guessed its occupant was trying to clamber out, though, even in the midst of my rising hysteria, I knew she must be dead to find a home there.

With trembling fingers, I prised open the front of the upright coffin, with its sculpted face caught in a rictus of pain. Then, overcome, I dropped the key I still held in my other hand. It dropped into the forming pool of her blood.

She was pierced, not by one but by a hundred spikes, this child of the land of the vampires who seemed so newly dead, so full of blood . . . oh God! how recently had he become a widower? How long had he kept her in this obscene cell? Had it been all the time he had courted me, in the clear light of Paris?

I closed the lid of her coffin very gently and burst into a tumult of sobbing that contained both pity for his other victims and also a dreadful anguish to know I, too, was one of them.

The candles flared, as if in a draught from a door to elsewhere. The light caught the fire opal on my hand so that it flashed, once, with a baleful light, as if to tell me the eye of God – his eye – was upon me. My first thought, when I saw the ring for which I had sold myself to this fate, was how to escape it.

I retained sufficient presence of mind to snuff out the candles round the bier with my fingers, to gather up my taper, to look around, although shuddering, to ensure I had left behind me no traces of my visit.

I retrieved the key from the pool of blood, wrapped it in my handkerchief to keep my hands clean, and fled the room, slamming the door behind me.

It crashed to with a juddering reverberation, like the door of hell.

*

I could not take refuge in my bedroom, for that retained the memory of his presence trapped in the fathomless silvering of his mirrors. My music room seemed the safest place, although I looked at the picture of St Cecilia with a faint dread; what had been the nature of her martyrdom? My mind was in a tumult; schemes for flight jostled with one another . . . as soon as the tide receded from the causeway, I would make for the mainland – on foot, running, stumbling; I did not trust that leather-clad chauffeur, nor the well-behaved housekeeper, and I dared not take any of the pale, ghostly maids into my confidence, either, since they were his creatures, all. Once at the village, I would fling myself directly on the mercy of the *gendarmerie*.

But – could I trust them, either? His forefathers had ruled this coast for eight centuries, from this castle whose moat was the Atlantic. Might not the police, the advocates, even the judge, all be in his service, turning a common blind eye to his vices since he was *milord* whose word must be obeyed? Who, on this distant coast, would believe the white-faced girl from Paris who came running to them with a shuddering tale of blood, of fear, of the ogre murmuring in the shadows? Or, rather, they would immediately know it to be true. But were all honour-bound to let me carry it no further.

Assistance. My mother. I ran to the telephone; and the line, of course, was dead.

Dead as his wives.

A thick darkness, unlit by any star, still glazed the windows. Every lamp in my room burned, to keep the dark outside, yet it seemed still to encroach on me, to be present beside me but as if masked by my lights, the night like a permeable substance that could seep into my skin. I looked at the precious little clock made from hypocritically innocent flowers long ago, in Dresden; the hands had scarcely moved one single hour forward from when I first descended to that private slaughterhouse of his. Time was his servant, too; it would trap me, here, in a night that would last until he came back to me, like a black sun on a hopeless morning.

And yet the time might still be my friend; at that hour, that very hour, he set sail for New York.

To know that, in a few moments, my husband would have left France calmed my agitation a little. My reason told me I had nothing to fear; the tide that would take him away to the New World would let me out of the imprisonment of the castle. Surely I could easily evade the servants. Anybody can buy a ticket at a railway station. Yet I was still filled with unease. I opened the lid of the piano; perhaps I thought my own particular magic might help me, now, that I could create a pentacle out of music that would keep me from harm for, if my music had first ensnared him, then might it not also give me the power to free myself from him?

Mechanically, I began to play but my fingers were stiff and shaking. At first, I could manage nothing better than the exercises of Czerny but simply the act of playing soothed me and, for solace, for the sake of the harmonious rationality of its sublime mathematics, I searched among his scores until I found *The Well-Tempered Clavier*. I set myself the therapeutic task of playing all Bach's equations, every one, and, I told myself, if I played them all through without a single mistake – then the morning would find me once more a virgin.

Crash of a dropped stick.

His silver-headed cane! What else? Sly, cunning, he had returned; he was waiting for me outside the door!

I rose to my feet; fear gave me strength. I flung back my head defiantly.

'Come in!' My voice astonished me by its firmness, its clarity.

The door slowly, nervously opened and I saw, not the massive, irredeemable bulk of my husband but the slight, stooping figure of the piano-tuner, and he looked far more terrified of me than my mother's daughter would have been of the Devil himself. In the torture chamber, it seemed to me that I would never laugh again; now, helplessly, laugh I did, with relief, and, after a moment's hesitation, the boy's face softened and he smiled a little, almost in shame. Though they were blind, his eyes were singularly sweet.

'Forgive me,' said Jean-Yves. 'I know I've given you grounds for dismissing me, that I should be crouching outside your door at midnight . . . but I heard you walking about, up and down – I sleep in a room at the foot of the west tower – and some intuition told me you could not sleep and might, perhaps, pass the insomniac hours at your piano. And I could not resist that. Besides, I stumbled over these –'

And he displayed the ring of keys I'd dropped outside my husband's office door, the ring from which one key was missing. I took them from him, looked round for a place to stow them, fixed on the piano stool as if to hide them would protect me. Still he stood smiling at me. How hard it was to make everyday conversation.

'It's perfect,' I said. 'The piano. Perfectly in tune.'

But he was full of the loquacity of embarrassment, as though I would only forgive him for his impudence if he explained the cause of it thoroughly.

'When I heard you play this afternoon, I thought I'd never heard such a touch. Such technique. A treat for me, to hear a virtuoso! So I crept up to your door now, humbly as a little dog might, *madame*, and put my ear to the keyhole and listened, and listened – until my stick fell to the floor through a momentary clumsiness of mine, and I was discovered.'

He had the most touchingly ingenuous smile.

'Perfectly in tune,' I repeated. To my surprise, now I had said it, I found I could not say anything else. I could only repeat: 'In tune . . . perfect . . . in tune,' over and over again. I saw a dawning surprise in his face. My head throbbed. To see him, in his lovely, blind humanity, seemed to hurt me very piercingly, somewhere inside my breast; his figure blurred, the room swayed about me. After the dreadful revelation of that bloody chamber, it was his tender look that made me faint.

When I recovered consciousness, I found I was lying in the piano-tuner's arms and he was tucking the satin cushion from the piano-stool under my head.

'You are in some great distress,' he said. 'No bride should suffer so much, so early in her marriage.'

His speech had the rhythms of the countryside, the rhythms of the tides.

'Any bride brought to this castle should come ready dressed in mourning, should bring a priest and a coffin with her,' I said.

'What's this?'

It was too late to keep silent; and if he, too, were one of my husband's creatures, then at least he had been kind to me. So I told him everything, the keys, the interdiction, my disobedience, the room, the rack, the skull, the corpses, the blood.

'I can scarcely believe it,' he said, wondering. 'That man . . . so rich; so well born.'

'Here's proof,' I said and tumbled the fatal key out of my handkerchief on to the silken rug.

'Oh God,' he said. 'I can smell the blood.'

He took my hand; he pressed his arms about me. Although he was scarcely more than a boy, I felt a great strength flow into me from his touch.

'We whisper all manner of strange tales up and down the coast,' he said. 'There was a *marquis*, once, who used to hunt young girls on the mainland; he hunted them with dogs, as though they were foxes. My grandfather had it from his grandfather, how the *marquis* pulled a head out of his saddle bag and showed it to the blacksmith while the man was shoeing his horse. "A fine specimen of the genus brunette, eh, Guillaume?" And it was the head of the blacksmith's wife.'

But, in these more democratic times, my husband must travel as far as Paris to do his hunting in the salons. Jean-Yves knew the moment I shuddered.

'Oh, *madame*! I thought all these were old wives' tales, chattering of fools, spooks to scare bad children into good behaviour! Yet how could you know, a stranger, that the old name for this place is the Castle of Murder?'

How could I know, indeed? Except that, in my heart, I'd always known its lord would be the death of me.

'Hark!' said my friend suddenly. 'The sea has changed key; it must be near morning, the tide is going down.'

He helped me up. I looked from the window, towards the mainland, along the causeway where the stones gleamed wetly in the thin light of the end of the night and, with an almost unimaginable horror, a horror the intensity of which I cannot transmit to you, I saw, in the distance, still far away yet drawing moment by moment inexorably nearer, the twin headlamps of his great black car, gouging tunnels through the shifting mist.

My husband had indeed returned; this time, it was no fancy.

'The key!' said Jean-Yves. 'It must go back on the ring, with the others. As though nothing had happened.'

But the key was still caked with wet blood and I ran to my bathroom and held it under the hot tap. Crimson water swirled down the basin but, as if the key itself were hurt, the bloody token stuck. The turquoise eyes of the dolphin taps winked at me derisively; they knew my husband had been too clever for me! I scrubbed the stain with my nail brush but still it would not budge. I thought how the car would be rolling silently towards the closed courtyard gate; the more I scrubbed the key, the more vivid grew the stain.

The bell in the gatehouse would jangle. The porter's drowsy son would push back the patchwork quilt, yawning, pull the shirt over his head, thrust his feet into his sabots . . . slowly, slowly; open the door for your master as slowly as you can . . .

And still the bloodstain mocked the fresh water that spilled from the mouth of the leering dolphin.

'You have no more time,' said Jean-Yves. 'He is here. I know it. I must stay with you.'

'You shall not!' I said. 'Go back to your room, now. Please.'

He hesitated. I put an edge of steel in my voice, for I knew I must meet my lord alone.

'Leave me!'

As soon as he had gone, I dealt with the keys and went to my bedroom. The causeway was empty; Jean-Yves was correct, my husband had already entered the castle. I pulled the curtains close, stripped off my clothes and pulled the bedcurtains round me as a pungent aroma of Russian leather assured me my husband was once again beside me.

'Dearest!'

With the most treacherous, lascivious tenderness, he kissed my eyes, and, mimicking the new bride newly wakened, I flung my arms around him, for on my seeming acquiescence depended my salvation.

'Da Silva of Rio outwitted me,' he said wryly. 'My New York agent telegraphed Le Havre and saved me a wasted journey. So we may resume our interrupted pleasures, my love.'

I did not believe one word of it. I knew I had behaved exactly according to his desires; had he not bought me so that I should do so? I had been tricked into my own betrayal to that illimitable darkness whose source I had been compelled to seek in his absence and, now that I had met that shadowed reality of his that came to life only in the presence of its own atrocities, I must pay the price of my new knowledge. The secret of Pandora's box; but he had given me the box, himself, knowing I must learn the secret. I had played a game in which every move was governed by a destiny as oppressive and omnipotent as himself, since that destiny was himself; and I had lost. Lost at that charade of innocence and vice in which he had engaged me. Lost, as the victim loses to the executioner.

His hand brushed my breast, beneath the sheet. I strained my nerves yet could not help but flinch from the intimate touch, for it made me think of the piercing embrace of the Iron Maiden and of his lost lovers in the vault. When he saw my reluctance, his eyes veiled over and yet his appetite did not diminish. His tongue ran over red lips already wet. Silent, mysterious, he moved away from me to draw off his jacket. He took the gold watch from his waistcoat and laid it on the dressing table, like a good bourgeois; scooped out his rattling loose change and now – Oh God! – makes a great play of patting his pockets officiously, puzzled lips pursed, searching for something that has been mislaid. Then turns to me with a ghastly, a triumphant smile.

'But of course! I gave the keys to you!'

'Your keys? Why, of course. Here, they're under the pillow; wait a moment – what – Ah! No . . . now, where can I have left them? I was whiling away the evening without you at the piano, I remember. Of course! The music room!'

Brusquely he flung my négligé of antique lace on the bed.

'Go and get them.'

'Now? This moment? Can't it wait until morning, my darling?'

I forced myself to be seductive. I saw myself, pale, pliant as a plant that begs to be trampled underfoot, a dozen vulnerable, appealing girls reflected in as many mirrors, and I saw how he almost failed to resist me. If he had come to me in bed, I would have strangled him, then.

But he half-snarled: 'No. It won't wait. Now.'

The unearthly light of dawn filled the room; had only one previous dawn broken upon me in that vile place? And there was nothing for it but to go and fetch the keys from the music stool and pray he would not examine them too closely, pray to God his eyes would fail him, that he might be struck blind.

When I came back into the bedroom carrying the bunch of keys that jangled at every step like a curious musical instrument, he was sitting on the bed in his immaculate shirtsleeves, his head sunk in his hands.

And it seemed to me he was in despair.

Strange. In spite of my fear of him, that made me whiter than my wrap, I felt there emanate from him, at that moment, a stench of absolute despair, rank and ghastly, as if the lilies that surrounded him had all at once begun to fester, or the Russian leather of his scent were reverting to the elements of flayed hide and excrement of which it was composed. The chthonic gravity of his presence exerted a tremendous pressure on the room, so that the blood pounded in my ears as if we had been precipitated to the bottom of the sea, beneath the waves that pounded against the shore.

I held my life in my hands amongst those keys and, in a moment, would place it between his well-manicured fingers. The evidence of that bloody chamber had showed me I could expect no mercy. Yet, when he raised his head and stared at me with his blind, shuttered eyes as though he did not recognize me, I felt a terrified pity for him, for this man who lived in such strange, secret places that, if I loved him enough to follow him, I should have to die.

The atrocious loneliness of that monster!

The monocle had fallen from his face. His curling mane was disordered, as if he had run his hands through it in his distraction. I saw how he had lost his impassivity and was now filled with suppressed excitement. The hand he stretched out for those counters in his game of love and death shook a little; the face that turned towards me contained a sombre delirium that seemed to me compounded of a ghastly, yes, shame but also of a terrible, guilty joy as he slowly ascertained how I had sinned.

That tell-tale stain had resolved itself into a mark the shape and brilliance of the heart on a playing card. He disengaged the key from the ring and looked at it for a while, solitary, brooding.

'It is the key that leads to the kingdom of the unimaginable,' he said. His voice was low and had in it the timbre of certain great cathedral organs that seem, when they are played, to be conversing with God.

I could not restrain a sob.

'Oh, my love, my little love who brought me a white gift of music,' he said, almost as if grieving. 'My little love, you'll never know how much I hate daylight!'

Then he sharply ordered: 'Kneel!'

I knelt before him and he pressed the key lightly to my forehead, held it there for a moment. I felt a faint tingling of the skin and, when I involuntarily glanced at myself in the mirror, I saw the heart-shaped stain had transferred itself to my forehead, to the space between the eyebrows, like the caste mark of a Brahmin woman. Or the mark of Cain. And now the key gleamed as freshly as if it had just been cut. He clipped it back on the ring, emitting that same, heavy sigh as he had done when I said that I would marry him.

'My virgin of the arpeggios, prepare yourself for martyrdom.'

'What form shall it take?' I said.

'Decapitation,' he whispered, almost voluptuously. 'Go and bathe yourself; put on that white dress you wore to hear *Tristan* and the necklace that prefigures your end. And I shall take myself off to the armoury, my dear, to sharpen my great-grandfather's ceremonial sword.'

'The servants?'

'We shall have absolute privacy for our last rites; I have already dismissed them. If you look out of the window you can see them going to the mainland.'

It was now the full, pale light of morning; the weather was grey, indeterminate, the sea had an oily, sinister look, a gloomy day on which to die. Along the causeway I could see trooping every maid and scullion, every pot-boy and pan-scourer, valet, laundress and vassal who worked in that great house, most on foot, a few on bicycles. The faceless housekeeper trudged along with a great basket in which, I guessed, she'd stowed as much as she could ransack from the larder. The *marquis* must have given the chauffeur leave to borrow the motor for the day, for it went last of all, at a stately pace, as though the procession were a cortège and the car already bore my coffin to the mainland for burial.

But I knew no good Breton earth would cover me, like a last, faithful lover; I had another fate.

'I have given them all a day's holiday, to celebrate our wedding,' he said. And smiled.

However hard I stared at the receding company, I could see no sign of Jean-Yves, our latest servant, hired but the preceding morning.

'Go, now. Bathe yourself; dress yourself. The lustratory ritual and the ceremonial robing; after that, the sacrifice. Wait in the music room until I telephone for you. No, my dear!' And he smiled, as I started, recalling the line was dead. 'One may call inside the castle just as much as one pleases; but, outside – never.'

I scrubbed my forehead with the nail brush as I had scrubbed the key but this red mark would not go away, either, no matter what I did, and I knew I should wear it until I died, though that would not be long. Then I went to my dressing-room and put on that white muslin shift, costume of a victim of an auto-da-fé, he had bought me to listen to the *Liebestod* in. Twelve young women combed out twelve listless sheaves of brown hair in the mirrors; soon, there would be none. The mass of lilies that surrounded me exhaled, now, the odour of their withering. They looked like the trumpets of the angels of death.

On the dressing table, coiled like a snake about to strike, lay the ruby choker.

Already almost lifeless, cold at heart, I descended the spiral staircase to the music room but there I found I had not been abandoned.

'I can be of some comfort to you,' the boy said. 'Though not much use.'

We pushed the piano stool in front of the open window so that, for as long as I could, I would be able to smell the ancient, reconciling smell of the sea that, in time, will cleanse everything, scour the old bones white, wash away all the stains. The last little chambermaid had trotted along the causeway long ago and now the tide, fated as I, came tumbling in, the crisp wavelets splashing on the old stones.

'You do not deserve this,' he said.

'Who can say what I deserve or no?' I said. 'I've done nothing; but that may be sufficient reason for condemning me.'

'You disobeyed him,' he said. 'That is sufficient reason for him to punish you.'

'I only did what he knew I would.'

'Like Eve,' he said.

The telephone rang a shrill imperative. Let it ring. But my lover lifted

me up and set me on my feet; I knew I must answer it. The receiver felt
heavy as earth.

'The courtyard. Immediately.'

My lover kissed me, he took my hand. He would come with me if I
would lead him. Courage. When I thought of courage, I thought of my
mother. Then I saw a muscle in my lover's face quiver.

'Hoofbeats!' he said.

I cast one last, desperate glance from the window and, like a miracle, I
saw a horse and rider galloping at a vertiginous speed along the causeway,
though the waves crashed, now, high as the horse's fetlocks. A rider, her
black skirts tucked up around her waist so she could ride hard and fast, a
crazy, magnificent horsewoman in widow's weeds.

As the telephone rang again.

'Am I to wait all morning?'

Every moment, my mother drew nearer.

'She will be too late,' Jean-Yves said and yet he could not restrain a note
of hope that, though it must be so, yet it might not be so.

The third, intransigent call.

'Shall I come up to heaven to fetch you down, St Cecilia? You wicked
woman, do you wish me to compound my crimes by desecrating the
marriage bed?'

So I must go to the courtyard where my husband waited in his London-
tailored trousers and the shirt from Turnbull and Asser, beside the
mounting block, with, in his hand, the sword which his great-grandfather
had presented to the little corporal, in token of surrender to the Republic,
before he shot himself. The heavy sword, unsheathed, grey as that November morning, sharp as childbirth, mortal.

When my husband saw my companion, he observed: 'Let the blind lead
the blind, eh? But does even a youth as besotted as you are think she was
truly blind to her own desires when she took my ring? Give it me back,
whore.'

The fires in the opal had all died down. I gladly slipped it from my
finger and, even in that dolorous place, my heart was lighter for the lack
of it. My husband took it lovingly and lodged it on the tip of his little
finger; it would go no further.

'It will serve me for a dozen more fiancées,' he said. 'To the block, woman. No – leave the boy; I shall deal with him later, utilizing a less exalted instrument than the one with which I do my wife the honour of her immolation, for do not fear that in death you will be divided.'

Slowly, slowly, one foot before the other, I crossed the cobbles. The longer I dawdled over my execution, the more time it gave the avenging angel to descend . . .

'Don't loiter, girl! Do you think I shall lose appetite for the meal if you are so long about serving it? No; I shall grow hungrier, more ravenous with each moment, more cruel . . . Run to me, run! I have a place prepared for your exquisite corpse in my display of flesh!'

He raised the sword and cut bright segments from the air with it, but still I lingered although my hopes, so recently raised, now began to flag. If she is not here by now, her horse must have stumbled on the causeway, have plunged into the sea . . . One thing only made me glad; that my lover would not see me die.

My husband laid my branded forehead on the stone and, as he had done once before, twisted my hair into a rope and drew it away from my neck.

'Such a pretty neck,' he said with what seemed to be a genuine, retrospective tenderness. 'A neck like the stem of a young plant.'

I felt the silken bristle of his beard and the wet touch of his lips as he kissed my nape. And, once again, of my apparel I must retain only my gems; the sharp blade ripped my dress in two and it fell from me. A little green moss, growing in the crevices of the mounting block, would be the last thing I should see in all the world.

The whizz of that heavy sword.

And – a great battering and pounding at the gate, the jangling of the bell, the frenzied neighing of a horse! The unholy silence of the place shattered in an instant. The blade did *not* descend, the necklace did *not* sever, my head did *not* roll. For, for an instant, the beast wavered in his stroke, a sufficient split second of astonished indecision to let me spring upright and dart to the assistance of my lover as he struggled sightlessly with the great bolts that kept her out.

The *marquis* stood transfixed, utterly dazed, at a loss. It must have been as if he had been watching his beloved *Tristan* for the twelfth, the thirteenth time and Tristan stirred, then leapt from his bier in the last act, announced in a jaunty aria interposed from Verdi that bygones were by-gones, crying over spilt milk did nobody any good and, as for himself, he proposed to live happily ever after. The puppet master, open-mouthed, wide-eyed, impotent at the last, saw his dolls break free of their strings, abandon the rituals he had ordained for them since time began and start to live for themselves; the king, aghast, witnesses the revolt of his pawns.

You never saw such a wild thing as my mother, her hat seized by the winds and blown out to sea so that her hair was her white mane, her black lisle legs exposed to the thigh, her skirts tucked round her waist, one hand on the reins of the rearing horse while the other clasped my father's service revolver and, behind her, the breakers of the savage, indifferent sea, like the witnesses of a furious justice. And my husband stood stock-still, as if she had been Medusa, the sword still raised over his head as in those clockwork tableaux of Bluebeard that you see in glass cases at fairs.

And then it was as though a curious child pushed his *centime* into the slot and set all in motion. The heavy, bearded figure roared out aloud, braying with fury, and wielding the honourable sword as if it were a matter of death or glory, charged us, all three.

On her eighteenth birthday, my mother had disposed of a man-eating tiger that had ravaged the villages in the hills north of Hanoi. Now without a moment's hesitation, she raised my father's gun, took aim and put a single, irreproachable bullet through my husband's head.

We lead a quiet life, the three of us. I inherited, of course, enormous wealth but we have given most of it away to various charities. The castle is now a school for the blind, though I pray that the children who live there are not haunted by any sad ghosts looking for, crying for, the husband who will never return to the bloody chamber, the contents of which are buried or burned, the door sealed.

I felt I had a right to retain sufficient funds to start a little music school here, on the outskirts of Paris, and we do well enough. Sometimes we can even afford to go to the Opéra, though never to sit in a box, of course. We know we are the source of many whisperings and much gossip but the three of us know the truth of it and mere chatter can never harm us. I can only bless the – what shall I call it? – the *maternal telepathy* that sent my mother running headlong from the telephone to the station after I had called her, that night. I never heard you cry before, she said, by way of explanation. Not when you were happy. And who ever cried because of gold bath taps?

The night train, the one I had taken; she lay in her berth, sleepless as I had been. When she could not find a taxi at that lonely halt, she borrowed old Dobbin from a bemused farmer, for some internal urgency told her that she must reach me before the incoming tide sealed me away from her for ever. My poor old nurse, left scandalized at home – what? interrupt *milord* on his honeymoon? – she died soon after. She had taken so much secret pleasure in the fact that her little girl had become a *marquise*; and now here I was, scarcely a penny the richer, widowed at seventeen in the most dubious circumstances and busily engaged in setting up house with a piano-tuner. Poor thing, she passed away in a sorry state of disillusion! But I do believe my mother loves him as much as I do.

No paint nor powder, no matter how thick or white, can mask that red mark on my forehead; I am glad he cannot see it – not for fear of his revulsion, since I know he sees me clearly with his heart – but, because it spares my shame.

# MELANIE RAE THON

# *The Snow Thief*

*Melanie Rae Thon grew up in Montana and is the author of* Meteors in August, *a novel. She gained a BA in English from the University of Michigan at Ann Arbor, where she won a Hopwood Award for her fiction. She received her MA from Boston University. She lives in Cambridge, Massachusetts, and teaches writing at Harvard University.*

My father fled without waking. Snow fell. The ghost of an elk drifted between trees. Mother called that November morning. *Gone,* she said, as if he might be missing. He was sixty-nine, still quick and wiry, a tow-truck driver who cruised county roads rescuing women like me.

A single vessel ruptures; blood billows in the brain. That fast. Impossible to believe. Eleven years since he'd caught me with his friend, Jack Fetters, in the backseat. No one could blame his bursting artery on me. No one except my father himself. He filled my one-room flat on Water Street. I smelled smoke in damp wool, saw the shadow of his hand pass close to my face.

Simply dead. How could this be? He'd wounded the elk at dawn, tracked it for miles down the ravine. Near dark, the bull became an owl and flew away.

Lungs freeze. Hearts fail. It's easy. I know it happens everywhere, hundreds of times a day, to daughters much younger than I was then. Still, each one leaves a mystery.

As my father slipped into bed that night, he said, *My shoulder hurts. Could you rub me?*

And Mother whispered, *I'm too sleepy.*

It drove her mad. Over and over she said the same thing: *I was going to rub his shoulder in the morning.*

I thought we'd lose her. She kept asking, *How could I sleep with your father dead beside me?* I remember how suddenly she shrank, how nothing she ate stayed with her. My brother wanted to put her away. *A home*, Wayne said, *for her own safety.*

One night we found all her windows open, the back door flapping. We caught her three miles up the highway. She stood in the middle of the road, as if she'd felt us coming and had paused to wait. Our headlights blasted through worn cloth, revealed small drooping breasts and tense legs, bare feet too cold to bleed. She wore only her tattered nightgown. No underpants beneath it. Nothing.

She wouldn't ride in the truck. I gave her my coat and boots. I wore Wayne's. He had to drive in stockinged feet. Mother and I walked together, silent the whole way. I held her arm to keep her steady. But this is the truth: she was the one to steady me. It made sense, this cold – a kind of prayer, this ceaseless walking.

When we got home, she let me wash her feet. I told her she was lucky, no frostbite, and she said, *Lucky?*

Then she slept, fifty-six hours straight.

The doctor said, *She needs this. She's healing.*

I washed her whole body. She hadn't bathed for twelve days. My mother, that smell! Air too thick to breathe, tight as skin around me.

She woke wanting sausages and steak. Eggs fried in bacon grease. A can of hash with corned beef. She ate like this for days and days, stayed skinny all the same. *It's your father*, she said. *He's hungry.*

He took her piece by piece. For thirteen years my mother stumbled in tracks she couldn't see. Every year another stroke left another tiny hole in her brain. I thought of it this way, saw our father standing at the edge of the pines, his gun raised. He was firing at Mother; but it was dusk, and since he was dead, his aim was unsteady. Each time he hit, she staggered toward him. He was a proud man, even now. It was his way of calling.

In the end, he defeated himself. All those scars left spaces empty. She forgot why she'd gone to the woods and who she wanted to find there.

She loved only her nurse, and almost forgot my father, and almost forgot my brother and me.

I caught the pretty boy smoothing her sheet. Thin as an angel, this Rafael, so graceful he seemed to be dancing. He held her wrist to feel the pulse. He checked her IV. He said, *What a beautiful way to eat.*

He loved her too. How can anyone explain? He wasn't afraid of burned thighs or skin peeling. He touched her feathery hair, sparse and fine as wet down on one of the not-born chicks my brother kept in jars of formaldehyde the year he was fourteen. *Specimens,* he called them, his eighth-grade science project. Every two days he cracked another egg to examine the fetus. I hated myself, remembering this, seeing my own mother curl up like one of these. But there they were, those jars of yellow fluid, those creatures floating.

I stroked her arm to make her wake.

*What do you want now?* she said.

*To say goodnight.*

*Not goodbye?*

*Not yet.*

*It's not up to you,* she said. She was seventy-seven years old, seventy-three pounds the last time anyone checked.

What did I want?

I wanted her big again. Tall as my father. Wide in the hips.

Think of me as a child. Once, when I was sick, my mother sat three days beside me, afraid to sleep because I might stop breathing. Sometimes when I woke, I smelled deerskin and tobacco, felt my father's cool hand on my forehead.

I have this proof they loved me.

What went wrong?

I turned fifteen. Jack Fetters said, *Someday, Marie.* Jack Fetters whispered, *We're not so different as you think.*

He was a guard at the state penitentiary. He said, *Man goes crazy watching other men all day.* His wife Edie had some terrible disease with a jungle name. Made her arms and legs puff up huge, three times their normal size. Jack Fetters said, *Sometimes the body is a cage.* They had a little girl just five, another seventeen, four boys in the middle. The one I knew had found his profession already: Nate Fetters was a sixteen-year-old car thief.

I thought, sooner or later his own daddy and a pack of dogs will chase him up a tree. Would Jack Fetters haul his son back to town, or would he chain the animals and let the thief escape?

A trap, either way.

I liked that boy, Nate Fetters. But he never noticed me. It was the father who touched my neck under my hair. It was the father I slapped away. The father who kept finding me. After school, at the edge of town, throwing rocks down the ravine. The patient father. *Someday, Marie.*

Was he handsome?

How can I explain?

He was the wolfman in a dream, a shape-shifter, caught halfway between what he was and what he was going to be. Even before I unbuttoned his shirt, I imagined silvery fur along his spine. Before I pulled his pants to his ankles, I saw his skinny wolf legs. I knew he'd grunt and moan on top of me. Bite too hard. Come too quickly.

This part I didn't see: a car pulled off the road, a backseat – my father with a flashlight, breaking glass above me. I never guessed my own belly would swell up huge like Edie's legs.

Wayne sat on the windowledge. Our mother's room. Another day.

*She's worse*, he said.

*At last*, I thought, *it's ending.*

But he didn't mean this.

He said, *She promised that little fairy her damn TV.*

I knew Wayne. He wanted the color television. He figured he'd earned it, living with Mother. Thirteen years. *I've done my time.* That's what he'd say.

Her eyelids fluttered. She was asking God, *What did I do to deserve children like these?*

Listen, I felt sorry for my brother. He was soon to be an orphan. Just like me.

Once we hid in the ravine, that dangerous place, forbidden, where fugitives dug caves, where terrified girls changed themselves to pine trees. We buried ourselves under dirt and damp leaves. We couldn't speak or see. We couldn't *be* seen. God only glanced our way. If he saw the pile of leaves, he thought it was his wind rustling. He turned his gaze. He let us do it. He let us slip our little hands under each other's clothes. Warm hands. So small! Child hands. So much the same. God didn't thunder in our ears. God didn't hurl his lightning.

But later, he must have guessed. He came as brittle light between black branches. He was each one blaming the other. He showed himself as blindness, the path through trees suddenly overgrown with thorns and briars. He came as fear. He turned to root and stone to trip us.

The man on my mother's windowledge had split knuckles, a stubbled beard, bloated face. He said, *It's late. I work tonight.* He said, *Call me if there's any change.*

First love gone to this. If I said, *Remember?*, Wayne would say I'd had a dream. He'd say I was a scrawny brat. He'd say the closest thing he ever gave me to a kiss was a rope burn around my wrist.

This is how God gets revenge: he leaves one to remember and one to forget.

The boy I loved had been struck dead.

At twenty, Wayne said, *This whole town is a penitentiary.* He meant to climb the wall and leap. No barbed wire. No snags. He moved up and down the coast, Anchorage to Los Angeles. He wrote once a year. Every time he was just about to make some real money. But after our father died, Wayne came home to Mother, safe, took a job from Esther McQuade at the 4-Doors Bar on Main Street. *It's a good business,* he said. *Everybody has to drink.*

Six months later, he married Esther's pregnant daughter. Some kind of trade. He said, *I know this first one's not gonna look much like me.* Now he was Esther's partner instead of her employee.

But he was still jealous, thought I must be smart and lucky. Because I went to college, two years. Because I got as far as Missoula and stayed. Eighty miles. I wanted to tell him, *No matter where I go I'm just the same.*

Did he blame himself for Mother's last accident?

I never asked. I knew what he'd say. *Just because she lives in my house doesn't mean I trot to the bathroom with her.*

She spent two days in bed before she told him. A tub of scalding water, thighs and buttocks burning. She was ashamed. *I just sat down,* she said. *I wasn't thinking.*

By the time she showed him, the skin was raw, the wounds infected.

She couldn't ride a single mile. The doctor who came to the house gave her morphine. He said, *How did you stand it?*

And she said, *I forgot my body.*

This doctor was a boy, blinking behind thick glasses. He couldn't grasp her meaning. Mother said, *Go ask your father. Maybe he can tell you.*

The doctor shook his head. No way to help her here in Deer Lodge. He said, *We'll have to fly you to Missoula.*

*Yes*, she said, *I'd like that.* She meant the ride, the helicopter.

Now this, three weeks of antibiotics and painkillers pumped into veins that kept collapsing. She had a doctor for each part of her: one for skin and one for brain, one to save her from pneumonia. But all of them together couldn't heal her whole body. The neurologist rubbed his clean hands as if they hurt him. He stood near the window – gray light, white jacket, all I remember. He tried to explain it. *Common with stroke victims, immune system impaired, the body can't fight infection.* He said, *It's one thing after another, like stomping out brush fires.*

We were alone at last. I smoothed her hair. She curled into herself, tiny bird of a woman, still shrinking, becoming my child, my unborn mother. I leaned close to whisper. *It's me*, I said, *Marie, your daughter.*

Rain hit the glass. Then Rafael appeared, off-duty, wearing his black coat draped around his shoulders. He washed her face. He said, *She likes this. See? She's smiling.* He said, *Go home if you're tired. I can stay awhile.*

His coat was frayed, not warm, not good in rain. Maybe he had nowhere else to go. No house, no room, no bed, no lover. Maybe this was the reason for his kindness. Who can know our secrets?

I saw my father in the parking lot, gun propped against a dumpster. He searched his pockets. Found no bullets. He knew Rafael was with my mother. So close at last, and he'd lost her all the same.

I meant to go home and bolt the door. But rain turned to sleet, sent me spinning. One wrong turn and I found myself at the Bearpaw Bar on Evaro.

Animals hung. Buffalo, moose, grizzly. This last one had its hide attached. I thought their bodies must be trapped behind these walls. I told the man beside me I'd break them free if I had a pick and axe. He had pointy teeth, a glad-dog grin. He said, *Where were you when they locked me down in Deer Lodge?* His skin was cracked, a Badlands face. When he smiled that way, I was afraid the scars might split open. This Tully bought my third beer, my first bourbon. He gripped my knee. He said, *I like you.*

By the jukebox, two sisters swayed, eyes closed, mouths moving. Sleep-dancers. My father leaned against the wall, watching their smooth faces and the dreamy tilt of their hips rolling. I passed him on my way to the bathroom. His coat was wet. I smelled metal and oil, a gun just cleaned, grease on his fingers.

Too many beers already. I knew how it would be, how I'd follow Tully to the Easy Sleep Motel, take off my clothes too fast to think.

But when I saw my father, I had hope I could be saved. I thought, *I won't do this if you'll talk to me.* I said his name. I whispered, *Daddy?*

He didn't hear. Deaf old man. He looked away.

*Listen.*

They never brought my son to me. They let me sob, sore and swollen. They let my breasts bleed milk for days.

In every room, another girl, just the same. In every room, the calm Catholic women said, *Gone, a good family.*

*Listen.* There were complications. Narrow pelvis, fetus turned the wrong way. They had to cut my child out of me. Days later, they cut again.

*Infection,* the doctor said, *it has to drain.*

One slip of the knife. And a girl becomes a childless mother forever. It's easy. The good women promised, *No more accidents.* Between themselves they murmured, *It's a blessing.*

*Listen.*

No father lets you tell him this.

In the bathroom, I tried to see myself, but I wasn't there. I was black eyebrows and lipstick smeared. The rest of me was hidden, inside the wavy glass. I imagined opening a door, falling on a bed. I saw the marks my mouth would leave, bright blooms on scarred flesh. I saw a spider's web tattooed on Tully's hairless chest.

What did I care if some old man judged me?

*Listen.* I'm snow in wind. No one leaves his imprint.

I went back to the bar, another beer, a third bourbon. Tully's hand moved up my leg. I'd hit black ice, locked my tires in a skid.

And then, a miracle, an angel sweet as Rafael sent to rescue stranded women. God spit him from the mouth of the buffalo head. Skinny boy in black jeans and leather. He pulled me off my stool. he said, *Maybe we should dance.*

The old man shot coins into the jukebox. My friend, after all. They were in this together, partners, a father and son with a tow truck, saviors with a hook and winch sent to pull me from the ditch.

Those thick-thighed sisters took care of Tully. One lit his cigarette, one stuck her tongue in his ear. They'd fallen with the snow, melted in my hair. They were my strange twins, myself grown fat. Their nails were long and hard, their lips a blazing red. Angels, both of them. You never know how they'll appear.

That boy's big hands were on my back. He whirled me in a dip and spin. His legs slipped between my legs.

*What are we doing?* I asked.

*Only dancing*, he said.

Yes, dancing. There's no harm in it. But later it was more a droop and drag, a slow waltz, one of us too drunk to stand.

The old man sat at a table in the back, holding his head in his hands. I saw how wrong I'd been. No angels here. The scarred man and the twins left. I was alone, reeling with the boy called Dez.

He ran his hands along my hips, pressed me into him. I said, *You're young enough to be my kid.*

*But I'm not*, he said.

He wrapped his fingers around my neck. He said, *Listen, baby, I'm low on cash.*

One last chance. I bought my freedom, gave him $52, all I had. He stuck it down his boot. I thought he'd vanish then, blow out the door, a swirl of smoke. But he said, *Let's go outside. This cowboy's got to get some air.*

In my car, he kissed me in that stupid way, all tongue and no breath. I lost my head. Then we were driving somewhere, snowblind, no seatbelts, nothing to strap us in. I saw broken glass, our bright bodies flying into tiny bits.

I took him home. Who can explain this? His long hair smelled of mud. I found damp leaves hidden in his pockets. His palms were cool on my forehead. He opened me. With his tongue, he traced the scar across my belly. It was wet and new. In a room years away I heard a child crying.

I expected him to steal everything. He touched the bones of my pelvis as if remembering the parts of me, veins of my hands, sockets of my eyes. *Like a sister*, he said. I thought he whispered, *Darling*, just before we slept.

In the morning he disappeared. Took my sleeping bag and cigarettes.

Then the phone rang and a voice said: *Your mother, gone.*

Imagine.

*Everyone you love is missing.* The voice on the phone never tells me this. The voice says, *Body, arrangements.* The voice says, *Your brother's on his way. You can meet him here.* I don't argue. I say, *Yes.* But I don't go to the hospital. I know I'll never catch them there.

Hours gone. *While you danced. While you lay naked in your bed.* That's what the voice in my own skull says.

I go to the ravine where the wounded elk staggers between pines. It's always November here, always snowing. It's the night my father died. It's the morning my mother is dying.

Sky is gray, snow fills it. Trees bend with ice, limbs heavy. I climb down, no tracks to follow. Snow higher than my boots already, a cold I hardly notice. I forget my body. How will I find them if they don't want me?

Flakes cluster, the size of children's palms now. They break against my head and back, so light I cannot feel them. I glimpse shapes, trees in wind shifting, clumps of snow blown from them, big as men's fists, big as stones falling. They burst. Silent bombs, scattering fragments.

Nothing nothing happens. Nothing hurts me.

And then I see them. He's wearing his plaid coat and wool pants, a red cap with earflaps. She wears only her pink nightgown. He carries her. She's thin as a child, but still a burden, and the snow is deep, and I see how he struggles. I could call out, but they'll never hear me. I can't speak in these woods. A shout would make the sky crumble. All the snow that ever was would bury me.

Deeper and deeper, the snow, the ravine. He never slows his pace. He never turns to look for me. Old man, slumped shoulders. All I ever wanted was to touch him, his body, so he could heal me, with his hair and bones, the way a saint heals. I hear my own breath. I stumble. How does he keep going?

Now I climb the steep slope. With every step I'm slipping. The distance between them and me keeps growing. I know I'll lose them. I know the place it happens. I know the hour. Dusk, the edge of the woods. The white elk takes flight as an owl in absolute silence. Wings open a hole in the sky, and a man and a woman walk through it.

No one says, *Go back*. No one says, *You'll die here*. But the cold, I feel it. My own body, I'm back in it.

I can stay. I can lie down. Let the snow fall on my face. Let its hands be tender.

Or I can walk, try to find my way in darkness.

I'm a grown woman, an orphan, I have these choices.

# The Violin

Translated by Sally Laird

*Ludmilla Petrushevskaya was born in Moscow in 1938. Her father disappeared when she was a baby, and because her mother could not feed her she was sent to a children's home when she was nine. During the 1950s mother and daughter shared a single room in a communal apartment with Petrushevskaya's grandfather, a distinguished professor of linguistics who had lost his job under Stalin, and his vast library. After school she studied journalism at Moscow University and worked on magazines and in radio and television. She is now a prestigious writer in Russia, a winner of the Pushkin Prize and runner-up for the first Russian Book Prize in 1992 for her novel* The Time: Night, *but for two decades she could not get her fiction published. She turned instead to plays, staging them in makeshift theatres and private apartments, and it was only under* glasnost *that her plays could be performed before wider audiences. Her play* Three Girls in Blue *has earned her the title of the 'feminist Chekhov'. Her novel and her short-story collection* Immortal Love *are published by Virago.*

She would lie unrestrainedly, muddle up her own stories, forget what she'd said just the day before and so on. It was a typical, easily recognizable case, fibbing to make oneself look important, presenting all one's actions as being somehow frightfully significant, of enormous consequence, bound to result in something momentous happening; but in fact nothing did happen; she went on trailing to and fro through the ward with the same self-important expression on her face, holding slightly aloft a certain pale-blue envelope, containing God only knows what message; but she carried it down the ward with tremendous dignity, demonstrating with her entire being the utmost urgency of having this letter dispatched. All the women in the ward were more or less familiar with the contents of the letter – although of course what they were familiar with was only the intention behind it, not the particular words in which this obvious intention had been couched, nor the particular form in which the author had chosen to hide all her longings, those pathetic, clear-as-daylight longings of hers, nor the particular lies she'd told this time in address-ing her heart's elect, a certain engineer called Valery who lived in another city.

None of this however meant that she was particularly chatty, this Lena, or that she was over-eager to enter into explanations of her present situation. On the contrary, she was rather taciturn, apt, if any-thing, to be over-ceremonious; and this tendency to stand on ceremony came to the fore especially when the consultant was making his rounds; for the consultant liked to sit and chat with Lena when he came on a Monday to see all his patients. With a fatherly frown he'd tell Lena that everything was going to form and if everything continued to do so our little student would soon be better and be able to get out and about again before it was time for the big event; and there was no reason to be afraid of going out, he'd say, forestalling Lena's objections; on the con-trary fresh air and strolls in the park were just what were needed, just what were needed to build up your strength before giving birth. 'And what about those hands of yours?' he'd ask Lena. 'Don't violinists' hands get out of practice if they don't keep at the old strings and bow? It's a well-known fact. How many hours a day are you supposed to practise, you budding musicians?' 'Four, sometimes five,' Lena answered without a hint of a blush. 'And before exams you're supposed to practise all the hours you can short of actually pulling a tendon – it's a question of sheer stamina then.'

Then the consultant would move on and finally vanish from the ward, leaving everyone to get on with their own affairs; and Lena, conscientious Lena, would sit down again with her notepaper and write and write and write, until it was time to seal up all these writings and triumphantly bear them down the entire ward to the exit. Or she'd go to make a phone call and in a low voice conduct long conversations with a certain person, obviously on some practical business of the utmost seriousness: from her expression it was evident that she needed to explain something of decisive importance to her; and it was the same thing each day with these telephone calls: the same preoccupied face, the same hushed voice, the same vague incomprehensible questions.

But despite all these immensely serious conversations on the phone, and the fact that there was evidently someone or other who was supposed to be doing something or other for Lena, nobody ever actually came to see her, and consequently there was nothing at all on her bedside cupboard but an empty glass covered with a paper napkin.

After her first few days in hospital, when she lay in bed in silence – she was not allowed to walk about; it was the rule of the hospital that no one was allowed to get up if there was the slightest hint of complications developing – after those first few days of compulsory bed rest, Lena was at last allowed to get up, and she set off somewhere out of the ward, taking with her the latest letter in its standard blue envelope. She began walking to and fro, engaging the nurses and orderlies in endless whispered, meaningful exchanges – though what all these furtive discussions amounted to, and quite why she had to engage all the nurses in them, was not entirely clear, since they never seemed to bring any concrete results: just as before not a soul came to see her, and just as before the clean glass yawned emptily on her bedside cupboard, and from time to time she'd take it off and get a drink of water. And still Lena busied herself with her letters, or went to the mirror in the hall to do her hair, or modestly ate up her hospital dinner. And all these activities, it must be said, she imbued with a lofty and quite impenetrable significance.

And the only channel through which at least a certain amount of information on Lena filtered out were her talks with the consultant on his Monday rounds, when, newly made-up, she lay back on the tall, stacked pillows and in her quiet voice answered all the consultant's questions, although the latter must by now have known everything there was to know about the history of her illness.

But the consultant asked his questions anyway, and Lena answered, and from these brief, quiet answers of hers the other patients in the hushed ward learned, for instance, that Lena had fainted in the street one day and that her friend had had to phone for an ambulance. In response to further queries from the consultant Lena said that she now felt extremely weak and dizzy, and that she sometimes had pains in the small of her back.

'You must rest up, rest here with us,' the consultant would say at the end of these conversations, turning to the next bed on his rounds.

And every Monday, as these brief conversations were resumed, Lena monotonously made the same complaint, of a certain dizziness and a certain weakness, although, as these same conversations revealed, all the results of her tests were just fine, and there was absolutely no problem with her heart; and then one fine day, on one of these Mondays, the consultant recommended that she be discharged, advising her to be as active as possible to overcome any weakness resulting from her rest in hospital, and to be a good girl and do her exercises and prepare herself properly for the birth so she'd be nice and strong and be able to take it all in her stride. The consultant jested that she ought to let him take care of her here at the hospital when the time came, and asked her for the hundredth time when she was going to send him the tickets to her solo concert, and then he vanished once more whence he'd come.

By that time, by that Monday, Lena had made herself at home in the ward and gradually told everyone about her husband Valery, an engineer who lived in another city and wasn't able to come and see her right now. And she told them all how she'd spent New Year's Eve at his parents' house and how welcome they'd made her feel, and so on and so forth.

And she still kept conscientiously writing those letters, and processing down the ward to the far doors with the same triumphant gait, and holding those secret conversations with the nurses; and she went on ringing up her friend and conversing in hushed tones with her over the phone – and all to no effect.

Meanwhile, however, it must be said that her bedside cupboard was no longer empty, but had started filling up with all sorts of fruits and vegetables and things to eat. And this development had occurred rather quickly, in fact as soon as the other women began to guess the real state of affairs. At first rather timidly and self-consciously, but ever more calmly and straightforwardly, they began putting their spare provisions in Lena's little cupboard, and Lena too began rather timidly and self-consciously, but gradually more freely to avail herself of these gifts: she was forever eating, nibbling away; she'd trail up to the washroom to wash a plateful of fruit and then set to and eat again. She ate apples, salad, cheese and sausage and chocolates and once even half a head of raw cabbage, which someone or other had brought in for a woman suffering from stomach problems.

And the nurses, too, started bringing Lena extra large portions and sometimes, when there was nothing else on offer, simply gave her a second bowl of soup – after they'd already served the dessert. And Lena, nodding her assent with great dignity, accepted these second helpings, calmly ate them up, then went off to comb her hair or sat down and wrote the next letter. The envelopes she used for this purpose, incidently, were no longer hers, for, as it emerged, there had been some delay in her husband's transferring her money, and her friend was unable to come. This friend of hers, it must be said, kept on not coming and not coming, and indeed, during the whole month that Lena spent in the hospital, the friend never showed up at all; she put in an appearance only at the very last, culminating moment, when Lena was leaving the hospital.

It's true that, before Lena left, the women in her ward had negotiated with the doctors to try and have Lena kept in the hospital for another two months, right up to the birth, but evidently this was quite impossible, and so Monday duly arrived, and the consultant sat down for his usual chat with Lena about the difficulties of studying at the conservatory, by that time well aware that there was no such conservatory, nor any trace, indeed, of a violin. However, this conversation was conducted with the utmost propriety, and soon afterwards Lena left the ward for good, taking with her the yellow comb that had become such a familiar sight over the last month.

Lena left the ward unmasked, so to speak, completely dethroned, but without for a moment losing her majestic poise, her mysteriousness – even after the whole ward, right in front of Lena, had started quite seriously discussing what she was going to do with her future child, and whether she could count on any help at all from that engineer, the one whom Lena claimed to be her husband – all these problems immediately rising to the surface the minute Lena started to say goodbye. She left the ward to a chorus of advice, one and all telling her to put the baby in a children's home, at least for a year, and during that year to somehow or other get herself on her feet, to find herself a job and somewhere to live so that she'd be able to fetch the child back and give it a proper home. Lena nodded grandly, sitting on the edge of her bed, and then just the same said farewell to everyone all over again and set off with her great belly before her, and then half an hour later she could be seen again, through the window, majestically sailing off into the distance in a crumpled yellow raincoat, on the arm of the famous friend, and it was quite clear to everyone then that the fainting fit in the street had quite simply been staged, and that in a while the two of them, out there on the street, would manage to think up another ruse – so long, of course, as Lena didn't actually faint before they'd managed between them to work out all the details.

# ACKNOWLEDGEMENTS

The editor and publishers wish to thank the following for permission to reprint copyright material:

Ama Ata Aidoo: to the author for 'A Gift from Somewhere' from *No Sweetness Here* (Longman, 1970; originally published in *Journal of New African Literature*).

Hanan Al Shaykh: to HarperCollins Publishers for 'The Fun-fair' from *I Sweep the Sun off Rooftops* (Allen & Unwin, 1994).

Isabel Allende: to Scribner, a Division of Simon & Schuster, for 'Two Words' from *The Stories of Eva Luna*, translated by Margaret Sayers Peden. Copyright © 1989 by Isabel Allende. English translation copyright © 1991 by Macmillan Publishing Company.

Barbara Anderson: to Bloomsbury Publishing and the Peters, Fraser & Dunlop Group Ltd for 'Tuataras' from *I Think We Should Go into the Jungle* (Secker & Warburg, 1993).

Margaret Atwood: to Bloomsbury Publishing for 'Hairball' from *Wilderness Tips* (1988).

Bi Shumin: to Chinese Literature Press for 'Broken Transformers', trans. Shi Junbao, from *Contemporary Chinese Women Writers: 3* (Panda Books, 1993).

Angela Carter: to the Estate of Angela Carter c/o Rogers, Coleridge & White Ltd, 20 Powis Mews, London W11 1JN, for 'The Bloody Chamber' from *The Bloody Chamber and Other Stories* (Gollancz, 1979). Copyright © Angela Carter, 1979.

Sandra Cisneros: to Bloomsbury Publishing and Susan Bergholz Literary Services, New York, for 'Woman Hollering Creek' from *Woman Hollering Creek*. Copyright © 1991 by Sandra Cisneros.

Anita Desai: to the author c/o Rogers, Coleridge & White Ltd for 'Games at Twilight' from *Games at Twilight* (Heinemann, 1978). Copyright © Anita Desai, 1978.

Irene Dische: to Bloomsbury Publishing for 'The Jewess' from *The Jewess Stories from Berlin and New York* (1992).

Mary Flanagan: to Random House UK Ltd for 'Cream Sauce' from *Bad Girls* (Cape, 1984).

Janet Frame: to Curtis Brown Ltd for 'The Reservoir' from *You Are Now Entering the Human Heart*. First published in Great Britain by the Women's Press Ltd, 1984, 34 Great Sutton Street, London EC1V ODX.

Ellen Gilchrist: to Bloomsbury Publishing and Little, Brown & Company for 'Too Much Rain, or, The Assault of the Mold Spores' from *The Age of Miracles*. Copyright © 1995 by Ellen Gilchrist.

Nadine Gordimer: to Bloomsbury Publishing, Farrar, Straus & Giroux Inc. and Penguin Books Canada Ltd. for 'Comrades' from *Jump and Other Stories*. Copyright © 1991 by Felix Licensing, B.V.

Bessie Head: to Heinemann Publishers (Oxford) Ltd and John Johnson (Authors' Agents) Ltd for 'Jacob' from *The Collector of Treasures and Other Botswana Village Tales* (Heinemann African Writers Series, 1977). Copyright the Estate of Bessie Head, 1996.

Elizabeth Jolley: to David Higham Associates Ltd and Australian Literary Management for 'Little Lewis Has Had a Lovely Sleep'. First published in *Cosmopolitan* (March 1992).

María Elena Llano: to Arte Publico Press, University of Houston, for 'In the Family', trans. Beatriz Teleki, from *Short Stories by Latin American Women: The Magic and the Real*, ed. Celia Correas de Zapata (1990).

Alison Lurie: to Reed Books Ltd for 'Fat People' from *Women and Ghosts* (William Heinemann, 1994).

Shena Mackay: to the author c/o Rogers, Coleridge & White Ltd and Reed Books for 'Perpetual Spinach' from *Dreams of Dead Women's Handbags*. Copyright © Shena Mackay, 1987.

Lorrie Moore: to Faber & Faber Ltd and Alfred A. Knopf Inc. for 'You're Ugly, Too' from *Like Life* (1990). Copyright © 1990 by Lorrie Moore.

Bharati Mukherjee: to Virago Press Ltd, Penguin Books Canada Ltd and Janklow & Nesbit Associates for 'A Wife's Story' from *The Middleman and Other Stories*. Copyright © 1988 by Bharati Mukherjee.

Alice Munro: to Random House UK Ltd, McClelland & Stewart Inc. and Alfred A. Knopf Inc. for 'A Wilderness Station' from *Open Secrets* (Chatto & Windus, 1994). Copyright © 1994 by Alice Munro.

Ludmilla Petrushevskaya: to Virago Press Ltd and Alfred A. Knopf Inc. for 'The Violin', trans. Sally Laird, from *Immortal Love* (1985).

Alifa Rifaat: to Quartet Books Ltd for 'Distant View of a Minaret' from *Distant View of a Minaret* (1983).

Annie Saumont: to Serpent's Tail Press for 'Before', trans. Christine Donougher, from *The Alphabet Garden* (1994).

462   ACKNOWLEDGEMENTS

Helen Simpson: to Reed Books Ltd and the Peters, Fraser and Dunlop Group Ltd for 'Heavy Weather' from *Dear George* (Heinemann, 1995).

Armonía Somers: to Libreria Linardi y Risso (Publishers), the translator and the Estate for 'The Burial' from *Women's Fiction from Latin America: Selections from Twelve Contemporary Authors*, edited and translated by Evelyn Picon Garfield (Wayne State University Press, 1988).

Melanie Rae Thon: to the author and Abner Stein Agency for 'The Snow Thief' from *First, Body* (Houghton Mifflin, 1997). Copyright © 1996 by Melanie Rae Thon.

Tatyana Tolstaya: to Virago Press Ltd and Alfred A. Knopf Inc. for 'The Circle', trans. Antonia Bovis, from *On the Golden Porch and Other Stories* (Penguin, 1990). Copyright © 1989 by Tatyana Tolstaya.

Luisa Valenzuela: to Rosario Santos (Literary & Cultural Services) and the translator for 'Blue Water-man' from *Women's Fiction from Latin America: Selections from Twelve Contemporary Authors*, edited and translated by Evelyn Picon Garfield (Wayne State University Press, 1988).

Alice Walker: to David Higham Associates Ltd and Harcourt Brace & Company (HBT) for 'Nineteen Fifty-five' from *The Complete Stories*. First published in Great Britain by the Women's Press Ltd, 1994, 34 Great Sutton Street, London EC1V 0DX. Copyright © 1981 by Alice Walker.

Banana Yoshimoto: to Grove/Atlantic Inc. for 'Newlywed', trans. Ann Sherif, from *Lizard* (Faber, 1995). Copyright © 1993 by Banana Yoshimoto; translation © 1995 by Ann Sherif.

Zhang Jie: to Chinese Literature Press for 'An Unfinished Record', trans. W. J. F. Jenner, from *Love Must Not Be Forgotten* (Panda Books, 1987).